T0214892

Communications
in Computer and Information Science 1095

Commenced Publication in 2007
Founding and Former Series Editors:
Phoebe Chen, Alfredo Cuzzocrea, Xiaoyong Du, Orhun Kara, Ting Liu,
Krishna M. Sivalingam, Dominik Ślęzak, Takashi Washio, Xiaokang Yang,
and Junsong Yuan

More information about this series at http://www.springer.com/series/7899

Weizhi Meng · Steven Furnell (Eds.)

Security and Privacy in Social Networks and Big Data

5th International Symposium, SocialSec 2019
Copenhagen, Denmark, July 14–17, 2019
Revised Selected Papers

 Springer

Editors
Weizhi Meng (ID)
Technical University of Denmark
Lyngby, Denmark

Steven Furnell (ID)
University of Plymouth
Devon, UK

ISSN 1865-0929   ISSN 1865-0937 (electronic)
Communications in Computer and Information Science
ISBN 978-981-15-0757-1   ISBN 978-981-15-0758-8 (eBook)
https://doi.org/10.1007/978-981-15-0758-8

This Springer imprint is published by the registered company Springer Nature Singapore Pte Ltd.
The registered company address is: 152 Beach Road, #21-01/04 Gateway East, Singapore 189721, Singapore

Preface

The 5th International Symposium on Security and Privacy in Social Networks and Big Data (SocialSec 2019) was held at Technical University of Denmark in Copenhagen, Denmark during July 14–17, 2019. It follows the success of SocialSec 2015 in Hangzhou, China; SocialSec 2016 in Fiji; SocialSec 2017 in Melbourne, Australia; and SocialSec 2018 in Santa Clara, CA, USA. The aim of the symposium is to provide a leading edge forum to foster interactions between researchers and developers with the security and privacy communities in social networks and big data, and to give attendees an opportunity to interact with experts in academia, industry, and government.

The conference program included 2 keynote speeches, 2 invited talks, and 21 contributed papers in addressing both theoretical and practical security and privacy challenges in social networks, Internet of Things, and big data. We would like to give our appreciation to our keynote speakers Dr. Manu Malek and Prof. Jaideep Vaidya for their talks "Internet of Things: Applications and Security Challenges" and "Privacy-preserving Analytics in the Big Data Environment" respectively. Also, our thanks go to our invited speakers Prof. Anthony TS Ho and Dr. Chunhua Su for their wonderful speeches.

This year, we received a total of 76 submissions, and each submission was reviewed by at least 3 Program Committee (PC) members. We finally accepted 18 full papers (with an acceptance rate of 25%) and 3 short papers, which cover a broad range of topics on security in Internet of Things, social networks, user authentication, algorithm design, artificial intelligence, and big data.

For the success of SocialSec 2019, we would like to first thank all the PC members for their great efforts in selecting the papers. We also thank all the external reviewers for assisting in the reviewing process. Further, we are thankful to the authors of all submitted papers.

For the conference organization, we would like to thank the general chairs – Yang Xiang (Swinburne University of Technology, Australia) and Anthony TS Ho (University of Surrey, UK) – for their kind support. We are grateful to other chairs – Jinguang Han (Queen's University Belfast, UK), Zhe Liu (Nanjing University of Aeronautics and Astronautics, China), Chunhua Su (University of Aizu, Japan), Ding Wang (Peking University, China), and Yu Wang (Guangzhou University, China) – for their help during the conference organization.

July 2019

Weizhi Meng
Steven Furnell

Organization

General Co-chairs

Yang Xiang   Swinburne University of Technology, Australia
Anthony T. S. Ho   University of Surrey, UK

Program Committee Co-chairs

Weizhi Meng   Technical University of Denmark, Denmark
Steve Furnell   University of Plymouth, UK

Program Committee

Man Ho Au	The Hong Kong Polytechnic University, Hong Kong, China
Patricia Arias Cabarcos	University Carlos III of Madrid, Spain
Joonsang Baek	University of Wollongong, Australia
Fei Chen	Shenzhen University, China
Rongmao Chen	National University of Defense Technology, China
Jiageng Chen	Central China Normal University, China
Xiaofeng Chen	Xidian University, China
Shaoying Cai	Hunan University, China
Aniello Castiglione	University of Salerno, Italy
Jintai Ding	University of Cincinnati, USA
Liming Fang	Nanjing University of Aeronautics and Astronautics, China
Jianming Fu	Wuhan University, China
Zhangjie Fu	Nanjing University of Information Science and Technology, China
Fuchun Guo	University of Wollongong, Australia
Muhammad Khurram Khan	King Saud University, Saudi Arabia
Jinguang Han	University of Surrey, UK
Gerhard Hancke	City University of Hong Kong, Hong Kong, China
Debiao He	Wuhan University, China
Xinyi Huang	Fujian Normal University, China
Qiong Huang	South China Agricultural University, China
Julian Jang-Jaccard	Massey University, New Zealand
Zoe L. Jiang	Harbin Institute of Technology, China
Georgios Kambourakis	University of the Aegean, Greece
Sokratis Katsikas	Norwegian University of Science and Technology, Norway
Romain Laborde	IRIT/SIERA, France

Kwok Yan Lam	Nanyang Technological University, Singapore
Yan Li	Singapore Management University, Singapore
Wenjuan Li	City University of Hong Kong, Hong Kong, China
Joseph Liu	Monash University, Australia
Zhiqiang Liu	Shanghai Jiao Tong University, China
Zheli Liu	Nankai University, China
Yang Liu	Nanyang Technological University, Singapore
Kaitai Liang	University of Surrey, UK
Bo Luo	The University of Kansas, USA
Entao Luo	Central South University, China
Xiapu Luo	The Hong Kong Polytechnic University, Hong Kong, China
Rongxing Lu	University of New Brunswick, Canada
Jiqiang Lu	Beihang University, China
Xiaobo Ma	Xi'an Jiaotong University, China
Felix Gomez Marmol	University of Murcia, Spain
Stefanos Gritzalis	University of the Aegean, Greece
Javier Parra-Arnau	Universitat Rovira i Virgili, Spain
Gerardo Pelosi	Politecnico di Milano, Italy
Rishikesh Sahay	Technical University of Denmark, Denmark
Zhiyuan Tan	Edinburgh Napier University, UK
Yizhi Ren	Hangzhou Dianzi University, China
Yu-An Tan	Beijing Institute of Technology, China
Jun Shao	Zhejiang Gongshang University, China
Seonghan Shin	National Institute of Advanced Industrial Science and Technology, Japan
Chunhua Su	University of Aizu, Japan
Hung-Min Sun	National Tsing Hua University, Taiwan
Guozi Sun	Nanjing University of Posts and Telecommunications, China
Willy Susilo	University of Wollongong, Australia
Jianfeng Wang	Xidian University, China
Wei Wang	Beijing Jiaotong University, China
Lei Wang	Shanghai Jiao Tong University, China
Hao Wang	Shandong University, China
Ding Wang	Peking University, China
Qianhong Wu	Beihang University, China
Zhe Xia	Wuhan University of Technology, China
Liang Xiao	Xiamen University, China
Bin Xiao	The Hong Kong Polytechnic University, Hong Kong, China
Lei Xue	The Hong Kong Polytechnic University, Hong Kong, China
Wun-She Yap	Universiti Tunku Abdul Rahman, Malaysia
Guomin Yang	University of Wollongong, Australia
Kuo-Hui Yeh	National Dong Hwa University, Taiwan

Yong Yu	Shaanxi Normal University, China
Xun Yi	RMIT University, Australia
Lei Zhang	East China Normal University, China
Jun Zhang	Swinburne University of Technology, Australia
Fangguo Zhang	Sun Yat-sen University, China
Haibo Zhang	University of Otago, New Zealand
Cliff Zou	University of Central Florida, USA

Additional Reviewers

Marios Anagnostopoulos
Xiaoying Jia
Xinyu Lei
Xingxin Li
Jing Pan
Nasrin Sohrabi
Zisis Tsiatsikas
Yunling Wang
Denis Chee Keong Wong
Zhiyan Xu
Xu Yang
Xuechao Yang
Zhichao Yang
Yunru Zhang
Yong Zhao
Rahman Ziaur

Contents

Web Scanner Detection Based on Behavioral Differences

Jianming Fu$^{(\boxtimes)}$, Lin Li, Yingjun Wang, Jianwei Huang, and Guojun Peng

Key Laboratory of Aerospace Information Security and Trusted Computing,
School of Cyber Science Engineering, Wuhan University, Wuhan 430072, China
{jmfu,yicoli,yjwang_cs,jw.huang,guojpeng}@whu.edu.cn

Abstract. Web scanners will not only take up the bandwidth of the server, but also collect sensitive information of websites and probe vulnerabilities of the system, which seriously threaten the security of websites. Accurate detection of Web scanners can effectively mitigate this kind of thread. Existing scanner detection methods extract features from log and differentiate between scanners and legal users with machine learning. However, these methods are unable to block scanning due to lack of behavior information of clients. To solve this problem, a Web scanner detection method based on behavioral differences is proposed. It collects request information and behavior information of clients by three modules named Passive Detection, Active Injection and Active Detection. Then, six kinds of features including fingerprint of scanners and execution ability of JavaScript code are extracted to detect whether a client is a scanner. This method makes full use of the behavior characteristics of clients and the behavioral differences between scanners and legal users. The experimental results showed the method is efficient and fast in scanner detection.

Keywords: Scanner detection · Behavioral difference · Online detection · Browsing behavior

1 Introduction

According to the 2016 Internet traffic report released by Imperva [1], about 52% of the Internet traffic worldwide comes from robots (i.e., automated programs), which means automation programs has dominated the Internet traffic. However, traffic of unsolicited robots such as automated vulnerability scanner, Web crawlers and DDoS attackers, accounted for 29% of the total Internet traffic [1]. In the 100,000 domains analyzed by Imperva, over 94% of the domains were attacked by robots within 30 days. Thus, earlier identification and blocking of unsolicited robot scanning can reduce the workload of Web servers and the risk of website information leakage.

WAF (Web Application Firewall) can detect scanning behavior with the scanner's fingerprint, dictionary, and the visiting frequency of Web page. But

© Springer Nature Singapore Pte Ltd. 2019
W. Meng and S. Furnell (Eds.): SocialSec 2019, CCIS 1095, pp. 1–16, 2019.
https://doi.org/10.1007/978-981-15-0758-8_1

scanners can modify the fingerprint and dictionary, reduce the scanning rate, and permute the scanning operations to bypass *WAF*. Upon detecting the scanning behavior, WAF will drop all the requests from the same IP address. But this response mechanism will result in a few false positive owing to *NAT* (Network Address Transfer) in some organizations or companies. Machine learning [2] can accurately identify scanning behaviors on the access log of Web servers, which is a kind of offline detection. But its accuracy depends on completeness of log information, which often misses behavior information including the mouse movements and clicking events. Moreover, it is a passive identification which is unable to stop attackers.

We observe that there are many behavior differences between scanner and legal user when they visit the same website, such as user often downloads resource files on demand while scanner doesn't show this behavior in order to speed up scanning. Based on these observations, a method of Web scanner detection is provided, this method injects specific label and JavaScript (JS) code into a Web page to achieve online recognition of scanning behavior, and blocks this scanning in time.

In summary, our main contributions with this work are as follows:

(1) We proposed a Web scanner detection method based on behavioral differences. The method actively interacts with the client to obtain browsing information via a way of injecting specific label and JS code into given Web page, and this browsing information will mend the limitation of offline detection.
(2) We designed and implemented a Web scanner detection prototype system-*Dome*. The prototype uses a proxy mechanism to accurately identify common scanners without sacrificing the user's browsing experience.
(3) We evaluated our method on common Web scanners and popular Web sites. The experimental results demonstrated that our method has obtained good accuracy in scanner detection, and kept good compatibility with known Web sites.

The other parts of this paper are arranged as follows. Section 2 describes related works about scanner detection. The detection model based on human-machine behavioral differences has been proposed in Sect. 3 and a prototype system-*Dome* has been implemented in Sect. 4. And Sect. 5 describes the experiment and our analysis. Finally, our conclusions are given in Sect. 6.

2   Related Work

Scanner detection can be divided into offline detection and online detection. Offline detection refers to detecting a scanner from Web log. Online detection is also called real-time detection, which means a scanner will be immediately alerted and processed once its scanning behavior is detected. In addition, some literatures focus on the design and implementation of scanners [3–8], which are helpful to understand the mechanism of these scanners and to extract the fingerprint and behavioral characteristics of scanners.

The simplest way of offline detection is to detect whether the *User-Agent* contains the fingerprints of common scanners, such as special *Referer*, visiting log of robots.txt and blacklisted IP address [9]. Moreover, machine learning algorithms can effectively construct visiting behavior of scanners and users, and this pattern is useful to identify unknown scanning behaviors in visiting log. Tan et al. [10] divided the visiting log session into four session types according to the IP address and *User-Agent*. The first type has the same IP address and *User-Agent*; the second has the same *User-Agent* and different IP addresses that correspond to the same domain; the third type has the same *User-Agent*, and the IP addresses belonging to the same C address segment; the fourth type has the same IP address and different *User-Agent*. They selected 25 features in each type as the feature vector, such as the total number of requests, the ratio of requests for image, the ratio of requests for document, the ratio of *GET* requests, the ratio of *HEAD* requests, the ratio of *POST* requests, the ratio of *Referer* requests, the request width, the request depth and so on, and the C4.5 algorithm acquires 90% detection rate finally.

The RDT [11] divided the log information of two adjacent requests that have the same IP address and *User-Agent* with an interval less than 30 min into a session. The features of RDT are different from that of Tan [10] according to some observations. For example, RDT believed that the ratio of requests for images is obvious indicator of resource visiting, so the number of requests for document and the ratio of *ZIP* requests are removed. At the same time, RDT removed the request width and request depth, because many crawlers have not used width-first traversal. And the link coverage (the ratio of links in the session to the total links in website), the ratio of *GET* requests, the ratio of *POST* requests, the ratio of *HEAD* are augumented as selective features in RDT. Finally, RDT combines the neural network, the decision tree and the logistic regression to model visiting behavior, and its accuracy is beyond 90%. In addition, other scholars have studied the Bayesian algorithm and Markov chains [12,13] to analyze log information to distinguish between normal traffic and robot traffic.

However, offline detection is a passive detection, greatly depending on the scanning log. Furthermore, the log information can be forged by scanner and this detection may bring the false negative. In addition, offline detection means no way to block the scanning behavior. In this paper, we firstly performs passive detection based on the detection features proposed by previous work, then detects the execution results of Cookie and JS code for active detection. Once scanning behavior is being detected, blockage action will be immediately triggered.

Online detection relies on the visiting frequency and the fingerprint of scanners [14]. There are a large amount of logs while the scanning happens. If an IP address visits the website with a high frequency, it can be inferred that the client corresponding to the IP address is a scanner. In addition, when the scanner initiates network request and vulnerability detection, it will add its own unique information to its *HTTP* request header or payload. For example, *Acunetix Web Vulnerability Scanner* (*AWVS*) will fill *Acunetix* in the request header [15], and this information can be used as the fingerprint of the scanner. So, the client can be speculated to be a scanner if an *HTTP* request contains *Acunetix*.

However, this kind of heuristic knowledge used by online detection is easily exploited and bypassed by attackers, resulting in false negatives. Moreover, if the scanner accesses the website through a proxy or *NAT*, the access frequency-based detection method will accumulate the access frequency of multiple normal websites, resulting in false positives.

In response to the problem of tampering with scanner fingerprint, Liu Xiaokai et al. proposed a detection method based on finite state machine [16]. The object survival detection, website fingerprint identification, website link crawling, and vulnerability scanning are constructed into a finite state machine. The cosine is used to calculate the similarity between the state machine of the scanner and the test sample, and this similarity is useful to identify the scanner with 91% accuracy rate. This method can counter the forgery of fingerprint and improve the detection accuracy. However, due to the lack of state machine, the unknown scanner cannot be detected, and the randomness of Web page crawling will disturb the transition between states.

In addition, Jocb et al. [17] designed a method of combining heuristic detection and traffic shape detection to detect crawlers. Heuristic detection identifies scanning behavior upon observing a large number of request errors (status code like 4xx, 5xx or 6xx), with no repeated visits to the same website, no *Referer* in the request, no cookies, and few parameters. Traffic shape detection discovers scanning behavior according to traffic log on every day with machine learning. Finally this method achieves a 90% accuracy rate, and the IP address related with scanners will be appended to the blacklist of IPS (Intrusion Prevention System). However, the effectiveness of online detection and blocking depends on the scanning window, the scanning will be stopped if the window is too small. Moreover, the distributed crawler always mimics the user's browsing behavior, so traffic shape detection may fail due to this imitative behavior. In addition, there exists a misjudgment under the *NAT* environment to block a scanner based on IP address.

Instead of using the IP-based method to block the scanning, our method propose a client identification module to identify the client that is visiting the website currently, reducing the misjudgment under the NAT environment. Moreover, in order to reduce the interference of tampered fingerprints on online detection, this paper studies the behavioral differences between legal user and scanner in the time information, mouse information, browsing information and dynamic code execution ability of Web pages. These information is captured and used by our active injection and active detection technology, which improves detection accuracy greatly.

3   Overview of Detection Model

This section observes the scanning process and scanning behavior of common scanners, then analyzes the difference between automated scanners and legal users when visiting Web pages, and explores the behavioral differences between them. Finally, we construct a online detection model.

3.1 Behavior Analysis on Scanners

In order to analyze the behavior characteristics of scanners effectively, we conducted experiments and analysis on the existing mainstream scanners. We divided these scanners into three categories, namely simple scanner, advanced scanner, and intelligent scanner according to their functions. The three classes of scanners are defined as follows.

- **Simple scanner.** Single functional scanner detects vulnerability by sending a large number of requests. It has obvious features, and a small number of configuration options, such as *Yujian*[18], *SQLmap*[19], *wpscan*[20], *wpsploit*[21], *DirBrute* [22], *wfuzz*[23].
- **Advanced scanner.** Scanner combining crawlers and vulnerability detection, can discover common Web vulnerabilities. It has a large nuber of configuration options to avoid fingerprint detection. *BurpSuite* and *AWVS* belong to this kind of scanner.
- **Intelligent scanner.** Scanner has certain capability of anti-detection, and defines the scanning strategy recognition engine and a professional knowledge database. *Appscan* is one of the typical representatives.

Based on the analysis of scanning principles and characteristics of crawler detection [6,8,14], we summed up the behavioral differences between scanners and legal users, as shown in Table 1. These differences are basis for the detection model.

When a user browses a Web page, the browsing speed and order are related to the user's habit, accompanied with mouse click. And the content parsing and rendering of Web page are implemented by the browser. When a scanner scans a Web page, the browsing speed and order are defined by the scanner, and there is no content presentation. In order to speed up the scanning, resources are generally not be downloaded, and JS in Web page may be not executed. These differences in browsing behavior between scanners and users, can be useful for distinguishing scanners and users.

Table 1. Behavioral difference

Behavioral difference	Legal user	Scanner
Mouse click	Yes	Na
Browsing speed	User habit	Pre-defined
Browsing order	User habit	Pre-defined
Execution of JS	Yes	Na
Visiting frequency	Normal	Frequent
Resource downloading	User demand	Na
Content presentation	Browser	Na

3.2 Behavioral Difference Modeling

In view of the problems in log analysis, we proposed an online detection model based on behavioral differences between scanners and legal users. Our model includes a client identification module, a passive detection module, an active injection module, and an active detection module.

The Client Identification Module. This module is to identify the client that is visiting the website currently, and to be able to associate the client's previous requests with subsequent requests. In addition, under the *NAT* environment, all computers share the same public IP address. If our defense scheme only distinguishes users by IP address, it will inevitably lead to misjudgment.

The Passive Detection Module. This module samples and observes the past requests of Web page, or detects the content of specific fields in traffic. Through the summary of previous research work [10–12,24,25], it was found that some of features have a good effect on the scanner detection. These features include the visiting frequency, the scanner fingerprint, the number of resource requests, and the number of failed requests of Web page.

- **Frequency-based.** The scanner frequently visits the website in a short period of time, and the number of requests per unit time is significantly higher than the number of manual requests sent by legal user. This feature makes the simple scanner easy to be detected.
- **Fingerprint-based.** By default, the scanner will have its own unique fingerprint information. Based on this information, we can infer which scanner the request was sent from. To this end, we collected the fingerprint of common scanners, which could be found in Appendix A.
- **Resource-based.** In order to speed up the visiting to the Web page, the scanner will ignore the resource files such as image files (jpg, png, gif), css, js, etc. The study by Doran [26] also confirmed the validity of resource-based detection method in scanner detection.

The Active Injection Module. This module injects specific label or JS code into the Web page according to a security policy to serve the active detection module. Its main purpose is to solve the problem of loss of behavior information when the client browses the Web page during the log analysis.

- ***Cookie.*** Through our previous analysis of scanners, the simple scanners and some advanced scanners ignore the interaction with the website, they does not carry *Cookie* returned by the Web server in subsequent request. So we add a specific *Cookie* in the *HTTP* request, for determining whether the subsequent request carries the Cookie.
- **JS code.** By injecting JS code into the Web page, we perceive the interaction between the Web page and client in browser, and collect the browsing behavior information of the client, help the active detection module to identify the scanner.

The Active Detection Module. This module detects the usage of the injected *Cookie* and the execution result of JS code, and we can identify whether the client is a scanner with these information.

- *Cookie*-**based.** The module distinguishes between the scanner and the legal user by detecting whether there is a cookie injected by the active injection module in the response header. If there is no *Cookie*, then the client is a scanner.
- **Mouse-click-based.** A legal user visits the website with a mouse click (excluding visiting via the bookmark bar or directly by entering an address in the address bar), but the scanner does not have a mouse click when visiting the website. So the scanner can be identified by calculating the ratio of number of mouse clicks to number of page requests and comparing it with a pre-defined threshold.
- **JS-based.** Through our previous analysis of scanners, only some intelligent scanners are able to execute the JS code in the Web page. To this end, the injected JS code in the active injection module is detected to determine whether the injected JS code is executed. If it is not executed, the client is a scanner.

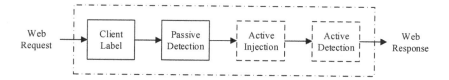

Fig. 1. Workflow of online detection model

Figure 1 shows the workflow of the four modules. The client identification module identifies the request to facilitate analysis of subsequent requests. The passive detection module uses the characteristics proposed by the predecessors to detect the scanner. The active injection module and the active detection module collect the browsing behavior of client to detect the scanner by injecting *Cookie* and JS code. If the passive detection module determines the client is a scanner, then it will block the subsequent requests sent by the scanner. If the passive detection module cannot distinguish the current request, the current request will be processed by the active injection module and the active detection module. If all modules can not discriminate the request, then we think the current request is from a legal user, and is normally handled.

4   Overview of Dome

Based on the behavioral difference model, we developed a detection prototype, *Dome* which is implemented on *OpenResty* [27]. *OpenResty* is a high performance Web platform based on *Nginx* and *Lua*. *OpenResty* can obtain and modify the content of *HTTP* request and response.

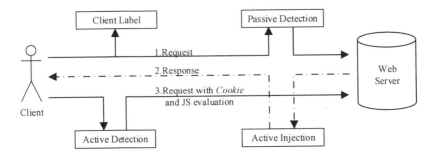

Fig. 2. Overview of the Dome infrastructure

Figure 2 is the overview of the *Dome* infrastructure. *Dome* uses ClientInfo to label a client, ClientInfo comes from the *User-Agent*, hostname and client IP address in the request header. These information together with the predefined salt in *Dome* are used as the input of Hash parameter. Finally, the output of the Hash algorithm is used as the Label of client.

The detection points of the passive detection module are the scanner fingerprint, the visiting frequency, and the number of requests for resource(png, gif, pig, txt, pdf, css, js, etc.). The detected information is mainly from the *HTTP* request information sent by the client, including the client identifier (Label), the request header information (*User-Agent*, Content-Type, *URL*), and the request parameters. Based on the Label, we increase the number of visiting once the client visits the website. If the number for a certain time exceeds the pre-defined threshold, the client is considered to be a scanner. And we use the suffix of the type of requested *URL* file and the Content-Type in the request header to determine the type of requested resource file, calculating the ratio of requested resource files in a certain number of HTTP requests. If the ratio of requested resource files is less than a pre-defined threshold, the client is considered to be a scanner. Once a client is recognized as scanner, its request will be rejected. On the contrary, this request will continue.

Active injection is performed after the server responds to the request. Algorithm 1 describes the detailed process of active injection, we can obtain the browsing information of the client by inject *Cookie* into the response header and content. *CookieValue* is derived from the Cookie in HTTP request. *CookieVerify* is obtained by the Hash algorithm, the Label of client and the string Cookie are used as the input of Hash algorithm; *JSVerify* is obtained by the Hash algorithm, the Label of client and the string JS are used as the input of Hash algorithm. Both of them are used to detect whether the corresponding client of the Label can carry the Cookie and whether the JS code can be executed.

Firstly, we detect whether there is a *CookieVerify* in the *CookieValue*. If *CookieVerify* is not found, we add the *CookieVerify* to the response header. If it exists, we continue to judge whether *JSVerify* exists in the *CookieValue*. If there is *JSVerify*, we add the JS code *Click_HOOK* to the response content to detect the mouse click when the client browses the Web page; if not, we add *JSVerify* to the response header, at the same time, we use JS to jump and re-request the current page.

Algorithm 1. Algorithm of Active Injection

INPUT: Response Header and Content of Original URL
OUTPUT: Injected Header and Content
1: $CookieValue = extractCookie(HTTPrequest)$
2: $CookieVerify = Hash(Label, "Cookie")$
3: $JSVerify = Hash(Label, "JS")$
4: **if** $CookieVerify$ in $CookieValue$ **then**
5:    **if** $JSVerify$ in $CookieValue$ **then**
6:       $injResponseContent = responseContent.injectJS(Click\_HOOK)$
7:    **else**
8:       $injResponseHeader = responseHeader.injectTag(JSVerify)$
9:       $redirect(Orginal\,URL)$
10:    **end if**
11: **else**
12:    $injectedresponseHeader = responseHeader.injectTag(CookieVerify)$
13: **end if**
14: **return** $injResponseContent$ and $injResponseHeader$

The active detection mainly uses the injected *Cookie* and JS code to analyze and judge the browsing behavior of the current client.

First, we judge whether the current client is the first access, and the judging method is based on whether the Label of client is already in log. If not, we think it is the first access, it is directly processed by the Web server and the active injection module. If the Label is in log, it is a consecutive request. The detection points of active detection module mainly include whether the client can carry the Cookie returned by the server, whether the client can execute the JS code, and whether the client has a mouse click after accessing a large number of Web pages.

(1) We assign the *Cookie* in the client by inserting the JS code. If the client is able to execute the JS code, then the *JSVerify* will be present in the client. If the JS code cannot be executed, JSVerify will not exist, which means the client is a scanner.

(2) We use *Click_HOOK* to listen all mouse click on Web page. If there is a mouse click, *Click_HOOK* will send a request to the Active detection module, and this module will record the number of click of the current client. If there is no mouse click after the current client has accessed a certain number of pages (which can be predefined according to the website), then the client is a scanner.

5   Experiments

In this section, we first elaborate on the system setting for *Dome* experiments. Then, we show the experimental design for *Dome* evaluation, which include that (1) Domes recognition ability (2) Domes compatibility with websites (3) the impact on website access delay when *Dome* is turned on or off (4) performance comparison with similar tools including *SafeDog* [28] and *ModSecurity* [29].

5.1   Setting

In the experimental server, we built an Ubuntu Server on the LAN and deployed *Dome* in it. 21 scanners used in the experiment are composed of common scanners and open source scanners on *Github* [26]. And we selected the top 100 websites of Top sites in China in Alexa as test sites for website compatibility testing. However, there are 30 websites using *HTTPS* so that they can not use the Dome proxy, so the final number of tested sites is 70.

5.2   Experimental Design

In the recognition capability testing, we used scanners to scan the tested server, observing whether *Dome* can block the scanning or it can affects the scanning results. Besides, according to the predefined behavior characteristics of scanners, we also detected the existence of scanners based on accessing frequency, fingerprint, resource downloading, Cookie carrying, JS execution, mouse-click respectively.

In the compatibility testing, we firstly implemented the proxy through *Dome*, and configured the browsers proxy options so that all requests from the browser are handled by *Dome*. Then we used the browser to visit the selected 70 websites, observing whether the Web pages could be normally displayed.

To test the impact of *Dome* on the visiting delay of website, we tested two different situations: directly visiting the website, and visiting the website when the proxy and *Dome* are turned on. The test was done by visiting the test site 50 times in Chrome in two cases, using Load Time in Chromes Dev Tools to record the time the page was loaded. Besides, we also tested the loading delay of page for each detection function in *Dome*. The loading delay is the difference of the loading time of the Web page between with and without the *Dome*.

In order to verify the recognition ability of *Dome*, we also compared *Dome* with the similar detection tools, including *SafeDog* and *ModSecurity*. The testing method is to deploy *Dome* and other tools to the same website separately, use the scanners to scan and attack the website, and observe whether the scanner can be recognized.

5.3   Experimental Result

In this section, we showed the results of the experiment from four aspects: recognition capability, compatibility, access delay, and performance comparison.

Recognition Capability. Final testing results are shown in Table 2 (Detail of the result can be found in Appendix B). It can be found that the active detection and the combination of passive detection achieved a 100% detection rate while passive detection only has a 90.5% detection rate. And we can find that frequency-based function in passive detection module and JS-based function in active detection performed have the best performance, achieving a 76.2% and 95.2% detection rate respectively.

Table 2. Detection result based on function

Detection	Total	Success	Fail	Rate(%)
Passive	21	19	2	90.5
Active	21	21	0	100
Passive & Active	21	21	0	100
Frequency-based	21	16	5	76.2
Fingerprint-based	21	15	6	71.4
Resource-based	21	14	7	66.7
Cookie-based	21	12	9	57.1
JS-based	21	20	1	95.2
Mouse-click-based	21	19	2	90.5

Compatibility. In the compatibility testing, we totally tested 70 websites based on *HTTP*, only one websites (www.cctv.com) were found it had a compatibility problem with *Dome*. The reason is that this site do not support additional parameters, but in the identification phase of scanners, *Dome* needs add a time stamp parameter when accessing the page, asking the browser not to cache the page content but to re-request the page. As a result, the page content couldn't be displayed properly.

Visiting Delay. Figure 3 depicts the load time for direct access to each website and the load time for access to each website when the Dome is turned on. It can be seen that Dome will delay the access to website to a certain extent. Websites with longer visiting time (>10 s) and slightly longer visiting time (≤10 s and >8 s) increased by 10% respectively, but websites with shorter visiting time (<2 s) reduced by 28%, and websites with short visiting time (≤8 s and >2 s) have been increased by 6%, indicating that Dome's delay on websites with short visiting time is more heavier. There are three main reasons: (1) When testing, we force the browser to prohibit the use of cache to avoid the test results affected by cacheing. In fact, when the browser normally accesses the website, the cache will effectively reduce the overall load time; (2) the proxy server is used as the deployment point of Dome during the test, and the proxy service will cause a certain delay; (3) the proxy server is built on a virtual machine with a low level of configuration, which will also have an impact on the results when we do batch testing.

In order to accurately calculate the loading delay of the detection functions, the research method of Liang [30] is adopted, the median is used as the time of loading the Web page after the maximum value is removed. We tested 12 times for each function. The final experimental results are shown in Table 3. The delay of the function based on mouse click-based is not very large, but the loading delay of JS-based detection function is larger than other functions. The reason is that JS-based function involves both the active injection module and

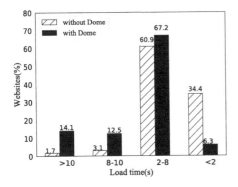

Table 3. Detection delay

Function	Delay (s)
Fingerprint	0.016
Frequency	0.013
Media file	0.015
Cookie	0.0125
JS	0.027
Mouse-Click	0.0195

Fig. 3. Diagram of load time

the active detection module, which increases the time cost. Other functions such as fingerprint, access frequency, and resource files only analyze the content of the request, so there is no significant delay for the Web page.

Performance Comparison. In the experiment of the *SafeDog*, the scanners couldn't be detected were *Appscan*, *Burpsuite*, *WebCrusier*, *Cangibrina*, *BruteXSS*, *Shuriken*. The reason why *Appscan* couldn't be detected is that the times of scanning is too few. Burpsuite only crawls but has no attack behavior, so the *SafeDog* couldn't recognize it. *WebCrusier* couldn't be recognized by *SafeDog* because the number of visits is too few, but Dome could identify it through the JS-based function. *Cangibrina* only detected the directory but didn't initiate the attack, so the *SafeDog* couldn't recognize it. *SafeDog* is a protection software, the principle of the scanner detection is the existence of attack behavior, but *BruteXSS* didn't show the attack behavior. *Shuriken* sent too few payloads so the *SafeDog* couldn't recognize it.

In the experiment of *ModSecurity*, the scanners that couldn't be detected were *Appscan*, *WebCrusier*, *Shuriken*, *Pentestdb*, *Lcyscan*. *Appscan*, *WebCrusier* and *Shuriken* had too few scans so they couldn't be blocked by *ModSecurity*. In addition,*Pentestdb* and *Lcyscan* showed aggressive behavior that caused them to be identified.

6   Conclusion and Future Work

This paper presented a method for online scanner detection based on behavioral differences. Conventional detection methods firstly analyze the log, then select features from log, and use machine learning algorithms to analyze the extracted features to identify the scanner. However, scanner detection based on log analysis does not allow real-time analysis and blocking of scanner behavior. Based on the analysis and characteristics of scanners, we proposed the online scanner detection model combined by the client label module, the passive detection module, the active detection module and the active injection module. Our model makes up for the shortcomings of offline identification, effectively distinguishes between scanners and legal users based on behavioral differences. Moreover, our model joints use of feature-based passive detection and JS-based active detection effectively reduces the false positives. But the limitation is that it is not effective for scanners that support JS. Based on the detection model, a detection prototype *Dome* is implemented on the *OpenResty* platform, considering that it is easy to implement the migration of old functions and the addition of new functions in the future. By analyzing the *HTTP* request and response packets and the behavior of the client while browsing the Web page, *Dome* can detect whether the client is a scanner. Experiments showed that our method is feasible and effective.

But our work also has certain shortcomings. Firstly, the JS injection module can cause delays in website visits. In addition, whether the attacker can use the module to pose side effects on Web servers and legal users, which is to be studied in the future. Secondly, *HTTPS*-based websites cannot use *Dome* for proxying, which means that Dome will be difficult to apply to WAF in the future. In the future, we will migrate and integrate our detection model into Web server, and build *Dome* as plugin of Web Server to support *HTTPS*.

Acknowledgements. We sincerely thank SociaSec anonymous reviewers for their valuable feedback. This research was supported in part by the National Natural Science Foundation of China (U1636107, 61373168).

A   Fingerprint Information of Common Scanners

Name	Fingerprint	Location
wpscan	wpscan	*User-Agent*
SQLmap	Sqlmap/version/#stable(http://sqlmap.org)	*User-Agent*
AppScan	APPSCAN	Requset parameter, *URL*
AWVS	Acunetix-Aspect	Request header
W3af	w3af.org	*User-Agent*
Burpsuite	burpcollaborator.net	Request header, parameter, *URL*
WebCruiser	WebCruiser, HEAD method	*User-Agent*
NetSpark	X-Scanner:Netsparker or Netsparker	Request header, parameter
FileSensor	Scrapy/1.4.0 (+http://scrapy.org)	*User-Agent*
Yujian	HEAD method, User-Agent:-	*User-Agent*, RM
BBScan	BBScan/version	*User-Agent*
DirBrute	whoami=wyscan_dirfuzz	*Cookie*
Nikto	(Nikto/version) (Evasions:None) (Test:map_codes)	*User-Agent*

B   Testing Results of Scanners

Scanners	Visiting frequency	Fingerprint	Resource file	Carrying cookie	JS execution	Mouse click	All methods
Appscan	√	√	√	×	×	√	√
w3af	√	√	√	√	√	√	√
Burpsuite	√	√	√	×	√	√	√
AWVS	√	√	√	×	√	√	√
netsparker	√	√	√	×	√	√	√
htpwdScan	√	×	√	√	√	√	√
NagaScan	√	×	×	×	×	×	√
WebCrusier	√	√	×	√	√	√	√
Yujian directory scanning	√	√	√	√	√	√	√
Yujian website identification	√	√	√	√	√	√	√
SQLmap	√	√	√	√	√	√	√
BBScan	√	√	√	√	√	√	√
Cangibrina	√	√	√	√	√	√	√
BruteXSS	×	√	×	×	√	×	√
Shuriken	×	×	×	×	√	×	√
Weakfilescan	√	×	√	×	√	√	√
Dirsearch	√	×	×	√	√	√	√
Pentestdb	×	√	√	√	√	√	√
Lcyscan	√	√	√	√	√	√	√
DirBrute	√	√	√	×	√	√	√
wpscan	×	√	×	×	√	√	√

References

1. Imperva. Bot traffic report 2016 [EB/OL] (2016). https://www.incapsula.com/blog/bot-traffic-report-2016.html
2. Asselin, E., Aguilar-Melchor, C., Jakllari, G.: Anomaly detection for web server log reduction: a simple yet efficient crawling based approach. In: 2016 IEEE Conference on Communications and Network Security (CNS), pp. 586–590. IEEE (2016)
3. Stock, B., Pellegrino, G., Rossow, C., Johns, M., Backes, M.: Hey, you have a problem: on the feasibility of large-scale web vulnerability notification. In: 25th USENIX Security Symposium (USENIX Security 16), pp. 1015–1032 (2016)
4. Kals, S., Kirda, E., Kruegel, C., Jovanovic, N.: SecuBat: a web vulnerability scanner. In: Proceedings of the 15th International Conference on World Wide Web, pp. 247–256. ACM (2006)
5. Zhao, T., Yuliang, L., Liu, J.H., Sun, H., Shi, F.: Web vulnerability detection based on form crawler. Comput. Eng. **34**(9), 186–188 (2008)

6. Akrout, R., Alata, E., Kaaniche, M., Nicomette, V.: An automated black box approach for web vulnerability identification and attack scenario generation. J. Braz. Comput. Soc. **20**(1), 4 (2014)

7. Cetin, O., Ganan, C., Korczynski, M., van Eeten, M.: Make notifications great again: learning how to notify in the age of large-scale vulnerability scanning. In: Workshop on the Economy of Information Security (2017)

8. Stock, B., Pellegrino, G., Li, F., Backes, M., Rossow, C.: Didnt you hear me? Towards more successful web vulnerability notifications (2018)

9. Geens, N., Huysmans, J., Vanthienen, J.: Evaluation of web robot discovery techniques: a benchmarking study. In: Perner, P. (ed.) ICDM 2006. LNCS (LNAI), vol. 4065, pp. 121–130. Springer, Heidelberg (2006). https://doi.org/10.1007/11790853_10

10. Tan, P.N., Kumar, V.: Discovery of web robot sessions based on their navigational patterns. In: Zhong, N., Liu, J. (eds.) Intelligent Technologies for Information Analysis, pp. 193–222. Springer, Heidelberg (2004). https://doi.org/10.1007/978-3-662-07952-2_9

11. Bomhardt, C., Gaul, W., Schmidt-Thieme, L.: Web robot detection - preprocessing web logfiles for robot detection. In: Bock, H.H., et al. (eds.) New Developments in Classification and Data Analysis. Studies in Classification, Data Analysis, and Knowledge Organization, pp. 113–124. Springer, Heidelberg (2005). https://doi.org/10.1007/3-540-27373-5_14

12. Stassopoulou, A., Dikaiakos, M.D.: A probabilistic reasoning approach for discovering web crawler sessions. In: Dong, G., Lin, X., Wang, W., Yang, Y., Yu, J.X. (eds.) APWeb/WAIM -2007. LNCS, vol. 4505, pp. 265–272. Springer, Heidelberg (2007). https://doi.org/10.1007/978-3-540-72524-4_29

13. Lu, W.-Z., Yu, S.-Z.: Web robot detection based on hidden Markov model. In: 2006 International Conference on Communications, Circuits and Systems, vol. 3, pp. 1806–1810. IEEE (2006)

14. Huntington, P., Nicholas, D., Jamali, H.R.: Web robot detection in the scholarly information environment. J. Inf. Sci. **34**(5), 726–741 (2008)

15. Seay. Waf realized scanner recognition, completely resisted hacker scanning [EB/OL] (2016). http://www.freebuf.com/articles/web/16806.html

16. Liu, X., Fang, Y., Huang, C., Liu, L.: Research of identifying web vulnerability scanner based on finite state machine. J. Inf. Secur. Res. **3**(2), 123–128 (2017)

17. Jacob, G., Kirda, E., Kruegel, C., Vigna, G.: {PUBCRAWL}: protecting users and businesses from crawlers. In: Presented as part of the 21st USENIX Security Symposium (USENIX Security 12), pp. 507–522 (2012)

18. SEO optimization. Yujian [EB/OL] (2019). https://www.chabug.org/tools/655.html

19. Netsparker Web Application Security Scanner. Sqlmap [EB/OL] (2019). https://sqlmap.org/

20. Wpscanteam. Wpscan [EB/OL] (2019). https://github.com/wpscanteam/wpscan

21. Espreto. Wpsploit [EB/OL] (2019). https://github.com/espreto/wpsploit

22. OWASP Project. Dirbrute [EB/OL] (2019). https://github.com/Xyntax/DirBrute

23. Xmendez. Wfuzz [EB/OL] (2019). https://github.com/xmendez/wfuzz

24. Yu, J.X., Ou, Y., Zhang, C., Zhang, S.: Identifying interesting visitors through web log classification. IEEE Intell. Syst. **20**(3), 55–59 (2005)

25. Stevanovic, D., Vlajic, N., An, A.: Unsupervised clustering of web sessions to detect malicious and non-malicious website users. Procedia Comput. Sci. **5**, 123–131 (2011)

26. Doran, D., Gokhale, S.S.: An integrated method for real time and offline web robot detection. Expert Syst. **33**(6), 592–606 (2016)
27. OpenResty. Openresty - official site [EB/OL] (2017). https://openresty.org/en/
28. Fuyun. Safedog [EB/OL] (2018). http://www.safedog.cn/
29. Trustwave. Modsecurity [EB/OL] (2019). https://modsecurity.org/
30. Liang, S., Li, M., Liang, J., Chen, Z.: An experimental study of response times of web applications. J. Comput. Res. Dev. **40**(7), 1076–1080 (2003)

DMU-ABSE: Dynamic Multi-user Attribute-Based Searchable Encryption with File Deletion and User Revocation

Jiming Liu[1], Zhenfu Cao[1,2(✉)], Xiaolei Dong[1], and Jiachen Shen[1(✉)]

[1] Shanghai Key Laboratory of Trustworthy Computing,
East China Normal University, Shanghai, China
51174500107@stu.ecnu.edu.cn, {zfcao,dongxiaolei,jcshen}@sei.ecnu.edu.cn
[2] Cyberspace Security Research Center, Peng Cheng Laboratory, Shenzhen, Shanghai Institute of Intelligent Science and Technology, Tongji University, Shanghai, China

Abstract. Searchable encryption (SE) is a new cryptographic technique that allows data users searching for the files of their interests over huge amounts of encrypted files on the cloud. When it comes to multi-user setting, more issues should be addressed comparing to single-user setting, including key distribution, search privilege control and access control. In this paper, we propose DMU-ABSE, a dynamic multi-user ciphertext-policy attribute-based searchable encryption scheme with file deletion and user revocation. We manipulate an attribute-based encryption to achieve fine-grained search privilege control and hidden policy in multi-user setting while searching time of the proposed scheme is constant ($O(1)$). With the help of proxy re-encryption, we build one searchable index matrix by different owners in order to improve the searching efficiency. Furthermore, our scheme implements access control by embedding decryption keys into the index matrix. The proposed scheme is proved IND-CKA and IND-CPA semantically secure and experimental results shows that our scheme is efficient.

Keywords: Dynamic multi-user searchable encryption · Cipher-policy attribute-based encryption · Proxy re-encryption

1 Introduction

With the rapid growth of cloud computing technology, an increasing number of files, including documents, emails, videos, music and so on, have been outsourced to third-party cloud servers to make full use of powerful calculation capacity and massive storage space of cloud. These outsourced data usually contains sensitive information and business secrets which should not be leaked to the dishonest cloud server. To ensure data confidentiality and user privacy, data owners have to encrypt their data before outsourcing them to cloud. However, it is usually difficult to perform computation or search tasks over encrypted data. It is also infeasible for a user to download the entire archive when he needs to

© Springer Nature Singapore Pte Ltd. 2019
W. Meng and S. Furnell (Eds.): SocialSec 2019, CCIS 1095, pp. 17–31, 2019.
https://doi.org/10.1007/978-981-15-0758-8_2

search within it. Searchable encryption is proposed to solve this problem [15]. It enables users to search over encrypted data that have been outsourced to the cloud servers. In searchable encryption, data owners encrypt the files and generate associated indexes, which can be used to search over the whole data set without leaking information, before upload them to the cloud server [1]. When a data user wants to search for the files of his interest, he first generates a search trapdoor with keyword and then submits it to the cloud server. Finally, the cloud server performs the search operation and return the matched files to the data user without leaking any information [4]. According to the number of data owners and data users, SE schemes can be categorized into four models: one-to-one SE, one-to-many SE, many-to-one SE, and many-to-many SE.

When it comes to the many-to-many scenario, which is also called multi-user searchable encryption (MUSE) [6], access control is usually required to manage who is allowed to search and access the data. For example, different position in a company or university should be granted different search privileges over different files. Attribute-based encryption (ABE), in which data user is defined by a set of attributes, is known as a typical way to achieve fine-grained access control. There are two types of ABE schemes: key-policy ABE (KP-ABE) [7] and ciphertext-policy ABE (CP-ABE) [11], distinguished by the access policy embed in whether the ciphertext or the private key. In 2014, attribute-based encryption searchable encryption (ABSE) was introduced by Khader [9], and he discussed the security of the ABSE scheme. In ABSE schemes, only the data users whose attribute set satisfies the access policy have the access to search for the corresponding keywords. Zheng [18] proposed a verifiable attribute-based keyword search (VABKS), which enables user to verify whether the cloud has faithfully executed the search operation and return the true search result. In 2016, Sun [16] proposed a more general construction which supports user revocation and expressive search capability. However, the access policy is exposed in the air in [16]. In 2017, Wang [17] proposed a multi-value-independent ABKS scheme which makes the search time constant, irrelevant to the number of attributes, and hides the access policy. However it does not support dynamic update. Moreover, comparing to the single-user scheme, the multi-user scheme faces a series number of additional challenges. For example, how to distribute different private keys of different users and prevent collusion between users, and meanwhile keep high search efficiency in the same time is a challenging problem.

In this paper, we focus on the multi-user searchable encryption scheme which enables dynamic deletion operation while keeping highly efficiency and semantic security and propose a dynamic multi-user attribute-based searchable encryption, DMU-ABSE. In order to support access control, we improve an attribute-based encryption [17] to achieve fine-grained access control in multi-user searchable encryption, which is hidden-policy, constant size and non-deterministic. Besides, inspired by a single-user dynamic searchable encryption [8], we adopt index matrix and proxy re-encryption (PRE) to improve the proposed multi-user searchable scheme with respect to allowing update and deletion operations and reducing search time overhead. Proxy re-encryption (PRE) [3] is based on the public-key system. In a PRE system, proxy server can use a proxy re-encryption key to transform the ciphertext to another ciphertext under different secret keys without leaking any information about the plaintext and keys [14]. At last we will give security proof of DMU-ABSE. Experiments will also be given to show that it is efficient. In summary, we contribute a multi-user attribute-based searchable encryption scheme that is:

1. Hidden policy: Existing ABE schemes usually store access policy in the plaintext form in the encrypted index. Our scheme hides the access policy to prevent cloud server from learning the exact access policy of each file.
2. Constant trapdoor: The length of search tokens in existing attribute-based searchable encryption is usually linear to the number of attributes. But they are irrelevant in the proposed scheme.
3. Non-deterministic: Search trapdoor is non-deterministic in our scheme so that the trapdoor generated for an arbitrary keyword varies every time.
4. User revocation & File deletion: Our scheme provides the revocation algorithm to revoke the search authority to a user and deletion algorithm of a file on the cloud to support dynamic archives.
5. Decryption function: In traditional searchable encryption schemes, the search function is separated from decryption function. Our scheme supports access control on both searching and decryption functions.
6. Security: Security proofs will be given to show that our scheme is IND-CKA and IND-CPA secure in the generic bilinear group model which prevents collusion between different users.

2   System Model

2.1   System Roles

Our scheme mainly consists of five entities, namely trusted authority, data owners, data users, cloud server and proxy server in Fig. 1. The trusted authority is responsible for generating independent secret keys for data owners and data users, and system public keys. Each data owner firstly uses symmetric encryption to encrypt his original files and generate corresponding keyword indexes embed with access policy. And then data owners send these encrypted files and keyword indexes to the proxy server. Then, the proxy server re-encrypts these indexes and sends to the cloud server. The cloud server stores the re-encrypted indexes into an index matrix. While a data user wants to search for the files with target keyword, he firstly creates a search trapdoor by the keyword and secret key, and then sends the trapdoor to the proxy server. The proxy server re-encrypts the trapdoor and sends it to the cloud server to search in the index matrix. Finally, the cloud server returns all the matched files and corresponding decryption keys to the data owner.

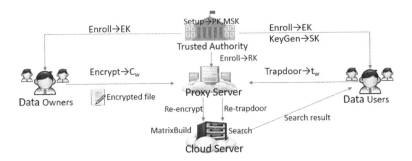

Fig. 1. System model

2.2   Application Scenario

The proposed scheme can be applied to many scenarios, such as personal health records (PHR) systems in which a huge amounts of patients updating their health records to the cloud and doctors can search for the target population or symptoms for research. Besides, it also can be applied to online subscription system where commercial publishers share charging data like videos or music with online subscribers.

2.3   Definition

- **Setup**$(1^\lambda) \to PK, MSK, MPK$
  Setup takes as input a security parameter λ, returns a public key PK, a master key MSK, and a master proxy key MPK.
- **Enroll**$(MSK, ID) \to EK_{ID}, RK_{ID}$
  Enroll algorithm is run by trusted authority, that takes as input the master key MSK and the new enrolled user ID. It returns enroll key EK_{ID} and corresponding proxy re-encryption key RK_{ID}.
- **KeyGenUser**$(MSK, S) \to SK$
  KeyGenUser algorithm is run by trusted authority, which takes as input the master key MSK and attributes set of a data user. It returns secret key SK for the data user.
- **Encrypt**$(PK, M \in \mathbb{G}_2, EK_{ID}, W, \mathbb{A}) \to C_w$
  Encrypt algorithm takes as input the public key PK, a decryption key of the file $M \in \mathbb{G}_1$, the enroll key EK_{ID}, keywords list $W = (w_1, w_2, ..., w_m)$ and the corresponding access structure $\mathbb{A}$, and generates an index ciphertext C_w. Only the secret keys satisfies S $= \mathbb{A}$ have access to search and decrypt index ciphertext C_w. Besides, the original file is supposed to be encrypted in symmetric encryption such as AES with symmetric key $M \in \mathbb{G}_1$.
- **Re-Encrypt**$(MPK, C_w, RK_{ID}) \to C'_w$
  Re-Encrypt algorithm is run by proxy server, which takes as input the master proxy key MPK, an encrypted index C_w and the re-encryption key RK_{ID} of the user ID, and outputs the re-encrypted index C'_w which will be send to the cloud server.

- **MatrixBuild**$(C'_w, id, \mathbb{M}) \rightarrow \mathbb{M}'$
  MatrixBuild algorithm is run by cloud server after receiving the re-encrypted index C'_w and file id from proxy server. It inserts the encrypted indexes into the index matrix $\mathbb{M}$ in Fig. 2.
- **Trapdoor** $(SK, EK_{ID}, w) \rightarrow t_w$
  Trapdoor algorithm is run by data user, which takes as input the secret key SK and a keyword w, it returns a search token t_w.
- **Re-Trapdoor**$(MPK, t_w, RK_{ID}) \rightarrow t'_w$
  Re-encryption algorithm is run by proxy server, which takes as input the master proxy key MPK, a search token t_w, and returns a re-encrypted token t'_w and sends it to cloud server.
- **Search**$(t'_w, \mathbb{M}) \rightarrow \mathcal{R}$
  Search algorithm is run by the cloud server to search for the target files in the index matrix $\mathbb{M}$ with t'_w. It returns the list $\mathcal{R}$ of all matched files and corresponding index ciphertext.
- **Decrypt**$(SK, C_{id}) \rightarrow M$
  Decrypt algorithm takes as input an index ciphertext C_{id} and a secret key SK, and returns the message M if S satisfies $\mathbb{A}$ embed in the ciphertext C_{id}. S is the attribute set used to generate SK. And then M can used to decrypt the file id.
- **FileDeletion**$(id, \mathbb{M})$
  File-Deletion algorithm takes as input the id of the file to be deleted, and the cloud server deletes the file and all corresponding index blocks in the index matrix $\mathbb{M}$ logically.
- **Revocation**(ID)
  Because of graduation, retirement or anything else, when a user wants to leave the system, his search privilege should be revoked. Revocation algorithm takes as input the user ID, and revokes his update and search permission.

2.4 System Adversarial Model

We now define the security for DMU-ABSE in the sense of semantic security in the generic bilinear group model.

We assume that cloud server and proxy server are semi-honest-but-curious, while proxy server won't collude with cloud server or any user. Firstly, we need to ensure that re-encrypt index label L_p which is send to the cloud server does not reveal any information about w. We define security against an active attacker who is able to obtain trapdoors for any w of his choice. Even under such attack, the attacker should not be able to distinguish an encryption of a keyword w_0 from an encryption of a keyword w_1 for which he did not obtain the trapdoor. Formally, we define security against an active adversary $\mathcal{A}$ using the following game between a challenger $\mathcal{B}$ and the adversary $\mathcal{A}$:

1. The challenger $\mathcal{B}$ runs the **Setup** algorithm and give public parameters PK to adversary $\mathcal{A}$.

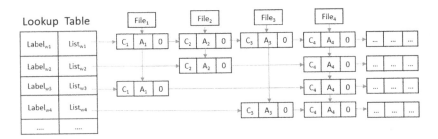

Fig. 2. Storage structure - Index matrix $\mathbb{M}$

2. The adversary $\mathcal{A}$ can adaptively ask the challenger $\mathcal{B}$ for the trapdoor for the keyword w
3. At some point, the adversary $\mathcal{A}$ sends the challenger $\mathcal{B}$ two keyword w_0, w_1 on which it wishes to be challenged. The challenger $\mathcal{B}$ picks a random $b \in \{0, 1\}$ and gives the adversary the challenge index label L_p^*.
4. Adversary $\mathcal{A}$ can continue to ask for re-trapdoor t'_w for any keyword w with the restriction that $w \neq w_0, w_1$.
5. Eventually, the adversary $\mathcal{A}$ outputs $b' \in \{0, 1\}$ and wins the game if $b = b'$

The advantage of an adversary is defined to be $Adv = |Pr[b = b'] - 1/2|$.

Definition 1. *(IND-CKA) DMU-ABSE is semantically secure against an adaptive chosen keyword attack if all probabilistic polynomial-time (PPT) attackers have at most negligible advantage in λ in the above security game.*

We now define security for DMU-ABSE to ensure that C_{id} does not reveal any information about M. We define security against an active attacker who is able to obtain secret keys which cannot decrypt the challenge ciphertext. Formally, we define security against an active adversary $\mathcal{A}$ using the following game between a challenger $\mathcal{B}$ and the adversary $\mathcal{A}$.

1. The challenger $\mathcal{B}$ runs the **Setup** algorithm and give public parameters PK to adversary $\mathcal{A}$.
2. The adversary $\mathcal{A}$ can adaptively ask the challenger $\mathcal{B}$ for the secret key for sets of $S_1, S_2, ..., S_{q1}$.
3. At some point, the adversary $\mathcal{A}$ sends the challenger $\mathcal{B}$ two message M_0, M_1 on which it wishes to be challenged. In addition the adversary $\mathcal{A}$ gives a challenge access structure $\mathbb{A}$. The only restriction is that such that none of the sets $S_1, S_2, ..., S_{q1}$ from phase (2) satisfy the access structure. The challenger $\mathcal{B}$ picks a random $b \in \{0, 1\}$ and gives the adversary the challenge ciphertext C_{id}^*.
4. Adversary $\mathcal{A}$ can continue to ask for secret SK for any sets with the restriction that none of the attributes $S_{q1+1}, S_{q1+2}, ..., S_q$ satisfy the challenge access structure.
5. Eventually, the adversary $\mathcal{A}$ outputs $b' \in \{0, 1\}$ and wins the game if $b = b'$

The advantage of an adversary is defined to be $Adv = |Pr[b = b'] - 1/2|$ in the game.

Definition 2. *(IND-CPA) DMU-ABSE is semantically secure against an adaptive chosen plaintext attack if all probabilistic polynomial-time (PPT) attackers have at most negligible advantage in λ in the above security game.*

3   Preliminaries

In this section, we will introduce some background on bilinear maps and generic group model.

3.1   Access Structure

There are several kinds of access structure in ABE scheme, such as threshold structure, tree-based structure and AND-gate structure. In our construction, we adopt a series of AND-gate on multi-value attribute as our access structure. It is assumed that the total number of attributes set is n, and all n attributes be indexed as $U = att_1, att_2, ..., att_n$. For every attribute $att_i \in U, (i = 1, 2, ..., n)$, $V_i = v_{i,1}, v_{i,2}, ..., v_{i,n_i}$ be a set of possible values of att_i, where n_i is the number of the possible values for att_i. Each user is defined as an attribute list $S = (x_1, x_2, ..., x_n)$, where $x_i \in V_i$. The access structure in ciphertext is defined as $\mathbb{A} = (W_1, W_2, ..., W_n)$, where $W_i \in V_i$. The attribute list S will satisfy the access structure $\mathbb{A}$ if and only if $x_i = W_i, (i = 1, 2, ..., n)$.

3.2   Bilinear Maps

A bilinear map is a map $e : \mathbb{G} \times \mathbb{G} \to \mathbb{G}_T$ with the following properties:

1. Bilinearity: $\forall u, v \in \mathbb{G}$ and $a, b \in \mathbb{Z}_p$, we have $e(u^a, v^b) = e(u, v)^{ab}$.
2. Non-degeneracy: $e(g, g) \neq 1$.
3. Computability: $e(u, v)$ is efficiently computable for any $u, v \in G$.

3.3   Generic Group Model

Let $\Upsilon = (p, \mathbb{G}, \mathbb{G}_T, e) \leftarrow Pair(1^\lambda)$. It is defined by [2] that: considering three random encodings $\psi_0, \psi_1 : \mathbb{Z}_p \to \{0, 1\}^m$, where $m > 3log(p)$. Let $\mathbb{G} = \{\psi_0(x) | x \in \mathbb{Z}_p\}$ and $\mathbb{G}_T = \{\psi_1(x) | x \in \mathbb{Z}_p\}$. Oracles are used to compute the induced group action on $\mathbb{G}, \mathbb{G}_T$ and compute a non-degenerate multilinear map $e : \mathbb{G} \times \mathbb{G} \to \mathbb{G}_T$. Random oracles are also given to present the hash functions H_1, H_2, H_3.

4 DMU-ABSE

4.1 Construction

1. **Setup**$(1^\lambda) \rightarrow PK, MSK, MPK$
   Let $\mathbb{G}$ and $\mathbb{G}_T$ be groups of order p, and let $e: \mathbb{G} \times \mathbb{G} \rightarrow \mathbb{G}_T$ be the bilinear map. The algorithm randomly chooses $\alpha, \beta, \nu \in \mathbb{Z}_p$, $g, h \in \mathbb{G}$ and three hash functions $H_1: \{0,1\}^* \rightarrow \mathbb{G}$, $H_2: \{0,1\}^* \rightarrow \mathbb{Z}_p$, $H_3: \{0,1\}^* \rightarrow \{0,1\}^\lambda$. let $A = e(g,g)^\alpha$, $B = g^\beta$, $V = h^\nu$. The system generates public key $PK = (\gamma, g, A, B, H_1, H_2, H_3)$, the master key $MSK = (\alpha, \beta, \nu)$, and the master proxy key $MPK = V$. MPK is send to the proxy server only.

2. **Enroll**$(MSK, ID) \rightarrow EK_{ID}, RK_{ID}$
   Trusted authority randomly chooses a number $r_{ID} \in \mathbb{Z}_p$ for the user ID and calculates $RK_{ID} = g^{\nu/r_{ID}}, M_1 = g^{r_{ID}}, M_2 = h^{r_{ID}}$. Finally, the enroll key $EK_{ID} = (M_1, M_2)$ is send to user ID, (ID, RK_{ID}) is send to proxy server.

3. **KeyGenUser**$(MSK, S) \rightarrow SK$
   Trusted authority takes input as a set of attributes $S = (x_1, x_2, ... x_n)$ and selects random $r, r_i \in \mathbb{Z}_p (i = 1, 2, ..., n)$, set $r_s = \sum_{i=1}^n r_i$. For each attribute $x_i \in S$, trusted authority calculates $\hat{D}_i = g^{r_i} \cdot H_1(x_i)^r$, $D_1 = g^{(\alpha + r_s)/\beta}$, $D_2 = \prod_{i=1}^n H_1(x_i)^\beta$, $D_3 = g^r$. The search key is send to data user as

$$<SK = (D_1, D_2, D_3, \{\hat{D}_i\} | x_i \in S)>$$

4. **Encrypt**$(PK, M \in \mathbb{G}_2, EK_{ID}, W, \mathbb{A}) \rightarrow C_w$
   Given a decryption key of the file $M \in \mathbb{G}_1$ and an AND gate policy $\mathbb{A} = (W_1, W_2..., W_n)$, and keywords list $W = (w_1, w_2, ..., w_m)$ in the file id, data owner selects random number $s_1, s_2 \in \mathbb{Z}_p^*$ and calculate $C_1 = B^{s_1}$, $C_2 = g^{s_1}$, $C_3 = M \cdot A^{s_1}$, $\hat{C}_i = H_1(W_i)^{s_1}$, $C_4^k = M_1^{H_2(w_k)} \cdot M_2^{s_2}$, where $w_k \in (w_1, w_2, ... w_m)$, $C_5 = g^{s_2}$. Finally, encrypted file id and all these encrypted indexes will be send to proxy server.

$$<\{C_{w_k}\}_{k=1,...,m} | C_{w_k} = (C_1, C_2, C_3, C_4^k, C_5, \hat{C}_i)>$$

5. **Re-Encrypt**$(MPK, C_w, RK_{ID}) \rightarrow C'_w$
   For every $\{C_{w_k}\}_{k=1,...,m}$, the proxy server calculates the re-encrypted label L_p^k and sends the re-encrypted indexes with corresponding encrypted file to the cloud server:

$$<\{C'_{w_k}\}_{k=1,...,m} | C'_{w_k} = (C_1, C_2, C_3, \hat{C}_i, L_p^k), L_p^k = H_3(\frac{e(C_4^k, RK_{ID})}{e(C_5, V)})>$$

6. **MatrixBuild**$(C'_w, id, \mathbb{M}) \rightarrow \mathbb{M}'$
   The cloud server firstly stores the file id and marks its address as A_{id}. Then it queries the look-up table $\mathbb{T}$ for every label L_p^k in $\{C'_{w_k}\}$:
   (a) If $\mathbb{T}[L_p^k] = NULL$, create a linked list $\mathbb{L}$ and sets the value of $\mathbb{T}[L_p^k]$ as the pointer of the list $\mathbb{L}$;
   (b) If $\mathbb{T}[L_p^k] \neq NULL$, set $\mathbb{L}$ as the value of $\mathbb{T}[L_p^k]$;

(c) Finally it creates a new index block value $< C_{id}, A_{id}, tagbit >$, where $C_{id} = (C_1, C_2, C_3, \hat{C}_i)$, and $tagbit = 0$ and adds it to the end of the linked list $\mathbb{L}$.

(d) After all $\{C'_{w_k}\}$ have been inserted, it creates a file array list $\mathbb{L}_f^{id}$ indexed by the file id and adds all the blocks above into the list.

7. **Trapdoor** $(SK, EK_{ID}, w) \rightarrow t_w$

Data user randomly selects $t \in \mathbb{Z}_p^*$ and calculates $tk_1 = D_2^t$, $tk_2 = B^t$, $tk_3 = M_1^{H_2(w)} \cdot M_2^t$, $tk_4 = g^t$, then sets the trapdoor of the chosen keyword w as:

$$<t_w = (tk_1, tk_2, tk_3, tk_4)>$$

8. **Re-Trapdoor** $(MPK, t_w, RK_{ID}) \rightarrow t'_w$

Proxy server calculates re-encrypted label L_p, and sends the re-encrypted trapdoor t'_w to the cloud server:

$$<t'_w = (tk_1, tk_2, L_p), L_p = H_3\left(\frac{e(tk_3, RK_{ID})}{e(tk_4, V)}\right)>$$

9. **Search** $(t'_w, \mathbb{M}) \rightarrow \mathcal{R}$

The cloud server searches for L_p in the look-up table, sets $P_w = \mathbb{T}[L_p]$ and creates a new empty result list $\mathcal{R}$, then follows:

(a) If $P_w = NULL$, return $\mathcal{R}$ and abort;

(b) If $tagbit = 1$, delete this linked list block and go to step (d);

(c) Retrieve index ciphertext $C_{id} = (C_1, C_2, C_3, \hat{C}_i)$ in P_w and run the **Test Equation** $e(tk_1, C_2) = e(\prod_{i=1}^n \hat{C}_i, tk_2)$ to check whether data user's attributes satisfy the access policy embed in the ciphertext. If the equation holds, add P_w to $\mathcal{R}$;

(d) Set P_w = next pointer of P_w and go to step (a);

After searching, cloud server finds out all encrypted files according to the A_{id} in the list $\mathcal{R}$, and returns them with corresponding index ciphertext C_{id} in $\mathcal{R}$ to the data user.

10. **Decrypt** $(SK, C_{id}) \rightarrow M$

After receiving the encrypted files and corresponding encrypted ciphertext C_{id}, data user can calculate E if his attribute list S satisfies the access policy $\mathbb{A}$, i.e. $x_i = W_i (i = 1, 2, ..., n)$.

$$E = \prod_{i=1}^n \frac{e(\hat{D}_i, C_2)}{e(D_3, \hat{C}_i)} = e(g, g)^{r_s s_1}$$

Then data user can get the corresponding decryption key M of the encrypted file by calculating

$$M = \frac{C_3}{(e(D_1, C_1)/E)}$$

11. **FileDeletion** $(id, \mathbb{M})$

The cloud server takes file id to find the file list $\mathbb{L}_f^{id}$ in the index matrix $\mathbb{M}$, and alters the tag bits from '0' to '1' in the index blocks in the list $\mathbb{L}_f^{id}$.

12. **Revocation**(ID)

The trusted authority uses ID to instruct the proxy server to delete the corresponding tuple (ID, RK_{ID}) in the proxy server. Without RK_{ID}, user's indexes and trapdoors won't be re-encrypted by the proxy server.

4.2 Correctness

Correctness (PRE): We now show that the **Re-encryption** and **Re-trapdoor** generate same labels of the same keyword:

$$L_p = H_3\left(\frac{e(C_4, RK)}{e(C_5, V)}\right) = H_3\left(\frac{e(M_1^{H_2(w)} \cdot M_2^{s_2}, g^{\nu/r_{ID}})}{e(g^{s_2}, h^\nu)}\right)$$

$$= H_3\left(\frac{e(g^{r_{ID}H_2(w)} \cdot h^{r_{ID}s_2}, g^{\nu/r_{ID}})}{e(g^{s_2}, h^\nu)}\right) = H_3(e(g,g)^{H_2(w)\nu}) = H_3\left(\frac{e(tk_3, RK)}{e(tk_4, V)}\right)$$

Correctness (Search): We now show the correctness of the **Test Equation** in the **Search** phase:

$$e(tk_1, C_2) = e(D_2^t, g^{s_1}) = e\left(\prod_{i=1}^n H(x_i)^{\beta t}, g^{s_1}\right) = e\left(\prod_{i=1}^n \hat{C}_i, tk_2\right)$$

Correctness (Decrypt): We now show the correctness of the **Decrypt** phase:

$$\frac{C_3}{(e(D_1, C_1)/E)} = \frac{C_3}{e(g^{\alpha+r_s/\beta}, g^{\beta s_1})/e(g.g)^{r_s s_1}} = \frac{M \cdot e_o(g,g)^{\alpha s_1}}{e(g.g)^{\alpha s_1}} = M$$

5   Security Analysis

In this section, we will give the security analysis of our dynamic multi-user attribute-based searchable encryption system proposed in Sect. 4.

We now prove that DMU-ABSE is IND-CKA secure in the generic bilinear group model.

Theorem 1. *Let $\gamma = (p, \mathbb{G}, \mathbb{G}_T, e)$ be defined as above. For any adversary $\mathcal{A}$ let q be a bound on the total number of group elements it receives from queries it makes to the oracles for the hash functions, groups $\mathbb{G}, \mathbb{G}_T$, the bilinear map e, and from its interaction with the IND-CKA security game. Then we have that the advantage of the adversary in the IND-CKA security game is negligible in λ.*

Proof. we initialize $g = \psi_0(1), g_T = \psi_1(1)$. We will write $g^x = \psi_0(x)$, $e(g,g)^y = \psi_1(y)$. In the following queries, the adversary $\mathcal{A}$ will communicate with the simulator $\mathcal{B}$ using the ψ-representations of the group elements. $\mathcal{B}$ interacts with $\mathcal{A}$ in the security game as follows:

1. The challenger $\mathcal{B}$ randomly selects $\alpha, \beta \in \mathbb{Z}_p$, $g, h \in \mathbb{G}$ and set public key as $A = e(g,g)^\alpha$, $B = g^\beta$, $V = h^\nu$, and sends the public key to adversary $\mathcal{A}$. When the adversary (or simulation) calls for the evaluation of H_1, H_2, H_3 on any string x_i, a new random value t_i is chosen from $\mathbb{Z}_p$ (unless it has already been

chosen), and the simulation provides g^{t_i} as the response to $H_1(x_i)$, $H_2(x_i)$ and $k_i = \{0,1\}^\lambda$ as the response to $H_3(x_i)$.

2. On $\mathcal{A}$'s secret key query for keyword w and user ID, a new random value $r^{(j)}$ is chosen from $\mathbb{Z}_p$, and for every attribute $x_j \in S_j$, new random values $r_i^{(j)}$, r_j' are chosen from $\mathbb{Z}_p$. The simulator $\mathcal{B}$ computes: $D_1 = g^{\frac{\alpha+r^{(j)}}{\beta}}$, $D_2 = \prod_{i=1}^{n} g^{t_i^{(j)}\beta}$, $D_3 = g^{r_j'}$, and for each attribute $x_i \in S_i, i = (1,2,...,n)$, $\mathcal{B}$ sets: $\hat{D}_i = g^{r_i^{(j)}+t_i^{(j)}r_j'}$. The secret key is defined as $SK = (D_1, D_2, D_3, \{\hat{D}_i\})$. Finally, $\mathcal{B}$ randomly chooses t_k, r_k from $\mathbb{Z}_p$ and generates the trapdoor of the chosen keyword w by: $tk_1 = D_2^{t_k}$, $tk_2 = B_k^t$, $tk_3 = g^{H_2(w)r_k}h^{r_k t_k}$, $tk_4 = g_k^t$ and then re-encrypts t_w by: $L_p = H_3(\frac{e(tk_3, g^{\nu/r_k})}{e(tk_4, h^\nu)}) = H_3(e(g,g)^{H_2(w)v})$. Then simulator $\mathcal{B}$ sends the re-encrypted trapdoor $t_w' = (tk_1, tk_2, L_p)$ to adversary $\mathcal{A}$.

3. Eventually adversary $\mathcal{A}$ produces a pair of keyword w_0 and w_1 that it wishes to be challenged on. The challenger $\mathcal{B}$ picks a random $b \in \{0,1\}$ and creates the challenging trapdoor as follows: $tk_1 = D_2^{t_k}$, $tk_2 = B^{t_k}$, $L_{p_b} = H_3(e(g,g)^{H_2(w_b)v})$. Finally, simulator $\mathcal{B}$ sends $t_{w_b}' = (tk_1, tk_2, L_{p_b})$ to adversary $\mathcal{A}$.

4. $\mathcal{A}$ repeats the query of phase (2) with the restriction that $\mathcal{A}$ did not previously ask for the trapdoors t_{w_0}', t_{w_1}'.

5. Eventually, the adversary $\mathcal{A}$ outputs $b' \in \{0,1\}$

We can instead consider a modified game in which the real challenging ciphertext via substituting $H_3(e(g,g)^{H_2(w_b)v})$ for $H_2(e(g,g)^\theta)$. The probability for distinguishing $H_3(e(g,g)^{H_2(w_0)v})$ from $e(g,g)^\theta$ is equal to half of the probability for distinguishing $H_3(e(g,g)^{H_2(w_0)v})$ from $H_3(e(g,g)^{H_2(w_1)v})$.

Suppose hash functions H_2 and H_3 are respectively modeled as two random oracles, and random value $k_i = \{0,1\}^\lambda$ is the response of $H_3(x_i)$. Then the ideal game for adversary $\mathcal{A}$ is to distinguish two random values k_1 and k_2 which are randomly choose from $\{0,1\}^\lambda$. Obliviously the probability for distinguish k_1 and k_2 is 0 unless there is a collision of H_3.

The probability that "unexpected collision" occurs is at most $O(q^2/p)$ before substitution by the Schwartz-Zipple lemma [13]. On the other hand, even if the adversary could distinguish $e(g,g)^{H_2(w_0)v}$ and $e(g,g)^\theta$, he is still unable to distinguish between $H_3(e(g,g)^{H_2(w_0)v})$ and $H_3(e(g,g)^\theta)$.

Therefore, we can conclude that $\mathcal{A}$ gains no unneglegible advantage in the modified game, which means that $\mathcal{A}$ gains a negligible advantage in the IND-CKA game. This completes the proof.

We now prove that DMU-ABSE is IND-CPA secure in the generic bilinear group model.

Theorem 2. *Let $\gamma = (p, \mathbb{G}, \mathbb{G}_T, e)$ be defined as above. For any adversary $\mathcal{A}$ let q be a bound on the total number of group elements it receives from queries it makes to the oracles for the hash functions, groups $\mathbb{G}, \mathbb{G}_T$, the bilinear map e, and from its interaction with the IND-CPA security game. Then we have that the advantage of the adversary in the IND-CPA security game is $O(q^2/p)$.*

Proof. we initialize $g = \psi_0(1), g_T = \psi_1(1)$. We will write $g^x = \psi_0(x), e(g, g)^y = \psi_1(y)$. In the following queries, the adversary $\mathcal{A}$ will communicate with the simulator $\mathcal{B}$ using the ψ-representations of the group elements. $\mathcal{B}$ interacts with $\mathcal{A}$ in the security game as follows:

1. The challenger $\mathcal{B}$ randomly selects $\alpha, \beta \in \mathbb{Z}_p$, and set public key as $A = e(g, g)^\alpha$, $B = g^\beta$, and sends the public key to adversary $\mathcal{A}$. When the adversary (or simulation) calls for the evaluation of H_1, H_2 on any string x_i, a new random value t_i is chosen from $\mathbb{Z}_p$ (unless it has already been chosen), and the simulation provides g^{t_i} as the response to $H_1(x_i), H_2(x_i)$.

2. On $\mathcal{A}$'s secret key query for set $S_j = \{x_1, x_2, ..., x_n\}$, a new random value $r^{(j)}$ is chosen from $\mathbb{Z}_p$, and for every attribute $x_j \in S_j$, new random values $r_i^{(j)}, r_j'$ are chosen from $\mathbb{Z}_p$. The simulator $\mathcal{B}$ computes: $D_1 = g^{\frac{\alpha + r^{(j)}}{\beta}}$, $D_2 = \prod_{i=1}^n g^{t_i^{(j)}\beta}$, $D_3 = g^{r_j'}$, and for each attribute $x_i \in S_i, i = (1, 2, ..., n)$, $\mathcal{B}$ sets: $\hat{D}_i = g^{r_i^{(j)} + t_i^{(j)} r_j'}$. The secret key is defined as $SK = (D_1, D_2, D_3, \{\hat{D}_i\})$ Then send the secret key SK to adversary $\mathcal{A}$.

3. Eventually adversary $\mathcal{A}$ produces a pair of message M_0 and M_1 and a challenge access structure $\mathbb{A}$. The challenger $\mathcal{B}$ selects random number $s_1 \in \mathbb{Z}_p^*$, picks a random $b \in \{0, 1\}$ and sets $C_1 = g^{\beta s_1}$, $C_2 = g^{s_1}$, $C_3 = M_b \cdot e(g, g)^{\alpha s_1}$. For each attribute in the AND gate $\mathbb{A}$, let $\hat{C}_i = g^{t_i s_1}, i = (1, 2, ..., n)$. These values are sent to $\mathcal{A}$.

4. $\mathcal{A}$ repeats the query of phase (2) with the restriction that $\mathcal{A}$ did not previously ask for the secret key for the attribute set S_i which satisfy the challenge access structure $\mathbb{A}$.

5. Eventually, the adversary $\mathcal{A}$ outputs $b' \in \{0, 1\}$

We can instead consider a modified game in which the real challenging ciphertext via substituting $M_b \cdot e(g, g)^{\alpha s_1}$ for $e(g, g)^\theta$. The probability for distinguishing $M_0 \cdot e(g, g)^{\alpha s_1}$ from $e(g, g)^\theta$ is equal to half of the probability for distinguishing $M_0 \cdot e(g, g)^{\alpha s_1}$ from $M_1 \cdot e(g, g)^{\alpha s_1}$.

We suppose that $\mathcal{B}$' simulation is prefect as long as no "unexpected collision" happens. More precisely, we think of an oracle query as being a rational function $\nu = \eta/\xi$ in the variables θ, α, β, $t_i^{(j)}$, $t^{(j)}$, $r_i^{(j)}$, r_j', $r^{(j)}$, s_1, s_2. An unexpected collision would be when two queries corresponding to two distinct formal rational functions $\eta/\xi = \eta'/\xi'$ but where due to the random choices of these variables values, we have that the values of $\eta/\xi = \eta'/\xi'$.

The probability that "unexpected collision" occurs is at most $O(q^2/p)$ before substitution by the Schwartz-Zipple lemma [13]. The adversary's view would have been identically distributed even if $\mathcal{B}$ substitutes αs_1 for variable θ. Since θ only occurs as $e(g, g)^\theta$, we must have that $\nu - \nu' = \gamma \alpha s_1 - \gamma'\theta$. The adversary can almost never construct a query for $e(g, g)^{\gamma \alpha s_1}$. To construct the term αs_1, the adversary can pairing $s_1\beta$ with $(\alpha + r^{(j)})/\beta$. In this way, $\mathcal{A}$ must create a query polynomial containing $\gamma \alpha s_1 + \Sigma \gamma' s_1 r^{(j)}$. In order to obtain a query of form αs_1, $\mathcal{A}$ must cancel the terms of form $\Sigma \gamma' s_1 r^{(j)}$.

To construct the term αs_1, the adversary can pairing $s_1\beta$ with $(\alpha + r^{(j)})/\beta$. But according to the simulation, $\mathcal{A}$ cannot get the secret key. Thus $\mathcal{A}$ is unable to get the form of αs_1 and construct the query for $e(g, g)^{\gamma \alpha s_1}$. By the

Schwartz-Zipple lemma, we can conclude that $\mathcal{A}$ gains a negligible advantage in the modified game, which means that $\mathcal{A}$ gains no unnegligible advantage in the IND-CPA game. This completes the proof.

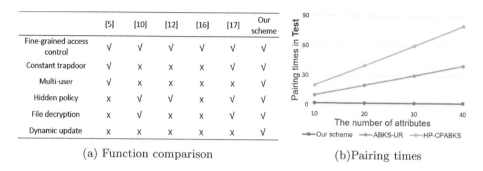

(a) Function comparison   (b)Pairing times

Fig. 3. Performance comparison with other related works

6 Comparison and Experiments

Functionality Comparisons: We list the key features of our scheme in Fig. 3(a) and make a comparison with several schemes, including MUSE-CK [5], KSF-OABE [10], HP-CPABKS [12], ABKS-UR [16], and CP-ABKS [17], in terms of supporting multi-user, constant-size trapdoor, hidden policy, file decryption and dynamic operation. Among these schemes, [5,10,12] and [17] are based on AND gate access structure. From the comparison, we can see that only [5] and our scheme achieve multi-user setting. Only in [5,17] and our scheme, the size of trapdoor are non-linear with the number of attributes involved in the access policy. Besides, only our scheme and [17] support decryption of the encrypted files in the search result. In particular, our multi-user attribute-based searchable encryption system also supports dynamic operations on the cloud including file updating and deleting.

Figure 3(b) demonstrates the comparison of pairing times of one search overhead between HP-CPABKS [12], ABKS-UR [16] and our scheme. It shows the number of pairing operations of our scheme does not change with the number of attributes during encryption, while the number of pairing operation of [12] and [16] are linear to the number of attributes. This makes our scheme more efficient in the complicated attribute scenarios.

Experimental Evaluation: In order to show the efficiency of our system, we conduct experiments with JPBC library on java8, which are executed on an AMD Ryzen5 2500U at 2.0 GHz and 8 GB memory. We exploit the Type A pairings conducted on the curve $y^2 = x^3 + x$ over the field $\mathbb{Z}_p$ for some prime $p = 3$ (*mod* 4). Experiments in Fig. 4(a) shows the relation between search time and the number of attributes in archives of 1000 files. It can be seen that the number of attributes barely influences the search time, which verifies that our scheme is independent of the number of attributes. Then in the scenario that the size of

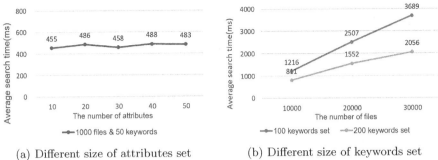

(a) Different size of attributes set   (b) Different size of keywords set

Fig. 4. Experimental results of average search time

the attribute set is 50, Fig. 4(b) shows the relation between search time and the number of files. It indicates that even in a huge archive, the search time will be reduced if the keywords set is increased, which implies our system is efficient in practical scenarios.

7 Conclusion

In this paper, a dynamic multi-user ciphertext-policy attribute-based searchable encryption system, DMU-ABSE, is presented. In DMU-ABSE, data owners authorize data users in a fine-grained manner by specifying access policy in the index ciphertexts. Meanwhile, DMU-ABSE achieves hidden-policy, constant size and non-deterministic properties. With the collaboration of the proxy server, the indexes and trapdoors will be re-encrypted before being sent to the cloud server so that the cloud server can merge them into one index matrix and search within it without learning any information. Furthermore, DMU-ABSE supports dynamic archives and user revocation, which is more practical in the scenario of PHR and online subscription systems. A concrete and formal proof is given to show that the proposed scheme is IND-CKA and IND-CPA secure in the sense of semantic security. The performance analysis demonstrates that the proposed scheme is efficient and practical.

Acknowledgement. This work was supported in part by the National Natural Science Foundation of China (Grant No. 61632012, 61672239, 61602180 and U1509219), in part by Natural Science Foundation of Shanghai (Grant No. 16ZR1409200), and in part by "the Fundamental Research Funds for the Central Universities". Zhenfu Cao and Jiachen Shen are the corresponding authors.

References

1. Bellare, M., Boldyreva, A., O'Neill, A.: Deterministic and efficiently searchable encryption. In: Menezes, A. (ed.) CRYPTO 2007. LNCS, vol. 4622, pp. 535–552. Springer, Heidelberg (2007). https://doi.org/10.1007/978-3-540-74143-5_30

2. Boneh, D., Boyen, X., Goh, E.-J.: Hierarchical identity based encryption with constant size ciphertext. In: Cramer, R. (ed.) EUROCRYPT 2005. LNCS, vol. 3494, pp. 440–456. Springer, Heidelberg (2005). https://doi.org/10.1007/11426639_26

3. Cao, Z.: New Directions of Modern Cryptography. CRC Press, Boca Raton (2012)

4. Chang, Y.-C., Mitzenmacher, M.: Privacy preserving keyword searches on remote encrypted data. In: Ioannidis, J., Keromytis, A., Yung, M. (eds.) ACNS 2005. LNCS, vol. 3531, pp. 442–455. Springer, Heidelberg (2005). https://doi.org/10.1007/11496137_30

5. Chang, Y.J., Wu, J.L.: Multi-user searchable encryption scheme with constant-size keys. In: 2017 IEEE 7th International Symposium on Cloud and Service Computing (SC2), pp. 98–103. IEEE (2017)

6. Curtmola, R., Garay, J., Kamara, S., Ostrovsky, R.: Searchable symmetric encryption: improved definitions and efficient constructions. J. Comput. Secur. **19**(5), 895–934 (2011)

7. Goyal, V., Pandey, O., Sahai, A., Waters, B.: Attribute-based encryption for fine-grained access control of encrypted data. In: Proceedings of the 13th ACM Conference on Computer and Communications Security, pp. 89–98. ACM (2006)

8. Hahn, F., Kerschbaum, F.: Searchable encryption with secure and efficient updates. In: Proceedings of the 2014 ACM SIGSAC Conference on Computer and Communications Security, pp. 310–320. ACM (2014)

9. Khader, D.: Introduction to attribute based searchable encryption. In: De Decker, B., Zúquete, A. (eds.) CMS 2014. LNCS, vol. 8735, pp. 131–135. Springer, Heidelberg (2014). https://doi.org/10.1007/978-3-662-44885-4_11

10. Li, J., Lin, X., Zhang, Y., Han, J.: KSF-OABE: outsourced attribute-based encryption with keyword search function for cloud storage. IEEE Trans. Serv. Comput. **10**(5), 715–725 (2017)

11. Nishide, T., Yoneyama, K., Ohta, K.: Attribute-based encryption with partially hidden encryptor-specified access structures. In: Bellovin, S.M., Gennaro, R., Keromytis, A., Yung, M. (eds.) ACNS 2008. LNCS, vol. 5037, pp. 111–129. Springer, Heidelberg (2008). https://doi.org/10.1007/978-3-540-68914-0_7

12. Qiu, S., Liu, J., Shi, Y., Zhang, R.: Hidden policy ciphertext-policy attribute-based encryption with keyword search against keyword guessing attack. Sci. China Inf. Sci. **60**(5), 052105 (2017)

13. Schwartz, J.: Fast polynomial algorithms for verification of polynomial identities. J. Assoc. Comput. **27**(4), 701–717 (1980)

14. Shao, J., Cao, Z.: CCA-Secure proxy re-encryption without pairings. In: Jarecki, S., Tsudik, G. (eds.) PKC 2009. LNCS, vol. 5443, pp. 357–376. Springer, Heidelberg (2009). https://doi.org/10.1007/978-3-642-00468-1_20

15. Song, D.X., Wagner, D., Perrig, A.: Practical techniques for searches on encrypted data. In: Proceeding 2000 IEEE Symposium on Security and Privacy, S&P 2000, pp. 44–55. IEEE (2000)

16. Sun, W., Yu, S., Lou, W., Hou, Y.T., Li, H.: Protecting your right: verifiable attribute-based keyword search with fine-grained owner-enforced search authorization in the cloud. IEEE Trans. Parallel Distrib. Syst. **27**(4), 1187–1198 (2016)

17. Wang, H., Dong, X., Cao, Z.: Multi-value-independent ciphertext-policy attribute based encryption with fast keyword search. IEEE Trans. Serv. Comput. (2017). https://doi.org/10.1109/TSC.2017.2753231

18. Zheng, Q., Xu, S., Ateniese, G.: VABKS: verifiable attribute-based keyword search over outsourced encrypted data. In: IEEE INFOCOM 2014-IEEE Conference on Computer Communications, pp. 522–530. IEEE (2014)

A Novel Lattice-Based Ciphertext-Policy Attribute-Based Proxy Re-encryption for Cloud Sharing

Juyan Li[1,3], Chunguang Ma[2,3], and Kejia Zhang[1(✉)]

[1] College of Data Science and Technology, Heilongjiang University,
Harbin 150080, People's Republic of China
lijuyan587@163.com, zhangkejia@hlju.edu.cn
[2] College of Computer Science and Technology, Harbin Engineering University,
Harbin 150001, People's Republic of China
machunguang@hrbeu.edu.cn
[3] State Key Laboratory of Information Security, Institute of Information Engineering,
Chinese Academy of Sciences, Beijing 100093, People's Republic of China

Abstract. Proxy re-encryption plays an important role in cloud sharing. Ciphertext-policy attribute-based proxy re-encryption (CP-ABPRE) scheme supports access control and can convert the ciphertext under an access policy to a ciphertext under another access policy, which is flexible and efficient for cloud sharing. The existing CP-ABPRE schemes are constructed by bilinear pairing or multi-linear maps which are fragile when the post-quantum comes. In this paper, a unidirectional single-hop CP-ABPRE scheme with small size of public parameters was presented by using trapdoor sampling, and proved secure under learning with errors assumption which is widely believed secure in quantum computer attacks.

Keywords: LWE · Proxy re-encryption · Attribute-based encryption · Cloud sharing

1 Introduction

Proxy re-encryption (PRE) allows the proxy to convert the ciphertext of delegator to the ciphertext of delegatee who can be specified by the delegator, while the proxy will not know the message in this process, which can be used for cloud sharing. At present, many types of PRE have been constructed such as conditional proxy re-encryption (CPRE) [1], homomorphic proxy re-encryption (HPRE) [2], proxy broadcast re-encryption (PBRE) [3], identity-based proxy re-encryption (IBPRE) [4], Attribute-Based Proxy Re-Encryption (ABPRE) [5].

Attribute-Based Encryption (ABE) was introduced by Sahai et al. [6] which is an extension of identity-based encryption (IBE). ABE can achieve fine-grained access control of encrypted data and provide a one-to-many encryption. Goyal et al. [7] introduced two variants of ABE, that is key policy attribute-based

© Springer Nature Singapore Pte Ltd. 2019
W. Meng and S. Furnell (Eds.): SocialSec 2019, CCIS 1095, pp. 32–46, 2019.
https://doi.org/10.1007/978-981-15-0758-8_3

encryption (KP-ABE) and ciphertext policy attribute-based encryption (CP-ABE). In a KP-ABE (CP-ABE) system, the ciphertext (private key) is associated with an attribute set S, the private key (ciphertext) is associated with an access structure W, the private key can decrypt the ciphertext if and only if S satisfies W.

Because of the resource-limited of the terminal device, it is impossible for users to backup all data (in the plain format) and make heavy compute. In cloud networks, a user (e.g., Alice) can use CP-ABE to encrypt her data with access structure W, and then store the ciphertext to cloud for sharing data and protecting her privacy. Suppose the access structure W needs to be updated to another policy W' for the new needs of other users (e.g., Bob), then Alice should download and decrypt the ciphertext, and then again encrypt the data with W'. If the access structure is renewed frequently, the computational overhead of this strategy at Alice will be too heavy.

Ciphertext-policy attribute-based proxy re-encryption (CP-ABPRE) can make data cloud sharing more effective. ABPRE only needs Alice to generate a re-encryption key and send it to proxy who can convert the ciphertext under W to a ciphertext under another W'. Cloud sharing should also consider issues such as authentication [8–10]. Liang et al. [11] constructed the first CP-ABPRE supporting AND gates over positive and negative attributes. Luo et al. [12] extended [5]to a CP-ABPRE supporting AND gates on multi-valued and negative attributes. Liang et al. [13] constructed the first adaptively CCA-secure CP-ABPRE. Zhang et al. [14] presented a ciphertext policy attribute-based encryption (ABE) scheme based on LWE which is widely believed secure in quantum computer attacks.

In this paper, we constructed a CP-ABE scheme by modifying the ABE scheme of Zeng et al. [15]. Compared with the ABE scheme of [14,15], our CP-ABE scheme has smaller size of public parameters. The existing CP-ABPRE schemes are constructed by bilinear pairing or multi-linear maps which are fragile when the post-quantum comes. We constructed a CP-ABPRE based on the new CP-ABE scheme by using trapdoor sampling from LWE which is widely believed secure in quantum computer attacks. Our CP-ABPRE scheme is the first CP-ABPRE from LWE and can implement the transfer of ciphertext access structure.

The rest of this paper is organized as follows. Section 2 is preliminaries. Section 3 describes the constructed ABPRE scheme. At last, our work is concluded in Sect. 4.

2   Preliminaries

In this section, we introduce some notations, Gaussian distribution, the LWE hardness assumption and the definition of CP-ABPRE.

2.1 Notation

We employ some initial notations listed in Table 1. For an integer q and a vector $\boldsymbol{x} \in \mathbb{Z}_q{}^n$, let $l = \lceil \log q \rceil$, $P2(\boldsymbol{x}) = (1\boldsymbol{x}; 2\boldsymbol{x}; \cdots; 2^{l-1}\boldsymbol{x}) \in \mathbb{Z}_q^{nl}$, $BD(\boldsymbol{x}) = (\boldsymbol{u}_1 | \cdots | \boldsymbol{u}_l) \in \{0,1\}^{nl}$, where $\boldsymbol{x} = \sum_{k=1}^{l} 2^{k-1} \boldsymbol{u}_k$. When A is a matrix, let $P2(A)$ $(BD(A))$ be the matrix formed by applying the operation to each row (column) of A.

Table 1. Notation

x	Scalar
$\boldsymbol{x}$	Vector
A	Matrix or set
$\|\boldsymbol{x}\|_\infty$	l_∞ norm of $\boldsymbol{x}$
$\|\boldsymbol{x}\|$	l_2 norm of $\boldsymbol{x}$
$[k]$	Set $\{1, 2, \cdots, k\}$
$|L|$	The order of set L
$S \vDash (\nvDash)W$	Attribute set S satisfies (or does not satisfy) access structure W
$[X|Y] \in \mathbb{Z}_q^{m \times (n_1+n_2)}$	The concatenation of the columns of $X \in \mathbb{Z}_q^{m \times n_1}, Y \in \mathbb{Z}_q^{m \times n_2}$
$[X;Y] \in \mathbb{Z}_q^{(n_1+n_2) \times m}$	The concatenation of the rows of $X \in \mathbb{Z}_q^{n_1 \times m}, Y \in \mathbb{Z}_q^{n_2 \times m}$
$x \leftarrow \chi$	x is sampled according to a probability distribution χ
$x \leftarrow S$	x is sampled uniformly from a set S
$X \approx_c (\approx_s)Y$	X and Y are computationally (statistically) indistinguishable

2.2 Gaussian Distributions and the LWE Hardness Assumption

For any positive parameter $\sigma > 0$, define the Gaussian function on $\mathbb{R}^m$, centered at $\boldsymbol{c}$: $\forall \boldsymbol{x} \in \mathbb{R}^m$,

$$\rho_{\sigma,\boldsymbol{c}}(\boldsymbol{x}) = \exp\left(-\pi \|\boldsymbol{x} - \boldsymbol{c}\|^2 / \sigma^2\right).$$

Let Λ be a discrete subset of $\mathbb{Z}^m$. For any vector $\boldsymbol{c} \in \mathbb{R}^m$ and any positive parameter $\sigma > 0$, define the discrete Gaussian distribution over Λ as: $\forall \boldsymbol{x} \in \mathbb{R}^m$,

$$\chi_{\Lambda,\sigma,\boldsymbol{c}}(\boldsymbol{x}) = \frac{\rho_{s,\boldsymbol{c}}(\boldsymbol{x})}{\rho_{\sigma,\boldsymbol{c}}(\Lambda)},$$

where $\rho_{\sigma,\boldsymbol{c}}(\Lambda) = \sum_{\boldsymbol{x} \in \Lambda} \rho_{\sigma,\boldsymbol{c}}(\boldsymbol{x})$.

Lemma 1 *([16]). For any $c \in \Lambda \subset \mathbb{Z}^m$, let $x \leftarrow D_{\Lambda+c,\sigma}$, $\sigma > \eta_\epsilon(\Lambda)$ for some $\epsilon \in (0,1)$, then with overwhelming probability $\|x\| < \sigma\sqrt{m}$. Moreover, if $c = 0$ then the bound holds for any $\sigma > 0$, with $\epsilon = 0$.*

Lemma 2 *([17]). Let q, n, m be positive integers with $q \geq 2$ and $m \geq 6n\log q$. There is a probabilistic polynomial-time algorithm $TrapGen(q, n, m)$ that outputs a pair $(A, T) \in \mathbb{Z}_q^{n \times m} \times \mathbb{Z}^{m \times m}$ such that A is statistically close to uniform in $\mathbb{Z}_q^{n \times m}$ and T is a basis for $\Lambda_q^\perp(A) = \{e \in \mathbb{Z}^m, s.t. Ae = 0 \bmod q\}$, satisfying $\|T\| \leq O(n\log q)$ and $\|\tilde{T}\| \leq O\left(\sqrt{n\log q}\right)$ (Alwen and Peikert assert that the constant hidden in the first $O(\cdot)$ is no more than 20).*

Lemma 3 *([18]). Let $q \geq 2$ and a matrix $A \in \mathbb{Z}_q^{n \times m}$. Let T_A be a basis for $\Lambda_q^\perp(A)$, $\sigma \geq \|\tilde{T}\| \omega\left(\sqrt{\log m}\right)$. Then for $c \in \mathbb{Z}^m$, $u \in \mathbb{Z}_q^n$. There is a PPT algorithm $SamplePre(A, T_A, u, c)$ that returns $x \in \Lambda_q^u(A) = \{e \in \mathbb{Z}^m, s.t. Ae = u \bmod q\}$ sampled from a distribution statistically close to $D_{\Lambda_q^u(A),\sigma,c}$.*

For the correctness of our CP-ABPRE, we recall a distribution $\overline{\Psi}_\alpha$ over $\mathbb{Z}_q$ in which the random variable is $\lfloor qX \rceil \bmod q$, where $\alpha \in (0,1)$ is a real, p is a prime, X is a normal random variable with mean 0 and deviation $\alpha^2/2\pi$.

Lemma 4 *([18]). Let $r \in \mathbb{Z}^m$, $e \leftarrow \overline{\Psi}_\alpha^m$. Then with overwhelming probability in m*

$$\left|r^T e\right| \leq \|r\| q\alpha\omega\left(\sqrt{\log m}\right) + \|r\|\sqrt{m}/2.$$

In particularly, we have $|e| \leq q\alpha\omega\left(\sqrt{\log m}\right) + 1/2$ with overwhelming probability in m if $e \leftarrow \overline{\Psi}_\alpha$.

The LWE (learning with errors) problem is a classic hard problem on lattices, which is as hard as the worst-case SIVP and GapSVP with certain noise distributions χ, such as $\overline{\Psi}_\alpha$.

Theorem 1 *([19]). Let $q \geq 2$, and χ be a distribution over $\mathbb{Z}$. The decisional $LWE_{n,q,\chi}$ problem is to distinguish the following two distributions: one is $(a_i; b_i) \leftarrow \mathbb{Z}_q^{n+1}$, the other is $(a_i, b_i) \in \mathbb{Z}_q^{n+1}$, where $a_i \leftarrow \mathbb{Z}_q^n, b_i = a_i^T s + e_i$, $s \leftarrow \mathbb{Z}_q^n, e_i \leftarrow \chi$. The $LWE_{n,q,\chi}$ assumption is that the $LWE_{n,q,\chi}$ problem is infeasible.*

2.3   Attribute and Access Structure

In this paper, we study CP-ABE that supports and-gates on positive and negative attributes. Let $L = [\|L\|]$ be the set of all attributes in system. For $i \in [L]$, each user has or does not have attribute i. If a user does not have attribute i, we say the user has attribute $-i$ which means each attribute i is associated with $-i$. We use i and $-i$ as positive and negative attribute, respectively.

Definition 1. *For an access structure W organized by and-gates on positive and negative attributes, an attribute set S satisfies W if and only if*

$$S^+ \subseteq S, S^- \subseteq L \backslash S,$$

where $S^+ (S^-)$ is the positive (negative) attribute set in W, L is the set of all attributes in system.

For instance, let $L = [4]$, access structure $W = (1 and - 3)$, if $S \vDash W$, then we only need $1 \in S, 3 \notin S$, and don't need consider $2, 4$. The attribute sets $S_1 = \{1\}, S_2 = \{1, 2\}, S_3 = \{1, 4\}, S_4 = \{1, 2, 4\}$ all satisfy W.

2.4   Definition and Security Model of CP-ABPRE

A Single-Hop Unidirectional CP-ABPRE scheme has four participants.

(1) Trusted Authority (TA). TA generates public parameters, master secret key, re-encryption key and can be trusted by all participants.
(2) Cloud Services Provider (CSP). CSP can store data which were uploaded by DO, compute the re-encrypted ciphertext by the original ciphertext and re-encryption key. CSP is semi-trusted.
(3) Data Owner (DO). DO encrypts his data and stores the encrypted data in cloud.
(4) Data User (DU). DU queries the CSP for re-encrypted data which belongs to DO.

Based on the definition and the security model of Liang et al. [5], we give the following definition.

Definition 2. *A single-hop unidirectional CP-ABPRE scheme consists of the following six algorithms:*

1. *Setup (κ, L): Given a security parameter κ, a set of attribute L, the TA returns public parameters pp and master secret key msk.*
2. *KeyGen (pp, msk, S): Given pp, msk and an attribute set S of the DO or DU, the TA returns secret key sk_S for S. Note that each secret key sk_S is associated with an attribute set S.*
3. *Encrypt (pp, W, μ): Given pp, a message μ, and an access structure W over the attribute set L, the DO returns ciphertext C_W. Note that each ciphertext C_W is associated with an access structure W.*
4. *Decrypt (pp, sk_S, C_W, S): Given pp, C_W, S and its corresponding secret key sk_S, the DO or DU returns plaintext μ if $S \vDash W$ or a symbol $\perp$ indicating either C_W is invalid or $S \nvDash W$.*
5. *ReKeyGen (pp, S, W, W^1): Given pp, attribute set S and two access structures W, W^1, the TA returns a re-encryption key $rk_{W \rightarrow W^1}$ which can be used to transform a ciphertext with W to another ciphertext with W^1 if $S \vDash W$ or a symbol $\perp$ if $S \nvDash W$. The access structure W and W^1 are required to be disjoint, that is $S^+ \subseteq S^{1,-}, S^- \subseteq S^{1,+}$, where $S^+, S^{1,+}(S^-, S^{1,-})$ are the positive (negative) attribute set in W, W^1.*

6. *ReEnc* $(pp, C_W, rk_{W \to W^1})$: *Given* pp, C_W, $rk_{W \to W^1}$, *the CSP outputs the re-encrypted ciphertext* C_{W^1} *or a symbol* $\perp$ *indicating* W *and* W^1 *are not disjoint.*

Correctness: There are two requirements for correctness,

1. Decrypt$(pp, sk_S, C_W)= \mu$, where $C_W = Encrypt(pp, W, \mu)$ and $S \vDash W$.
2. Decrypt$(pp, sk_{S^1}, C_{W^1})= \mu$, where $C_{W^1} = ReEnc(pp, rk_{W \to W^1}, C_W)$, $C_W = Encrypt(pp, W, \mu)$, $rk_{W \to W^1} = ReKeyGen(pp, W, W^1)$, $S^1 \vDash W^1$.

Definition 3. *For a single-hop unidirectional CP-ABPRE scheme, let* κ *be a security parameter. Consider the following games, denoted by* $Expt_{CP-ABPRE,\mathcal{A}}^{IND-sAS-CPA-Or}(\kappa)$, *between challenger and adversary.*

Initialization. *The adversary chooses a challenge access structure* W^* *to challenger.*

Setup Phase: *The challenger runs Setup* (κ, L) *and sends pp to adversary.*

Learning Phase: *In this phase, the adversary can access to the following oracles polynomially many times, and the challenger needs to answer these oracles.*

(1) *Secret key oracle* $\mathcal{O}_{sk}(S)$: *The adversary inputs an attribute set S. If* $S \nvDash W^*$, *then the challenger returns* $sk_S \leftarrow KeyGen(pp, msk, S)$. *Otherwise, the challenger returns* $\perp$.

(2) *Re-encryption key oracle* $\mathcal{O}_{rk}(W, W')$: *The adversary inputs two access structure* W, W'. *If* $W = W^*$ *and* $\mathcal{O}_{sk}(S')$ *has been accessed for any* $S' \vDash W'$, *then challenger returns* $\perp$. *Otherwise, the challenger returns* $rk_{W \to W'} \leftarrow ReKeyGen(pp, W, W')$.

(3) *Re-encryption oracle* $\mathcal{O}_{re}(rk_{W \to W'}, W', C_W)$: *The adversary inputs* W', C_W, $rk_{W \to W'}$. *If* $rk_{W \to W'} \leftarrow ReKeyGen(pp, W, W')$, $sk_S \leftarrow KeyGen(pp, msk, S)$, $S \vDash W$, *then the challenger returns* $C_{W'} \leftarrow ReEnc(pp, C_W, rk_{W \to W'})$. *Otherwise, the challenger returns* $\perp$.

Challenge: *If the adversary finishes all of the oracles' queries, then he sends* $\mu \in \{0, 1\}$ *to the challenger. For a coin* $b \in \{0, 1\}$, *the challenger returns a random ciphertext* C *if* $b = 0$ *or the real ciphertext* $C_{W^*} \leftarrow Encrypt(pp, W^*, \mu)$ *if* $b = 1$.

Gauss: *Finally, the adversary outputs a guess* $b' \in \{0, 1\}$. *If* $b' = b$, *the adversary wins.*

We say a single-hop unidirectional CP-ABPRE scheme is IND-sAS-CPA secure at original ciphertext if for any PPT adversary, the advantage

$$Adv_{CP-ABPRE,\mathcal{A}}^{IND-sAS-CPA-Or}(\kappa) = \left| Pr\left[b = b'\right] - \frac{1}{2} \right|$$

of adversary is negligible.

Definition 4. *For a single-hop unidirectional CP-ABPRE scheme, let κ be a security parameter. We say a single-hop unidirectional CP-ABPRE scheme is IND-sAS-CPA secure at re-encrypted ciphertext if for any PPT adversary, the advantage*

$$\text{Adv}_{\text{CP-ABPRE},\mathcal{A}}^{\text{IND-sAS-CPA}-Re}(\kappa) = \left| Pr \left[\begin{array}{l} b = b' : \\ (W^*, state_1) \leftarrow \mathcal{A}(1^\kappa); \\ (pp, msk) \leftarrow Setup(1^\kappa, L); \\ (\mu, W, state_2) \leftarrow \mathcal{A}^{\mathcal{O}_1}(pp, state_1); \\ b \leftarrow \{0,1\}; \\ C_{W^*}^* \leftarrow ReEnc(rk_{W \to W^*}, C_W); \\ b' \leftarrow \mathcal{A}^{\mathcal{O}_1}(C_{W^*}^*, state_2) \end{array} \right] - \frac{1}{2} \right|$$

of adversary is negligible, where $\mathcal{O}_1 = \{\mathcal{O}_{\text{sk}}, \mathcal{O}_{\text{rk}}, \mathcal{O}_{\text{re}}\}$ and $\mathcal{O}_{\text{sk}}$ (it is forbidden to $S \vDash W^*$), $\mathcal{O}_{\text{rk}}, \mathcal{O}_{\text{re}}$ (it is forbidden to C_W is an valid original ciphertext or a re-encrypted ciphertext) as in Definition 3, $State_1$ and $State_2$ are the state information, W^* is challenge access structure and W, W^* are disjoint, C_W is a random ciphertext C if $b = 0$ or the real ciphertext $C_W \leftarrow \text{Encrypt}(pp, W, \mu)$ if $b = 1$, $\mu \in \{0, 1\}$.

3   A CP-ABPRE Scheme

In this section, a single-hop unidirectional CP-ABPRE scheme was presented at first, then the correctness and security of CP-ABPRE were proved.

3.1   Concrete Scheme

A single-hop unidirectional CP-ABPRE scheme consists of the following six algorithms.

1. Setup(n, m, q, L): Given positive integers n, m, q, and a set of attribute L, the TA samples $\boldsymbol{u} \leftarrow \mathbb{Z}_q^n$, computes $(A_{i,b}, T_{i,b}) \leftarrow TrapGen(q, n)$ for $i \in L$, where $b \in \{0, 1\}$ and returns public parameters $pp = \left(\{A_{i,b}\}_{i \in L}^{b \in \{0,1\}}, \boldsymbol{u} \right)$ and master secret key $msk = \left(\{T_{i,b}\}_{i \in L}^{b \in \{0,1\}} \right)$.

2. KeyGen(pp, msk, S): Given pp, msk and an attribute set S of the DU, where $S \subseteq L$, the TA lets $A_i = \begin{cases} A_{i,0}, & i \in L \backslash S \\ A_{i,1}, & i \in S \end{cases}$, computes $\boldsymbol{s} \leftarrow$ SamplePre $(A, T, \boldsymbol{u})$ and returns secret key $sk_S = \boldsymbol{s}$, where $A = (A_1 | \cdots | A_{|L|})$, $T = \begin{bmatrix} T_1 & & \\ & \ddots & \\ & & T_{|L|} \end{bmatrix}$, T_i is the basis for $\Lambda_q^\perp(A_i)$, $i \in L$.

3. Encrypt(pp, W, μ): Given pp, a message $\mu \in \{0, 1\}$, and an access structure W, the DO denotes S^+ (S^-) as the positive (negative) attribute set in W, computes

$$c = \boldsymbol{u}^T \boldsymbol{f} + x_c + \left\lfloor \frac{q}{2} \right\rfloor \mu,$$

$$c_{i,0} = \begin{cases} z_{i,0}, & i \in S^+ \\ A_{i,0}^T f + x_{i,0}, & i \in S^- \end{cases},$$

$$c_{i,1} = \begin{cases} A_{i,1}^T f + x_{i,1}, & i \in S^+ \\ z_{i,1}, & i \in S^- \end{cases},$$

$$\begin{pmatrix} c_{j,0} \\ c_{j,1} \end{pmatrix} = \begin{pmatrix} A_{j,0}^T \\ A_{j,1}^T \end{pmatrix} f + \begin{pmatrix} x_{j,0} \\ x_{j,1} \end{pmatrix},$$

$j \in L \backslash (S^+ \cup S^-)$, and returns ciphertext

$$C_W = \left(c; \{ c_{i,0}, c_{i,1} \}_{i \in L} \right),$$

where $x_c \leftarrow \chi$, $f \leftarrow \chi^n$, $z_{i,0}, z_{i,1}, x_{i,0}, x_{i,1} \leftarrow \chi^m$.

4. Decrypt(pp, C_W, sk_S, S): After receiving the cipthertext C_W from CSP, the DU computes $y = \left(y_1; \cdots; y_{|L|} \right)$ by $y_i = \begin{cases} c_{i,1}, & i \in S \\ c_{i,0}, & else \end{cases}$, and then outputs 0 if $\left(-s^T | 1 \right) \left(y^T; c \right) \doteq c - y^T s$ is closer to 0 than to $\lfloor \frac{q}{2} \rfloor$ modulo q, and 1 otherwise.

5. ReKeyGen(pp, S, W, W^1): After receiving pp, S, two access structures W, W^1 from DO, If W, W^1 are not disjoint or $S \nvDash W$, then the TA outputs $\bot$, otherwise, denotes the positive (negative) attribute set in W^1 as $S^{1,+} \left(S^{1,-} \right)$, noting $S^{1,+} \subseteq L, S^{1,-} \subseteq L$, then computes

$$Q_{i,0} \leftarrow \begin{cases} \overline{X_i}, & i \in S^{1,+} \\ P2 \left(R_{i,1\to0}^T \right) + X_i, & i \in S^{1,-} \end{cases},$$

$$Q_{i,1} \leftarrow \begin{cases} P2 \left(R_{i,0\to1}^T \right) + X_i, & i \in S^{1,+} \\ \overline{X_i}, & i \in S^{1,-} \end{cases},$$

$$Q_{i,0} \leftarrow P2 \left(R_{i,1\to0}^T \right) + X_{i,0}, i \in \left(L \backslash \left(S^{1,+} \cup S^{1,-} \right) \right),$$

$$Q_{i,1} \leftarrow P2 \left(R_{i,0\to1}^T \right) + X_{i,1}, i \in \left(L \backslash \left(S^{1,+} \cup S^{1,-} \right) \right),$$

Where $R_{i,1\to0} \leftarrow$ SamplePre$(A_{i,1}, T_{i,1}, A_{i,0})$, $R_{i,0\to1} \leftarrow$ SamplePre$(A_{i,0}, T_{i,0}, A_{i,1})$, $X_i, X_{i,0}, X_{i,1} \leftarrow \chi^{m \times m \lceil \log q \rceil}$, $\overline{X_i} \leftarrow \mathbb{Z}_q^{m \times m \lceil \log q \rceil}$ and finally returns re-encryption key $rk_{S \to W^1} = \left(\{ Q_{i,0}, Q_{i,1} \}_{i \in L} \right)$.

6. ReEnc$(pp, C_W, rk_{W \to W^1})$: Given $pp, C_W, rk_{W \to W^1}$, the CSP computes

$$c_{i,0}^1 = \begin{cases} Q_{i,0} BD \left(c_{i,1} \right) + x_{i,0}^1, & i \in S^{1,-} \\ z_{i,0}^1, & i \in S^{1,+} \end{cases},$$

$$c_{i,1}^1 = \begin{cases} Q_{i,1} BD \left(c_{i,0} \right) + x_{i,1}^1, & i \in S^{1,+} \\ z_{i,1}^1, & i \in S^{1,-} \end{cases},$$

$$c_{j,0}^1 = Q_{i,0} BD\left(c_{j,1}\right) + x_{j,0}^1,$$

$$c_{j,1}^1 = Q_{i,1} BD\left(c_{j,0}\right) + x_{j,1}^1,$$

$$j \in \left(L \backslash \left(S^{1,+} \cup S^{1,-}\right)\right),$$

where $x_{i,0}^1, x_{j,0}^1 \leftarrow \chi^m$, $z_{i,0}^1, z_{i,1}^1 \leftarrow \mathbb{Z}_q^m$ and outputs the re-encrypted cipher-text

$$C_{W^1} = \left(c; \left\{c_{i,0}^1, c_{i,1}^1\right\}_{i \in L}\right).$$

3.2 Correctness and Parameters

We show the correctness and parameters in this subsection.

Firstly, we prove that $\text{Decrypt}(pp, sk_S, C_W) = \mu$, where $C_W = \text{Encrypt}(pp, W, \mu)$ and $S \models W$.

For an attribute set S, let $A_i = \begin{cases} A_{i,0}, & i \in L \backslash S \\ A_{i,1}, & i \in S \end{cases}$, $A = \left(A_1 | \cdots | A_{|L|}\right)$. Since

T_i is the basis for $\Lambda_q^\perp(A_i)$, $i \in L$, $AT = \left(A_1 | \cdots | A_{|L|}\right) \begin{bmatrix} T_1 & & \\ & \ddots & \\ & & T_{|L|} \end{bmatrix} = 0$, and

$|T| = \prod_{i \in L} |T_i| \neq 0$, we have $T = \begin{bmatrix} T_1 & & \\ & \ddots & \\ & & T_{|L|} \end{bmatrix}$ is the basis for $\Lambda_q^\perp(A)$, then TA

can compute $s = \left(s_1; \cdots, s_{|L|}\right) \leftarrow \text{SamplePre}(A, T, u)$ such that $u = As = \sum_{i=1}^{|L|} A_i s_i$. Since $S \models W$, we know that

$$y = \left(y_1; \cdots; y_{|L|}\right) = A^T f + x,$$

where $x = \left(x_1; \cdots; x_{|L|}\right)$, $x_i = \begin{cases} x_{i,0}, & i \in L \backslash S \\ x_{i,1}, & i \in S \end{cases}$. Thus,

$$\begin{aligned} & c - s^T y \\ & = u^T f + x_c + \lfloor \tfrac{q}{2} \rfloor \mu - s^T \left(A^T f + x\right). \\ & = \lfloor \tfrac{q}{2} \rfloor \mu + \left(x_c - s^T x\right). \end{aligned}$$

If $\left|x_c - s^T x\right| < \lfloor \tfrac{q}{2} \rfloor / 2$, then we can get μ.

Then, we prove that $\text{Decrypt}(pp, sk_{S^1}, C_{W^1}) = \mu$, where $C_{W^1} = ReEnc(pp, rk_{W \to W^1}, C_W)$, $rk_{W \to W^1} = ReKeyGen(pp, W, W^1)$, $C_W = Encrypt(pp, W, \mu)$, $S^1 \models W^1$.

Let $S^{1,+}, S^{1,-}$ are the positive and negative attribute set in W^1, $C_W = \left(c; \left\{c_{i,0}, c_{i,1}\right\}_{i \in L}\right)$ is a ciphertext under W, and $rk_{W \to W^1} = \left(\left\{Q_{i,0}, Q_{i,1}\right\}_{i \in L}\right)$ is a re-encryption key. Since the access structure W and W^1 are disjoint, we know that if $i \in S^{1,-}$, then

$$
\begin{aligned}
c^1_{i,0} &= Q^T_{i,0} B D \left(c_{i,1}\right) + x^1_{i,0} \\
&= \left[\text{P2}\left(R^T_{i,1\to0}\right) + X_i\right] B D \left(c_{i,1}\right) + x^1_{i,0} \\
&= R^T_{i,1\to0} c_{i,1} + X_i B D \left(c_{i,1}\right) + x^1_{i,0} \\
&= R^T_{i,1\to0} A^T_{i,1} f + R^T_{i,1\to0} x_{i,1} + X_i B D \left(c_{i,1}\right) + x^1_{i,0} \\
&= A^T_{i,0} f + R^T_{i,1\to0} x_{i,1} + X_i B D \left(c_{i,1}\right) + x^1_{i,0}
\end{aligned}
$$

that is

$$
c^1_{i,0} = \begin{cases} A^T_{i,0} f + x^2_{i,0}, & i \in S'^- \\ z^1_{i,0}, & i \in S'^+ \end{cases},
$$

where $x^2_{i,0} = R^T_{i,1\to0} x_{i,1} + X_i B D \left(c_{i,1}\right) + x^1_{i,0}$. Similarly, we have

$$
c^1_{i,1} = \begin{cases} A^T_{i,1} f + x^2_{i,1}, & i \in S'^+ \\ z^1_{i,1}, & i \in S'^- \end{cases},
$$

where $x^2_{i,1} = R^T_{i,0\to1} x_{i,0} + X_i B D \left(c_{i,0}\right) + x^1_{i,1}$,

$$
c^1_{j,0} = A^T_{j,0} f + x^2_{j,0},
$$

$$
c^1_{j,1} = A^T_{j,1} f + x^2_{j,1},
$$

where $x^2_{i,0} = R^T_{i,1\to0} x_{i,1} + X_{i,0} B D \left(c_{i,1}\right) + x^1_{i,0}$, $x^2_{i,1} = R^T_{i,0\to1} x_{i,0} + X_{i,1} B D \left(c_{i,0}\right) + x^1_{i,1}$, $i \in \left(L\backslash\left(S^{1,+} \cup S^{1,-}\right)\right)$.

For the attribute set S^1, let $A_i = \begin{cases} A_{i,0}, & i \in L\backslash S^1 \\ A_{i,1}, & i \in S^1 \end{cases}$, $A^1 = \left(A_1 | \cdots | A_{|L|}\right)$. TA can compute $s^1 \leftarrow \text{SamplePre}\left(A^1, T^1, u\right)$ such that $A^1 s^1 = u$, where

$$
T^1 = \begin{pmatrix} T_1 & & \\ & \ddots & \\ & & T_{|L|} \end{pmatrix}
$$

is the basis for $\Lambda^\perp_q \left(A^1\right)$. Since $S^1 \vDash W^1$, we know

that $y^1 = \left(y^1_1; \cdots; y^1_{|L|}\right) = A^{1T} f + x^1$, where $x^1 = \left(x^1_1; \cdots; x^1_{|L|}\right)$, $x^1_i = \begin{cases} x^2_{i,0}, & i \in L\backslash S^1 \\ x^2_{i,1}, & i \in S^1 \end{cases}$. Thus,

$$
c - s^{1T} y^1 = \left\lfloor \frac{q}{2} \right\rfloor \mu + \left(x_c - s^{1T} x^1\right).
$$

If $\left|x_c - s^{1T} x^1\right| < \left\lfloor \frac{q}{2} \right\rfloor / 2$, then we can get μ.

Finally, we set the parameters.

(1) Algorithm TrapGen requires $m \geq 6n \log q$.
(2) Algorithm SamplePre requires $\sigma \geq \left\|\tilde{T}\right\| \omega\left(\sqrt{\log m}\right)$.

(3) Correctly decrypt the ciphertext requires $|x_c - s^T x| < \lfloor \frac{q}{2} \rfloor / 2$.
(4) Correctly decrypt the re-encrypted ciphertext requires $|x_c - s^{1T} x^1| < \lfloor \frac{q}{2} \rfloor / 2$.
(5) The hardness of LWE requires $\alpha q > 2\sqrt{n}$.

Let $\chi = \overline{\Psi}_\alpha$, we set the parameters as follows:
$n = \kappa$, q=the prime nearest to 2^{n^δ}, $m = 6n \lceil \log q \rceil$, $\sigma = m\omega \left(\sqrt{\log m} \right)$, $\alpha = \left[5m^3 \sigma^2 |L| \omega \left(\sqrt{\log m} \right) \right]^{-1}$, where δ is constant between 0 and 1.
We only verify (4) that is $|x_c - s^{1T} x^1| < \lfloor \frac{q}{2} \rfloor / 2$. The others can be easily computed.
From the element of x^1, we know

$$\left\| x^1 \right\|_\infty \leq \left| r^T x' \right| + m \lceil \log q \rceil \left\| x'' \right\|_\infty + \left\| x''' \right\|_\infty,$$

where $x', x''' \leftarrow \chi^m$, $x'' \leftarrow \chi^{m \times m \lceil \log q \rceil}$, r is a column of $R_{i,1 \to 0}, R_{i,0 \to 1}$. By Lemmas 1 and 3, we have $\|r\| \leq \sigma \sqrt{m}$. By Lemma 4, we have

$$\begin{aligned}
\left\| x^1 \right\|_\infty &\leq \left| r^T x' \right| + m \lceil \log q \rceil \left\| x'' \right\|_\infty + \left\| x''' \right\|_\infty \\
&\leq \sigma \sqrt{m} q\alpha\omega \left(\sqrt{\log m} \right) + \sigma m/2 + m \lceil \log q \rceil \left(q\alpha\omega \left(\sqrt{\log m} \right) + 1/2 \right) + q\alpha\omega \left(\sqrt{\log m} \right) + 1/2 \\
&= q\alpha\omega \left(\sqrt{\log m} \right) \left[\sigma\sqrt{m} + m \lceil \log q \rceil + 1 \right] + \sigma m/2 + m \lceil \log q \rceil / 2 + 1/2 \\
&\leq 2\sigma \sqrt{m} q\alpha\omega \left(\sqrt{\log m} \right) + \sigma m
\end{aligned}$$

Thus,

$$\begin{aligned}
\left| x_c - s^{1T} x^1 \right| &\leq |x_c| + \left| s^{1T} x^1 \right| \leq |x_c| + m\sqrt{|L|} \left\| s^1 \right\| \left\| x^1 \right\|_\infty \\
&\leq q\alpha\omega \left(\sqrt{\log m} \right) + 1/2 + m\sqrt{|L|}\sigma\sqrt{|L| m} \left[2\sigma\sqrt{m} q\alpha\omega \left(\sqrt{\log m} \right) + \sigma m \right] \\
&= q\alpha\omega \left(\sqrt{\log m} \right) \left[1 + 2m^2\sigma^2 |L| \right] + 1/2 + m^{\frac{5}{2}}\sigma^2 |L| \\
&< q\alpha\omega \left(\sqrt{\log m} \right) m^3 \sigma^2 |L| \\
&\leq \frac{q}{5}
\end{aligned}$$

3.3   Security

Theorem 2. *Let n, q, m, σ, α be as in the aforementioned. Then if LWE is hard, our CP-ABPRE scheme is IND-sAS-CPA secure at original ciphertext.*

Proof. Consider the following games.
   $Game_0^b$: This is the real game $\text{Expt}_{CP-ABPRE,\mathcal{A}}^{IND-sAS-CPA-Or}(\kappa)$ with $b \in \{0,1\}$. Suppose W^* is the adversary's access structure, the challenger denotes the positive (negative) attribute set in W^* as $S^{*,+}$ $(S^{*,-})$. The challenger answers the ciphertext of the adversary's issue about $\mu \in \{0,1\}$ as follow,

- If $b = 0$, output $c \leftarrow \mathbb{Z}_q^{1+2|L|m}$.
- If $b = 1$, output $C_{W^*} \leftarrow \text{Encrypt}(pp, W^*, \mu)$.

Finally, the adversary outputs a guess $b' \in \{0,1\}$.

$Game_1^b$: We modify the secret key oracle $\mathcal{O}_{sk}(S)$. If the adversary inputs an attribute set S and $S \models W^*$, then the challenger returns $\perp$. If $S \not\models W^*$, the challenger lets $A_i = \begin{cases} A_{i,0}, i \in L \backslash S \\ A_{i,1}, \quad i \in S \end{cases}$, samples $s_i^+ \leftarrow D_{\mathbb{Z}^m,\sigma}$, $i \in [|L|-1]$, computes $u' = u - \sum_{i=1}^{|L|-1} A_i s_i^+$, $s_{|L|}^+ \leftarrow \text{SamplePre}\left(A_{|L|}, T_{|L|}, u'\right)$ and outputs the secret key $s^+ = \left(s_1^+, \cdots, s_{|L|}^+\right)$. The others are the same as $Game_0^b$.

Since the distribution of s^+ is same as the real secret key s, and $As^+ = u$, we have $s^+ \approx_s s$. Thus, $Game_0^b \approx_s Game_1^b$.

$Game_2^b$: We modify the re-encryption key oracle $\mathcal{O}_{rk}(W, W')$. We replace $P2\left(R_{i,1\to0}^T\right) + X_i$, $i \in S^{1,-}$, $P2\left(R_{i,0\to1}^T\right) + X_i$, $i \in S^{1,+}$, and $Q_{i,0}, Q_{i,1}$, $i \in \left(L \backslash \left(S^{1,+} \cup S^{1,-}\right)\right)$ with $Q_{i,1\to0}^*, Q_{i,0\to1}^*, Q_{i,0}^*, Q_{i,1}^* \leftarrow D_{\mathbb{Z}^{m \times m \lceil \log q \rceil},\sigma}$, respectively. The others are the same as $Game_1^b$.

Since the distribution of $Q_{i,0}^*, Q_{i,1}^* \leftarrow D_{\mathbb{Z}^{m \times m \lceil \log q \rceil},\sigma}$ are the same as $Q_{i,0}, Q_{i,1}$, respectively, we have $Q_{i,0}^* \approx_s Q_{i,0}$, $Q_{i,1}^* \approx_s Q_{i,1}$. Thus, $Game_0^b \approx_s Game_1^b$.

$Game_3^b$: We modify the re-encryption oracle $\mathcal{O}_{re}(rk_{S \to W'}, W', C_W)$. We replace $c_{i,0}^1, c_{i,1}^1$ with $c_{i,0}^{1,+}, c_{i,1}^{1,+} \leftarrow D_{\mathbb{Z}_q^m,\sigma}$, respectively, $i \in [|L|]$. The others are the same as $Game_2^b$.

Since $Q_{i,0}^*, Q_{i,1}^* \leftarrow D_{\mathbb{Z}^{m \times m \lceil \log q \rceil},\sigma}$ and $x_{i,0}^1, x_{i,1}^1 \leftarrow D_{\mathbb{Z}^m,\sigma}$, we have the distribution of $c_{i,0}^1, c_{i,1}^1$ and $c_{i,0}^{1,+}, c_{i,1}^{1,+}$ are same. Thus, $c_{i,0}^{1,+} \approx_s c_{i,0}^1$, $c_{i,1}^{1,+} \approx_s c_{i,1}^1$. Furthermore, $Game_3^b \approx_s Game_2^b$.

$Game_4^b$: we replace $C_{W^*} \leftarrow \text{Encrypt}(pp, W^*, \mu)$ with $c^+ \leftarrow \mathbb{Z}_q^{1+2|L|m}$, where $c^+ = \left(c^+; \left\{c_{i,0}^+, c_{i,1}^+\right\}_{i \in L}\right)$. The others are the same as $Game_3^b$.

We have $c^+ \approx_c c$, $c_{i,1}^+ \approx_c c_{i,1}, i \in S^+ \cup L \backslash (S^+ \cup S^-)$, $c_{i,0}^+ \approx_c c_{i,0}, i \in S^- \cup L \backslash (S^+ \cup S^-)$ under the LWE assumption and $c_{i,1}^+ \approx_s c_{i,1}$, $i \in S^-$, $c_{i,0}^+ \approx_s c_{i,0}$, $i \in S^+$. Thus $C_{W^*} \approx_c c^+$. Furthermore, $Game_3^b \approx_c Game_4^b$.

Finally, we can get $Game_0^0 \approx_c Game_0^1$ by $Game_4^0 \approx_c Game_4^1$. This completes the proof.

Theorem 3. *Let n, q, m, σ, α be as in the aforementioned. Then if LWE is hard, our CP-ABPRE scheme is IND-sAS-CPA secure at re-encrypted ciphertext.*

Proof. For $(W^*, state_1) \leftarrow \mathcal{A}(1^\kappa)$, $(\mu, W, state_2) \leftarrow \mathcal{A}^{\mathcal{O}_1}(pp, state_1)$ which are chosen by the adversary, The challenger encrypts $\mu \in \{0,1\}$ under access structure W and gets a corresponding ciphertext C_W which is a random ciphertext C if $b = 0$ or the real ciphertext $C_W \leftarrow \text{Encrypt}(pp, W, \mu)$ if $b = 1$. By the $Game_4^b$ of Theorem 2, we know that the adversary can't distinguish a random ciphertext C from the real ciphertext $C_W \leftarrow \text{Encrypt}(pp, W, \mu)$. For the re-encryption key $rk_{W \to W^*}$, the adversary can't distinguish the real $rk_{W \to W^*}$ from a random Gaussian distribution by the $Game_2^b$ of Theorem 2. Thus, the adversary can't obtain any useful things for winning the game. At last, the challenger outputs the challenge re-encrypted ciphertext $C_{W^*}^* \leftarrow ReEnc(rk_{S \to W^*}, C_W)$. By the LWE, we have $Q_{i,0}BD\left(c_{i,1}\right) + x_{i,0}^1$, $i \in S^{1,-} \cup \left(L\backslash\left(S^{1,+} \cup S^{1,-}\right)\right)$ and the random uniform distribution are computationally indistinguishable, $Q_{i,1}BD\left(c_{i,0}\right) + x_{i,1}^1$, $i \in S^{1,+} \cup \left(L\backslash\left(S^{1,+} \cup S^{1,-}\right)\right)$ and the random uniform distributions are computationally indistinguishable. Thus, the advantage $\mathrm{Adv}_{CP-ABPRE,\mathcal{A}}^{\mathrm{IND-sAS-CPA-Re}}(\kappa)$ of adversary is negligible.

3.4   Comparison

We compare the related works in this subsection.

(1) Our scheme was constructed based on [14]. Compared with the ABE scheme of [14,15], our scheme not only supports proxy re-encryption but also has smaller size of public parameters. The comparison results in Table 2. The S is a set of all attribute in access structure.
(2) The existing CP-ABPRE schemes are constructed by bilinear pairing [5, 13,20], which are fragile when the post-quantum comes. Our CP-ABPRE was constructed based on LWE which is widely believed secure in quantum computer attacks.
(3) Compared with the PRE based on LWE, our scheme is the first CP-ABPRE scheme based on LWE and has the same computational complexity $O(n^2)$. The comparison results in Table 3.

Table 2. Comparison for CP-ABE

Cryptosystem	The size of pp		The size of sk	The size of ciphertext
[14]	$(2\left|L\right|+1)\,n \times (2\left|L\right|+1)\,m+n$	$\left|L\right|m$		$(2\left|L\right|+1-\left|S\right|)m$
[15]	$(2\left|L\right|+1)\,n \times (2\left|L\right|+1)\,m+n$	$\left|L\right|m$		$1+(2\left|L\right|+1)m$
our scheme	$2\left|L\right|n \times 2\left|L\right|m+n$		$\left|L\right|m$	$1+2\left|L\right|m$

Table 3. Comparison for PRE

Cryptosystem	Interactivity	Directionality	Security	LWE assumption	Access control
[2]	NO	Unidirectional	CPA	YES	NO
[21]	YES	Bidirectional	CPA	YES	NO
[22]	NO	Unidirectional	CPA	YES	NO
[23]	NO	Unidirectional	CPA	YES	NO
Our scheme	NO	Unidirectional	CPA	YES	YES

4   Conclusion

This paper constructs a ciphertext-policy attribute-based proxy re-encryption over lattice. The lattice-based cryptography is an alternative to resist quantum computer attacks. The constructed scheme not only supports access control but also can convert the ciphertext C_W under access structure W to a ciphertext $C_{W'}$ under another access structure W' without decrypt the ciphertext C_W. Thus, the scheme is flexible for cloud sharing. At last, the scheme is proved secure under LWE assumption.

Acknowledgements. This work was supported by the National Natural Science Foundation of China (61472097), the Natural Science Foundation of Heilongjiang Province of China (JJ2019LH1770), the Special Funds of Heilongjiang University of the Fundamental Research Funds for the Heilongjiang Province (RCCXYJ201812) and the Open Fund of the State Key Laboratory of Information Security (2019-ZD-05).

References

1. Ma, C., Li, J., Ouyang, W.: Lattice-based identity-based homomorphic conditional proxy re-encryption for secure big data computing in cloud environment. Int. J. Found. Comput. Sci. **28**(6), 645–660 (2017)
2. Ma, C., Li, J., Ouyang, W.: A homomorphic proxy re-encryption from lattices. In: Chen, L., Han, J. (eds.) ProvSec 2016. LNCS, vol. 10005, pp. 353–372. Springer, Cham (2016). https://doi.org/10.1007/978-3-319-47422-9_21
3. Chow, S.S.M., Weng, J., Yang, Y., Deng, R.H.: Efficient unidirectional proxy re-encryption. In: Bernstein, D.J., Lange, T. (eds.) AFRICACRYPT 2010. LNCS, vol. 6055, pp. 316–332. Springer, Heidelberg (2010). https://doi.org/10.1007/978-3-642-12678-9_19
4. Green, M., Ateniese, G.: Identity-based proxy re-encryption. In: Katz, J., Yung, M. (eds.) ACNS 2007. LNCS, vol. 4521, pp. 288–306. Springer, Heidelberg (2007). https://doi.org/10.1007/978-3-540-72738-5_19
5. Liang, K., Fang, L., Susilo, W., et al.: A ciphertext-policy attribute-based proxy re-encryption with chosen-ciphertext security. In: Proceedings of the 5th International Conference on Intelligent Networking and Collaborative Systems, INCoS 2013, Xi'an, China, October, pp. 55–559 (2013)
6. Sahai, A., Waters, B.: Fuzzy identity-based encryption. In: Cramer, R. (ed.) EURO-CRYPT 2005. LNCS, vol. 3494, pp. 457–473. Springer, Heidelberg (2005). https://doi.org/10.1007/11426639_27
7. Goyal, V., Pandey, O., Sahai, A., Waters, B.: Attribute-based encryption for fine-grained access control of encrypted data. In: Wright, R., Vimercati, S. (eds.) Proceedings of the 13th ACM Conference on Computer and Communications Security, Alexandria, Virginia, USA, pp. 89–98 (2006)
8. Wang, D., Ma, C., Shi, L., Wang, Y.: On the security of an improved password authentication scheme based on ECC. In: Liu, B., Ma, M., Chang, J. (eds.) ICICA 2012. LNCS, vol. 7473, pp. 181–188. Springer, Heidelberg (2012). https://doi.org/10.1007/978-3-642-34062-8_24
9. He, D., Wang, D., Wu, S.: Cryptanalysis and improvement of a password-based remote user authentication scheme without smart cards. Inf. Technol. Control **42**(2), 105–112 (2013)

10. Wang, D., Ma, C., Zhang, Q., et al.: Secure password-based remote user authentication scheme against smart card security breach. J. Netw. **8**(1), 148 (2013)
11. Liang, X., Cao, Z., Lin, H., Shao, J.: Attribute based proxy re-encryption with delegating capabilities. In: Safavi-Naini, R., Varadharajan, V. (eds.) proceedings of the 4th International Symposium on Information, Computer, and Communications Security, Sydney, Australia, pp. 276–286 (2009)
12. Luo, S., Hu, J., Chen, Z.: Ciphertext policy attribute-based proxy re-encryption. In: Soriano, M., Qing, S., López, J. (eds.) ICICS 2010. LNCS, vol. 6476, pp. 401–415. Springer, Heidelberg (2010). https://doi.org/10.1007/978-3-642-17650-0_28
13. Liang, K., Man, H., Liu, J., et al.: A secure and efficient ciphertext-policy attribute-based proxy re-encryption for cloud data sharing. Futur. Gener. Comput. Syst. **52**, 95–108 (2015)
14. Zhang, J., Zhang, Z.: A ciphertext policy attribute-based encryption scheme without pairings. In: Wu, C.-K., Yung, M., Lin, D. (eds.) Inscrypt 2011. LNCS, vol. 7537, pp. 324–340. Springer, Heidelberg (2012). https://doi.org/10.1007/978-3-642-34704-7_23
15. Zeng, F., Xu, C.: A novel model for lattice-based authorized searchable encryption with special keyword. Math. Probl. Eng. (2015). Article ID 314621 https://doi.org/10.1155/2015/314621
16. Micciancio, D., Peikert, C.: Trapdoors for lattices: simpler, tighter, faster, smaller. In: Pointcheval, D., Johansson, T. (eds.) EUROCRYPT 2012. LNCS, vol. 7237, pp. 700–718. Springer, Heidelberg (2012). https://doi.org/10.1007/978-3-642-29011-4_41
17. Alwen, J., Peikert, C.: generating shorter bases for hard random lattices. Theory Comput. Syst. **48**(3), 535–553 (2011)
18. Agrawal, S., Boneh, D., Boyen, X.: Efficient Lattice (H)IBE in the standard model. In: Gilbert, H. (ed.) EUROCRYPT 2010. LNCS, vol. 6110, pp. 553–572. Springer, Heidelberg (2010). https://doi.org/10.1007/978-3-642-13190-5_28
19. Regev, O.: On lattices, learning with errors, random linear codes, and cryptography. In: STOC, pp. 84C93. ACM (2005)
20. Zeng, P., Choo, K.: A new kind of conditional proxy re-encryption for secure cloud storage. IEEE Access. **6**, 70017–70024 (2018)
21. Xagawa, K.: Cryptography with Lattices. Ph.D. thesis. Department of Mathematical and Computing Sciences Tokyo Institute of Technology (2010)
22. Jiang, M., Hu, Y., Wang, B., et al.: Lattice-based multi-use unidirectional proxy re-encryption. Secur. Commun. Netw. **8**(18), 3796–3803 (2016)
23. Hou, J., Jiang, M., Guo, Y., Song, W.: Identity-based multi-bit proxy re-encryption over lattice in the standard model. In: Li, F., Takagi, T., Xu, C., Zhang, X. (eds.) FCS 2018. CCIS, vol. 879, pp. 110–118. Springer, Singapore (2018). https://doi.org/10.1007/978-981-13-3095-7_9

Blockchain-Based Asymmetric Group Key Agreement Protocol for Mobile Ad Hoc Network

Qikun Zhang[1]([✉]), Yongjiao Li[1], Jianyong Li[1], Yong Gan[2], Yanhua Zhang[1], and Jingjing Hu[3]

[1] Computer and Communication Engineering,
Zhengzhou University of Light Industry, Zhengzhou 450002, China
zhangqikun04@163.com
[2] Zhengzhou Institute of Technology, Zhengzhou 450044, China
[3] School of Computer Science and Technology, Beijing Institute of Technology,
Beijing 100081, China
hujingjing@bit.edu.cn

Abstract. Group key agreement is one of the key technologies for ensuring information exchange security among group members. It is widely used in secure multiparty computation, resource security sharing, and distributed collaborative computing et al. The current group key agreement requires personal privacy protection, lightweight computing and more efficient and secure group key agreement technology. Aiming at these requirements, this paper proposed a lightweight group key agreement protocol based on blockchain, which uses the technical advantages of blockchain and asymmetric group key agreement combined. In this protocol, the blockchain anonymous authentication technology is used to implement personal privacy protection in the identity authentication process of the group key agreement, and the blockchain decentralized computing technology is adopted to reduce the computational and communication overhead of each participant. So it also suite able to use in resource-constrained mobile network, It also uses blockchain recording techniques for traceability and accountability (if some participants impersonate or falsify data, they can be recorded by the blockchain. No malicious attempts can be made undetected). This protocol is proved secure under the decisional bilinear Diffie-Hellman (DBDH) problem assumption and the performance analysis shows that the proposed scheme is more efficient than existing works.

Keywords: Group key agreement · Blockchain · Anonymous authentication · Information exchange

1 Introduction

Mobile ad hoc networks (MANETs) have been used in many application areas such as sensors, file sharing, video conferencing and collaborative applications.

© Springer Nature Singapore Pte Ltd. 2019
W. Meng and S. Furnell (Eds.): SocialSec 2019, CCIS 1095, pp. 47–56, 2019.
https://doi.org/10.1007/978-981-15-0758-8_4

Since entities in MANETs are mobile, providing secure communications among participants are a significant issue. To overcome this issue, group key exchange protocols are used. Such protocols are categorized as key distribution and key agreement protocols. In key distribution protocols, there exists a centralized authority, such as an entity in the network or a trusted third party, to distribute group keys to participants. In key agreement protocols, all participants in the group compute a shared key by using some public parameters and functions. Since MANETs are decentralized mobile networks, group key agreement protocols are better candidates than key distribution protocols for providing secure communications.

In MANETs, the group information security sharing among nodes has some obvious constraints [1], for example, the nodes communication area is limited, nodes energy is limited, nodes easily to be captured and nodes join or leave group frequently et al. In this environment, the computational and communication load is required to be a lightweight, authenticated dynamic group key agreement protocol.

1.1 Contributions

Since MANETs are decentralized mobile networks, it is unsuitable for centralized trusted server [2,3]. During the group key agreement, anyone can verify the identities of other nodes by digital signatures in a blockchain system. The computation overhead of authentication and key calculation can be distributed on different nodes to achieve load balance and reduce the calculation amount of a single node. If a malicious participant attempts to disrupt the establishment of a group key among honest participants, it will be recorded by the blockchain. The malicious attempts can be made detected and these will be tracked and punished.

For above analysis, the contribution of this protocol is as follows:

(1) privacy preserving. For security, group key agreement requires the participants must to be mutual authentication before negotiating the group keys to avoid illegal members to participate in group key agreement. This protocol uses anonymous identity authentication to avoid disclosure of identity information and protect personal privacy.

2) Eliminate the computation task. For the resource-constrained of mobile terminals, B-AGKA protocol ensures that the computing and communication as simple and small as possible.

(3) Key self-certified. All participants can verify the group key correctness without any other additional communication.

2   Basic Knowledge

2.1 Bilinear Mapping

Let G_1 and G_2 be two multiplicative groups, the discrete logarithm over G_1 and G_2 is difficult, $g_1 \in G_1$ is a generator of G_1, G_1 and G_2 have the same large prime number q, where $q \geq 2^k + 1$, and k is a security parameter. Group G_1 and G_2 is a pair of bilinear group, there exists a bilinear map e and $e : G_1 \times G_1 \rightarrow G_2$, and it has the following properties.

(1) Bilinearty: For all $g_1, g_2 \in G_1$, and $a, b \in \mathbb{Z}_q^*$, there is $e\left(g_1^a, g_2^b\right) = e\left(g_1, g_2\right)^{ab}$;
(2) Non-degeneracy: Namely $e(g_1, g_2) \neq 1$.
(3) Computability: For all $g_1, g_2 \in G_1$, there exists an efficient algorithm to calculate $e(g_1, g_2)$.

Inference1.   For all $\mu_1, \mu_2, v \in G_1$, there is $e(\mu_1.\mu_2, v) = e(\mu_1, v)e(\mu_2, v)$.

2.2   Computational Complexity Problems

For given group G_1 is generated by g_1. For the above definition, the following difficult problems are defined.

Definition 1: Discrete Logarithm problem (DLP). Given an equation $y = g^a$, where $a \in \mathbb{Z}_q^*$ and $y, g \in G_1$, $a < q$. If a and g are given, it is easy to calculate y. But if g and y are given, it is difficult to calculate a.

Definition 2: Decisional Bilinear Diffe-Hellman (DBDH) Problem: Suppose the following two triples (g_1^{ab}, g_1^a, g_1^b) and (g_1^{ab}, g_1^a, π), for any $a, b \in \mathbb{Z}_q^*$ and $\pi \in G_1$, are computationally indistinguishable. In other words, there is no efficient algorithm $\mathcal{A}$ that satisfies $\left|\Pr[\mathcal{A}(g_1^{ab}, g_1^a, g_1^b, e) = 1] - \Pr[\mathcal{A}(g_1^{ab}, g_1^a, \pi, e) = 1]\right| \geq \frac{1}{Q(|2^k|)}$.

Definition 3: Bilinear Inverse Diffe-Hellman (BIDH) Problem: The BIDH problem is given g_1, g_1^{ab} and g_1^{ac} for some $a, c \in \mathbb{Z}_q^*$ to compute $e(g_1, g_1)^{abc}$.

2.3   Initialization

In this section, we describe an asymmetric group key agreement protocol based on blockchain. The protocol consists of KGC (Key Generation Center) and network terminals. KGC is a key entity who generates system parameters and master keys. Especially, KGC is mainly used to verify the identity of the terminal entity for tracking the identity of anonymous members in the blockchain.

In this work, it is assumed that the protocol contains a KGC and n terminals. Let $U = \{u_1, u_2, ..., u_n\}$ be the set of terminals. And the corresponding identity set is $ID = \{id_{u_1}, id_{u_2}, ..., id_{u_n}\}$.

Initial: on input a security parameter ℓ, the KGC chooses two multiplicative groups G_1 and G_2, the discrete logarithm over G_1 and G_2 is difficult, $g_1 \in G_1$ is a generator of G_1, G_1 and G_2 have the same large prime number q, and there exists a bilinear map e and $e : G_1 \times G_1 \rightarrow G_2$, $H_1 : \{0, 1\}^* \rightarrow \mathbb{Z}_q^*, H_2 : G_1 \rightarrow \mathbb{Z}_q^*, H_3 : G_2 \rightarrow \mathbb{Z}_q^*$ are three hash functions.

Setup(1^λ) $\to$ (m_{pk},m_{sk}) The Setup(1^λ) algorithm is run by KGC. It takes the security parameter λ as input, and outputs the system master key $m_{sk} \in \mathbb{Z}_q^*$ and public key $m_{pk} = g_1^{m_{sk}}$.

All the members before participated in group key agreement need to register for KGC. The registration is as follows:

(1) Any member $u_i \in U(1 \le i \le n)$ chooses a random positive integer $x_i \in \mathbb{Z}_q^*$, and calculates $y_i = g_1^{x_i}$, $t_{u_i} = H_1(id_{u_i})$ and $T_{u_i} = (m_{pk})^{x_i t_{u_i}}$, where the (y_i, x_i) is the public/private key pairs of u_i, then it sends (id_{u_i}, y_i, T_{u_i}) to KGC.

(2) After received the messages (id_{u_i}, y_i, T_{u_i}) from u_i, KGC computes $r_{u_i} = T_{u_i}^{H_1(id_{u_i})^{-1}}$ and verifies the equation $e(r_{u_i}, g_1) = e(y_i, m_{pk})$. If the equation holds, KGC selects a random number $r \in \mathbb{Z}_q^*$ and computes $T_i = y_i^r$, $R_{u_i} = (y_i)^{r \cdot m_{sk}}$ and sends R_{u_i} to u_i as register message.

(3) KGC creates a new group session with identifier $S_{id} \in \mathbb{Z}_q^*$, and orders all the participating users into a ring structure using their IP addresses, public keys and register messages. Suppose the ring of n users is $R_{S_{id}} = (R_{u_1}, R_{u_2}, ..., R_{u_i}, ..., R_{u_n})$, where $R_{u_{i-1}}$ and $R_{u_{i+1}}$ are respectively left and right neighbors of R_{u_i} for $1 \le i \le n$, $R_{u_0} = R_{u_n}$ and $R_{u_1} = R_{u_{n+1}}$. KGC broadcasts the messages $\{S_{id}, T_i, (IP_1, y_1, R_{u_1}), (IP_2, y_2, R_{u_2}), ..., (IP_n, y_n, R_{u_n})\}$ to all the users.

(4) After received the messages $\{S_{id}, T_i, (IP_1, y_1, R_{u_1}), (IP_2, y_2, R_{u_2}), ..., (IP_n, y_n, R_{u_n})\}$ broadcasted from KGC, every member $u_j(1 \le j \le n)$ keeps the messages $(IP_{j-1}, y_{j-1}, R_{u_{j-1}})$ of the one before it, as well as keeps the messages $(IP_{j+1}, y_{j+1}, R_{u_{j+1}})$ of the one after it.

The system parameters are $params = (G_1, G_2, g_1, q, e, H_1, H_2, H_3, m_{pk})$.

2.4   Computation of Group Key

The Computation of group key proposed in this protocol is depicted as follows:

(1) The sponsor u_i of group key agreement computes a left key $K_i^L = (y_{i-1})^{x_i}$ and a right key $K_i^R = (y_{i+1})^{x_i}$ secret preservation, and computes a group key parameter $Y_i = \frac{K_i^R}{K_i^L}$, signing message $\sigma_i = (Y_i)^{x_i}$ and $M_i = H_2(g_1^{S_{id}}|\sigma_i|R_{u_i}|y_i|T_i)$ as block transaction information. u_i sends $(IP_{i+1}, S_{id}, R_{u_i}, Y_i, y_i, \sigma_i, M_i, T_i)$ to member u_{i+1} in the network that its IP address is IP_{i+1}, Then, u_i records time information $time_i$ and encapsulates the messages $(IP_{i+1}, S_{id}, R_{u_i}, Y_i, y_i, \sigma_i, M_i, T_i, time_i)$ into a block as transaction.

(2) After the member u_{i+1} received the messages $(IP_{i+1}, S_{id}, R_{u_i}, Y_i, y_i, \sigma_i, M_i, T_i)$ from u_i, it compares his IP address with the address of IP_{i+1} in the message block. If the two IP addresses are equal, u_{i+1} will write a new block. u_{i+1} computes $g_1^{S_{id}}$. S_{id} is the one that keeps and verifies whether the two formulas $H_2(g_1^{S_{id}}|\sigma_i|R_{u_i}|y_i|T_i)$ $=?M_i$ and $e(\sigma_i \cdot R_{u_i}, g_1) = e(Y_i, y_i)e(T_i, m_{pk})$ hold. If their hold, u_{i+1} computes a left

key $K_{i+1}^L = (y_i)^{x_{i+1}}$ and a right key $K_{i+1}^R = (y_{i+2})^{x_{i+1}}$ secret preservation, and computes a group key parameter $Y_{i+1} = \frac{K_{i+1}^R}{K_{i+1}^L}$, signing message $\sigma_{i+1} = (Y_{i+1})^{x_{i+1}}$, group public key parameters $pk_{u_{i+1}} = e(y_i, y_{i+1})$ and $M_{i+1} = H_2(g_1^{S_{id}}|\sigma_{i+1}|R_{u_{i+1}}|y_{i+1}|T_{i+1})$ as block transaction information. u_{i+1} sends $\{IP_{i+2}, S_{id}, R_{u_{i+1}}, y_{i+1}, \sigma_{i+1}, M_{i+1}, T_{i+1}, (pk_{u_{i+1}}), (Y_i, Y_{i+1})\}$ to member u_{i+2} in the network that its IP address is IP_{i+2}, Then, u_{i+1} records time information $time_{i+1}$ and encapsulates the messages $\{IP_{i+2}, S_{id}, R_{u_{i+1}}, T_{i+1}, y_{i+1}, \sigma_{i+1}, M_{i+1}, (pk_{u_{i+1}}), (Y_i, Y_{i+1}), time_{i+1}\}$ into a block as transaction.

(3) After a series of block transaction, until u_i received its left neighbour node u_{i-1}'s messages $\{(IP_i, S_{id}, R_{u_{i-1}}, T_{i-1}, Y_{i-1}, y_{i-1}, \sigma_{i-1}, M_{i-1}, (pk_{u_{i+1}}, ..., pk_{u_n}, pk_{u_1}, ..., pk_{u_{i-1}}), (Y_{i+1}, ..., Y_n, Y_1, ..., Y_{i-1})\}$, then u_i computes $g_1^{S_{id}}$, S_{id} is the one that keeps and verifies whether the two formulas $H_2(g_1^{S_{id}}|\sigma_{i-1}|R_{u_{i-1}}|y_{i-1}|T_{i-1}) = ?M_{i-1}$ and $e(\sigma_{i-1} \cdot R_{u_{i-1}}, g_1) = e(Y_{i-1}, y_{i-1})e(T_{i-1}, m_{pk})$ hold. If they hold, the Blockchain transaction ends. u_i computes group public key parameter $pk_{u_i} = e(y_i, y_{i-1})$ and group public key $PK_{enc}^i = \prod_{i=1}^{n} pk_{u_i}$, then it broadcasts the messages $\{(IP_i, S_{id}, R_{u_i}, T_i, y_i, \sigma_i, M_i, PK_{enc}^i, (Y_{i+1}, ..., Y_n, Y_1, ..., Y_i)\}$ to all the members.

(4) After each the member $u_j (1 \le j \le n, j \ne i)$ received the messages $\{(IP_i, S_{id}, R_{u_i}, T_i, y_i, \sigma_i, M_i, PK_{enc}^i, (Y_{i+1}, ..., Y_n, Y_1, ..., Y_i)\}$ from u_i, each member $u_k (1 \le k \le n, k \ne i)$ verifies the authenticity of these messages by formula $e(\sigma_i \cdot R_{u_i}, g_1) = e(Y_i, y_i)e(T_i, m_{pk})$. If it holds, each member $u_k (1 \le k \le n)$ computes $\widetilde{K_{k+1}^R}, \widetilde{K_{k+2}^R}, ..., \widetilde{K_{k+(n-1)}^R}$ and uses its own right key K_k^R as follows:

$$\begin{cases} \widetilde{K_{k+1}^R} = Y_{k+1} \times K_k^R \\ \widetilde{K_{k+2}^R} = Y_{k+2} \times \widetilde{K_{k+1}^R} \\ \quad ...... \\ \widetilde{K_{k+(n-1)}^R} = Y_{k+(n-1)} \times \widetilde{K_{k+(n-2)}^R} \end{cases}$$

u_k can compute the group decryption key $SK_{dec} = \prod_{i=1}^{n} \widetilde{K_i^R}$ and obtain the group encryption key $PK_{enc} = \prod_{i=1}^{n} pk_{u_i}$ from u_i.

It is obvious that all honest users obtain the same group encryption key $PK_{enc} = e(g_1, g_1)^{(x_1 x_2 + x_2 x_3 +, ..., + x_n x_1)}$ and compute the same group decryption key $SK_{dec} = g_1^{(x_1 x_2 + x_2 x_3 +, ..., + x_n x_1)}$.

(5) Group keys self-certified

All the group members $u_i (1 \le i \le n)$ have calculated group keys, they needn't broadcast the hash values of the group keys to other members in its group to verify whether the group keys are correctness. They can verify whether the two formulas $\widetilde{K_{i+(n-1)}^R} = ?K_i^L$ and $PK_{enc} = ?e(g_1, SK_{dec})$ hold to check the correctness of group keys they computed.

2.5 Group Secure Communication Among Group Nodes

For any plaintext $m \in \mathcal{M}^*$ ($\mathcal{M}^*$: plaintext space), any member u_i has its own group encryption key PK_{enc} and group decryption key SK_{dec}, they operate as the follows:

Encryption: The message sender u_i randomly chooses an integer $t \in \mathbb{Z}_q^*$ and calculates $\delta_i = g_1^t, \eta_i = m \oplus H_3(PK_{enc})^t$, then broadcasts ciphertext $c = \langle \delta_i, \eta_i \rangle$.

Decryption: when receiving the ciphertext message $c = \langle \delta_i, \eta_i \rangle$ broadcasted by sender u_i, any other members $u_j (1 \leq j \leq n, j \neq i)$ who have the group decryption key SK_{dec} can calculate the plaintext $m = \eta_i \oplus H_3(e(\delta_i, SK_{dec}))$ by the group decryption key SK_{dec}.

3 Security Analysis

Theorem 1. The proposed B-AGKA protocol is security against passive adversary: A group key agreement protocol is secure against a passive adversary if a passive attacker is unable to obtain information about the established session key by eavesdropping on messages transmitted over the broadcast channel. To prove that, we need a well-known security assumption. Here we adopt the DLP problem and DBDH problem assumption to prove that the new protocol is secure against a passive adversary. Several works have already demonstrated the security and the variants of the decision bilinear Diffie-Hellman problem.

Assumption 1 (DLP problem and DBDH problem). Let G_1 and G_2 be two multiplicative cyclic groups, both of the two groups have the same large prime order q, where $q \geq 2^k + 1$, and k is a security parameter, the discrete logarithm on G_1 and G_2 is difficult, $G_1 = \langle g_1 \rangle$ is generated by g_1, G_1 and G_2 is a pair of bilinear group, $e : G_1 \times G_1 \rightarrow G_2$ is a calculable bilinear mapping.

Discrete Logarithm problem (DLP). For given $\phi_1 = g_1^a$, $\varphi_1 = g_1^b$, and $\eta_1 = g_1^{ab}$, where $b, a \in \mathbb{Z}_q^*$ and $\phi_1, \varphi_1, \eta_1 \in G_1$, $a < q$ and $b < q$. If a and φ_1 are given, it is easy to calculate η_1. But if φ_1 and η_1 are given, it will be difficult to calculate a.

Decisional Bilinear Diffe-Hellman (DBDH) Problem: Suppose the following two triples $(g_1, g_2, g_1^a, g_1^b, g_1^c, e(g_1, g_1)^{abc})$ and $(g_1, g_2, g_1^a, g_1^b, g_1^c, \pi)$, for any $a, b \in \mathbb{Z}_q^*$, $g_2 \in G_2$ and $\pi \in G_2$, are computationally indistinguishable. In other words, there is no efficient algorithm $\mathcal{A}$ that satisfies

$$\left| \Pr[\mathcal{A}(g_1, g_2, g_1^a, g_1^b, g_1^c, e(g_1, g_1)^{abc}) = 1] - \Pr[\mathcal{A}(g_1, g_2, g_1^a, g_1^b, g_1^c, \pi) = 1] \right| \geq \frac{1}{Q(|2^k|)}$$

for any polynomial Q, where the probability is over the random choice of a, b, c and π.

In Step 1, An attacker $\mathcal{C}$ can obtain the messages $\{(IP_i, S_{id}, R_{u_i}, y_i, \sigma_i, M_i, (pk_{u_{i+1}}, ..., pk_{u_n}, pk_{u_1}, ..., pk_{u_i}), (Y_{i+1}, ..., Y_n, Y_1, ..., Y_i)\}$ broadcasted by u_i over the blockchain, and the group decryption key is $SK_{dec}^i = \prod_{k=i}^{i+(n-1)} \widetilde{K_k^R} = \prod_{k=i}^{i+(n-1)}$

$(y_{k+1})^{x_k} = g_1^{x_{i+1}x_i} \times g_1^{x_{i+2}x_{i+1}} \times \dots \times g_1^{x_{i+(n-1)}x_i}$. The attacker $\mathcal{C}$ want to know SK_{dec}^i, without knowing x_i is unable to compute $(g_1^{x_{i+1}})^{x_i}$ directly from y_i, y_{i+1}, Y_i and Y_{i+1}, because it is equal to the difficulty of DLP problem (the security proof will be demonstrated in Lemma 1).

In Step 2, we will demonstrate that $(g_1, g_2, y_i, y_{i+1}, \delta_i, (PK_{enc})^t)$ and $(g_1, g_2, y_i, y_{i+1}, \delta_i, \pi)$ are computationally indistinguishable, where $t \in \mathbb{Z}_q^*$, $\delta_i = g_1^t \in G_1$ and $\pi \in G_2$. We know that obtaining the group decryption key SK_{dec} from the parameters $(PK_{enc})^t$ and bilinear mapping e is equal to the difficulty of DBDH problem. In other words, there is no efficient algorithm to calculate the plaintext $m = \eta_i \oplus H_3(e(\delta_i, SK_{dec}))$ without group decryption key SK_{dec} (the security proof will be demonstrated in Lemma 2).

Lemma 1. Under the random oracle model, if computing the DLP is hard, any malicious adversary $\mathcal{C}$ without knowing x_i will be unable to compute $(g_1^{x_{i+1}})^{x_i}$ directly from y_i, y_{i+1}, Y_i and Y_{i+1}. Thence, it cannot compute the group decryption key $SK_{dec}^i = \prod\limits_{k=i}^{i+(n-1)} \widetilde{K_k^R} = \prod\limits_{k=i}^{i+(n-1)} (y_{k+1})^{x_k} = g_1^{x_{i+1}x_i} \times g_1^{x_{i+2}x_{i+1}} \times \dots \times g_1^{x_{i+(n-1)}x_i}$.

Proof. $\mathcal{C}$ can receive the parameters $\{(IP_i, S_{id}, R_{u_i}, y_i, \sigma_i, M_i, T_i, (pk_{u_{i+1}}, \dots, pk_{u_n}, pk_{u_1}, \dots, pk_{u_i}), (Y_{i+1}, \dots, Y_n, Y_1, \dots, Y_i)\}$ from u_i, and also obtain the value y_i, y_{i+1}, Y_i and Y_{i+1} from the transaction record of the block packaged by u_i. Since $SK_{dec}^i = g_1^{x_{i+1}x_i} \times g_1^{x_{i+2}x_{i+1}} \times \dots \times g_1^{x_{i+(n-1)}x_i}$, if $\mathcal{C}$ wants to calculate SK_{dec}^i, it first needs to calculate $g_1^{x_{i+1}x_i}(1 \leq i \leq n)$. $\mathcal{C}$ can compute $Y_i = \frac{K_i^R}{K_i^L} = \frac{(y_{i+1})^{x_i}}{(y_{i-1})^{x_i}} = \left(\frac{y_{i+1}}{y_{i-1}}\right)^{x_i} = (g_1^{x_{i+1}-x_{i-1}})^{x_i}$ and $f_i = \frac{y_{i+1}}{y_{i-1}} = (g_1)^{x_{i+1}-x_{i-1}}$. If $\mathcal{C}$ wants to calculate the group key parameter $g_1^{x_{i+1}x_i}$ without knowing x_i, it must compute x_i from Y_i. We assume that $\mathcal{C}$ can compute the value x_i from Y_i by an efficient algorithm $\mathcal{A}$. Then, $\mathcal{C}$ uses $Y_i = g_1^{ab}$ and $f_i = g_1^a$ as input, and outputs $b = x_i$, where $a = (x_{i+1} - x_{i-1})$. So it can use $\mathcal{A}$ to construct an efficient algorithm $\mathcal{A}'$ to solve the DLP problem, which is a contradiction for the hard of DLP problem.

Lemma 2. Under the decision bilinear Diffie-Hellman assumption, $(g_1, g_2, y_i, y_{i+1}, \delta_i, (PK_{enc})^t)$ and $(g_1, g_2, y_i, y_{i+1}, \delta_i, \pi)$ are computationally indistinguishable, where $t \in \mathbb{Z}_q^*$, $\delta_i = g_1^t \in G_1$ and $\pi \in G_2$. Using the contradiction proof, assume that there exists an efficiently algorithm $\mathcal{A}$, which can obtain the plaintext $m = \eta_i \oplus H_3(e(\delta_i, SK_{dec}))$ without the group decryption key SK_{dec}. Based on the algorithm $\mathcal{A}$, we can construct another algorithm $\mathcal{A}'$ that can efficiently distinguish $(g_1, g_2, y_i, y_{i+1}, \delta_i, (PK_{enc})^t)$ and $(g_1, g_2, y_i, y_{i+1}, \delta_i, \pi)$.

Proof. A passive attacker tries to learn secret information about the group key by listening to the communication channel. The passive attacker can obtain all messages $(g_1, y_i, \sigma_i, R_{u_i}, Y_i)(1 \leq i \leq n)$ over communication channel and the ciphertext $c = \langle \delta_i, \eta_i \rangle$ broadcasted by u_i, where $\delta_i = g_1^t$, $t \in \mathbb{Z}_q^*$ and $\eta_i = m \oplus$

$H_3(PK_{enc})^t$. Here we show that the passive attacker cannot get any information about the group decryption key SK_{dec}.

Without loss of generality, let $f_1 = y_1 = g_1^{x_1}$ and $\beta_i = \delta_i = g_1^t$. Then, Algorithm $\mathcal{A}'$ randomly selects $(\lambda_1, \lambda_2, \cdots, \lambda_n)$ from $\mathbb{Z}_q^*$ and calculates values are as follows:

$$f_1 = \gamma_1 = g_1^{x_1}, p_1 = (\beta_i)^{\lambda_1};$$
$$f_2 = \gamma_2 = g_1^{x_2}, p_2 = (\beta_i)^{\lambda_2};$$
$$\vdots$$
$$f_n = \gamma_n = g_1^{x_n}, p_n = (\beta_i)^{\lambda_n}.$$

Therefore, the algorithm $\mathcal{A}'$ constructs all message pairs (f_i, p_j), for $1 \leq j \leq n$, and computes $\pi = \prod_{j=1}^n e(f_j, p_j) = \prod_{j=1}^n e(g_1^{x_j}, g_1^{t\lambda_j}) = e(g_1, g_1)^{x_1\lambda_1 t + x_2\lambda_2 t + \ldots + x_n\lambda_n t}$
$= e(g_1, g_1)^{t(x_1\lambda_1 + x_2\lambda_2 + \ldots + x_n\lambda_n)}$, then $\mathcal{A}'$ calls $\mathcal{A}$ with these values to compute $m = \eta_i \oplus H_3(e(\delta_i, SK_{dec}))$. It is obvious that $SK_{dec} = g_1^{(x_1\lambda_1 + x_2\lambda_2 + \ldots + x_n\lambda_n)}$ based on property of bilinear map if $e(g_1, g_1)^{t(x_1\lambda_1 + x_2\lambda_2 + \ldots + x_n\lambda_n)} = e(g_1^t, g_1^{(x_1\lambda_1 + x_2\lambda_2 + \ldots + x_n\lambda_n)}) = e(\delta_1, SK_{dec})$ holds. $\mathcal{A}'$ can apply $\mathcal{A}$ to efficiently distinguish $(g_1, g_2, g_1^a, g_1^b, g_1^c, e(g_1, g_1)^{abc})$ and $(g_1, g_2, g_1^a, g_1^b, g_1^c, \pi)$, where $g_1^{x_1} = g_1^a$, $g_1^t = g_1^b$ and $g_1^{(x_1\lambda_1 + x_2\lambda_2 + \ldots + x_n\lambda_n)} = g_1^c$, which is a contradiction for the DBDH problem assumption. Thus, the proposed protocol is secure against passive attacks under the DBDH problem assumption.

3.1   Performance Analysis

During the process of designing protocol, besides security, the computational complexity is important performance measures of the group key agreement. In this paper, we compare and analyze the literature that can be quantified in recent years. We compare the proposed protocol with the related works [4–6] in computational complexity.

Table 1 lists comparison and analysis between the B-AGKA protocol and other three group-key agreement protocols in the calculation complexity.

From Table 1, B-AGKA protocol and Ranjani et al.'s protocol [4] have similar computational complexity and have the lowest computational complexity. Zhang et al's protocol [6] have the higher computational complexity. Lv et al.'s protocol [5] has the highest computational complexity.

In communication, B-AGKA protocol, Ranjani et al.'s protocol [4] and Lv et al.'s protocol [5] protocol have similar communication complexity. Zhang et al's protocol [6] has the higher communication complexity.

Table 1. Complexity analysis of the four protocols

	Zhang et al. [6]	Ranjani et al. [4]	Lv et al. [5]	B-AGKA
Computational complexity of each ordinary node (online)	$12T_{bp}$ + $(3n + 2)T_{exp}$ + $(12n - 4)T_{mul}$ + $5(n + 1)T_h + 6T_{sm-bp}$	$(3n + 4nT_{mul} + nT_h$	$(n - 1)T_{bp}$ + nT_{sm-bp} + nT_{pa-bp} + nT_{pa-ecc}	$+ 5T_{bp}$ + $4T_{exp}$ + $(2n - 1)T_{mul}$ + $2T_h + 4T_{pa-ecc}$ + $1T_{inv}$
Computational complexity required by the sponsor node	$12T_{bp}$ + $(3n + 2)T_{exp}$ + $(12n - 4)T_{mul}$ + $5(n + 1)T_h$	$(3n + T_{bp}+nT_{exp}$ $- 5nT_{mul} + (2n + 2)T_{mul}$ $1)T_h + 6T_{sm-bp}$	$+ (n - 1)T_{bp}+(n$ + nT_{sm-bp} + nT_{pa-bp} + $nT_{pa-ecc} + nT_h$	$+ 3T_{bp}$ + $4T_{exp}$ + $(2n - 1)T_{mul}$ + $(n - 1)T_{sm-bp}$ + $2T_h + 2T_{pa-ecc}$ + $1T_{inv}$
Average number of messages received per ordinary node	$(n - 1)(n + 3)|q|$	$(n + 3)|q|$	$(n + 4)|q|$	$(n + 5)|q|$
Average number of messages sent per ordinary node	$(n + 3)|q|$	$5(n - 1)|q|$	$(n + 3)|q|$	$(n + 7)|q|$

4 Conclusions

This paper analyzed the application requirements of group key agreement in a mobile ad hoc network and the problems that need to be solved of group key negotiation in this network environment, and proposed a blockchain-based asymmetric group key agreement protocol for ad hoc network. It used the technical advantages of blockchain to achieve a non-centralized authentication, lightweight calculation and key self-certified group key agreement. It solves the technical bottleneck of group key agreement in ad hoc network, and satisfies the application requirements of key information exchange in this network environment. The protocol is proven secure under the DLP and DBDH problem assumption, and the performance analysis shows that the proposed scheme is highly efficient. It is suitable for security group communication in ad hoc network.

Acknowledgements. This work is supported by National Natural Science Foundation of China under Grant No. 61772477, 61572445 and U1804263, the Beijing Municipal Natural Science Foundation (No. 4172053), the Natural Science Foundation of Henan Province (No. 162300410322).

References

1. Lin, T., Hsu, C.: Anonymous group key agreement protocol for multi-server and mobile environments based on Chebyshev chaotic maps. J. Supercomput. **74**(9), 4521–4541 (2018)
2. Tan, Y., Zhang, X., Sharif, K., et al.: Covert timing channels for IoT over mobile networks. IEEE Wirel. Commun. **25**(6), 38–44 (2018)
3. Zhang, X., Liang, C., Zhang, Q., et al.: Building covert timing channels by packet rearrangement over mobile networks. Inf. Sci. **445–446**, 66–78 (2018)
4. Ranjani, R., Bhaskari, D., Avadhani, P.: An extended identity based authenticated asymmetric group key agreement protocol. IJ Netw. Secur. **17**(5), 510–516 (2015)
5. Lv, X., Li, H., Wang, B.: Authenticated asymmetric group key agreement based on certificateless cryptosystem. Int. J. Comput. Math. **91**(3), 447–460 (2014)
6. Zhang, L., Wu, Q., Domingo-Ferrer, J., et al.: Round-efficient and sender-unrestricted dynamic group key agreement protocol for secure group communications. IEEE Trans. Inf. Forensics Secur. **10**(11), 2352–2364 (2015)

Development of an Early Warning System for Network Intrusion Detection Using Benford's Law Features

Liuying Sun[1], Anthony Ho[1,2], Zhe Xia[1(✉)], Jiageng Chen[3],
and Mingwu Zhang[4]

[1] Department of Computer Science and Technology,
Wuhan University of Technology, Wuhan 430063, China
xiazhe@whut.edu.cn
[2] Department of Computer Science, University of Surrey,
Guildford, Surrey GU2 7XH, UK
[3] Department of Computer Science and Technology,
Central China Normal University, Wuhan 430079, China
[4] School of Computers, Hubei University of Technology,
Wuhan 430068, China

Abstract. In order to ensure a high level of security in computer networks, it is important to prevent malicious behaviours from the intruders. However, high volumes of network traffic make it difficult for intrusion detection systems (IDSs) to separate abnormal network traffic from the normal ones. To alleviate this problem, a window-based feature extraction method using the Benford's law has been proposed in this paper. Our method employs six features of the divergence values, including the first digit and the first three digits of size difference between traffic flows. Experiments are performed and evaluated using the KDD99 dataset. To illustrate the advantages of our proposed method, three popular classifiers, Multi-Layer Perceptron (MLP), Support Vector Machine (SVM) and Naïve Bayes are analysed using different combinations of these six features as the input feature sets. The results demonstrated that the MLP classifier performs the best in classifying the normal, mixed and malicious windows by correctly classifying the normal and malicious windows. This is particularly useful to reduce the amount of network traffic that needs to be analysed. The only exception is the mixed window which contains both normal flows and attack flows, and it needs to be further analysed to distinguish normal flows from malicious ones. Our method is fast and can be used as an early warning system to trigger other more advanced IDSs to focus on the specific regions of the network traffic. The combined system, incorporating our method with a traditional IDS, can provide a lower FAR of 0.27% compared with 9.87% of the isolated IDS, along with no significant reduction of the detection performance. Moreover, the whole accuracy of the combined system achieves 92.09%.

© Springer Nature Singapore Pte Ltd. 2019
W. Meng and S. Furnell (Eds.): SocialSec 2019, CCIS 1095, pp. 57–73, 2019.
https://doi.org/10.1007/978-981-15-0758-8_5

1 Introduction

The Internet has become an indispensable component of our daily life and it affects all aspects of people's lives. This has led to a great deal of attentions in the area of network security both in the industry and academia. This is because any malicious intrusion or attack against a network would cause serious consequences for an organization, potentially impacting their reputation and financial stability. Therefore, unauthorized access to communication or computer network must be detected, prevented and repelled as soon as possible. Intrusion Detection Systems (IDSs) can be used to prevent unauthorized access to network resources by monitoring and analysing the network traffic.

To distinguish the attacks from the normal network access, various artificial intelligence methods have been developed for solving problems that are related to the intrusion detection, and the following methods are most commonly used in the literature [1–8]: support vector machine (SVM), decision tree, genetic algorithm (GA), principal component analysis (PCA), Particle Swarm Optimization (PSO), K-nearest neighbours, Naïve Bayes networks, and Neural Networks such as Multi-Layer perceptron and Self-organizing map. Their detection targets vary from any class of anomalies to just a single class.

In general, IDSs deal with a tremendous amount of data which contains redundant and irrelevant features resulting in excessive training and predictive time. To minimize the computational costs and the number of data patterns need to be searched, various feature selection and extraction techniques have been developed. The feature selection techniques generally first rank the existing features according to their predictive significance, and then select the most meaningful feature subset from the original features. However, feature extraction techniques actually transform the features into linear combinations of the original attributes. There are various techniques that can be used for the feature extraction and selection. These include Genetic Algorithm (GA), Information Gain, correlation coefficient, Partial Least Square (PLS), and Kernel Principal Component Analysis (KPCA) [9–13].

In this paper, we propose a fast window-based feature extraction method based on the Benford's law to analyse and classify the KDD99 dataset. The proposed method is an extension of a previous work [14], and it can be used as an early warning system and incorporated into other IDSs. It composes of two phases. In the first phase, three machine learning techniques, Multi-Layer Perceptron (MLP), Support Vector Machine (SVM) and Naïve Bayes are implemented and compared to evaluate the performance of the features extracted over different training datasets reconstructed from the KDD99, and then the classifier and the subset of features that perform the best are selected. In the second phase, experiments are performed to compare the performance of when our proposed method is used as an early warning system incorporated into an IDS that was proposed in [15] with that of the IDS alone. The work in [15] has trained a classifier using 19 critical features chosen by the proposed feature reduction strategy called gradually feature removal method rather than 41 original features in KDD99, which resulted in contributing a more efficient intrusion system. The classifier used in the second phase is MLP. Classifiers used in these two phases are trained and designed independently, and the final results are aggregated from the individual ones in each model.

The remainder of this paper is organized as follows. Section 2 introduces the dataset used and Benford's law. Section 3 describes the proposed method. Experiments are conducted in Sect. 4. Results and analysis are presented in Sect. 5. Finally, we conclude and discuss some future works in Sect. 6.

2 Materials and Methods

2.1 Data Set

The experimental data used in our experiments is a benchmark database KDD99. Till now, KDD CUP'99 dataset is the only publicly available and widely used labelled dataset for IDS. The KDD99 dataset contains two types of data, training data and test data. Training data is consisted of seven weeks of network traffic, and the test data contains two weeks of network traffic. The network traffic contains network-based attacks inserted in the normal background data. The full dataset (18 MB, 743 MB Uncompressed) contains 22 types of attacks and is employed for the purpose of training. For testing, the "Corrected KDD" dataset containing 17 additional attacks is used. These attacks are grouped into four major categories: denial of service (DOS), unauthorized access from a remote machine (R2L), unauthorized access to local supervisor privileges (U2R), probing, surveillance and other probing (Probe) [16]. Since our focus is the TCP transmission, these data are therefore extracted from the KDD99 dataset for the experiments. The extracted data sets are composed of the training data and test data, containing 1,820,596 records and 119,357 records, respectively.

2.2 Benford's Law

Benford's law is an empirical law that states the probability distribution of the leading digits for naturally occurring sets of numbers. According to Benford's law, its significant digits for a collection of numbers are not uniformly distributed. Instead, they obey the distribution shown in Eq. (1). It was first proposed by Newcomb [17] in 1881. In 1938, Frank Benford, whom this law was named after, re-discovered this phenomenon by testing it on data from 20 different domains including the sizes of populations, the surface areas of rivers, physical constants, molecular weights and so on [18]. In 1995, Hill provided a statistical interpretation of this law and also generalized it for all significant digits in [19].

$$P_d = \log_{10}\left(1 + \frac{1}{d}\right) \tag{1}$$

Where P_d denotes the probability of d, d = 1,2,3,…,9.

Although Benford's law has been applied in various fields for a long time, such as forensic accounting, auditing, nature science and image forensics [20–23], its use in network security has only been investigated until recently. Nevertheless, Benford's law has been demonstrated to be very effective and reliable in anomaly detection [24–26].

3 Our Proposed Method

3.1 Construction of Feature Sets

KDD 99 consists of 41 features excluding the target-class label. In our recent research [14], src_bytes, dst_bytes and bytes which are the sum of src_bytes and dst_bytes have been proved to be effective parameters of the network flows that could be used for Benford's law in distinguishing the normal network flows from the malicious ones. Thus, new features are reconstructed based on these three basic features.

Since the first-digit law is a distribution, a window-based method proposed in [28] is employed to collect sufficient samples for a given feature. This is then used to construct an observed distribution which can then be compared with the target distribution for deviation detection. To compare the conformity of first-digit frequencies with the logarithmic distribution in different windows, we use chi-square goodness-of-fit statistics test [29]. The chi-square divergence is given as in Eq. (2).

$$\chi^2 = \sum_{d=1}^{9} \frac{\left(\hat{P}_d - P_d\right)^2}{P_d} \tag{2}$$

Where P_d is the expected frequency of digit, d is the first digit according to the logarithmic distribution and $\hat{P}_d$ is the actual observed frequency in the data set. In all cases, the lower the discrepancy measure, the higher the similarity will be obtained between the data set and the distribution.

In this paper, the Benford's law divergence value is taken as a new feature of the window. Firstly, the following features, src_bytes, dst_bytes and bytes of each flow, are extracted and then divided into sets of consecutive windows. Window size is chosen as W = 2000, which is a reasonable choice according to [14]. The difference is calculated between every two contiguous flows in each window. The frequency of the first-digit in each window is then computed. Finally, the results are compared with the expected logarithmic distribution by applying the chi-square measure. Thus, three features are constructed and they are denoted as src_bytes_chi, dst_bytes_chi and bytes_chi, respectively. Since the results have been shown previously that the Benford's Law can be very effective in distinguishing between normal and malicious network flows [24–26], especially when using multiple digits of the Benford's Law [14], its first three digits are also calculated, resulting in three features, src_bytes_chi_3, dst_bytes_chi_3 and bytes_chi_3.

To evaluate the performance of features extracted, the six features are divided into three feature sets. Different feature sets are used to construct different data sets. Detailed properties of each feature set have been tabulated in Table 1.

3.2 ClassLabelling of Instances

KDD99 has labels at the flow level, but our features works at the flow window level, so flow labels need to be converted to flow window labels. Depending on whether the windows contain attack flows or not, they are classified into three groups: normal,

Table 1. Constructed feature sets and the corresponding features

Feature set	Feature	Dimension
F_set1	src_bytes_chi, dst_bytes_chi, bytes_chi	3
F_set2	src_bytes_chi_3, dst_bytes_chi_3 and bytes_chi_3	3
F_set3	src_bytes_chi, dst_bytes_chi, bytes_chi src_bytes_chi_3, dst_bytes_chi_3, bytes_chi_3	6

mixed, and malicious. The normal group, as the name implies, contains all TCP flows that are normal. The windows labeled mixed contain both normal and attack flows. A window is labeled malicious if all TCP flows in this window are malicious.

3.3 Construction of Datasets

As already mentioned, the traffic flows in KDD99, which is used as the base dataset, are divided into consecutive windows using a window-based method. Firstly, non-overlapping is used with a window size W = 2000, resulting 317 normal windows, 83 mixed windows, 535 malicious windows and a total of 935. In order to obtain sufficient instances, an overlapping window is then applied with sliding window steps of 1000 and 100, respectively.

Similarly, non-overlapping strategy is adopted to reconstruct the test dataset from the original test data set "Corrected KDD". However, the new test dataset contains only one normal window. To increase the number of normal windows, all normal traffic flows in "Corrected KDD" are extracted, and non-overlapping is then re-applied to the normal traffic flows. Thus, the final test dataset consists of 23 normal windows, 49 mixed windows and 9 malicious windows. The results of the constructed datasets are illustrated in Table 2.

Table 2. The list of constructed datasets with their corresponding composition information

Dataset name	Feature	Normal	Mixed	Malicious	Total
Trainset data 1	F_set1	317	83	535	935
Trainset data 1-1	F_set1	637	167	1065	1869
Trainset data 1-2	F_set1	6374	1638	10674	18686
Trainset data 2	F_set2	317	83	535	935
Trainset data 2-1	F_set2	637	167	1065	1869
Trainset data 2-2	F_set2	6374	1638	10674	18686
Trainset data 3	F_set3	317	83	535	935
Trainset data 3-1	F_set3	637	167	1065	1869
Trainset data 3-2	F_set3	6374	1638	10674	18686
Test data 1	F_set1	23	49	9	81
Test data 2	F_set2	23	49	9	81
Test data 3	F_set3	23	49	9	81

3.4   Machine Learning Algorithms Applied to Intrusion Detection

3.4.1   Multilayer Perceptron

A neural network (NN) consists of information processing units which can mimic the neurons of human brain [30]. It works by accepting input data, extracting rules and then making decisions. Multilayer perceptron (MLP) is a feed-forward type of NN, which is usually trained with the standard back propagation algorithm. A MLP network consists of an input layer, one or more hidden layers, and an output layer of calculation nodes. The layers are fully connected from one layer to the next one. Each node in hidden layer and output layer has a nonlinear activation function, which enables MLP to distinguish data that is not linearly separable. MLPs are very powerful pattern classifiers that they can approximate virtually any input-output map with one or two hidden layers [31].

3.4.2   Support Vector Machine

SVM (Support Vector Machine) is based on statistical learning theory by finding an optimal hyperplane in the feature space that separates input dataset with maximum margin [31]. It uses just a portion of the data called the support vectors that represent the training data to train a model. Although linear SVM classifiers are efficient and work well in many cases, it often happens that many datasets are not even close to being linearly separable. To solve this problem, a kernel trick is applied, which implicitly maps the inputs into high-dimensional feature spaces. There are three major kernel functions, Sigmoid kernel, Polynomial kernel and Gaussian kernel which are used to build SVM classifier. In addition to binary classification, SVMs can also handle multiclass problems by reducing the multi-class task to several binary problems via One-vs-One or One-vs-All strategy. One-vs-One multiclass SVMs are used for the experiments in this paper.

3.4.3   Naive Bayes

A Naïve Bayes classifier is a simplified probabilistic classification model based on applying Bayes's theorem, which estimates the conditional and prior probabilities to generate a learning model, with a naive independence assumption between the features [27]. It assumes that all features are conditionally independent given class. Despite the fact that the strong independence assumption is generally poor and rarely true in real-world applications, the naive Bayes classifiers perform surprisingly well in practice and can be as effective as other more sophisticated classifiers. However, for intrusion detection, the strong independent relation assumption may result in lower attack detection accuracy when the features are correlated [34].

4   Our Proposed Method

The experiments consist of two phases: In the first phase, the windows passing through are classified into three classes, normal, mixed and malicious, which can be used as an early warning system. In the second phase, the network flows in mixed windows are further classified into normal and attack using the IDS proposed in [15]. And then, we show the performance that our method is used as an early warning system combined with the IDS. To show the advantages of our proposed method, the performances of whole test data set detected by the single IDS are compared with the results of the combined system.

4.1   Phase-1: Multiclass Classification

To perform multi-class classification, the models are first trained using different training sets (Table 2). Each training set is evaluated with the corresponding test dataset using three different machine learning algorithms, MLP, SVM, and Naïve Bayes.

The structure of MLP is composed of 3 layers, input, hidden and output layer. This structure is commonly chosen as a basic structure for many applications such as image processing. Whereas the number of units at the input layer is equal to the number of selected features, the output layer consists of three softmax output neurons which is the equal number of categories to be classified to make the network's prediction. The number of units at the hidden layer is set up based on the rules-of-thumb proposed in [32]. Hyper-parameters which show the best performance are selected through trial and error. ReLU function is used as a neuron function and MLP is learned using back propagation.

The test dataset is then predicted to evaluate the performance of the trained models. The trained models are divided into three groups based on the feature sets selected. In each group, comparisons are performed to select the best performing model. Finally, the comparison among the selected best models is made to determine the feature set that performs best.

4.2   Phase-2: Anomaly Detection in Mixed Window

The main purpose of this phase is to further classify the traffic flows in mixed window from phase-1 into corresponding two classes, i.e., normal or anomalies. The classification returns back to flow level, and so does the features. The features used in this phase are 19 original features in KDD99. For explicit information of the 19 features, refer to [15].

In this phase, 10% of the KDD99 dataset is used as the training data. After training the model, two test experiments are conducted using two different test datasets. One consists of TCP traffic flows in the "mixed" windows classified by the best model chosen in phase-1. The other is the whole test dataset of the group the best model belongs to, and it is converted to flow level.

5   Results and Discussion

For MLP, Keras backend theano is used. SVM and Naïve Bayes classifiers are constructed using a machine learning package called scikit-learn. The experiments are conducted with Windows 10 as the test bed operating system on Intel i7-6700 HQ CPU @ 2.60 GHz processor, 8 GB of RAM. All the codes are written in python.

5.1 Phase-1

5.1.1 Classification Using MLP

Classifier is evaluated with a 10-fold cross validation, which is a standard technique for estimating the performance of a classifier. The results of three groups are listed in Tables 3, 4 and 5. It can be observed that the gap between the training accuracy and validation accuracy narrows as the volume of training data sets grows, which means a lower probability of overfitting. The best model in each group is chosen based on two factors: validation accuracy and training time. Validation accuracy shows the generalization ability of a model, to some extent, the higher the better. On the contrary, the lower the training time, the less the system overhead. To summarize, the best models are those trained by Trainset data 1, Trainset data 2-1 and Trainset data 3, as can be seen from Table 3, 4 and 5, respectively.

Table 3. Performance comparisons among training data sets composed of F_set1

Dataset name	Training accuracy	Validation accuracy	Training time
Trainset data 1	93.48%	92.62% (2.28%)	17.682498 s
Trainset data 1-1	92.51%	92.29% (2.56%)	32.524289 s
Trainset data 1-2	92.93%	93.20% (0.79%)	150.547682 s

Table 4. Performance comparisons among training data sets composed of F_set2

Dataset name	Training accuracy	Validation accuracy	Training time
Trainset data 2	89.09%	90.79% (4.99%)	20.983321 s
Trainset data 2-1	92.88%	92.03% (2.45%)	14.954141 s
Trainset data 2-2	92.86%	92.80% (0.72%)	173.994690 s

Table 5. Performance comparisons among training data sets composed of F_set3

Dataset name	Training accuracy	Validation accuracy	Training time
Trainset data 3	93.69%	93.58% (1.91%)	15.837295 s
Trainset data 3-1	93.37%	92.88% (2.46%)	17.778418 s
Trainset data 3-2	93.59%	93.53% (0.51%)	236.564110 s

To evaluate the models obtained, data sets listed in Table 2 are tested by the corresponding trained models. Specifically, models which are trained separately by Trainset data 1, Trainset data 2-1 and Trainset data 3, are tested on Test data 1, Test data 2 and Test data 3, respectively. Figure 1(a)–(c) illustrates the classification results of test data sets via confusion matrices.

Confusion Matrixes show that all the normal and malicious windows in Test data 1 and 3 are correctly classified. In other words, the detection rate of both the normal and malicious is 1.0. Furthermore, classification results of normal and malicious among the three test sets have minor differences. The main difference lies in the classification of

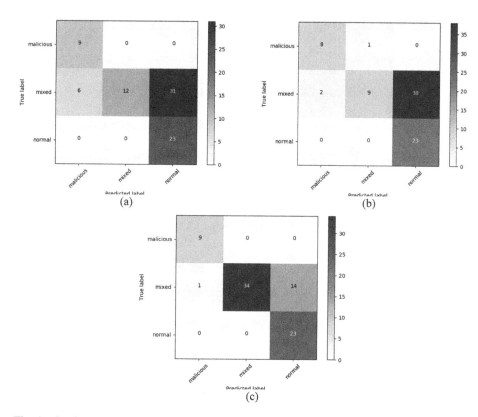

Fig. 1. Confusion matrixes for window classification using MLP: (a) Trainset data 1 with Test data 1; (b) Trainset data 2-1 with Test data 2; (c) Trainset data 3 with Test data 3

mixed windows. Trainset data 2 performs the worst with only 18% of mixed windows correctly classified, while the Trainset data 3 performs the best with 69% of mixed windows correctly classified. Nevertheless, the average classification accuracy of Test data 3, which achieved the best result, is as low as 81.48%. There is a gap of 12.1% between validation accuracy and test accuracy.

The main reason is that χ^2 divergence, the feature of the mixed window is sensitive to the number of attack flows in this window. Figure 2 shows the distributions of normal TCP traffic flows in mixed windows in Trainset data 3 and Test data 3, respectively. In Fig. 2, the percentage of normal flows on the total 2000 flows in a window is shown horizontally, and the count of windows corresponding to x-axis is shown vertically. As one can see, the majority of the normal TCP traffic flows in mixed windows in Trainset data 3 account for 90% to 100%, i.e. most of these mixed windows consist of more than 1800 normal TCP flows and less than 200 attack TCP flows. However, Test data 3 shows just the opposite. The difference of normal flow number between training set and test set results in different distributions of χ^2 divergence value. That is, the value range regarding the same feature of mixed windows in training set and test set is different, as can be seen in Fig. 3, resulting in incomplete

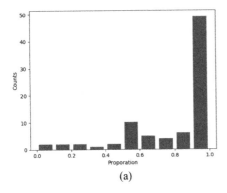
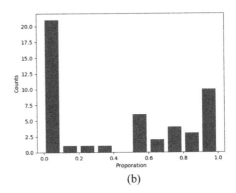

Fig. 2. The distribution of normal flows in training and test dataset: (a) Trainset data 3; (b) Test data 3

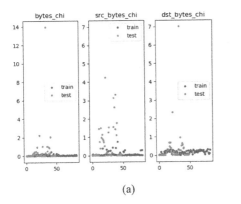
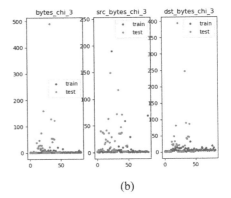

Fig. 3. The value of different features composing the mixed windows in training samples and test samples

training sets for mixed windows. Because the lower the attack flow number, the smaller difference between mixed window and normal window. Similarly, the higher the attack flow number, the smaller difference between mixed window and malicious window. Therefore, these characteristics make it difficult to distinguish mixed windows from normal and malicious ones.

Figure 4 shows the distribution of normal flows in mixed windows which were classified as normal windows. As one can see, seven of 14 misclassified mixed windows are those in which normal TCP traffic flow account for 90% to 100%. The windows that were misclassified as malicious consist of 1999 attack TCP flows and only one normal flow.

5.1.2   Classification Using SVM
For the SVM, the classifier is evaluated with 5-fold cross validation. The results achieved for these three groups are listed in Tables 6, 7 and 8. Based on the two factors

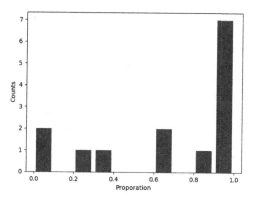

Fig. 4. The distribution of normal flows in misclassified mixed windows of Test data3

Table 6. Performance comparisons among training data sets composed of F_set1

Dataset name	Training accuracy	Validation accuracy	Training time
Trainset data 1	93.9%	93.40%	0.009569 s
Trainset data 1-1	93.63%	93.48%	0.036576 s
Trainset data 1-2	95.11%	94.70%	8.50749 s

Table 7. Performance comparisons among training data sets composed of F_set2

Dataset name	Training accuracy	Validation accuracy	Training time
Trainset data 2	94.65%	93.83%	0.026069 s
Trainset data 2-1	94.44%	93.69%	0.064608 s
Trainset data 2-2	95.75%	94.44%	1212.171683 s

Table 8. Performance comparisons among training data sets composed of F_set3

Dataset name	Training accuracy	Validation accuracy	Training time
Trainset data 3	94.55%	94.04%	0.021469 s
Trainset data 3-1	94.06%	93.8%	0.031255 s
Trainset data 3-2	96.91%	95.51%	294.210544 s

mentioned above in terms of accuracy and time efficiency, SVM classifiers trained by Trainset data 1-1, Trainset data 2-1 and Trainset data 3-1 are then chosen. This is because SVM classifiers achieve higher training accuracy and lower training time for generating a model as compared with MLP classifiers. Confusion matrices of classification results using selected SVM classifiers are depicted in Fig. 5(a)–(c).

From Fig. 5, it can be seen, classification accuracies of the three classifiers are approximately the same, with 66.67% having 416 support vectors, 62.96% having 290 support vectors and 64.20% having 312 support vectors, respectively. This indicates that the difference among feature sets in SVM does not cause a significant difference in classification results as it did in MLP. However, since nearly half of the mixed windows are misclassified as normal, the difficulty of classification in SVM still lies in the mixed windows, which is similar to the case in MLP. In addition, as shown in Fig. 5, one of nine malicious windows is classified as being mixed. Since mixed windows will be further classified, windows that are mistakenly classified as mixed theoretically do not affect the final result of anomaly detection in phase-2. However, in this case, the classification process in phase-1 will be meaningless. In addition, Fig. 5 (b) shows that one in 23 normal windows is misclassified as malicious, which may result in a tendency of higher false alarm rate that needs to be avoided.

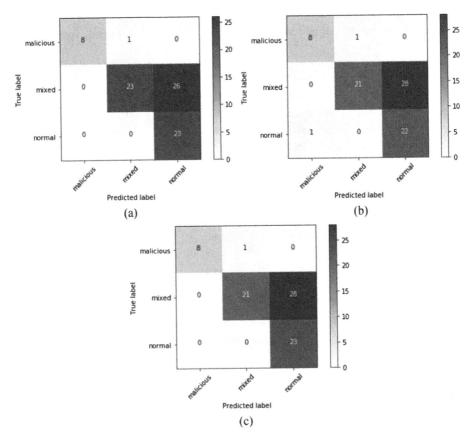

Fig. 5. Confusion matrixes for window classification using SVM: (a) Trainset data 1-1 with Test data 1; (b)Trainset data 2-1 with Test data 2; (c) Trainset data 3-1 with Test data 3

5.1.3 Classification Using Naïve Bayes

Tables 9, 10 and 11 illustrate the corresponding results of Naïve Bayes classifiers. The classification performance has been evaluated using a 10-fold cross validation procedure. As shown in Table 9, classifiers using F_set1 as the feature vector achieve the best performance. While Table 10 shows that F_set2 is not a good feature vector as the Naïve Bayes classifiers performed poorly in the learning process. In other words, features in F_set2, src_bytes_chi_3, dst_bytes_chi_3 and bytes_chi_3 are not sufficiently distinctive enough to use as features for Naïve Bayes classifiers. In addition, F_set3, combination of F_set1 and F_set2, did not show any advantages of using all these six features. In Tables 9, 10 and 11, the highest validation accuracy rates achieved were approximately 93.36% for Trainset data 1, 34.03% for Trainset data 2-2 and 91.37% for Trainset data 3-2, respectively. As such, considering accuracy and time efficiency, Naïve Bayes classifiers trained by Trainset data 1, Trainset data 2-2 and Trainset data 3-2 are chosen. The classification results of the chosen features are shown in Fig. 6(a)–(c) via confusion matrices.

Table 9. Performance comparisons among training data sets composed of F_set1

Dataset name	Training accuracy	Validation accuracy	Training time
Trainset data 1	93.37%	93.36%	0.003971 s
Trainset data 1-1	91.17%	90.53%	0 s
Trainset data 1-2	91.44%	91.22%	0.019967 s

Table 10. Performance comparisons among training data sets composed of F_set2

Dataset name	Training accuracy	Validation accuracy	Training time
Trainset data 2	8.45%	10.39%	0 s
Trainset data 2-1	34.08%	33.43%	0 s
Trainset data 2-2	34.42%	34.03%	0.019979 s

Table 11. Performance comparisons among training data sets composed of F_set3

Dataset name	Training accuracy	Validation accuracy	Training time
Trainset data 3	67.59%	68.47%	0.004002 s
Trainset data 3-1	91.06%	90.53%	0 s
Trainset data 3-2	91.64%	91.37%	0.01994 s

Figure 6(a)–(c) show that Trainset data 1 with test data 1, Trainset data 2-2 with test data 2 and Trainset data 3-2 with test data 3 achieving classification results of approximately 41.98%, 38.27% and 46.91%, respectively. Figure 6(a) shows that all malicious and normal windows are correctly classified. However, only 4.08% mixed window are detected. Figure 6(b) shows that the majority of the samples are classified as normal. Since eight of nine malicious windows are misclassified as normal, the classifier trained by Trainset data 2-2 is too insensitive to detect abnormal activities. Figure 6(c) shows similar results to Fig. 6(a). However, there is a slight improvement in distinguishing mixed windows from malicious windows.

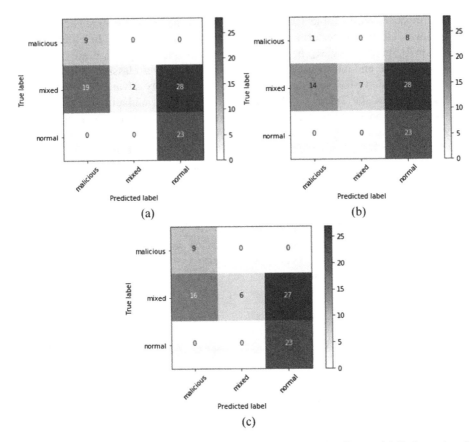

Fig. 6. Confusion matrixes for window classification using Naïve Bayes: (a) Trainset data 1 with Test data 1; (b) Trainset data 2-2 with Test data 2; (c) Trainset data 3-2 with Test data 3

From the above analysis, MLP classifier trained by all six features achieved the highest accuracy with 81.48% when compared to SVM with 66.67% and Naïve Bayes with 46.91%. Thus, the 34 mixed windows detected by the MLP classifier will be further analyzed and then classified in phase-2.

5.2 Phase-2

Phase-2 further classifies the mixed window recognized in phase-1 into normal and malicious traffic flows. Since the samples classified in phase-1 are all windows containing 2000 traffic flows, windows classified as mixed need further classification to obtain a better performance in accuracy of the whole dataset. Furthermore, the superiority of the combined model compared to a single model will be evaluated in detail via five metrics: accuracy, precision, recall, f1-score and false alarm rate. They are commonly defined as follows:

$$Accuracy = \frac{TP + TN}{TP + TN + FP + FN}$$

$$Precision = \frac{TP}{FP + FP}$$

$$Recall = \frac{TP}{TP + FN}$$

$$F1 - score = \frac{2TP}{2TP + FP + FN}$$

$$False\ alarm\ rate = \frac{FP}{TP + FP}$$

Where TP, FP, FN and TN are the number of True Positives, False Positives, False Negatives and True Negative, respectively.

The reason for measuring the false alarm rate is that the cost incurred when IDS misclassifies a normal flow as malicious could be very high. In addition, it is well known that the false alarm occurs frequently in IDS experiments, so that it should be considered when developing IDSs [33]. The time incurred for processing will also be evaluated. The results obtained with respect to the evaluation metrics are provided in Table 12.

Table 12. Performance comparisons between proposed combined system and single IDS

Approach	Accuracy	Precision	Recall	F1-score	False alarm rate	Testing time (sec)
combined IDS	92.09%	99.73%	87.48%	93.2%	0.27%	0.34
single IDS	93%	90.13%	97.83%	93.82%	9.87%	0.80

Table 12 shows that the accuracy and F1-score of proposed method combining an IDS is slightly lower as compared to the IDS alone, but it outperforms with a much lower rate of only 0.27% FAR. Besides, the proposed approach consumes less time for training and testing.

6 Conclusion

This paper presented an application of Benford's law for anomaly-based network flow IDS based on six new features as an early warning system for the detection of malicious attacks. The six features used were src_bytes_chi, dst_bytes_chi, bytes_chi, src_bytes_chi_3, dst_bytes_chi_3 and bytes_chi_3. Based on these six features, three feature sets were selected to train the classifiers. The MLP classifier trained by all six features was shown to perform the best in accurately distinguishing and classifying the normal or malicious windows from the mixed windows. The mixed windows were further classified by combining our proposed method with existing IDSs to detect the malicious network flows. The experimental results showed that the proposed IDS improved the performance by reducing the computational complexity and decreasing the FAR by approximately 9.6%. Our future work will focus on finding other optimum subsets of features for the Benford's law and the window size, in order to further improve the overall performance of the proposed system.

Data Availability
The data used to support the findings of this study are available at http://kdd.ics.uci.edu/databases/kddcup99/kddcup99.html.

Acknowledgments. This work was partially supported by the National Natural Science Foundation of China (Grant No. 61702212, 61672010) and the Natural Science Foundation of Hubei Province (Grant No. 2017CFB303).

References

1. Khan, L., Awad, M., Thuraisingham, B.: A new intrusion detection system using support vector machines and hierarchical clustering. VLDB J. **16**(4), 507–521 (2007)
2. Amor, N.B., Benferhat, S., Elouedi, Z.: Naive Bayes vs decision trees in intrusion detection systems. In: Proceedings of the 2004 ACM Symposium on Applied Computing, pp. 420–424. ACM (2004)
3. Shafi, K., Abbass, H.A.: An adaptive genetic-based signature learning system for intrusion detection. Expert Syst. Appl. **36**(10), 12036–12043 (2009)
4. Wang, W., Battiti, R.: Identifying intrusions in computer networks with principal component analysis. In: International Conference on Availability, Reliability and Security, pp. 270–279. IEEE (2006)
5. Kennedy, J.: Particle swarm optimization. In: Encyclopedia of Machine Learning, pp. 760–766. Springer, Heidelberg (2011)
6. Li, Y., Guo, L.: An active learning based TCM-KNN algorithm for supervised network intrusion detection. Comput. Secur. **26**(7–8), 459–467 (2007)
7. Moradi, M., Zulkernine, M.: A neural network based system for intrusion detection and classification of attacks. In: Proceedings of the IEEE International Conference on Advances in Intelligent Systems-Theory and Applications, pp. 15–18 (2004)
8. Labib, K., Vemuri, R.: NSOM: a real-time network-based intrusion detection system using self-organizing maps. Netw. Secur. 1–6 (2002)
9. Aslahi-Shahri, B.M., Rahmani, R., Chizari, M., et al.: A hybrid method consisting of GA and SVM for intrusion detection system. Neural Comput. Appl. **27**(6), 1–8 (2016)
10. Kayacik, H.G., Zincir-Heywood, A.N., Heywood, M.I.: Selecting features for intrusion detection: a feature relevance analysis on KDD 99 intrusion detection datasets. In: Proceedings of the Third Annual Conference on Privacy, Security and Trust (2005)
11. Parsazad, S., Saboori, E., Allahyar, A.: Fast feature reduction in intrusion detection datasets. In: 2012 Proceedings of the 35th International Convention MIPRO, pp. 1023–1029. IEEE (2012)
12. Gan, X.S., Duanmu, J.S., Wang, J.F., et al.: Anomaly intrusion detection based on PLS feature extraction and core vector machine. Knowl.-Based Syst. **40**(1), 1–6 (2013)

13. Kuang, F., Zhang, S., Jin, Z., et al.: A novel SVM by combining kernel principal component analysis and improved chaotic particle swarm optimization for intrusion detection. Soft. Comput. **19**(5), 1187–1199 (2015)

14. Sun, L., Anthony, T.S.H., Xia, Z., et al.: Detection and classification of malicious patterns in network traffic using Benford's law. In: 2017 Asia-Pacific Signal and Information Processing Association Annual Summit and Conference (APSIPA ASC), pp. 864–872. IEEE (2017)

15. Li, Y., Xia, J., Zhang, S., et al.: An efficient intrusion detection system based on support vector machines and gradually features removal method. Expert Syst. Appl. **39**(1), 424–430 (2012)

16. Elkan, C.: Results of the KDD'99 classifier learning. ACM SIGKDD Explor. Newslett. **1**(2), 63–64 (2000)

17. Newcomb, S.: Note on the frequency of use of the different digits in natural numbers. Am. J. Math. **4**(1), 39–40 (1881)

18. Benford, F.: The law of anomalous numbers. Proc. Am. Philos. Soc., 551–572 (1938)

19. Hill, T.P.: A statistical derivation of the significant-digit law. Stat. Sci. **10**, 354–363 (1995)

20. Nigrini, M.: Benford's Law: Applications for Forensic Accounting, Auditing, and Fraud Detection. Wiley, Hoboken (2012)

21. Durtschi, C., Hillison, W., Pacini, C.: The effective use of Benford's law to assist in detecting fraud in accounting data. J. Forensic Account. **5**(1), 17–34 (2004)

22. Fu, D., Shi, Y.Q., Su, W.: A generalized Benford's law for JPEG coefficients and its applications in image forensics. In: Security, Steganography, and Watermarking of Multimedia Contents IX. International Society for Optics and Photonics, vol. 6505, p. 65051L (2007)

23. Sambridge, M., Tkalčić, H., Jackson, A.: Benford's law in the natural sciences. Geophys. Res. Lett. **37**(22) (2010)

24. Arshadi, L., Jahangir, A.H.: An empirical study on TCP flow interarrival time distribution for normal and anomalous traffic. Int. J. Commun. Syst. **30**(1), e2881 (2017)

25. Asadi, A.N.: An approach for detecting anomalies by assessing the inter-arrival time of UDP packets and flows using Benford's law. In: 2015 2nd International Conference on Knowledge-Based Engineering and Innovation (KBEI), pp. 257–262. IEEE (2015)

26. Iorliam, A., Tirunagari, S., Ho, A.T.S., et al.: "Flow size difference" can make a difference: detecting malicious TCP network flows based on Benford's law. arXiv preprint arXiv:1609.04214 (2016)

27. Lewis, D.D.: Naive (Bayes) at forty: the independence assumption in information retrieval. In: Nédellec, C., Rouveirol, C. (eds.) ECML 1998. LNCS, vol. 1398, pp. 4–15. Springer, Heidelberg (1998). https://doi.org/10.1007/BFb0026666

28. Sperotto, A., Pras, A.: Flow-based intrusion detection. In: 2011 IFIP/IEEE International Symposium on Integrated Network Management (IM), pp. 958–963. IEEE (2011)

29. Plackett, R.L.: Karl Pearson and the chi-squared test. Int. Stat. Rev., 59–72 (1983)

30. Haykin, S.: Neural Networks: A Comprehensive Foundation. Prentice Hall PTR, Upper Saddle River (1994)

31. Vapnik, V.: The Nature of Statistical Learning Theory. Springer, Heidelberg (2013)

32. Panchal, G., Ganatra, A., Kosta, Y.P., et al.: Behaviour analysis of multilayer perceptrons with multiple hidden neurons and hidden layers. Int. J. Comput. Theory Eng. **3**(2), 332–337 (2011)

33. Ghorbani, A.A., Lu, W., Tavallaee, M.: Network Intrusion Detection and Prevention: Concepts and Techniques. Springer, Heidelberg (2009). https://doi.org/10.1007/978-0-387-88771-5

34. Ibrahim, H.E., Badr, S.M., Shaheen, M.A.: Adaptive layered approach using machine learning techniques with gain ratio for intrusion detection systems. arXiv preprint arXiv:1210.7650 (2012)

An RTP Extension for Reliable User-Data Transmission over VoIP Traffic

Jinbao Gao[1], Yuanzhang Li[1], Hongwei Jiang[1], Lu Liu[1], and Xiaosong Zhang[2(✉)]

[1] School of Computer Science, Beijing Institute of Technology,
Beijing 100081, China
2537907878@qq.com, 1411038349@qq.com,
{popular, liulu}@bit.edu.cn
[2] Department of Computer Science and Technology, Tangshan University,
Tangshan 063000, China
zxs0224@163.com

Abstract. Covert channels are those breaking the restrictions of the legitimate channel and transmitting covert messages secretly. According to the modulation methods, the covert channels are separated into two types, which are the covert storage channel and the covert timing channel. Since the covert storage channel modulates a covert message into the shared storage space, both capacity and throughput exceed the covert timing channel, which guarantees the effectiveness of covert communication. In this paper, a covert storage channel over RTP is proposed and evaluated. Since mobile multimedia communication requires low transmission latency, the RTP based on UDP is widely utilized by VoIP applications. Through modifying the packet layout of RTP packets and embedding secret message sections into the target position, the covert message could be delivered to the receiver. However, since the RTP is not a reliable protocol, the transmission procedure could be infected by the network noise. To solve this, a transmission control mechanism with retransmission is designed for the scheme. Besides, the secret message is also encrypted with a secure encryption algorithm, which prevents message leakage. To evaluate the scheme, several experiments are deployed, and the scheme is proved to be reliable and secure.

Keywords: Covert storage channel · RTP · Reliable protocol · VoIP

1 Introduction

With the rapid development of the Internet, the protocols for user data transmission are becoming more and more significant. Meanwhile, in order to adapt to different application requirements, we need to make some extensions for existing network protocols. Covert channels are widely used to send some especially significant and secret information on the Internet. These channels are designed to modify the data packets. If we consider modifying the header of the data packet, the modified data header will be detected as illegal easily. Therefore, we are supposed to modify the data section and insert some significant data in this section. The covert channel represents

© Springer Nature Singapore Pte Ltd. 2019
W. Meng and S. Furnell (Eds.): SocialSec 2019, CCIS 1095, pp. 74–86, 2019.
https://doi.org/10.1007/978-981-15-0758-8_6

invisibility and will not affect normal packet transmission and parsing. There are roughly two classifications of covert channels. One is the covert timing channel and the other is the covert storage channel. The covert timing channel uses a generalized storage unit which is not controlled by security policy to transmit information through connecting processes in the system. The sender changes the content of the generalized storage unit, while the receiver observes the change of the generalized storage unit and measures it with coordinates such as a real-time clock. The covert storage channel transmits information through two processes in the system using storage units that are not controlled by security policies. The sender changes the content of the storage unit, while the receiver decodes the content and finds the modified message.

The RTP (Real-Time Transmission Protocol) is widely used for delivering audio and video, which is not reliable. When the network condition is very terrible, a significant amount of data will lose. Because RTP runs over User Datagram Protocol (UDP). As we all know that UDP uses a very simple connectionless transmission model while a minimum of protocol mechanism. It does not have three-way handshake at the begin of the dialogues and four-way handshake at the end of dialogues. Therefore, UDP is an unreliable underlying network protocol.

When we embed some user data in RTP packets, if RTP packets loss, the user data embedded in RTP packets will lose at the same time. To make up for losing data in this condition, we proposed a new protocol which can resolve this problem. Meanwhile, we need to guarantee that the embedded user data cannot be resolved correctly when the RTP packets are grabbed by using some software.

Our contributions:

1. Adding some marks into the begin of RTP data section. These marks will control the embedded user data when to send or stop and this method will provide acknowledgment mechanism to ensure the opposite side to continue to do the next work.
2. Adding the user data into the RTP data section and sending the user data over RTP. Meanwhile, this method ensures that the user data will be retransmitted if the data is lost.
3. Using the AES algorithm to encrypt and decrypt the user data, when it is sent and is received. The key of the AES algorithm needs to be negotiated by both parties.

2   Background

In this section, the format of the RTP packet and its extension are introduced. The extension RTP packet format is briefly described. And we can set two modes used for communication (see Fig. 1).

2.1   RTP Packet Format

The RTP packet format is divided into two sections. The one is called RTP header section, the other is called RTP data section. The RTP header section includes some information such as version, sequence number, timestamp, Synchronization source

(SSRC), Contributing source (CSRC) and so on. The header information will make the RTP packets to be resolved easily when the receivers receive these packets. For instance, timestamp stands for when the video and audio are created. Only in this way can the receiver resolve the video and audio correctly. The RTP data section only includes the video and audio source data.

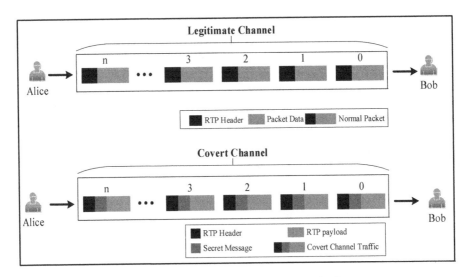

Fig. 1. The two mode used for communication

2.2 RTP Packet Format Extension

In order to realize reliable transmission, we need to modify the RTP packet format. As mentioned above, the RTP packet has two sections and we can modify the two sections to fit our requirement.

We consider whether the RTP header section can be modified. Due to the RTP header section is fixed and has become a standard, if we modify this, when we send the modified RTP packets, the RTP packets will be recognized and will be sent abortively. Therefore, we try to modify the RTP data section because this section will not be examined (see Fig. 2).

The modified RTP packet includes three sections that are RHS (RTP Header Section), EDS (Embedded Data Section) and RDS (RTP Data Section). For RHS, this section will not be modified and it is as same as its original header section. The RDS is the video and voice data and will ensure normal communication between the two sides. The EDS is particularly significant and it's the important section that we embed into the RTP packet. In order to realize reliability, we need to have a similar three-way handshake, four-way handshake and the length of user data that needs to be sent. Therefore, we divide the embedded data section into two categories.

The one is for controlling when to start or stop sending data or telling the receiver the length of embedded user data which is called marked data and is shown in Fig. 3.

The "Related Data" domain is set according to the "Specific String "domain. The specific correspondence is described below. The other includes the real user data which can be combined into a whole file eventually and is shown in Fig. 4.

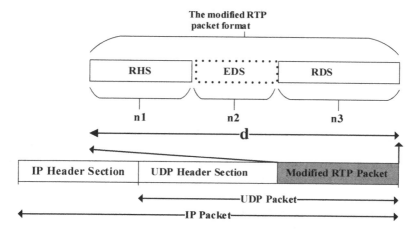

Fig. 2. The modified RTP packet.

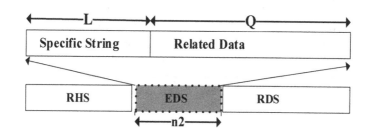

Fig. 3. The format of control.

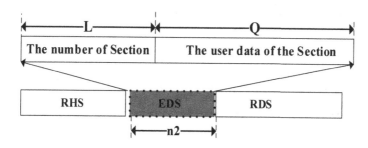

Fig. 4. The format of sending user data

In Figs. 3 and 4, n2 is equal to L + Q. The length of "Specific String" and "The number of Section" is the same. The length of EDS is fixed and its length is n2. The length of "Specific String" domain and "The number of Section" domain is L. After creating the RTP packets following modified RTP packet format, these RTP packets will be submitted to creating UDP packets which is the next layer network protocol packets.

3   Reliable User Data Transmission

3.1   Establish Connection

Before we start to send user data, we are supposed to establish a connection. Firstly, we should distinguish between two sides who are the sender and the receiver. In this experiment, we think the side who has the user data which needs to be sent. If the two sides both have the data to send, we consider them both to be sender and receiver. For the sake of simplicity, we discuss only the one side is sender who is called Alice and the other side is receiver who is called Bob. Secondly, establish connection need to be conducted. Alice needs to set the "Specific String" as "AAAA". Then, this embed the special string will be sent to Bob over RTP and Alice expects that Bob will react to this embed special string and send a special string to him. When Bob receives the embed special string, Bob also needs to set the "Specific String" as "BBBB" and set his connect condition as WFRRDS (Waiting For Receiving Real Data Size). If Bob does not receive the special string, he just processes normal RTP packets and waits for the specific string "BBBB". When Alice receives the embed specific string "BBBB", he will set his link state as SSRD (Start Sending Real Data). If Alice does not receive the specific string from Bob, he thinks that Bob does not receive the string "AAAA" or has sent the string "BBBB" but lost. Therefore, Alice continues to send "AAAA" to Bob. The establish connection algorithm is summarized as shown in Algorithm 1.

Algorithm 1 Establish connection algorithm

---

1 **initialize** the state of Alice and *Bob*.
2 Alice ← sender
3 *Bob* ← receiver
4 **While** Alice does not receive the string "BBBB"
5   Alice sends the string "AAAA" to *Bob*
6   **if** !(*Bob* receive the string "AAAA") **then**
7   *Bob* does not change his link state and just processes normal RTP packets.
8   **else**
9   *Bob*'s link state ← WFRRDS
10   *Bob* sends the string "BBBB" to Alice.
11 Alice's link state ← SSRD

3.2   Encrypt and Decrypt the User Data

When Alice sends the user data and Bob receives that, the user data need to be encrypted and decrypted in order to make the process of transmission more secure. Therefore, they use the AES algorithm to encrypt and decrypt the user data. As we all know that the AES algorithm needs to set the value of the key. Both encryption and decryption need the key to encrypt and decrypt the data. However, if the value of the key is fixed, some attackers who get the code about the key will decrypt the encrypted user data. In this situation, the transmission will become very dangerous. In order to solve this problem, the value of the key is not fixed and will be set dynamically.

Firstly, we analyze the format of the RTP header section and find the SSRC (Synchronization source) can help us solve this problem. In a specific session, SSRC is globally unique and fixed and it will not change until a new session is created. SSRC is generated randomly and we take to use the SSRC to generate the key of AES algorithm together.

More specifically, we use the SSRC of the sender and receiver to generate the key. Then, Alice and Bob need to send the message to one another. Alice needs to send the SSRC of his session to Bob. When Bob receives this SSRC that sent by Alice, he will combine the first eight bytes of Alice's SSRC and the first eight bytes of his own SSRC. Then, Bob will get the key value and send the value of the generated key to Alice. Therefore, Alice will get the same key as Bob's. Ultimately, the key of the AES algorithm has been generated randomly and avoid the dangerous conditions above. The complete algorithm is shown in Algorithm 2.

Algorithm 2 generate the key of AES algorithm

1 Alice's SSRD ← SSRD$_1$
2 Bob's SSRD ← SSRD$_2$
3 *Alice's* link state ← GKA
4 Bob's link state ← GKA
5 **while** *Alice's link state == GKA*
6   Alice sends SSRD$_1$ to Bob.
7   **if** Bob receives the SSRD$_1$ successfully **then**
8   Bob's *key* ← Generate_Key(SSRD$_1$, SSRD$_2$)
9   Bob sends *key* to Alice
10   **if** Alice receives the *key* successfully **then**
11   Alice's *key* ← *key*
12   **break**
13   **end while**
14   Alice's send_data ← my_encrypt(original_data, *key*)
15   Bob's received_data(original_data) ← my_decrypt(Alice's send_data, *key*)

3.3   Start Sending Real User Data

Firstly, for the sender, Alice needs to compute the size of the user data and divide the user data into fixed length data packets. The proposed scheme is shown in Fig. 5. Because the user data has N bytes and its length is too long, it needs to be divided into P sections and the length of each section is Q bytes. In this article, the value of Q is equal to n2-L (the length of "The number of Section" domain) above. Besides, Alice also need to mark the P sections with 0, 1, 2 …. P. And the relationships among them are shown in (1).

Secondly, Alice needs to send the number N to Bob over our modified RTP packets. Of course, the number N also is embedded into the beginning of the RTP data section. Once Bob receives the number N, he will allocate a buffer of fixed length. It is unnecessary for Bob to allocate a buffer with too large in length..

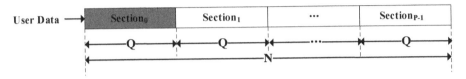

Fig. 5. The division of the sent user data

Because if the length of the allocated buffer is too large, this will take up a lot of memory. The length of the allocated buffer is set at d (M*Q) bytes, which means if Bob has received d bytes, he need to write the d bytes into the temporary file. The length of the temporary file is increasing and the temporary file will become the whole file. Here, the allocated buffer is called D_Buffer and it's shown in the Fig. 6. In this figure, each "Temp_File" domain is a D_Buffer and the concrete relationships is shown clearly. Eventually, these "Temp_File" files become the complete file.

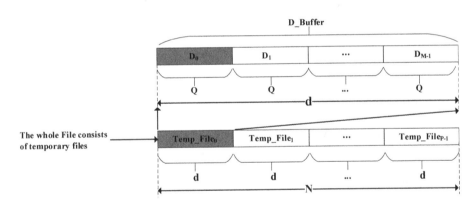

Fig. 6. The combination of the received user data.

Thirdly, if Bob has allocated the buffer, he need to send the specific string "CCCC" to Alice and set his link state as WFRRD (Waiting For Receiving Read Data). Therefore, Bob needs to create a new "EDS" and set the "Specific String" domain (Fig. 3) as "CCCC". When Alice receives the string "CCCC", he sets his link state as SSRD (Starting Sending Real Data) and starts to send the user data. Here, Alice also needs create a new "EDS". Alice adds the number of P sections into the "The number of Section" domain (Fig. 4) and adds the user data into the "The user data of the Section" domain. Then, Alice sends the modified RTP packet to Bob.

Fourthly, Bob needs P (the number of the section of the user data) bytes to mark whether the specific section received and uses 0 which stands for having not received and 1 which means having received. Therefore, Bob also need to allocate a buffer whose length is P bytes. By default, the value of the allocated buffer starts at 0. Here, this allocated buffer is called M_Buffer. When Bob receives the RTP packets which include the number of the P sections and user data, he will parse the RTP packets. If the number of the P sections is P_p, the P1th byte value of the M_Buffer is set to 1 and the user data will be added into the specific position of D_Buffer. As for the specific position, he needs to compute. If he receives the P_{th} section, he is supposed to skip (P mod M)*Q bytes of D_Buffer and write the user data he received into D_Buffer. If D_Buffer is full, Bob needs to write the data of D_Buffer into the temporary file.

Whereas, the network is not reliable and sometimes the user data may lose. Therefore, Bob needs to have the retransmission mechanism. When Alice has sent M*Q bytes, Bob has to check to see if some bytes has not been received successfully by looking for the value of the M_Buffer. When Alice has sent the user data between m0th section and m1-th section (m1 − m0 = M), Bob will examine the value of M_Buffer and if the value of m2-th byte of M_Buffer is zero, Bob needs to send the retransmission message to Alice. For the retransmission message, Bob sets the "Specific String" domain as "RESENT" and the "Related Data" as m2. If Alice received the retransmission message, he will send the m2-th section of user data again until Bob confirms he has received the m2-th section of user data. After Bob received the retransmission, the D_Buffer will be full and the data of D_Buffer will be written into the temporary file. Then, Bob will clear D_Buffer and waits for receiving the leftover user data according to the above steps.

Eventually, when the user data has been sent by Alice completely, the temporary file will become the complete user data (Fig. 5), which means Bob has received the data sent by Alice completely. The algorithm is shown in the Algorithm 3.

Algorithm 3 Send user data algorithm

1　set the values of N, Q, P
2　*Alice* sends N, Q, P to *Bob*
3　**while** *Bob* does not receive the values of N, Q, P
4　　*Alice* sends these value again.
5　**end while**
6　D_Buffer, M_Buffer ← allocate_Buffer(N, Q, P)
7　**if** D_Buffer != NULL and M_Buffer !=NULL **then**
8　　Bob sends message to *Alice* to start sending the user data
9　**if** *Alice* receives the message **then**
11　*Alice*'s link state ← SSRD
12 **while** *Alice*'s link state == SSRD and !(data has been sent completely)
13　*Alice* sends the user data in the number of the divided sections order or
　　　retransmits the user data according to the number of the retransmission user data
14　**if** D_Buffer's == full **then**
15　　the temporary ← the data of D_Buffer
16　**if** all the value of the M_Buffer == 1 **then**
17　　the final complete file ← the temporary file
18　　Bob sends message to *Alice*
19　**if** *Alice* received the message **then**
20　　Alice stops sending the user data
21　　**break**
22　**end while**

3.4 Close the Connection

When Bob has received all the user data, the connection between Alice and Bob will be closed, because this action will reduce the usage of network and send more normal RTP packets besides the modified RTP packets.

Firstly, after Bob receives all the user data, he sets his state as Stop receiving the user data (SRUD). Meanwhile, he will send a specific message to Alice to inform him to stop sending the user data. At this time, Alice's state is still SSRD and Alice needs to change his state according to the message sent by Bob. In here, the acknowledgment mechanism is extraordinarily necessary. When Alice changes his link state from SSRD to STOP (this state stands for Alice does not need to send the user data again) according to Bob's message, Alice is supposed to send the acknowledgment message ("ACK") to Bob. Otherwise, Bob will think that Alice does not receive the stop message and continue to send the stop message to Alice. Only when Bob receives the acknowledgement message sent by Alice, Bob will stop sending the stop message. Eventually, the connection between Alice and Bob will be broken. The specific algorithm is shown in Algorithm 4.

Algorithm 4 Close the connect algorithm

1 **if** *Bob* has received all the user data completely **then**
2   Bob's link state ← SRUD.
3 *Alice*'s link state ← SSRD.
4 **while** *Bob's* link state == SRUD
5   *Bob* sends "STOP SEND" to *Alice.*
6   **while** *Alice*'s link state ← SSRD
7   **if** *Alice* receives the string == "STOP SEND" **then**
8   *Alice*'s link state ← "STOP"
9   **if** *Alice*'s link state == "STOP" **then**
10   *Alice* sends "ACK" to *Bob*
11   **if** *Bob* receives the string == "ACK" **then**
12   *Bob*'s link state ← "Close Connect"
13   **end while**
14 **end while**

---

4   Experiment Result

In order to verify the proposed method, we carried out the experiment by using open source software. We use some files as the user data and transmit these files when we start voice calls. We are supposed to find the oRTP module because of the creation process of the RTP packet in this module. We just modify the RTP packets in this time and send the user data.

This experiment is done on Huawei Mate 10 Pro mobile phone, Android 8. 0, 6 GB RAM. In our experiment, we will use many different files to evaluate the performance of the proposed method. The types of these files include tiff, pdf, jpeg, and rar. In this experiment, we set the value of the length of d as 1000 bytes and the value of Q as 975 bytes.

Table 1. The data of this experiment.

File name	File type	File size (B)	Retransmission section number	Total section number	Packet Loss Rate (%)
SailBoat	tiff	786572	78	807	9.67
House	tiff	786572	2	807	0.25
Paper0	pdf	4912050	0	5038	0.00
Paper1	pdf	4458938	3	4574	0.06
Picture0	jpeg	2266320	56	2325	2.41
Picture1	jpeg	6506175	37	6673	0.55
File0	rar	5543213	45	5686	0.79
File1	rar	3426543	21	3514	0.60

Table 1 shows that the user data been embedded into the RTP packets has been sent successfully and been received successfully. We can see the retransmission mechanism will work when the data is lost and ensure the receiver get the whole data successfully (Table 2).

Table 2. The speed of the user data transfer.

File name	File size (B)	Transmission time (s)	Transmission Speed (KB/s)
SailBoat	786572	17	45.18
House	786572	17	45.18
Paper0	4912050	107	44.83
Paper1	4458938	98	44.43
Picture0	2266320	50	44.26
Picture1	6506175	143	44.43
File0	5543213	118	45.87
File1	3426543	73	45.84

Our test mobile phone are connected to WIFI hotspots and in this condition, we start to send the user data and get the result of the speed of the user data transfer. We can know that the speed of transmission is about 45 KB/s.

5 Related Works

Covert channel [5, 11, 13, 15, 16, 21], is a communication mechanism that can transmitter data covertly and guarantees that the data can not be detected easily. Every hour and every minute, there are a lot of data packets transmitted over the network. With the development of instant message application, many covert channels have been proposed for some applications, such as Wechat, Linphone, Skype [18] and so on.

We can create a covert channel by modifying the data packet. And this covert channel belongs to storage covert channel. Many researchers have focused on storage covert channel [1, 2, 4, 6–8, 10]. [18] discussed how to use Skype video traffic to provide secret communication. For covert timing channel [3, 9, 12, 17, 19, 22], they modified silence periods, which modulates covert message by the postponing or extending silence periods in VoLTE traffic. [20] proposed a method to support voice over VoLTE and it is difficult to be detected if IPDs of VoLTE traffic changed. Aiming at the problem of the lack of feedback on network state between two RTCP packets, a new solution is proposed [22].

Some researchers create the storage covert channel according to TCP/IP stack (such as IP, TCP/UDP) or higher[18]. [8] proposed to construct a covert channel by dividing the length distribution of the legal packet service and mapping the packet length partition to the data symbols.[14] proposed a balanced approach to eliminate packet length-based covert channels. [1] adjusted the silence time to create a covert channel. They used Gray code and silence period grouping to achieve robust noise for both anticipated and unexpected channels. [23] proposed to build the covert timing channel over VoLTE and dropped out packets to make sure it is feasible for VoLTE video stream.

6 Conclusion

In this paper, we proposed a cover storage channel by modifying the RTP packets. We modified the data section of RTP packets and inserted our data into these instead of modifying the header of RTP packets. Meanwhile, in order to guarantee the security of data transmission, we proposed a mechanism of AES key negotiation. Before sending the user data, the two sides need to negotiate to get the AES key. After the two sides get the same AES key, they can use the same AES key to encrypt and decrypt data. Of course, we also proposed retransmission to make sure that the lost data can be resent, because the RTP can not ensure the reliability and the RTP packets may be lost when the network is in bad condition. Finally, this cover storage channel can send our data completely and successfully.

Acknowledgment. This work is supported by the National Key R&D Program of China (No. 2018YFB1004402), the Beijing Municipal Natural Science Foundation (No. 4172053).

References

1. Zhang, X., Tan, Y., Liang, C., Li, Y., Li, J.: A covert channel over VoLTE via adjusting silence periods. Access IEEE **6**, 9292–9302 (2018). https://doi.org/10.1109/acces-s.2018. 2802783
2. Tuptuk, N., Hailes, S.: Covert channel attacks in pervasive computing. In: 2015 IEEE International Conference on Pervasive Computing and Communications (PerCom), pp. 236–242, St. Louis, MO, USA (2015). https://doi.org/10.1109/percom.2015.7146534

3. Rezaei, F., Hempel, M., Shrestha, P., Sharif, H.: Achieving robustness and capacity gains in covert timing channels. In: 2014 IEEE International Conference on Communications (ICC), pp. 969–974. IEEE, Sydney (2014). https://doi.org/10.1109/icc.2014.6-883445

4. Denney, K., Uluagac, A., Akkaya, K., Bhansali, S.: A novel storage covert channel on wearable devices using status bar notifications. In: 2016 13th IEEE Annual Consumer Communications & Networking Conference (CCNC). IEEE, Las Vegas (2016). https://doi.org/10.1109/ccnc.2016.7444898

5. Epishkina, A., Kogos, K.: Covert channels parameters evaluation using the information theory statements. In: 2015 5th International Conference on IT Convergence and Security (ICITCS). IEEE Press, Kuala Lumpur (2015). https://doi.org/10.1109/icitcs.2015.7-292966

6. Singh, A., Manchanda, K.: Establishment of bit selective mode storage covert channel in VA-NETS. In: 2015 IEEE International Conference on Computational Intelligence and Computing Research (ICCIC). IEEE Press, Madurai (2015). https://doi.org/10.1109/icc-ic.2015.7435732

7. Liang, C., Wang, X., Zhang, X., Zhang, Y., Sharif, K., Tan, Y.: A payload-dependent packet rearranging covert channel for mobile VoIP traffic. Inf. Sci. **465**, 162–173 (2018). https://doi.org/10.1016/j.ins.2018.07.011

8. Liang, C., Tan, Y., Zhang, X., Wang, X., Zheng, J., Zhang, Q.: Building packet length covert channel over mobile VoIP traffics. J. Netw. Comput. Appl. **118**, 144–153 (2018). https://doi.org/10.1016/j.jnca.2018.06.012

9. Archibald, R., Ghosal, D.: A covert timing channel based on fountain codes. In: 2012 IEEE 11th International Conference on Trust, Security and Privacy in Computing and Communications. IEEE Press, Liverpool (2012). https://doi.org/10.1109/trustcom.2012.21

10. Chaari, H., Mnif, K., Kamoun, L.: Multimedia quality transmission evaluation over wireless networks: a survey. Wirel. Netw. **22**, 2607–2621 (2016). https://doi.org/10.1007/s11276-015-1127-5

11. Hovhannisyan, H., Qi, W., Lu, K., Yang, R., Wang, J.: Whispers in the cloud storage: a novel cross-user deduplication-based covert channel design. Peer-to-Peer Netw. Appl. **11**, 277–286 (2018). https://doi.org/10.1007/s12083-016-0483-y

12. Archibald, R., Ghosal, D.: Design and analysis of a model-based Covert Timing Channel for Skype traffic. In: 2015 IEEE Conference on Communications and Network Security (CNS). IEEE Press, Florence (2015). https://doi.org/10.1109/cns.2015.7346833

13. Garcia, L., Senyondo, H., McLaughlin, S., Zonouz, S.: Covert channel communication through physical interdependencies in cyber-physical infrastructures. In: 2014 IEEE International Conference on Smart Grid Communications (SmartGridComm). IEEE Press, Venice (2014). https://doi.org/10.1109/smartgridcomm.2014.7007771

14. Elsadig, M., Fadlalla, Y.: A balanced approach to eliminate packet length-based covert channels. In: 2017 4th IEEE International Conference on Engineering Technologies and Applied Sciences (ICETAS). IEEE Press, Salmabad (2017). https://doi.org/10.1109/ice-tas.2017.8277839

15. El-Atawy, A., Duan, Q., Al-Shaer, E.: A novel class of robust covert channels using out-of-order packets. IEEE Trans. Dependable and Secure Comput. **14**(2), 116–129 (2017). https://doi.org/10.1109/tdsc.2015.2443779

16. Lin, Y., Malik, S., Bilal, K., Yang, Q., Wang, Y., Khan, S.: Designing and modeling of covert channels in operating systems. IEEE Trans. Comput. **65**(6), 1706–1719 (2016). https://doi.org/10.1109/tc.2015.2458862

17. Shrestha, P., Hempel, M., Sharif, H., Chen H.: An event-based unified system model to characterize and evaluate timing covert channels. IEEE Syst. J. **10**(1) (2016). https://doi.org/10.1109/jsyst.2014.2328665

18. Mazurczyk, W., Karaś, M., Szczypiorski, K., Janicki, A.: YouSkyde: information hiding for Skype video traffic. Multimedia Tools Appl. **75**(21), 13521–13540 (2016). https://doi.org/10.1007/s11042-015-2740-0
19. Tan, Y., Zhang, X., Sharif, K., Liang, C., Zhang, Q., Li, Y.: Covert timing channels for IoT over mobile networks. IEEE Wirel. Commun. **25**(6), 38–44 (2018). https://doi.org/10.1109/mwc.2017.1800062
20. Zhang, X., Liang, C., Zhang, Q., Li, Y., Zheng, J., Tan, Y.: Building covert timing channels by packet rearrangement over mobile networks. Inf. Sci. **445–446**, 66–78 (2018). https://doi.org/10.1016/j.ins.2018.03.007
21. Zhang, X., Zhu, L., Wang, X., Zhang, C., Zhu, H., Tan, Y.: A packet-reordering covert channel over VoLTE voice and video traffics. J. Netw. Comput. Appl. **126**, 29–38 (2019). https://doi.org/10.1016/j.jnca.2018.11.001
22. Zhang, Q., Gong, H., Zhang, X., Liang, C., Tan, Y.: A sensitive network jitter measurement for covert timing channels over interactive traffic. Multimedia Tools Appl. **78**(3), 3493–3509 (2019). https://doi.org/10.1007/s11042-018-6281-1
23. Tan, Y., Xu, X., Liang, C., Zhang, X., Zhang, Q., Li, Y.: An end-to-end covert channel via packet dropout for mobile networks. Int. J. Distrib. Sensor Netw. 14(5) (2018). https://doi.org/10.1177/155014771877956-8

A Hybrid Covert Channel with Feedback over Mobile Networks

Xiaosong Zhang[1], Linhong Guo[1], Yuan Xue[2], Hongwei Jiang[2], Lu Liu[2], and Quanxin Zhang[2(✉)]

[1] Department of Computer Science and Technology,
Tangshan University, Tangshan 063000, China
[2] School of Computer Science, Beijing Institute of Technology University,
Beijing 100081, China
zhangqx@bit.edu.cn

Abstract. In the existing network covert channel research, the transmission of secret messages is one-way, lacking confirmation feedback on whether the secret message is successfully accepted. However, VoLTE has real-time interactive features, and the data packets between the sender and the receiver are transmitted in both directions, which facilitates the construction of a two-way covert channel with feedback. Therefore, we propose a hybrid covert channel over mobile networks, which includes a sender-to-receiver covert timing channel that modulates covert message through actively dropping packets during the silence periods and a reverse covert storage channel that hides the acceptance of the covert message as feedback information into the feedback control information field of the RTCP packet. The sender evaluates the current attack severity according to the feedback and adjusts the real-time parameters of the covert timing channel to weigh the robustness and other performance. Experimental results show that this solution can effectively feedback the transmission of the covert message while keeping undetectable and robust.

Keywords: Covert channel · VoLTE · Mobile networks · Feedback

1 Introduction

The concept of covert channels was first proposed by Lampson [1], who saw covert communication as a process of communicating data through a transmission channel that is neither designed nor expected. The emergence of information theory, coding theory, and high-performance systems interconnected by high-speed networks has led to the development of covert channels, especially covert timing channels, from conceptual ideas to potential practical tools. The network covert channels that use the network communication medium to transmit information in a covert manner have become the focus of covert channel research.

Covert channels are generally classified into two types: covert storage channels (CSCs) and covert timing channels (CTCs) [2]. The storage covert channel

© Springer Nature Singapore Pte Ltd. 2019
W. Meng and S. Furnell (Eds.): SocialSec 2019, CCIS 1095, pp. 87–94, 2019.
https://doi.org/10.1007/978-981-15-0758-8_7

means that the sender directly or indirectly writes information to certain storage locations (memory unit, resource status, network data packet, etc. [3–8]), and the receiver restores the information from the sender by observing the storage location. The covert timing channel means that the influence of the sender on system events (performance, behavior, etc. [9–15]) can be observed by the receiver, and the two parties use the sequence of events, interval, frequency and other time factors to transmit covert message. Covert channels have both legitimate and malicious applications. An example of a malicious use of a covert channel is that criminals use it to leak the secret information of a business.

In order to build an effective covert channel, many research solutions have been proposed [16–18]. However, the existing covert channel construction scheme based on inter-packet delay (IPD) cannot be directly applied to VoLTE because the IPDs of VoLTE traffic is limited to a small range and has strong regularity, which makes the modulation of IPDs easy to detect, and it is difficult to hide covert message into the IPDs of VoLTE traffic. Therefore, based on the research of VoLTE traffic characteristics, we propose a VoLTE two way covert channel, which includes a sender-to-receiver covert timing channel that modulates covert message through actively dropping packets during the silence periods and a reverse covert storage channel that hides the acceptance of the covert message as feedback information into the feedback control information field of the RTCP packet. In order to verify the effectiveness of the covert channel created, we conducted experiments and analysis in the real VoLTE environment, and gave the test results. In this paper, the research on the construction method of VoLTE covert channel will provide useful reference for construction and detection technology of covert channels over mobile networks.

2   Preliminaries

With the in-depth deployment of LTE networks and the popularity of smartphones, data services are beginning to emerge. LTE has successfully penetrated into the cellular communication market and has become the mainstream of communication technology. As an all-IP technology, LTE has many advantages, including robustness, low latency, and high bandwidth. However, since all-IP networks are inherently incompatible with voice processing and cannot utilize traditional circuit-switched-based voice services, there are many challenges in providing voice services based on an all-IP architecture. To compensate for the shortcomings of circuit-switched voice, VoLTE is widely used in the mobile industry as an IP-based LTE voice and video calling solution.

In order to analyze the characteristics of VoLTE traffic, we developed packet capture software for mobile devices to capture packets in the VoLTE video calling. Two Samsung A5108 mobile phones that support VoLTE calling are selected, where Android system version is 5.1.1 and the kernel version is 3.10.61. The network environment is China Mobile 4G network. Figure 1 shows the IPDs of VoLTE voice traffic. Comparing (a) and (b), we can see the difference between the IPDs of the sender and the receiver. For voice traffic, as shown in Fig. 1, the

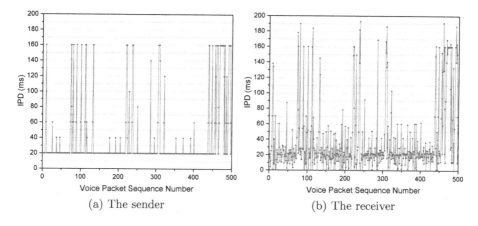

(a) The sender   (b) The receiver

Fig. 1. The IPDs of VoLTE voice traffic

IPDs of the voice packets sent by the sender are basically 20 ms. The IPDs of the voice packet at the receiver vary greatly from the IPDs at the sender, and the regularity is not obvious. Jitter is the amount of network delay variation. It is generated by any two adjacent packets of the same application during network transmission.

By analyzing the IPD and jitter of VoLTE traffic, it can be seen that the IPDs of VoLTE traffic are limited to a small range and have obvious regularity, and both video traffic and voice traffic have a large jitter variation. According to the characteristics analysis of VoLTE traffic, since the IPDs of VoLTE traffic are obviously regular when the sender sends, if the traditional IPD-based covert timing channel construction method is used, the modulation and modification of the IPDs of the VoLTE traffic will be easily detected by the opponent. At the same time, due to the large variation of the jitter of VoLTE traffic, the IPD-based covert timing channel construction scheme will also face challenges in decoding and accurate secret information cannot be obtained, which will result in high bit error rate. These features make the IPD-based hidden channel construction method not suitable for VoLTE traffic. Therefore, this paper proposes a covert channel construction method by packet rearrangement for VoLTE traffic, which can ensure the constructed covert channel undetectable and robust.

3   The Hybrid Covert Channel

The hybrid covert channel is composed of a covert timing channel from the sender to the receiver and a reverse covert storage channel. On one hand, the covert timing channel from the sender to the receiver is implemented by actively dropping packets during the silence periods, and the covert message is modulated into the numbers of silence insertion descriptor (SID) packets in the silence periods. The silence period is a normal phenomenon in a voice call, and a moderate change in the silent period is not easily detected. At the same time, the use of Gray coding ensures the robustness of the covert channel against the adversary's intentional packet loss attack. The changes of silent periods may affect the covert channel undetectability and reduce the voice quality of the conversation, so the variable length coding is employed to meet the undetectability and voice quality requirements. On the other hand, a covert storage channel is built for feedback from the receiver to the sender, and it hides the acceptance of the covert message as feedback information into the feedback control information field of the RTCP packet back to the sender. These certain bits of the fields are selected to serve as acknowledgment bits for the covert message transmission. The sender evaluates the current attack severity according to the feedback and adjusts the real-time parameters of the covert timing channel to weigh the relationship between the robustness of the adversary's active attack and other performance of the covert timing channel. After many rounds of feedback, the security confrontation against the active attack of the adversary is finally realized. The two-way feedback covert channel is shown in Fig. 2.

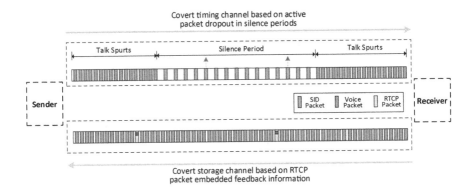

Fig. 2. The two-way feedback covert channel

4   Covert Channel Construction

4.1   Encoding

We use Gray code to mitigate channel noise since Gray code is characterized by two consecutive values that differ only in one bit resulting in robustness to packet reordering and packet loss. The covert message is encoded by the Gray code according to the variable length bl determined by the number of SID packets in the silence period. The covert information bits are encoded into code symbols with a variable length of bl, where each silent period carries one piece of information bits of length bl. The larger the average bit length of the symbol, the higher the transmission efficiency of the covert message. Therefore, if you want to increase the capacity of the covert channel, you can select the voice traffic with a longer average silence period as the carrier.

4.2   Modulation

In our covert timing channel, the encoded covert information is modulated into the numbers of SID packets in the silence period. We consider a one-to-one mapping as the conversion of a symbol s_i to the numbers of SID packets n_i must be invertible: $n_i := G(s_i)$ where $G(\cdot)$ is an invertible function. Correspondingly, $n_i' := G^{-1}(s_i')$ represents that the demodulation is done at the receiver, where n_i' is the received numbers of SID packets, and s_i' denotes the symbols which the numbers of SID packets demodulated into.

The first SID packet is used as a synchronization identifier to mark the beginning of the covert timing channel. At the end of the silence period, the sender calculates the number of SID packets in the silence period to determine how many covert information bits can be transmitted. According to the number of SID packets n_i and covert message, the maximum bl can be found that satisfies $GraytoDec(Getmessage(bl)) \le n_i - 2 < GraytoDec(Getmessage(bl + 1))$. If the number of SID packets n_i is not equal to the symbol value, the sender will actively discard the extra SID packets to make the two values equal. Moreover, the sender will modify the tail SID packet so that the time interval between the tail packet and the previous SID packet is $bl * 20$. In this way, the size of bl can be judged by the tail packet interval.

4.3   RTCP Feedback

A covert storage channel is built for feedback from the receiver to the sender, and it hides the acceptance of the covert message as feedback information into the feedback control information field of the RTCP packet back to the sender. We use the 16 bits of the bitmask of the lost packet in the feedback control information field to feed back the receiver's confirmation of the covert message. Among them, 8 bits are used to indicate the number of received covert information bits, and the other 8 bits are used to store the last eight bits of the received covert message. Moreover, in order to ensure undetectability of the covert storage channel, not all RTCP packets are used to feedback the reception of covert message, and the interval frequency of the selected RTCP is determined according to the capacity of the sender-to-receiver covert timing channel.

5   Experimental Results and Analysis

To analyze the performance of the proposed covert channel, we used VoLTE traffic between two mobile phones. As long as the devices and systems support VoLTE, our solution can be successfully implemented on different mobile devices and different versions of android. We chose two Samsung A5108 phones, of which the Android version is 5.1.1 and the kernel version is 3.10.61. We test our solution by the two phones as sender and receiver. We capture the VoLTE voice traffic of the sender and receiver in the experiment. Due to that the existing software cannot capture the VoLTE voice packets processed by the baseband program, we have developed a capture program based on the Android kernel. According to our solution, covert traffic is generated by encoding and modulating overt traffic.

5.1   Undetectability

We use KS test, a standard statistical test, to visualize and verify undetectability. In Fig. 3(a), the KS p-values are all greater than 0.05 for the number of SID packets in the silence period of the five overt traffic, which indicates that the number of SID packets of these traffics fit the same distribution. On the other hand, Fig. 3(b) shows that KS p-values are all greater than 0.05 for the number of SID packets of the five corresponding covert traffics which represents that the covert traffics fit the same distribution with the overt traffic.

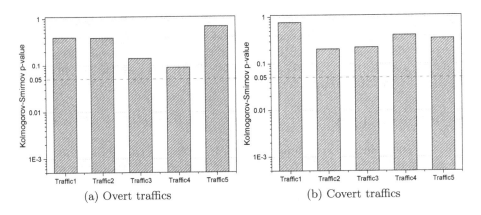

(a) Overt traffics   (b) Covert traffics

Fig. 3. KS test for the number of SID packets in the silence period

5.2   Robustness

We measure the robustness of covert channels with BER of the decoded covert message. In Fig. 4, the BER of the proposed covert channel reaches 10^{-3} when R_l is less than 0.2%, whereas the BER increases to 10^{-1} when R_l is greater than 5%. The sort of performance for all covert traffics are similar in different network conditions. In summary, the proposed covert channel remains valid even under high network jitter. Specifically, the covert channel with larger average number of SID packets can achieve better robustness.

At the same time, the receiver-to-sender covert storage channel feedbacks the transmission of the covert message through RTCP packets. If the feedback information indicates that the current bit error rate is high, the sender will adjust the covert timing channel modulation parameters or even suspend the delivery of the covert message to resist the active attack of the adversary.

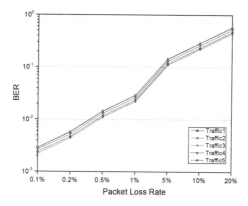

Fig. 4. BER of our covert channels under different packet loss rate

6   Conclusion

The existing covert channel solution based on IPD cannot be applied to VoLTE due to the limited and regular IPDs. Therefore, we proposed a VoLTE two-way covert channel, which includes a sender-to-receiver covert timing channel that modulates covert message through actively dropping packets during the silence periods and a reverse covert storage channel that hides the acceptance of the covert message as feedback information into the feedback control information field of the RTCP packet. To improve the robustness, we employ Gray code to encode the covert message for mitigating the packet loss. To remain undetectable, we employ controllable active packet dropout to fit the distribution of overt traffic. Our scheme implements a covert channel with feedback while considering robustness and undetectability. An interesting future direction for this work is employing silence periods to hide covert message by different modulation algorithm to increase the capacity of covert channels.

Acknowledgment. This work has been supported by the National Natural Science Foundation of China under grant No. U1636213 and No. 61876019.

References

1. Lampson, B.W.: A note on the confinement problem. Commun. ACM **16**(10), 613–615 (1973)
2. Department of Defense Trusted Computer System Evaluation Criteria, pp. 69–72. Palgrave Macmillan UK, London (1985)
3. Mazurczyk, W., Szczypiorski, K.: Evaluation of steganographic methods for oversized IP packets. Telecommun. Syst. **49**(2), 207–217 (2012)
4. Sadeghi, A.-R., Schulz, S., Varadharajan, V.: The silence of the LANs: efficient leakage resilience for IPsec VPNs. In: Foresti, S., Yung, M., Martinelli, F. (eds.) ESORICS 2012. LNCS, vol. 7459, pp. 253–270. Springer, Heidelberg (2012). https://doi.org/10.1007/978-3-642-33167-1_15

5. Rios, R., Onieva, J.A., Lopez, J.: Covert communications through network configuration messages. Comput. Secur. **39**(4), 34–46 (2013)
6. Muchene, D.N., Luli, K., Shue, C.A.: Reporting insider threats via covert channels. In: 2013 IEEE Security and Privacy Workshops, pp. 68–71, May 2013
7. Do, Q., Martini, B., Choo, K.K.R.: Exfiltrating data from android devices. Comput. Secur. **48**, 74–91 (2015)
8. Wu, Z., Cao, H., Li, D.: An approach of steganography in G. 729 bitstream based on matrix coding and interleaving. Chin. J. Electron. **24**(1), 157–165 (2015)
9. Cabuk, S.: Network covert channels: design, analysis, detection, and elimination. Ph.D. thesis, Purdue University, West Lafayette, IN, USA (2006)
10. Houmansadr, A., Borisov, N.: CoCo: coding-based covert timing channels for network flows. In: Filler, T., Pevný, T., Craver, S., Ker, A. (eds.) IH 2011. LNCS, vol. 6958, pp. 314–328. Springer, Heidelberg (2011). https://doi.org/10.1007/978-3-642-24178-9_22
11. Tan, Y., Zhang, X., Sharif, K., Liang, C., Zhang, Q., Li, Y.: Covert timing channels for iot over mobile networks. IEEE Wirel. Commun. **25**(6), 38–44 (2018)
12. Tan, Y., Xinting, X., Liang, C., Zhang, X., Zhang, Q., Li, Y.: An end-to-end covert channel via packet dropout for mobile networks. Int. J. Distrib. Sens. Netw. **14**(5), 1–14 (2018)
13. Zhang, X., Liang, C., Zhang, Q., Li, Y., Zheng, J., Tan, Y.: Building covert timing channels by packet rearrangement over mobile networks. Inf. Sci. **445–446**, 66–78 (2018)
14. Zhang, X., Tan, Y., Liang, C., Li, Y., Li, J.: A covert channel over VoLTE via adjusting silence periods. IEEE Access **6**, 9292–9302 (2018)
15. Zhang, X., Zhu, L., Wang, X., Zhang, C., Zhu, H., Tan, Y.: A packet-reordering covert channel over VoLTE voice and video traffics. J. Netw. Comput. Appl. **126**, 29–38 (2019)
16. Luo, X., Chan, E.W.W., Chang, R.K.C.: TCP covert timing channels: design and detection. In: 2008 IEEE International Conference on Dependable Systems and Networks with FTCS and DCC (DSN), pp. 420–429, June 2008
17. Wu, J., Wang, Y., Ding, L., Liao, X.: Improving performance of network covert timing channel through huffman coding. Math. Comput. Model. **55**(1C2), 69–79 (2012)
18. Ahmadzadeh, S.A., Agnew, G.: Turbo covert channel: an iterative framework for covert communication over data networks. In: 2013 Proceedings IEEE INFOCOM, pp. 2031–2039, April 2013

Cloud-Aided Privacy Preserving User Authentication and Key Agreement Protocol for Internet of Things

Chenyu Wang[1], Ding Wang[2], Haowei Wang[2], Guoai Xu[1(✉)], Jing Sun[1], and Huaxiong Wang[3]

[1] Beijing University of Posts and Telecommunications, Beijing, China
xga@bupt.edu.cn
[2] Peking University, Beijing, China
[3] Nanyang Technological University, Jurong West, Singapore

Abstract. With the exponential growth of interconnected devices, Internet of Things has played an indispensable part of our modern life. However, the constraint of the devices greatly limits the development of IoT and has become one of the major bottlenecks for the large-scale deployment of the devices. Cloud computing, as a technique for the analysis and storage of a large amount of heterogeneity data, is a key solution to this. However, the integrating of IoT and cloud computing also brings new security and privacy challenge. Therefore, an authentication mechanism must be provided to verify user's identity and ensure the data be accessed without authorization. However, we found most of the authentication schemes for IoT do not truly integrate the cloud computing thus are not suitable for IoT. To improve this unsatisfactory condition, we depicted the architecture of the cloud-assisted IoT environment, and for the first time designed a new secure and privacy preserving user authentication scheme for cloud-assisted IoT environment. Furthermore, we compared the proposed scheme with several related schemes from security functions and performance, the result showed the superiority of our scheme.

Keywords: Multi-factor user authentication · Internet of Things · Cloud computing

1 Introduction

Internet of Things (IoT) is a dynamic and global network with self configuring interconnected objects. It aims to let the things be able to be measured, connected, communicated and understood, and then further to make decisions or self-regulation intelligently. IoT is one of the most influential technologies and will play an important role in our further life without doubt. Internet of Things will digitize the real world and have a wide range of applications, like smart home, smart city, video surveillance and smart grid. According to [8], the

© Springer Nature Singapore Pte Ltd. 2019
W. Meng and S. Furnell (Eds.): SocialSec 2019, CCIS 1095, pp. 95–109, 2019.
https://doi.org/10.1007/978-981-15-0758-8_8

number of the interconnected devices even exceeded the number of people in 2011. Furthermore, this number was estimated to be 9 billion in 2012, and will reach the value of 24 billions by 2020 [3]. With the popularization of the interconnected devices, Internet of Things is bound to be one of the most essential techniques of our inter-connected world. Certainly, cloud computing, as a model for enabling ubiquitous, convenient, on-demand network to access to a shared configurable computing resources [16], is regarded as the most appropriate technology which can collaborate with IoT to maximize benefits of the both sides. The basic principle of cloud computing is to make the computation finished across a large number of distributed computers via virtualization technology. Therefore, cloud computing has become a promising technique for the future of information technology industry.

Consequently, integrating IoT and cloud computing has become an inevitable trend, many researchers have been devoted into it [1,3,9]. To IoT, cloud computing compensate its storage and computation constraints via providing virtually unlimited storage space and capabilities, furthermore, cloud computing can maximize the data collected from IoT to rich the services for users; to cloud computing, IoT extends its scope and perception of the real world via providing a large amount of data. The integrating of IoT and cloud computing will greatly improve the applications in smart city, smart home, environmental monitoring and smart grid.

However, we also should note the integrating of IoT and cloud computing brings benefits as well as new security challenges. In cloud computing environment, people already worry about their personal information being acquired by the third party or adversary with ulterior motives. When integrating IoT, such concerns on privacy protection will be more prominent since IoT brings the data from the real world to the cloud and more actions can be performed in the real world. Therefore, preventing the data from unauthorized access means a lot to user's privacy protection. Among the security measures, user authentication, as the first line to the security of the system, has attracted more and more attentions. Considering such an occasion where a user wants to access the data collected from the smart device directly, for example, the user wants to know his/her heartbeats from the wearable device, a more effective and secure method to achieve this is that the user and the smart device authenticate each other and then negotiate a session key to encrypt the communication with the help of cloud center and the gateway. The aim of the paper is to provide a secure authentication scheme for this occasion.

1.1 Related Works

In 2009, Das et al. [4] for the first time presented a smart card based user authentication scheme for real-time data access for wireless sensor network, while this scheme was shortly identified that it is vulnerable to serious security flaws [11,12,20] including offline dictionary attack, insider attack and impersonation attack. Since then, many authentication schemes for wireless sensor network are proposed [6,10,17,21], while most of them have unsatisfactory aspects more or less. For example, Fan et al.'s scheme [6] cannot provide user anonymity and forward secrecy; Jiang et al.'s scheme [10] does not achieve forward secrecy too. Furthermore, these schemes more focus on wireless sensor network (the part of IoT), rather than take the whole big network (IoT) into consideration. Thus most of these schemes are not suitable for IoT.

Recently, with the prevalence of the idea of IoT, more and more user authentication schemes for IoT are presented. For example, in 2016, Farash et al. [7] introduced a user authentication and key agreement scheme for heterogeneous wireless sensor network for IoT, while their scheme then was found insecure against offline dictionary attack, no user anonymity and forward secrecy; in 2017, Wu et al. [27] also designed a temporary certificate based authentication scheme for IoT which suffers from impersonation attack, offline dictionary attack and no forward secrecy; in 2018, Wazid et al. [25] then presented a lightweight scheme for IoT again and proved it security with formal provable security, but unfortunately, their scheme is not secure against offline dictionary attack, no user anonymity and forward secrecy. Note that most schemes [5,14,19] including the above schemes though claimed to be designed for IoT environment, only have three participants: the user, the gateway and the sensor nodes, thus have many limitations and are not suitable for IoT environment according to our introduction above.

Among these authentication schemes for IoT, only a limited number of schemes evolve the cloud computing, for example, in 2018, Amin et al. [2] identified the importance of integrating of IoT and cloud computing and proposed an authentication scheme, while they not only cannot withstand various attacks, but also does not involve IoT elements; similar situation also happens on Shen et al.'s scheme [18]; in 2017, Wazid et al. [26] proposed a remote user authentication scheme for smart home environment with formal security proof, since the smart home is an important application of IoT, their scheme also can be regard as the one for IoT. Furthermore, in their scheme, a register server evolves which takes a part task of cloud center and can be reviewed as the cloud center directly when considering the cloud-assisted IoT environment. Therefore, we chose their scheme as a study case to explain the role of the cloud center in user authentication and identify challenges in the design of the scheme for cloud-assisted IoT environment.

In conclusion, from the related work of the remote multi-factor user authentication schemes for cloud-assisted IoT environment, we can see that: (1) designing a secure authentication scheme for IoT environment is difficult; (2) the authentication scheme for cloud-assisted IoT environment still lacks.

1.2 Motivations and Contributions

On one hand, the integrating of IoT and cloud computing enables a large number of application scenarios, and has been a foreseen trend. On the other hand, this new architecture also brings new security challenges, especially in privacy protection. User authentication as the first line of security is bound to attract many attentions. However, when reviewing the history of user authentication

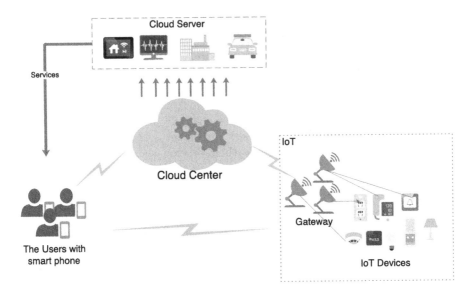

Fig. 1. Illustration of cloud-assisted IoT architecture

protocol for IoT or cloud computing related environment, it can be seen that most of schemes are only designed for either cloud or IoT environment. Several schemes designed for the cloud-assisted IoT usually do not maximize the advantage of cloud computing, for example, the cloud center in their scheme just acts as a register center, and does not join in authentication process. In this case, the bottleneck of IoT in communication and computation cost still exists. To change this unsatisfactory situation, we first clearly depict the architecture of the cloud-assisted IoT environment, then for the first time propose a truly privacy preserving user authentication scheme for cloud-assisted IoT environment. In short, our contributions are summarized as follows:

(1) Firstly, we depict the architecture of the cloud-assisted IoT environment, including the communication model of the user authentication.
(2) Then, we for the first time design a truly secure and privacy preserving user authentication scheme for cloud-assisted IoT environment.
(3) Finally, we analyze the security of the proposed scheme and compare it with several related schemes from security functions and performance, the result shows the superiority of our scheme.

1.3   The Organization of the Paper

The rest of the paper is organized as follows. Section 2 describes the system architecture and communication model; In Sect. 3, we firstly review a recent scheme, then demonstrate the scheme suffers from many serious attacks; to provide a secure authentication scheme suitable for the IoT environment, we design a new scheme based on elliptic curve algorithm; its security and performance analysis are given in Sects. 4 and 5, respectively. Finally, Sect. 6 concludes the whole paper.

2   System Overview

In this section, we provide an introduction to the cloud-aided Internet of Things environment. Note that the notations and abbreviations are described in Table 1. As shown in Fig. 1, the cloud-assisted IoT system may include four participants representing different stakeholders. The IoT consists of quantities of smart devices such as smart doorbells, smart locks and some gateways. The smart devices collect various data from the environment and can interconnect to each other to finish a common goal. The gateway is responsible for lightweight data processing, and it also collects data from the smart devices and upload them to the cloud center. Then the cloud center will do a series of complicated computations on the data from the real world to get some useful findings. Furthermore, based on these findings, the cloud center can also help the server provider to offer better and more precise services to the users.

Usually, the users do not communicate with the IoT network directly. Once the users want to access a certain resource, he/she can get the information from the cloud center. Furthermore, to enjoy the service provided by the cloud server, the users also only need to authenticate with the cloud center or the cloud server, without IoT networks. However, considering such a scenario, where the users want to know the real-time data from the smart devices, such as his/her heartbeats, then it is inefficient and impossible to get these data from cloud center, since the smart devices usually upload the data within certain time interval. Under this situation, to ensure the user can securely access the data, it is necessary to let the user and the target smart device authenticate each other, and negotiate a secret session key. Then the user and the smart device can transmit sensitive information with the session key securely. Note that, we recommend to let the cloud center join in this authentication since it can greatly alleviate the storage and computation load of the gateway (even the smart devices). If the cloud center does not join in the authentication and just acts as a register center, then to verify the legitimation of the user, the gateway has to store some information related to the user and do more computation to finish the authentication, which will limit the scale of the IoT networks. Therefore, an ideal authentication process in the scenario mentioned above is: firstly, the user initiates an access request to the cloud center; secondly, the cloud center verifies the legitimation of the user, and forwards the request to the gateway; thirdly, the gateway authenticates the cloud center, then transmits the message to the target smart devices; fourthly, the smart devices verify the gateway and give a response to it; fifthly, the gateway checks the response and gives it to the cloud center; sixthly, after testing the response, the cloud center transmits it to the user; seventhly, the user verifies the response and computes the session key shared with the smart device to finish the authentication successfully.

Table 1. Notations and abbreviations

Symbol	Description	Symbol	Description
U_i	i^{th} user	x/y	Secret key of $CloCen$
S_j	j^{th} sensor node	X_{S_j}	Secret key of GWN for S_j
x_{G_k}	Secret key of GWN_k	X_{G_k}	Secret key of CC for GWN_k
GWN_k	k^{th} gateway	K_{GWN-U_i}	Secret key of GWN for U_i
$CloCen.$	The cloud center	K_{GWN-S_j}	Secret key of GWN for S_j
$\mathcal{A}$	The adversary	$\oplus$	Bitwise XOR operation
SK	The session key	$\rightarrow$	A common channel
ID_i	Identity of U_i	$\Rightarrow$	A secure channel
SID_j	Identity of S_j	$h(\cdot)$	One-way hash function
GID_j	Identity of S_j	$Gen(\cdot)/Rep(\cdot)$	Fuzzy extractor
PW_i/Bio_i	Password/biometrics of U_i	$\|$	Concatenation operation

3 Proposed Scheme

According to our analysis in Sect. 2, making the cloud center join in the authentication benefits improving the performance and network capacity of the system. While in some schemes like [26], the cloud center (register center) only is responsible for registering, or rather, assigning some parameters to other participants, which almost does not take the advantages of cloud computing. Therefore, these schemes are not so suitable for the further smart home environment with larger-scale smart devices. To present a more suitable communication framework and overcome the identified weaknesses, we propose a new enhanced user authentication scheme which is a cloud-assisted Internet of Things network with larger-scale smart devices. In our scheme, the cloud center acts as the trust bridge among the other three participants and undertake most complicated computations. For security consideration, to provide truly multi-factor security, we follows Wang et al.'s suggestion [22] to deploy a public key algorithm; to achieve forward secrecy, we let the sensor node do two elliptic curves point multiplication [15]; and since temporary certificate based schemes usually have desynchronization attack, we adopt the public key algorithm to achieve the similar function like user anonymity. All in all, our scheme is processed as follows:

3.1 Smart Device and Gateway Registration Phase

Since we consider the As we mentioned before, in practice, the gateway and the sensor nodes may be provided by a company, and the cloud center may be provided by another company. In this network, the gateway acts as an interface between the wireless sensor networks and the internet. Therefore, on one hand, the cloud center should distribute a secret key to the gateway as their authenticated credentials; on the other hand, the gateway and the sensor nodes should keep their own secret key to stop their data from unauthorized access by the third party (the cloud center). Similarly, for the security consideration, we let

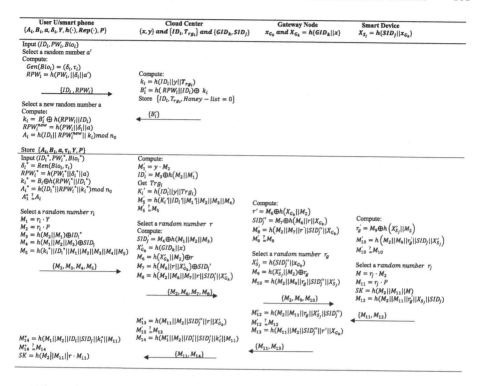

Fig. 2. The user registration and authentication phase of the proposed scheme

the cloud center own two secret keys (x and y), one for the users, the other for the gateways. Furthermore, our scheme is built on an elliptic curve E (generated by P with a large prime order q) over prime finite field F_p, the public key $Y = yP$. Accordingly, in our scheme, the smart device and the gateway can register to the cloud-assisted Internet of Things system as follows:

The gateways register to the cloud center:

Step 1. $GWN_k \Longrightarrow CloCen$: registration request.
Step 2. $CloCen \Longrightarrow GWN_k$: $\{GID_k, X_{G_k}(= h(GID_k||x))\}$.
Step 3. GWN_k keeps $X_{G_k} = h(x||GID_k)$.

The smart device register to the gateway as follows:

Step 1. $S_j \Longrightarrow GWN_k$: registration request.
Step 2. $GWN_k \Longrightarrow S_j$: $\{SID_j, X_{S_j} = h(SID_j||x_{G_k})\}$, where x_{G_k} is the secret key of the gateway.
Step 3. S_j keeps $X_{S_j} = h(SID_j||x_{G_k})$.

3.2 User Registration Phase

Step 1. $U_i \Longrightarrow CloCen$: $\{ID_i, RPW_i\}$.
U_i selects its identity ID_i and password PW_i, enters the biometric Bio_i, then the smart phone computes: $Gen(Bio_i) = (\delta_i, \tau_i)$, $RPW_i = h(PW_i||\delta_i||a')$, where a' is a random number chosen by the phone.

Step 2. $CloCen \Longrightarrow U_i$: $\{A_i, B_i, Y, n_0, h(\cdot), Gen(\cdot)\}$.

The cloud center first picks the timestamps T_{rg_i}, computes $k_i = h(ID_i \| y \| T_{rg_i})$, $B_i' = h(RPW_i \| ID_i) \oplus k_i$, and stores $\{ID_i, T_{rg_i}, Hoeny-list = NULL\}$.

Step 3. the smart phone selects a new random number a to avoid privilege insider attack, and computes: $k_i' = B_i' \oplus h(RPW_i \| ID_i)$, $RPW_i^{new} = h(PW_i \| \delta_i \| a)$, $A_i = h(ID_i \| RPW_i^{new} \| k_i) \bmod n_0$, $B_i = h(RPW_i^{new} \| ID_i) \oplus k_i$, keeps $\{A_i, B_i, a, \tau_i, Y, n_0, h(\cdot), Rep(\cdot)\}$ in its database.

3.3   Login Phase

Step 1. $U_i \longrightarrow CloCen$: $\{M_2, M_3, M_4, M_5\}$.

U_i inputs $\{ID_i^*, PW_i^*, Bio_i^*\}$, the smart phone computes: $\delta_i^* = Rep(Bio_i^*, \tau_i)$, $RPW_i^* = h(PW_i^* \| \delta_i^* \| a)$, $k_i^* = B_i \oplus RPW_i^*$, $A_i^* = h(ID_i^* \| RPW_i^* \| k_i^*) \bmod n_0$, then verifies U_i via comparing A_i^* with A_i.

If they are not equal, the smart phone rejects the request, otherwise, selects a random number, and computes: $M_1 = r_i Y$, $M_2 = r_i P$, $M_3 = h(M_2 \| M_1) \oplus ID_i^*$, $M_4 = h(M_1 \| M_2 \| M_3) \oplus SID_j$, $M_5 = h(k_i^* \| ID_i^* \| M_1 \| M_2 \| M_3 \| M_4)$.

3.4   Authentication Phase

1. $CloCen \longrightarrow GWN_k$: $\{M_2, M_6, M_7, M_8\}$.

The cloud center first do some computations to checks the valid of U_i: computes $M_1' = yM_2$, $ID_i' = M_3 \oplus h(M_2 \| M_1')$, retrieves T_{rg_i} with the computed ID_i', and continue computes $k_i = h(ID_i' \| y \| T_{rg_i})$, $M_5' = h(k_i' \| ID_i' \| M_1' \| M_2 \| M_3 \| M_4)$, then authenticates the user U_i with M_5'.

If $M_5' \neq M_5$, the cloud center thinks U_i is an adversary, thus rejects the session, and sets $Honey - list = Honey - list + 1$, once $Honey - list$ exceeds a preset value (such as 10), suspends U_i's account; otherwise, computes $SID_j' = M_4 \oplus h(M_1 \| M_2 \| M_3)$, and according to SID_j selects corresponding gateway GWN_k, computes $X_{G_k}' = h(x \| GID_k)$, $M_6 = h(X_{G_k}' \| M_2) \oplus r$, $M_7 = h(M_6 \| r \| X_{G_k}') \oplus SID_j'$, $M_8 = h(M_2 \| M_6 \| M_7 \| r \| SID_j' \| X_{G_k}')$, where r is a random number chosen by $CloCen$.

2. $GWN_k \longrightarrow S_j$: $\{M_2, M_9, M_{10}\}$.

The gateway first computes $r' = M_6 \oplus h(X_{G_k} \| M_2)$, $SID_j'' = M_7 \oplus h(M_6 \| r \| X_{G_k})$, $M_8' = h(M_2 \| M_7 \| r' \| SID_j' \| X_{G_k})$, then checks whether $M_8' \overset{?}{=} M_8$ to authenticate $CloCen$.

If $M_8' \neq M_8$, GWN_k exits the session, otherwise, selects a random number r_g, and computes: $X_{S_j}' = h(SID_j'' \| x_{G_k})$, $M_9 = h(X_{S_j}' \| M_2) \oplus r_g$, $M_{10} = h(M_2 \| M_9 \| r_g \| SID_j'' \| X_{S_j}')$.

3. $S_j \longrightarrow GWN_k$: $\{M_{11}, M_{12}\}$.

The smart device computes $r_g' = M_9 \oplus h(X_{S_j} \| M_2)$, $M_{10}' = h(M_2 \| M_9 \| r_g' \| SID_j \| X_{S_j})$. If $M_{10}' \neq M_{10}$, the smart device rejects the access, otherwise computes $M = r_j M_2$, $M_{11} = r_j P$, $SK = h(M_2 \| M_{11} \| M)$, $M_{12} = h(M_2 \| M_{11} \| r_g' \| X_{S_j} \| SID_j)$.

4. $GWN_k \longrightarrow CloCen$: $\{M_{11}, M_{13}\}$.

The gateway computes $M'_{12} = h(M_2||M_{11}||r_g||X'_{S_j}||SID''_j)$, compares M'_{12} with M_{12} to authenticate S_j. If the equation does not hold, terminates the session, otherwise computes $M_{13} = h(M_{11}||M_2||SID''_j||r'||X_{G_k})$.

5. $CloCen \longrightarrow U_i$: $\{M_{11}, M_{14}\}$.

The cloud center computes $M'_{13} = h(M_{11}||M_2||SID''_j||r||X'_{G_k})$. If $M'_{13} \neq M_{13}$, ends the session, otherwise, computes $M_{14} = h(M'_1||M_2|| ID'_i||SID'_j|| k'_i||M_{11})$.

6. The smart phone computes $M^*_{14} = h(M_1||M_2||ID_i||SID_j||k^*_i||M_{11})$, if $M^*_{14} == M_{14}$, the smart phone accepts $SK = h(M_2||M_{11}||r_iM_{11})$ as the session key, the authentication process finishes successfully. Otherwise, the smart phone terminates the session.

3.5   Password Change Phase

To achieve user friendliness, we allow the user to change his/her password locally as following steps:

Step 1. $U_i \longrightarrow smartphone$: $\{ID^*_i, PW^*_i, Bio^*_i, PW^{new}_i\}$.

Step 2. The smart phone computes $\delta^*_i = Rep(Bio^*_i, \tau_i)$, $RPW^*_i = h(PW^*_i ||\delta^*_i||a)$, $k^*_i = B_i \oplus RPW^*_i$, $A^*_i = h(ID^*_i|| RPW^*_i||k^*_i) \bmod n_0$.

If $A^*_i \neq A_i$, rejects the request; otherwise computes $RPW^{new}_i = h(PW^{new}_i||\delta^*_i||a)$, $A^{new}_i = h(ID^*_i||RPW^{new}_i||k^*_i) \bmod n_0$, $B^{new}_i = h(RPW^{new}_i ||ID_i) \oplus k_i$, and then replaces $\{A_i, B_i\}$ with $\{A^{new}_i, B^{new}_i\}$.

3.6   Re-registration Phase

Once the user's account has been suspended, he/she can re-register to the system with the same identity as follows:

Step 1. $U_i \Longrightarrow CloCen$: $\{ID_i, RPW_i, revoke - requst\}$, where $Gen(Bio_i) = (\delta_i, \tau_i)$, $RPW_i = h(PW_i||\delta_i||a')$.

Step 2. $CloCen \Longrightarrow U_i$: $\{A^{new}_i, B^{new}_i, Y, h(\cdot), Gen(\cdot)\}$.

The cloud center first finds ID_i from the database, if it does not exist, rejects the request; otherwise, picks the timestamps $T^{new}_{rg_i}$, computes $k_i = h(ID_i||y||T^{new}_{rg_i})$, $B^{new}_i = h(RPW_i||ID_i) \oplus k^{new}_i$, and stores $\{ID_i, T^{new}_{rg_i}, Hoeny - list = NULL\}$.

Step 3. the smart phone selects a random number a^{new}, computes: $k^{new}_i = B'_i \oplus h(RPW_i||ID_i)$, $RPW^{new}_i = h(PW_i||\delta_i||a^{new})$, $A^{new}_i = h(ID_i|| RPW^{new}_i||k^{new}_i) \bmod n_0$, $B^{new}_i = h(RPW^{new}_i||ID_i) \oplus k^{new}_i$, keeps $\{A^{new}_i, B^{new}_i, a^{new}, \tau_i, Y, n_0, h(\cdot), Rep(\cdot)\}$ in its database.

3.7   Dynamics Node Addition Phase

The dynamics smart devices addition phase is similar to the smart device registration phase in Sect. 3.1, so we do not repeat here.

4   Security Analysis

From the perspective of a real adversary, we give an informal analysis of the proposed scheme in this section.

4.1   User Anonymity

To preserve user anonymity, the scheme should stop a user from computing the identity and tracking the user. For identity protection, we transmit the identity ID_i in a form of $h(M_2||M_1) \oplus ID_i$, where M_1 is only known to the user and the cloud center with x, thus besides them, nobody can compute ID_i; for user untraceability, all the parameters transmitted in open channel are dynamically changing with the random numbers chosen by the four participants. Therefore, our scheme achieves user anonymity.

4.2   Forward Secrecy

Forward secrecy requires that the compromise of the whole system does not affect the previous session. Supposing the long term secret key x and y are exposed, then the adversary also eavesdrops the parameters M_2 and M_{11} consisted of the session key, while for the rest parameter M where $M = r_j M_2 = r_i M_{11}$. Note that r_j and r_i are not transmitted in the open channel and are only known to the smart device and the user, respectively. Therefore, the adversary can only directly compute the value of M with M_2 and M_{11}, that is, the adversary has to solve the Elliptic Curve Computational Diffie-Hellman (ECCDH) problem. Since the ECCDH problem cannot be solved within polynomial time, the adversary is bound to fail to compute M. Thus, our scheme achieves forward secrecy.

4.3   Mutual Authentication

Mutual authentication requires each participant to verify the other one's identity. In the proposed scheme, the cloud center authenticates the user through $M_5 = h(k_i||ID_i||M_1||M_2||M_3||M_4)$, k_i is their preset fixed shared secret and (M_1, M_2) is a pair of ciphertext and plaintext in public key algorithm. Thus k_i and M_1 are only known to the user and the cloud center, the authentication is effective; similarly, the user authenticates the cloud center with the same key parameters; then cloud center is authenticated by the gateway via M_8 which consists of their shared secret key X_{G_k}; the smart device and the gateway authenticate each other via M_{12} and M_{10}, respectively. In consequence, the proposed scheme achieves mutual authentication.

4.4   Privileged Insider Attack

Privileged insider attack requires the legitimate cloud center administrator to gain no advantage in attacking the security of the scheme. To achieve this goal, we let the user send $\{ID_i, RPW_i = h(PW_i||\delta_i||a)\}$ to the cloud center when he/she registers to avoid exposing sensitive information. Under this circumstance, the administrator of cloud center cannot gain any useful information since the password PW_i is protected by two parameters.

4.5 Smart Card Loss Attack

In [24], the smart card loss attack here refers to an adversary conduct attack with the help of parameters from the smart phone. In our scheme, if the adversary acquires $\{A_i, B_i, a, \tau_i, Y, h(\cdot), Rep(\cdot)\}$ in the phone, on one hand, if he/she wants to change the password without being noticed by the smart phone, then he/she has to construct correct $A_i = h(ID_i||RPW_i||k_i) \bmod n_0$ to pass the verification of the smart phone. Since the knowledge of $\{A_i, B_i, a, \tau_i, Y, n_0, h(\cdot), Rep(\cdot)\}$ makes no help to compute A_i, the adversary cannot change the password; on the other hand, if the adversary wants to guess the password correctly, he/she may either use A_i or M_5 as the verification parameter to test the correctness of the guessed password. To A_i, even the adversary with the biometric finds such a password and identity satisfying $h(ID_i^*||RPW_i^*||k_i) \bmod n_0 == A_i$, he/she still is not sure whether the password is right, since there are $|\mathcal{D}_{pw}| * |\mathcal{D}_{id}| \setminus n_0 \approx 2^{32}$ candidates of $\{ID_i, PW_i\}$ pair when $n_0 = 2^8$ and $|\mathcal{D}_{pw}| = |\mathcal{D}_{id}| = 2^6$ [23]. To further determine the correctness of the guessed password, the adversary has to conduct an online verification, which will be stopped by $Honey - list$; to M_5, as we explained before, M_5 consists of not only the preset secret shared parameter k_i which can be deduced from user's password and biometric, but also a dynamically changing M_1 which can only be known to the real user who selects r_i and the cloud center who knows y, in other words, the adversary though can "compute" k_i with the guessed password, cannot "compute" M_1, therefore, the adversary fails to construct such a M_5^* and then verifies it correctness with M_5 from the open channel. In conclusion, our scheme is secure against this attack.

4.6 Impersonation Attack

Firstly, we consider user impersonation attack. Note that in this attack, the adversary does not acquire the information from the smart card. On one hand, the adversary cannot gain user's password via offline dictionary attack according to our analysis of "smart card loss attack"; on the other hand, the adversary cannot directly construct such a valid access request $\{M_2, M_3, M_4, M_5\}$, where M_5 consists of k_i which can only be computed via user's sensitive information like the password, biometric and the smart phone or the long term secret y and verifier table, that is the adversary cannot impersonate the user.

Then, we talk about the cloud center impersonation attack. According to our protocol, both the user and the gateway will authenticate the cloud center via M_{14} and M_8, thus to impersonate the cloud center, the adversary has to compute M_{14} and M_8 correctly. However, to compute these two parameters, the adversary has to know k_i and X_{G_k} simultaneously. Since the two parameters are not transmitted directly or with "$\oplus$" operation in the open channel, the

Table 2. Performance comparison among relevant authentication schemes

Ref.	Evaluation criteria [24]												Computational cost in login & authentication			
	C1	C2	C3	C4	C5	C6	C7	C8	C9	C10	C11	C12	User	Cloud	Gateway	Device
ours													$3T_P + T_B + 8T_H$	$T_P + 10T_H$	$7T_H$	$2T_P + 4T_H$
[14]		×	×	×									$3T_P + T_B + 7T_H$	-	$T_P + 6T_H$	$2T_P + 4T_H$
[25]		×	×			×				×	×		$T_B + 13T_H + 2T_S$	-	$5T_H + 4T_S$	$4T_H + 2T_S$
[2]		×	×	×							×		$9T_H$	$10T_H$	-	$4T_H$
[13]		×			×	×	×				×		$2T_P + T_B + 7T_H$	-	$T_P + 9T_H$	$4T_H$
[26]		×	×	×							×		$T_B + 9T_H + T_S$	-	$11T_H + 2T_S$	$7T_H + T_S$

T_E, T_P, T_B, T_H, T_S denote the operation time for modular exponentiation, elliptic curve point multiplication, fuzzy extracting biometric data, hash, and symmetric encryption, respectively, Some lightweight operations like exclusive-OR and ∥ are omitted.
C1: No password verifier table; C2: Password friendly; C3: No password exposure; C4: No lost smart card attack; C5: Resistance to known attacks; C6: Sound repairability; C7: Provision of key agreement; C8: No clock synchronization; C9: Timely typo detection; C10: Mutual authentication; C11: User anonymity; C12: Forward secrecy.

adversary cannot get them when he/she is not a legitimate participant, that is the adversary cannot impersonate the cloud center.

As for the gateway and the smart device, similarly to our analysis above, the gateway and the smart device authenticate each other with X_{S_j} who is not transmitted directly or with "⊕" operation in the open channel, the adversary cannot get X_{S_j} except that he/she captures the smart device. But when the adversary has captured the device, it is not appropriate to consider smart device impersonation attack anymore. Thus, the adversary cannot impersonate the smart device. Then, to the gateway, the cloud center also authenticates it via X_{G_k} which cannot be acquired to the adversary as we mentioned above, that is $\mathcal{A}$ cannot impersonate the gateway.

In conclusion, our scheme can well withstand against impersonation attack.

De-synchronization Attack. We use the random number and the public key algorithm to achieve user anonymity and prevent replay attack, the participants are not required to keep the consistency of the clock synchronize or some temporary certificate related parameters. Therefore, our scheme can withstand against de-synchronization attack.

5   Performance Analysis

To check the performance of our proposed scheme, we compared it with several related schemes in this section. Note that, here we follow Wang et al.'s 12 independent criteria [24] as shown in Table ??. Though their criteria are proposed for wireless sensor networks, also suitable for cloud-assisted IoT. On one hand, the WSN is a significant part of Internet of Things, the security threats and requirements of WSN also apply to the cloud-assisted IoT environment. On the other hand, compared with WSN, the cloud-assisted IoT environment has two different aspects, one is the user's terminate device (smart card VS. smart phone), the other is the participation of the powerful cloud center. When considering the security, the parameters in the smart card and the smart phone both can be extracted by the adversary, so this difference has no essential affect on the 12 criteria. As for the cloud center, it is assumed to be trusted, thus also makes no change to the criteria. In conclusion, Wang et al.'s 12 criteria also apply to the cloud-assisted IoT environment.

From Table 2, it is easy to see that our scheme is more suitable to the cloud-assisted Internet of Things environment: our scheme satisfies all the attributes proposed by Wang et al. [24], also shows its competitiveness in computation cost. Other schemes all have several security flaws more or less, the best one can only provide 9 attributes. When considering the computational cost, it should note that the limitation of the IoT network is the gateway and the sensor nodes/ smart device. Since the cloud center has powerful capacity, and smart phone only works for one terminate user, while one gateway may connect thousands of smart devices or sensor nodes and serve for thousands of users, and under this circumstance, reducing the computational cost on gateway is even more significant than that on the sensor nodes or smart device. With the help of the cloud, our scheme greatly release the computation cost of the gateway, which means that our scheme can accommodate more network nodes, while other schemes, though claimed to be applicable to the IoT environment, are not well suited for IoT due to the limitations of gateways and sensor nodes. The only one that uses cloud computing to help the authentication is Amin et al.'s scheme [2], but unfortunately, this scheme does not take into account the important components (i.e. wireless sensor network) of the IoT. As for the computational cost on the sensor nodes/smart phone, our scheme performs not bad among these schemes armed with public key algorithm. Although, these schemes without deploying public key algorithm cost less, but definitely fail to achieve a secure authentication according to [23]. In conclusion, our scheme is more suitable for the Internet of Things environment.

6   Conclusion

To satisfy the exponential growth of interconnected devices and the demanding on large amounts of data processing, integrating of IoT and cloud computing has become an inevitable trend in the future. However, under this condition, we found most of the authentication schemes for IoT do not really integrate the cloud computing thus are not suitable for IoT. Thus, we firstly depict the architecture of the cloud-assisted IoT environment, and propose a new secure and privacy preserving user authentication scheme for cloud-assisted IoT, analyze its security and compare it with several related schemes, the result shows the superiority of our new scheme.

Acknowledgments. This work was supported by the National Key Research and Development Plan of China under Grant No. 2018YFB0803605, and by the National Natural Science Foundation of China under Grant No. 61802006, and by China Postdoctoral Science Foundation under Grants No. 2018M640026 and No. 2019T120019.

References

1. Alhakbani, N., Hassan, M.M., Hossain, M.A., Alnuem, M.: A framework of adaptive interaction support in cloud-based internet of things (IoT) environment. In: Proceedings of the IDCS (Internet and Distributed Computing System), pp. 136–146 (2014)
2. Amin, R., Kumar, N., Biswas, G., Iqbal, R., Chang, V.: A light weight authentication protocol for iot-enabled devices in distributed cloud computing environment. Future Gener. Comput. Sys. **78**, 1005–1019 (2018)
3. Botta, A., De Donato, W., Persico, V., Pescapé, A.: Integration of cloud computing and internet of things: a survey. Future Gener. Comput. Sys. **56**, 684–700 (2016)
4. Das, M.L.: Two-factor user authentication in wireless sensor networks. IEEE Trans. Wirel. Commun. **8**(3), 1086–1090 (2009)
5. Dhillon, P.K., Kalra, S.: Secure multifactor remote user authentication scheme for Internet of Things environments. Int. J. Commun Syst **30**(16), e3323 (2017)
6. Fan, R., He, D., Pan, X., Ping, L.: An efficient and dos-resistant user authentication scheme for two-tiered wireless sensor networks. J. Zhejinag Univ. Sci. C **12**(7), 550–560 (2011)
7. Farash, M.S., Turkanović, M., Kumari, S., Hölbl, M.: An efficient user authentication and key agreement scheme for heterogeneous wireless sensor network tailored for the Internet of Things environment. Ad Hoc Netw. **36**, 152–176 (2016)
8. Gubbi, J., Buyya, R., Marusic, S., Palaniswami, M.: Internet of Things (IoT): a vision, architectural elements, and future directions. Future Gener. Comput. Sys. **29**(7), 1645–1660 (2013)
9. Hossain, M.S., Muhammad, G.: Cloud-assisted Industrial Internet of Things (IIoT)-enabled framework for health monitoring. Comput. Netw. **101**, 192–202 (2016)
10. Jiang, Q., Zeadally, S., Ma, J., He, D.: Lightweight three-factor authentication and key agreement protocol for internet-integrated wireless sensor networks. IEEE Access **5**, 3376–3392 (2017)
11. Khan, M., Alghathbar, K.: Cryptanalysis and security improvements of two-factor user authentication in wireless sensor networks. Sensors **10**(3), 2450–2459 (2010)
12. Kumar, P., Gurtov, A., Ylianttila, M., Lee, S., Lee, H.: A strong authentication scheme with user privacy for wireless sensor networks. ETRI J. **35**(5), 889–899 (2013)
13. Li, X., Niu, J., Kumari, S., Wu, F., Sangaiah, A.K., Choo, K.K.R.: A three-factor anonymous authentication scheme for wireless sensor networks in Internet of Things environments. J. Netw. Comput. Appl. **103**, 194–204 (2018)
14. Li, X., Niu, J., Bhuiyan, M.Z.A., Wu, F., Karuppiah, M., Kumari, S.: A robust ecc-based provable secure authentication protocol with privacy preserving for industrial internet of things. IEEE Trans. Ind. Inform. **14**(8), 3599–3609 (2018)
15. Mal, C., Wang, D., Zhao, S.: Security flaws in two improved remote user authentication schemes using smart cards. Int. J. Commun Syst **27**(10), 2215–2227 (2012)
16. Mell, P., Grance, T., et al.: The nist definition of cloud computing. NatI. Inst. Stand. Technol **53**(6), 50 (2009)
17. Reddy, A.G., Das, A.K., Yoon, E.J., Yoo, K.Y.: A secure anonymous authentication protocol for mobile services on elliptic curve cryptography. IEEE Access **4**, 4394–4407 (2016)
18. Shen, J., Gui, Z., Ji, S., Shen, J., Tan, H., Tang, Y.: Cloud-aided lightweight certificateless authentication protocol with anonymity for wireless body area networks. J. Netw. Comput. Appl. **106**, 117–123 (2018)

19. Srinivas, J., Das, A.K., Wazid, M., Kumar, N.: Anonymous lightweight chaotic map-based authenticated key agreement protocol for industrial Internet of Things (2018). https://doi.org/10.1109/TDSC.2018.2857811

20. Sun, D., Li, J., Feng, Z., Cao, Z., Xu, G.: On the security and improvement of a two-factor user authentication scheme in wireless sensor networks. Pers. Ubiquitous Comput. **17**(5), 895–905 (2013)

21. Wang, C., Xu, G., Sun, J.: An enhanced three-factor user authentication scheme using elliptic curve cryptosystem for wireless sensor networks. Sensors **17**(12), 2946 (2017)

22. Wang, D., Wang, P.: On the anonymity of two-factor authentication schemes for wireless sensor networks: attacks, principle and solutions. Comput. Netw. **73**(C), 41–57 (2014)

23. Wang, D., Wang, P.: Two birds with one stone: two-factor authentication with security beyond conventional bound. IEEE Trans. Depend. Secur. Comput. **15**(4), 708–722 (2018)

24. Wang, D., Li, W., Wang, P.: Measuring two-factor authentication schemes for real-time data access in industrial wireless sensor networks. IEEE Trans. Ind. Inform. **14**(9), 4081–4092 (2018)

25. Wazid, M., Das, A.K., Khan, M.K., Al-Ghaiheb, A.D., Kumar, N., Vasilakos, A.: Design of secure user authenticated key management protocol for generic IoT networks. IEEE Internet of Things J. **5**(1), 269–282 (2018)

26. Wazid, M., Das, A.K., Odelu, V., Kumar, N., Susilo, W.: Secure remote user authenticated key establishment protocol for smart home environment (2017). https://doi.org/10.1109/TDSC.2017.2764083

27. Wu, F., et al.: An efficient authentication and key agreement scheme for multi-gateway wireless sensor networks in IoT deployment. J. Netw. Comput. Appl. **89**, 72–85 (2017)

Integer Version of Ring-LWE and Its Applications

Chunsheng Gu[(✉)]

School of Computer Engineering, Jiangsu University of Technology,
Changzhou, China
chunsheng_gu@163.com

Abstract. In this work, we introduce an integer version of ring-LWE (I-RLWE) over the polynomial rings and present a public key encryption based on I-RLWE. The security of our scheme relies on the computational hardness assumption of the I-RLWE problem.

Keywords: Ring-LWE · NTRU · Public key encryption · Ideal lattice

1 Introduction

Many cryptographic schemes based on discrete logarithms and integer factoring problems are no longer secure once the quantum computer becomes a reality. This is because Shor [21] presented an efficient quantum algorithm that solves these computational number theory problems. Currently, the most promising quantum-safe works are based on the hardness of lattice problems like LWE-based cryptosystems [20], Ring-LWE-based cryptosystems [13] and NTRU [11].

The LWE-based cryptographic schemes have strong security confidence. However, they also have key sizes and computation times that are at least quadratic in the security parameter. To improve the efficiency of these schemes, Lyubashevsky, Peikert, and Regev [13] defined a ring-based variant of LWE (RLWE) that uses algebraic structure, and described a polynomial time quantum reduction from worst-case problems on ideal lattices to the decisional RLWE. The LWE-based schemes can directly adapt to the RLWE-based analogues, whose key sizes and computation times reduce to almost linear in the security parameter. Furthermore, in recent years, several new cryptographic schemes have been proposed around the RLWE problem [4,6,14,15].

On one hand, the schemes based on RLWE over the polynomial rings (RLWE) have an advantage of efficiency. On the other hand, the RLWE-based schemes also have some shortcomings. Especially, for the RLWE problems over the different polynomial rings, their computational efficiency is different and needs to be re-optimized implementation for each of them.

This work is trying to solve the above problem. That is, we introduce an integer version of the ring-LWE (I-RLWE) over the polynomial ring that unifies the framework of RLWEs over the different polynomial rings, and present a new

© Springer Nature Singapore Pte Ltd. 2019
W. Meng and S. Furnell (Eds.): SocialSec 2019, CCIS 1095, pp. 110–122, 2019.
https://doi.org/10.1007/978-981-15-0758-8_9

public key encryption based on I-RLWE. We observe that the integer version of the hard problem recently appeared in the work [2]. In [2], Aggarwal, Joux, Prakash, and Santha proposed a new public-key cryptosystem (AJPS) using an integer version of NTRU, whose security relies on the conjectured hardness of the Mersenne low hamming ratio assumption. However, Beunardeau, Connolly, Géraud, and Naccache [3] presented an algorithm that recovers the secret key from the public key much faster than the security estimates in [2].

1.1 Our Contribution

Our main contribution is to describe an integer variant of ring-LWE over the polynomial ring (I-RLWE) and present a I-RLWE-based public key encryption.

In the RLWE over the polynomial ring, given q a prime integer, and a list of samples $(\mathbf{a}_l, \mathbf{b}_l = \mathbf{a}_l \mathbf{s} + \mathbf{e}_l) \in R_q^2$, where $R_q = \mathbb{Z}_q[x]/\langle x^n + 1 \rangle$, $\mathbf{s} \in R_q$, $\mathbf{a}_l \in R_q$ are chosen independently and uniformly from $\mathbb{Z}_q^n$, and $\mathbf{e}_l$ is chosen independently according to the probability distribution $\chi = D_{\mathbb{Z}^n, \sigma}$, find $\mathbf{s}$. In the first variant of LWE, $\mathbf{s}$ is chosen from the error distribution χ rather than uniformly at random, the choice of other parameters remains unchanged. This variant becomes no easier to solve than the decisional LWE [1,17].

In this work, we introduce an integer version of RLWE over the polynomial rings (I-RLWE). In the I-RLWE problem, we replace x with q and convert RLWE over the polynomial ring into I-RLWE. Given $p = q^n + 1$, we draw many samples $(a_l, b_l = a_l s + e_l) \in \mathbb{Z}_p^2$, where $\mathbf{a}_l, \mathbf{s} \leftarrow R_q$, $\mathbf{e}_l \leftarrow D_{\mathbb{Z}^n, \sigma}$, and $a_l = \sum_{i=0}^n a_{l,i} q^i$, $s = \sum_{i=0}^n s_i q^i$, $e_l = \sum_{i=0}^n e_{l,i} q^i$, the problem is to find s. Similarly, we can also generate a variant by sampling from the error distribution $\mathbf{s} \leftarrow \chi$ and generating s. For this case, we also call to sample s from χ.

Our second contribution is to present a public key encryption (PKE) based on I-RLWE. Given a sample of I-RLWE $(a, b = as + 2e) \in \mathbb{Z}_p^2$ that samples s, e from the error distribution χ, and plaintext $m = \sum_{i=0}^n m_i q^i$ with $\mathbf{m} \in \{0,1\}^n$, one first chooses r, e_1, e_2 from χ, and generates a ciphertext as $(c_1 = [ar + 2e_1]_p, c_2 = [br + 2e_2 + m]_p)$. To decrypt the ciphertext (c_1, c_2), one computes $c = [c_2 - c_1 s]_p = [2e_2 + m - 2e_1 s]_p = \sum_{i=0}^n c_i q^i$, and recovers the plaintext $\mathbf{m}$ from c. This is because all c_i's that only depend χ are "small". Concrete details see Sect. 4.

Organization. Section 2 recalls some background. Section 3 describes an integer variant of RLWE over the polynomial ring and some related properties. Section 4 presents a public key encryption using this variant of RLWE. Finally, we conclude this paper.

2 Preliminaries

2.1 Notations

Let $\mathbb{Z}, \mathbb{Q}, \mathbb{R}$ denote the ring of integers, the field of rational numbers, and the field of real numbers. Let n be a positive integer and power of 2. Notation

$[n]$ denotes the set $\{1, 2, ..., n\}$. Let $R = \mathbb{Z}[x]/\langle x^n + 1\rangle$, $R_q = \mathbb{Z}_q[x]/\langle x^n + 1\rangle$, and $\mathbb{K} = \mathbb{Q}[x]/\langle x^n + 1\rangle$. Vectors are denoted in bold lowercase (e.g. $\mathbf{a}$), and matrices in bold uppercase (e.g. $\mathbf{A}$). We denote by a_j the j-th entry of a vector $\mathbf{a}$, and $a_{i,j}$ the element of the i-th row and j-th column of $\mathbf{A}$. We denote by $\|\mathbf{a}\|_2$ (abbreviated as $\|\mathbf{a}\|$) the Euclidian norm of $\mathbf{a}$. For $\mathbf{A} \in R^{d\times d}$, we define $\|\mathbf{A}\| = \max\{\|a_{i,j}\|, i, j \in [d]\}$, where $\|a_{i,j}\|$ is the Euclidian norm corresponding to the coefficient vector of $a_{i,j}$.

We denote $[a]_q = a \mod q \in [0, q-1]$ throughout this work. Similarly, for $\mathbf{a} \in \mathbb{Z}^n$ (or $\mathbf{a} \in R$), $[\mathbf{a}]_q$ denotes each entry (or each coefficient) $[a_j]_q \in [0, q-1]$ of $\mathbf{a}$.

2.2 Lattices and Ideal Lattices

An n-dimensional full-rank lattice $L \subset \mathbb{R}^n$ is the set of all integer linear combinations $\sum_{i=1}^n y_i \mathbf{b}_i$ of n linearly independent vectors $\mathbf{b}_i \in \mathbb{R}^n$. If we arrange the vectors $\mathbf{b}_i$ as the columns of matrix $\mathbf{B} \in \mathbb{R}^{n\times n}$, then $L = \{\mathbf{By} : \mathbf{y} \in \mathbb{Z}^n\}$. We say that $\mathbf{B}$ spans L if $\mathbf{B}$ is a basis for L. Given a basis $\mathbf{B}$ of L, we define $P(\mathbf{B}) = \{\mathbf{By}|\mathbf{y} \in \mathbb{R}^n \text{ and } y_i \in [-1/2, 1/2)\}$ as the parallelization corresponding to $\mathbf{B}$. We let $\det(\mathbf{B})$ be the determinant of $\mathbf{B}$.

Given $\mathbf{g} \in R$, we let $I = \langle \mathbf{g}\rangle$ be the principal ideal lattice in R generated by g, whose $\mathbb{Z}$-basis is $Rot(\mathbf{g}) = (\mathbf{g}, x \cdot \mathbf{g}, ..., x^{n-1} \cdot \mathbf{g})$.

Given $\mathbf{c} \in \mathbb{R}^n$, $\sigma > 0$, the Gaussian distribution of a lattice L is defined as $D_{L,\sigma,\mathbf{c}} = \rho_{\sigma,\mathbf{c}}(\mathbf{x})/\rho_{\sigma,\mathbf{c}}(L)$ for $\mathbf{x} \in L$, where $\rho_{\sigma,\mathbf{c}}(\mathbf{x}) = \exp(-\pi\|\mathbf{x} - \mathbf{c}\|^2/\sigma^2))$, $\rho_{\sigma,\mathbf{c}}(L) = \sum_{\mathbf{x}\in L}\rho_{\sigma,\mathbf{c}}(\mathbf{x})$. In the following, we will write $D_{L,\sigma,\mathbf{0}}$ as $D_{L,\sigma}$. We denote a Gaussian sample as $\mathbf{x} \leftarrow D_{L,\sigma}$ (or $\mathbf{x} \leftarrow D_{I,\sigma}$) over the lattice L (or ideal lattice I).

Micciancio and Regev [16] introduced the smoothing parameter of lattices. For an n-dimensional lattice L, and positive real $\epsilon > 0$, we define its smoothing parameter $\eta_\epsilon(L)$ to be the smallest s such that $\rho_{1/s}(L^*\backslash\{\mathbf{0}\}) \leq \epsilon$, where L^* is the dual lattice of L.

Lemma 2.1 (Lemma 3.3 [16]). For any n-dimensional lattice L and positive real $\epsilon > 0$, $\eta_\epsilon(L) \leq \sqrt{\ln(2n(1 + 1/\epsilon))/\pi} \cdot \lambda_n(L)$.

Lemma 2.2 (Lemma 4.4 [16]). For any n-dimensional lattice L, vector $\mathbf{c} \in \mathbb{R}^n$ and reals $0 < \epsilon < 1$, $s \geq \eta_\epsilon(L)$, we have

$$\Pr_{\mathbf{x}\leftarrow D_{L,s,\mathbf{c}}}\{\|\mathbf{x} - \mathbf{c}\| > s\sqrt{n}\} \leq \frac{1+\epsilon}{1-\epsilon} \cdot 2^{-n}.$$

2.3 Ring-LWE in Polynomial Rings

Throughout this paper, we only consider the integer version of ring-LWE for the special ring R. However, we notice if the expansion factor of a polynomial ring $R = \mathbb{Z}_q[x]/\langle f(x)\rangle$ is small, then one can directly generate the integer version of this ring using our method. For the ring-LWE defined by the number fields [13], we will further study their integer versions.

For simplicity, we recall the ring-LWE over the polynomial rings. We sample a secret $s \in R$ from some Gaussian distribution instead of uniform distribution over R_q, since the latter is easily be transformed into the former [1,17].

Definition 2.3 (Ring-LWE Distribution). Let χ be a Gaussian distribution with parameter σ over R. Given a secret $\mathbf{s} \leftarrow R_{\mathbb{Z}^n,\sigma}$, a sample from the ring-LWE distribution $A_{\mathbf{s},\sigma}$ over $R_q \times R_q$ is generated by choosing $\mathbf{a} \leftarrow U(R_q)$, $\mathbf{e} \leftarrow D_{\mathbb{Z}^n,\sigma}$, and outputting $(\mathbf{a}, \mathbf{b} = \mathbf{as} + \mathbf{e}) \in R_q \times R_q$.

Definition 2.4 (Computational Ring-LWE). The computational ring-LWE problem, denoted $\text{RLWE}_{q,\sigma}$, is defined as follows: given arbitrary many independent samples from $A_{\mathbf{s},\sigma}$, find $\mathbf{s}$.

Definition 2.5 (Decisional Ring-LWE). The decisional ring-LWE problem, denoted $\text{DRLWE}_{q,\sigma}$, is to distinguish with non-negligible advantage between arbitrary many independent samples from $A_{\mathbf{s},\sigma}$, and the same number of uniformly random and independent samples from $R_q \times R_q$.

According to [7], the ring-LWE over the polynomial ring $R = \mathbb{Z}[x]/\langle x^n + 1\rangle$ is equivalent to the hard ring-LWE defined in [13].

Lemma 2.6 (Theorem 3.6 [13]). Let $\mathbb{K}$ be the mth cyclotomic number field having dimension $n = \varphi(m)$ and $R = O_{\mathbb{K}}$ be its ring of integers. Let $\alpha < \sqrt{\log n/n}$, and $q \geq 2$, $q = 1 \mod m$ be a poly(n)-bounded prime such that $\alpha q \geq \omega(\sqrt{\log n})$. Then there is a polynomial-time quantum reduction from $O(\sqrt{n}/\alpha)$-approximate SIVP (or SVP) on ideal lattices in $\mathbb{K}$ to $\text{DRLWE}_{q,\sigma}$, where $\sigma = \alpha(n/\log n)^{1/4}$.

3   Integer Version of Ring-LWE

This section introduces an integer variant of the ring-LWE over the polynomial rings, and describes some related properties.

For simplicity, we let n be the security parameter, $q > n^3$ a prime, $R = \mathbb{Z}[x]/\langle x^n + 1\rangle$ a ring, $p = q^n + 1$, χ be a Gaussian distribution with parameter $\sigma = \sqrt{n}$ over R, unless otherwise stated.

Definition 3.1 (I-RLWE Distribution). Given a secret $s = \sum_{i=0}^{n-1} s_i q^i$ with $\mathbf{s} \leftarrow D_{\mathbb{Z}^n,\sigma}$, a sample from the I-RLWE distribution $A_{s,\sigma}$ over $\mathbb{Z}_p \times \mathbb{Z}_p$ is generated by choosing at random $a \leftarrow \mathbb{Z}_p$, $e = \sum_{i=0}^{n-1} e_i q^i$ with $\mathbf{e} \leftarrow D_{\mathbb{Z}^n,\sigma}$, and outputting $(a, b = as + e) \in \mathbb{Z}_p \times \mathbb{Z}_p$.

Definition 3.2 (Computational I-RLWE). The computational integer ring-LWE problem, denoted $\text{I-RLWE}_{q,\sigma}$, is defined as follows: given arbitrary many independent samples from $A_{s,\sigma}$, find s.

Definition 3.3 (Decisional I-RLWE). The decisional integer ring-LWE problem, denoted I-DRLWE$_{q,\sigma}$, is to distinguish with non-negligible advantage between arbitrary many independent samples from $A_{s,\sigma}$, and the same number of uniformly random and independent samples from $\mathbb{Z}_p \times \mathbb{Z}_p$.

In the following, we describe several related properties of I-RLWE using lemmas.

Given an element $\mathbf{f} \in R$, if all coefficients $f_i, i \in \{0, \cdots, n-1\}$ of $\mathbf{f}$ are small, then we can generate an integer modulo p corresponding to $\mathbf{f}$.

Lemma 3.4. Suppose that $f = \left[\sum_{i=0}^{n-1} f_i q^i \right]_p = \sum_{i=0}^{n-1} h_i q^i$ with $|f_i| < q/2 - 1$.

Then

$$h_i = [f_i - \overline{h}_{i-1}]_q = \begin{cases} f_i - \overline{h}_{i-1} & f_i - \overline{h}_{i-1} \geq 0 \\ f_i - \overline{h}_{i-1} + q & f_i - \overline{h}_{i-1} < 0 \end{cases}$$

where for $i \in [n-1]$,

$$\overline{h}_{i-1} = \begin{cases} 0 & h_{i-1} \leq q/2 \\ 1 & h_{i-1} > q/2 \end{cases};$$

for $i = 0$,

$$\overline{h}_{-1} = \overline{h}_{n-1} = \begin{cases} 0 & h_{n-1} \leq q/2 \\ -1 & h_{n-1} > q/2 \end{cases}.$$

Proof. First, we determine $\overline{h}_{n-1}$ by f_{n-1} as follows:

Case 1: $f_{n-1} < 0$.

Since $h_{n-1} = [f_{n-1} - \overline{h}_{n-2}]_q$ and $\overline{h}_{n-2} \geq 0$, we have $f_{n-1} - \overline{h}_{n-2} < 0$. So, $h_{n-1} > q/2$ and $\overline{h}_{-1} = -1$.

Case 2: $f_{n-1} > 0$.

By $\overline{h}_{n-2} \leq 1$, we get $f_{n-1} - \overline{h}_{n-2} \geq 0$. So, $h_{n-1} < q/2$ and $\overline{h}_{n-1} = 0$.

Case 3: $f_{n-1} = 0$.

In this case, $\overline{h}_{n-1}$ depends on f_{n-2}. $\overline{h}_{-1} = -1$ when $f_{n-2} < 0$, and $\overline{h}_{n-1} = 0$ when $f_{n-1} > 0$.

Similarly, if $f_{n-2} = 0$, then $\overline{h}_{n-1}$ recursively depends on $f_{n-3}, \cdots, f_1$.

Now we use the induction method to prove the result.

For induction basis, consider $i = 0$.

If $\overline{h}_{n-1} = -1$, then $h_{n-1} > q/2$. So, $f = \sum_{i=0}^{n-1} h_i q^i > \sum_{i=0}^{n-1} |f_i| q^i$ by $|f_i| < q/2 - 1$. As a result, $f_{n-1} < 0$.

Again, by $|f_i| < q/2 - 1$, we have $-p < \sum_{i=0}^{n-1} f_i q^i < 0$. Hence,

$$f = \sum_{i=0}^{n-1} f_i q^i + p$$

$$= \sum_{i=0}^{n-1} f_i q^i + q^n + 1$$

$$= (f_{n-1} + q)q^{n-1} + \sum_{i=1}^{n-2} f_i q^i + f_0 + 1$$

$$= (f_{n-1} + q)q^{n-1} + \sum_{i=1}^{n-2} f_i q^i + f_0 - \overline{h}_{n-1}$$

That is, $h_0 = [f]_q = [f_0 - \overline{h}_{n-1}]_q$. Hence, if $f_0 - \overline{h}_{n-1} < 0$, then $h_0 = f_0 - \overline{h}_{n-1} + q$, otherwise $h_0 = f_0 - \overline{h}_{n-1}$.

If $\overline{h}_{n-1} = 0$, then $0 \leq h_{n-1} \leq q/2$. So, $f = \sum_{i=0}^{n-1} h_i q^i = \sum_{i=0}^{n-1} f_i q^i$ by $|f_i| < q/2 - 1$. Consequence, $f_{n-1} \geq 0$. Hence, $h_0 = [f]_q = [f_0]_q = [f_0 - \overline{h}_{n-1}]_q$. By induction step, we assume that h_i is correct for $i \leq k$.

Now, we prove $i = k + 1$.

Since $f = \left[\sum_{i=0}^{n-1} f_i q^i \right]_p = \sum_{i=0}^{n-1} f_i q^i + rp$ for some $r \in \{0, 1\}$, we have

$$[f]_{q^{k+2}} = \left[\sum_{i=0}^{n-1} f_i q^i + rp \right]_{q^{k+2}}$$

$$= \left[\sum_{i=0}^{k+1} f_i q^i + r \right]_{q^{k+2}}$$

$$= \sum_{i=0}^{k+1} h_i q^i$$

If $h_k > q/2$, then $\overline{h}_k = 1$ and $f_k - \overline{h}_{k-1} < 0$. So, $-q^{k+1}/2 < \sum_{i=0}^{k} f_i q^i + r < 0$ by $|f_i| < q/2 - 1$. That is, $\sum_{i=0}^{k} h_i q^i = q^{k+1} + \sum_{i=0}^{k} f_i q^i + r$. Thus,

$$\left[\sum_{i=0}^{k+1} f_i q^i + r \right]_{q^{k+2}} = \left[(f_{k+1} - 1)q^{k+1} + q^{k+1} + \sum_{i=0}^{k} f_i q^i + r \right]_{q^{k+2}}$$

$$= \left[(f_{k+1} - 1)q^{k+1} + \sum_{i=0}^{k} h_i q^i \right]_{q^{k+2}}$$

$$= \sum_{i=0}^{k+1} h_i q^i$$

Hence, we obtain $h_{k+1} = [f_{k+1} - 1]_q = [f_{k+1} - \overline{h}_k]_q$.

If $h_k < q/2$, then $\overline{h}_k = 0$ and $f_k - \overline{h}_{k-1} > 0$. Similarly, we can get $h_{k+1} = [f_{k+1}]_q = [f_{k+1} - \overline{h}_k]_q$. ∎

Given two ring elements $\mathbf{f}, \mathbf{g} \in R$, if their coefficients are all "small", then the corresponding integer of their product is equal to the product of their corresponding integers modulo p.

Lemma 3.5. Suppose that $f = \left[\sum_{i=0}^{n-1} f_i q^i \right]_p$, $g = \left[\sum_{i=0}^{n-1} g_i q^i \right]_p$ with $\mathbf{f} \leftarrow D_{\mathbb{Z}^n, \sigma}$, $\mathbf{g} \leftarrow D_{\mathbb{Z}^n, \sigma}$. Then $h = [fg]_p = \sum_{i=0}^{n-1} h_i q^i$, where

$$h_i = \left[\sum_{[j+k]_n = i} (-1)^{\lfloor (j+k)/n \rfloor} f_j g_k - \overline{h}_{i-1} \right]_q,$$

$$\overline{h}_{i-1} = \begin{cases} 0 & h_{i-1} \leq q/2 \\ 1 & h_{i-1} > q/2 \end{cases}, i \in [n-1];$$

$$\overline{h}_{i-1} = \overline{h}_{n-1} = \begin{cases} 0 & h_{n-1} \leq q/2 \\ -1 & h_{n-1} > q/2 \end{cases}, i = 0.$$

Proof. By $f = \left[\sum_{j=0}^{n-1} f_j q^j\right]_p$, $g = \left[\sum_{k=0}^{n-1} g_k q^k\right]_p$, we have

$$h = [fg]_p$$
$$= \left[\sum_{j=0}^{n-1} f_j q^j \times \sum_{k=0}^{n-1} g_k q^k\right]_p$$
$$= \left[\sum_{i=0}^{n-1} a_i q^i\right]_p,$$

where $a_i = \sum_{[j+k]_n = i} (-1)^{\lfloor (j+k)/n \rfloor} f_j g_k$, $i = 0, 1, \cdots, n-1$.

By Lemma 2.2, $|f_j| < n$, $|g_k| < n$ with overwhelming probability. So, we have $|a_i| \leq \sum_{[j+k]_n = i} |f_j||g_k| \leq n^3 < q/2 - 1$.

Hence, the result is directly obtained by Lemma 3.4. ∎

In Lemma 3.5, we only consider the product of two ring elements with "small" coefficients. However, in the RLWE problem over the polynomial ring, only the coefficients of one element are "small", the coefficients of another element are uniformly distributed modulo q. So, in the following lemma, we give the relationship between the product of the corresponding integers of two elements and the corresponding integer of the product of two elements.

Lemma 3.6. Given $\mathbf{a} \leftarrow R_q$, $\mathbf{s} \leftarrow D_{\mathbb{Z}^n, \sigma}$, $\mathbf{b} = \mathbf{as} \in R_q$, suppose that

$$a = \left[\sum_{i=0}^{n-1} a_i q^i\right]_p, b = \left[\sum_{i=0}^{n-1} b_i q^i\right]_p, s = \left[\sum_{i=0}^{n-1} s_i q^i\right]_p.$$

Then,

$$[as - b]_p = \sum_{i=0}^{n-1} r_i q^i,$$

where

$$\begin{cases} |r_i| < n^2 - n + 3 & r_i \leq q/2 \\ |r_i - q| < n^2 - n + 3 & r_i > q/2 \end{cases}.$$

Proof. By $\mathbf{b} = \mathbf{as} \in R_q$, we have

$$b_i = \left[\sum_{[j+k]_n = i} (-1)^{\lfloor (j+k)/n \rfloor} a_j s_k\right]_q$$
$$= \sum_{[j+k]_n = i} (-1)^{\lfloor (j+k)/n \rfloor} a_j s_k + c_{b_i} q$$

Since $\mathbf{s} \leftarrow D_{\mathbb{Z}^n, \sigma}$, $|s_k| < n$ by Lemma 2.2. By $\mathbf{a} \leftarrow R_q$, $|a_j| < q$. So

$$\left|\sum_{[j+k]_n = i} (-1)^{\lfloor (j+k)/n \rfloor} a_j s_k\right| \leq \sum_{[j+k]_n = i} |a_j||s_k|$$
$$\leq \sum_{[j+k]_n = i} (n-1)|a_j|$$
$$< n(n-1)q$$

Hence $|c_{b_i}| < n(n-1) + 1$.

Let $h = [as]_p = \sum_{i=0}^{n-1} h_i q^i$. Then,

$$h_i = \left[\sum_{[j+k]_n=i} (-1)^{\lfloor (j+k)/n \rfloor} a_j s_k + c_{b_{i-1}} - \overline{h}_{i-1} \right]_q$$
$$= [b_i - c_{b_i}q + c_{b_{i-1}} - \overline{h}_{i-1}]_q$$
$$= [b_i + c_{b_{i-1}} - \overline{h}_{i-1}]_q,$$

where for $i \in [n-1]$,

$$\overline{h}_{i-1} = \begin{cases} 0 & 0 \le b_{i-1} + c_{b_{i-2}} - \overline{h}_{i-2} < q \\ 1 & b_{i-1} + c_{b_{i-2}} - \overline{h}_{i-2} < 0 \\ -1 & b_{i-1} + c_{b_{i-2}} - \overline{h}_{i-2} \ge q \end{cases} ;$$

for $i = 0$,

$$\overline{h}_{-1} = \overline{h}_{n-1} = \begin{cases} 0 & 0 \le b_{n-1} + c_{b_{n-2}} - \overline{h}_{n-2} < q \\ -1 & b_{n-1} + c_{b_{n-2}} - \overline{h}_{n-2} < 0 \\ 1 & b_{n-1} + c_{b_{n-2}} - \overline{h}_{n-2} \ge q \end{cases} .$$

Thus, we obtain

$$[as - b]_p = [h - b]_p$$
$$= [\sum_{i=0}^{n-1} (h_i - b_i)q^i]_p$$
$$= [(-c_{b_{n-1}} + \overline{h}_{n-1})q^0 + \sum_{i=1}^{n-1} (c_{b_{i-1}} - \overline{h}_{i-1})q^i]_p$$
$$= \sum_{i=0}^{n-1} r_i q^i,$$

Since $|c_{b_i}| + |\overline{h}_i| < n^2 - n + 2 < q/2 - 1$, $i \in \{0, 1, \cdots, n-1\}$, so by Lemma 3.4

$$r_i = \begin{cases} [-c_{b_{n-1}} + \overline{h}_{n-1} + \overline{r}_{n-1}]_q & i = 0 \\ [c_{b_{i-1}} - \overline{h}_{i-1} - \overline{r}_{i-1}]_q & i \in [n-1]. \end{cases}$$

where, for $i \in [n-1]$,

$$\overline{r}_{i-1} = \begin{cases} 0 & r_{i-1} \le q/2 \\ 1 & r_{i-1} > q/2 \end{cases} ;$$

for $i = 0$,

$$\overline{r}_{-1} = \overline{r}_{n-1} = \begin{cases} 0 & r_{n-1} \le q/2 \\ -1 & r_{n-1} > q/2 \end{cases} .$$

The result follows by $|c_{b_i}| + |\overline{h}_i| + |\overline{r}_{i-1}| < n^2 - n + 3$.   ■

4 Public Key Encryption

In this section, we first present a public key encryption based on the I-RLWE problem. Then we show its correctness and give its security assumption.

4.1 Construction

Let n be the security parameter.

Key Generation: $(pk, sk) \leftarrow \text{KeyGen}(1^n)$.

(1) Choose a prime $q = O(n^3)$, and set $p = q^n + 1$.
(2) Choose at random $a \leftarrow \mathbb{Z}_p$.
(3) Sample $\mathbf{s} \leftarrow D_{\mathbb{Z}^n, \sigma}$, $\mathbf{e} \leftarrow D_{\mathbb{Z}^n, \sigma}$ with $\sigma = O(\sqrt{n})$.
(4) Set $s = \sum_{i=0}^{n-1} s_i q^i$, $e = \sum_{i=0}^{n-1} 2e_i q^i$.
(5) Set $b = [as + e]_p$.
(6) Output the public key $pk = \{q, (a, b)\}$, and the secret key $sk = \{s\}$.

Encryption: $(c_1, c_2) \leftarrow \text{Enc}(pk, \mathbf{m})$.

(1) Given a plaintext $\mathbf{m} \in \{0, 1\}^n$, set $m = \sum_{i=0}^{n-1} m_i q^i$.
(2) Sample $\mathbf{r} \leftarrow D_{\mathbb{Z}^n, \sigma}$, $\mathbf{e}_1, \mathbf{e}_2 \leftarrow D_{\mathbb{Z}^n, \sigma}$.
(3) Set $r = \sum_{i=0}^{n-1} r_i q^i$, $e_j = \sum_{i=0}^{n-1} 2e_{j_i} q^i, j \in [2]$.
(4) Compute $c_1 = [ar + e_1]_p$, $c_2 = [br + e_2 + m]_p$.
(5) Output (c_1, c_2) a ciphertext.

Decryption: $\mathbf{m} \leftarrow \text{Dec}(sk, (c_1, c_2))$.

(1) Given sk and a ciphertext (c_1, c_2), compute $t_0 = [c_2 - c_1 s]_p$.
(2) For $i = 0, 1, \cdots, n - 1$
    (2.1) Compute $d_i = [t_i]_q$.
    (2.2) Compute $t_{i+1} = \lfloor t_i / q \rfloor$.
    (2.3) If $d_i > q/2$, then set $d_i = d_i - q$, $t_{i+1} = t_{i+1} + 1$.
(3) Set $d_0 = d_0 - 1$ if $d_{n-1} < 0$.
(4) Set $m_i = [d_i]_2, i \in \{0, 1, \cdots, n - 1\}$.
(5) Output the plaintext $\mathbf{m}$.

Remark 4.1. (1) Our scheme uses the parity of noise in a ciphertext to encode a plaintext. Similar to [13], we can also use $\lfloor q/2 \rfloor$ to compute $m = \sum_{i=0}^{n-1} (m_i \lfloor q/2 \rfloor) q^i$ and generate a ciphertext. In this case, the decryption algorithm seem to be easier. That is, it directly determines the ith plaintext bit by checking d_i. If $q/4 < d_i < (3/4)q$, then $m_i = 1$; otherwise $m_i = 0$.

(2) To improve the efficiency of our scheme, we can use some special number $q = 2^t$ with a positive integer t. This is because the encryption and decryption algorithms take less time. Furthermore, the multiplication between two large integers can directly apply FFT-based algorithms [10], as a result, our scheme can use an arbitrary positive integer n instead of $n = 2^k$ in RLWE that is to use FFT-based algorithms.

(3) The NTRU scheme over the polynomial rings [11,22] can be directly converted into an integer scheme of NTRU. For example, consider the NTRU scheme in [22]. Let $q = 2^t, p = q^n - 1$ with a prime n, the public key $\mathbf{h} = \mathbf{3f}/(\mathbf{3g+1}) \in \mathbb{Z}_q[x]/\langle x^n - 1\rangle$, and the secret key $\mathbf{s} = \mathbf{3g+1} \in \mathbb{Z}[x]/\langle x^n - 1\rangle$. Then, one can generate an integer scheme of NTRU as follows: the public

key is $h = \left[\sum_{i=0}^{n-1} h_i q^i\right]_p$, and the secret key $s = \left[\sum_{i=0}^{n-1} s_i q^i\right]_p$.

4.2 Correctness

For the correctness of our scheme, we only require to prove that the algorithm Dec correctly recover the plaintext in a ciphertext.

Lemma 4.2. Given sk and a ciphertext (c_1, c_2), the algorithm Dec correctly decrypts the plaintext $\mathbf{m}$.

Proof. By Enc, we have $c_1 = [ar + e_1]_p$, $c_2 = [br + e_2 + m]_p$. Since $b = [as + e]_p$, by Dec, we get

$$
\begin{aligned}
t_0 &= [c_2 - c_1 s]_p \\
&= [br + e_2 + m - (ar + e_1)s]_p \\
&= [er + e_2 - e_1 s + m]_p \\
&= \sum_{i=0}^{n-1} d_i q^i.
\end{aligned}
$$

Since $r = \sum_{i=0}^{n-1} r_i q^i$, $s = \sum_{i=0}^{n-1} s_i q^i$, $e = \sum_{i=0}^{n-1} 2e_i q^i$, $e_j = \sum_{i=0}^{n-1} 2e_{j_i} q^i$, we obtain

$$er = [\sum_{i=0}^{n-1}(2\sum_{[j+k]_n=i}(-1)^{\lfloor(j+k)/n\rfloor} e_j r_k)q^i]_p = [\sum_{i=0}^{n-1} 2u_i q^i]_p$$

$$e_1 s = [\sum_{i=0}^{n-1}(2\sum_{[j+k]_n=i}(-1)^{\lfloor(j+k)/n\rfloor} e_{1_j} s_k)q^i]_p = [\sum_{i=0}^{n-1} 2v_i q^i]_p$$

$$t_0 = [er + e_2 - e_1 s + m]_p = [\sum_{i=0}^{n-1}(2u_i + 2e_{2_i} - 2v_i + m_i)q^i]_p = \sum_{i=0}^{n-1} d_i q^i$$

Using Lemma 2.2, we get $|2u_i| < 2n^3$, $|2v_i| < 2n^3$, $|2e_{1_i}| < 2n$. So,

$$|2u_i + 2e_{2_i} - 2v_i + m_i| < 4n^3 + 2n + 1 < q/2 - 1, i \in \{0, 1, \cdots, n-1\}.$$

By Lemma 3.4, $d_i = [2u_i + 2e_{2_i} - 2v_i + m_i - \overline{d}_{i-1}]_q, i \in \{0, 1, \cdots, n-1\}$.

For $i = 0$, we have

$$d_0 = [2u_0 + 2e_{2_0} - 2v_0 + m_0 - \bar{d}_{n-1}]_q$$

$$= \begin{cases} 2u_0 + 2e_{2_0} - 2v_0 + m_0 - \bar{d}_{n-1} & 2u_0 + 2e_{2_0} - 2v_0 + m_0 - \bar{d}_{n-1} \geq 0 \\ 2u_0 + 2e_{2_0} - 2v_0 + m_0 - \bar{d}_{n-1} + q & 2u_0 + 2e_{2_0} - 2v_0 + m_0 - \bar{d}_{n-1} < 0 \end{cases}$$

By Step (2.3), if $d_0 > q/2$, then $d_0 = d_0 - q = 2u_0 + 2e_{2_0} - 2v_0 + m_0 - \bar{d}_{n-1}$, otherwise $d_0 = 2u_0 + 2e_{2_0} - 2v_0 + m_0 - \bar{d}_{n-1}$.

Using Step (3), the algorithm Dec subtracts $\bar{d}_{n-1}$ according to the sign of d_{n-1}, and obtain $d_0 = 2u_0 + 2e_{2_0} - 2v_0 + m_0$. Thus, $m_0 = [d_0]_2$ by Step (4).

Similarly, Dec can correctly recover all other bits of the plaintext $\mathbf{m}$ by $m_i = [d_i]_2, i \in \{1, \cdots, n-1\}$.   ∎

4.3 Security Assumption

The security of our public key encryption is based on the following assumption.

Definition 4.3 I-DRLWE$_{q,\sigma}$ Assumption. For any probabilistic distinguisher D that solves the I-DRLWE$_{q,\sigma}$ problem, its advantage ϵ is negligible in security parameter n.

Lemma 4.4. Under I-DRLWE$_{q,\sigma}$ assumption, the public key encryption scheme (Enc, Dec) described in Sect. 4 is secure against chosen plaintext attack.

Proof. Given m_0, m_1 corresponding to plaintext vectors $\mathbf{m}_0, \mathbf{m}_1 \in \{0,1\}^n$, let $c_{i,1} = [ar_i + e_{i,1}]_p$, $c_{i,2} = [br_i + e_{i,2} + m_i]_p$ be the ciphertexts of $m_i, i = 0, 1$, where $\mathbf{r}_i \leftarrow D_{\mathbb{Z}^n,\sigma}$, $\mathbf{e}_{i,1}, \mathbf{e}_{i,2} \leftarrow D_{\mathbb{Z}^n,\sigma}$. We denote $\mathbf{c}_i = (c_{i,1}, c_{i,2}), i = 0, 1$.

By contradiction, assume that there exists a polynomial time algorithm B, so that

$$|\Pr[B(\mathbf{c}_0) = 1] - \Pr[B(\mathbf{c}_1) = 1]| \geq n^{-O(1)}. \tag{1}$$

We assume $\mathbf{c} \leftarrow U(\mathbb{Z}_p^2)$. By I-DRLWE$_{q,\sigma}$ assumption, for any polynomial time algorithm A

$$|\Pr[A(\mathbf{c}_i) = 1] - \Pr[A(\mathbf{c}) = 1]| \leq \text{negl}_i(n), \quad i = 0, 1. \tag{2}$$

Therefore,

$$\begin{aligned} &|\Pr[B(\mathbf{c}_0) = 1] - \Pr[B(\mathbf{c}_1) = 1]| \\ &\leq |\Pr[B(\mathbf{c}_0) = 1] - \Pr[A(\mathbf{c}) = 1] + \Pr[A(\mathbf{c}) = 1] - \Pr[B(\mathbf{c}_1) = 1]| \\ &\leq |\Pr[B(\mathbf{c}_0) = 1] - \Pr[A(\mathbf{c}) = 1]| + |\Pr[A(\mathbf{c}) = 1] - \Pr[B(\mathbf{c}_1) = 1]| \\ &\leq \text{negl}_0(n) + \text{negl}_1(n) \\ &= \text{negl}(n), \end{aligned} \tag{3}$$

where $\text{negl}_0(n), \text{negl}_1(n)$, and $\text{negl}(n)$ are negligible functions in n.

This is a contradiction for the expression (1) and (3).   ∎

5   Conclusions

In this work, we introduce an integer version of ring-LWE (I-RLWE) over the polynomial rings, and present a public key encryption based on I-RLWE whose security relies on a new computational hardness assumption of the I-RLWE problem.

In the future, we will build the relationship between RLWE over the polynomial ring and I-RLWE. We will also study between the one-dimensional LWE problem with structural noise and the hard one-dimensional LWE problem with non-structural noise [5].

Acknowledgement. This work was supported by the National Natural Science Foundation of China (Nos. 61672270, 61702236, and 61602216) and Changzhou Sci&Tech Program (Grant No. CJ20179027).

References

1. Applebaum, B., Cash, D., Peikert, C., Sahai, A.: Fast cryptographic primitives and circular-secure encryption based on hard learning problems. In: Halevi, S. (ed.) CRYPTO 2009. LNCS, vol. 5677, pp. 595–618. Springer, Heidelberg (2009). https://doi.org/10.1007/978-3-642-03356-8_35
2. Aggarwal, D., Joux, A., Prakash, A., Santha, M.: A new public-key cryptosystem via Mersenne numbers. Cryptology ePrint Archive, Report 2017/481 (2017). http://eprint.iacr.org/2017/481
3. Beunardeau, M., Connolly, A., Géraud, R., Naccache, D.: On the hardness of the Mersenne low hamming ratio assumption. Cryptology ePrint Archive, Report 2017/522 (2017). http://eprint.iacr.org/2017/522
4. Brakerski, Z., Gentry, C., Vaikuntanathan, V.: (Leveled) fully homomorphic encryption without bootstrapping. In: ICTS, pp. 309–325 (2012)
5. Brakerski, Z., Langlois, A., Peikert, C., Regev, O., Stehlè, D.: Classical hardness of learning with errors. In: STOC, pp. 575–584 (2013)
6. Brakerski, Z., Vaikuntanathan, V.: Fully homomorphic encryption from Ring-LWE and security for key dependent messages. In: Rogaway, P. (ed.) CRYPTO 2011. LNCS, vol. 6841, pp. 505–524. Springer, Heidelberg (2011). https://doi.org/10.1007/978-3-642-22792-9_29
7. Ducas, L., Durmus, A.: Ring-LWE in polynomial rings. In: Fischlin, M., Buchmann, J., Manulis, M. (eds.) PKC 2012. LNCS, vol. 7293, pp. 34–51. Springer, Heidelberg (2012). https://doi.org/10.1007/978-3-642-30057-8_3
8. Eisenträger, K., Hallgren, S., Lauter, K.: Weak instances of PLWE. In: Joux, A., Youssef, A. (eds.) SAC 2014. LNCS, vol. 8781, pp. 183–194. Springer, Cham (2014). https://doi.org/10.1007/978-3-319-13051-4_11
9. Elias, Y., Lauter, K.E., Ozman, E., Stange, K.E.: Provably weak instances of Ring-LWE. In: Gennaro, R., Robshaw, M. (eds.) CRYPTO 2015. LNCS, vol. 9215, pp. 63–92. Springer, Heidelberg (2015). https://doi.org/10.1007/978-3-662-47989-6_4
10. von zur Gathen, J., Gerhard, J.: Modern Computer Algebra, 3rd edn. Cambridge University Press, Cambridge (2013)
11. Hoffstein, J., Pipher, J., Silverman, J.H.: NTRU: a ring-based public key cryptosystem. In: Buhler, J.P. (ed.) ANTS 1998. LNCS, vol. 1423, pp. 267–288. Springer, Heidelberg (1998). https://doi.org/10.1007/BFb0054868

12. Lyubashevsky, V., Micciancio, D.: Generalized compact knapsacks are collision resistant. In: Bugliesi, M., Preneel, B., Sassone, V., Wegener, I. (eds.) ICALP 2006. LNCS, vol. 4052, pp. 144–155. Springer, Heidelberg (2006). https://doi.org/10.1007/11787006_13

13. Lyubashevsky, V., Peikert, C., Regev, O.: On ideal lattices and learning with errors over rings. In: Gilbert, H. (ed.) EUROCRYPT 2010. LNCS, vol. 6110, pp. 1–23. Springer, Heidelberg (2010). https://doi.org/10.1007/978-3-642-13190-5_1

14. Langlois, A., Stehlé, D.: Worst-case to average-case reductions for module lattices. Des. Codes Cryptogr. **75**(3), 565–599 (2015)

15. Lòpez-Alt, A., Tromer, E., Vaikuntanathan, V.: On-the-fly multiparty computation on the cloud via multikey fully homomorphic encryption. In: STOC, pp. 1219–1234 (2012)

16. Micciancio, D., Regev, O.: Worst-case to average-case reductions based on Gaussian measures. SIAM J. Comput. **37**(1), 267–302 (2007)

17. Micciancio, D., Regev, O.: Lattice-based cryptography. In: Bernstein, D.J., Buchmann, J., Dahmen, E. (eds.) Post Quantum Cryptography, pp. 147–191. Springer, Heidelberg (2009). https://doi.org/10.1007/978-3-540-88702-7_5

18. Peikert, C.: Public-key cryptosystems from the worst-case shortest vector problem. In: STOC, pp. 333–342 (2009)

19. Peikert, C.: How (Not) to instantiate Ring-LWE. In: Zikas, V., De Prisco, R. (eds.) SCN 2016. LNCS, vol. 9841, pp. 411–430. Springer, Cham (2016). https://doi.org/10.1007/978-3-319-44618-9_22

20. Regev, O.: On lattices, learning with errors, random linear codes, and cryptography. J. ACM **56**(6), 1–40 (2009)

21. Shor, P.W.: Polynomial-time algorithms for prime factorization and discrete logarithms on a quantum computer. SIAM J. Comput. **26**(5), 1484–1509 (1997)

22. Stehlé, D., Steinfeld, R.: Making NTRU as secure as worst-case problems over ideal lattices. In: Paterson, K.G. (ed.) EUROCRYPT 2011. LNCS, vol. 6632, pp. 27–47. Springer, Heidelberg (2011). https://doi.org/10.1007/978-3-642-20465-4_4

Correlate the Advanced Persistent Threat Alerts and Logs for Cyber Situation Comprehension

Xiang Cheng, Jiale Zhang, and Bing Chen[✉]

College of Computer Science and Technology,
Nanjing University of Aeronautics and Astronautics, Nanjing 21106, China
cb_china@nuaa.edu.cn

Abstract. With the emerging of the Advanced Persistent Threat (APT) attacks, many high-level information systems have faced a large number of serious threats with characteristics of concealment, permeability, and pertinence. However, existing methods and technologies cannot provide comprehensive and promptly recognition for APT attack activities. To address this problem, we propose an APT Alerts and Logs Correlation Method, named APTALCM, to achieve the cyber situation comprehension. We firstly proposed a cyber situation ontology for modeling the concepts and properties to formalize APT attack activities; For recognize the APT attack intentions we also proposed a cyber situation instances similarity measures method based on SimRank method. Combining with instance similarity, we proposed the APT alert instances correlation method to reconstruct APT attack scenarios and the APT log instances correlation method to detect log instance communities. Through the coalescent of these methods, APTALCM can accomplish the cyber situation comprehension effectively by recognizing the APT attack intentions. The exhaustive experimental results show that the two kernel modules, i.e., Alert Instance Correlation Module (AICM) and Log Instance Correlation Module (LICM) in our APTALCM can achieve a high true positive rate and a low false positive rate.

Keywords: Cyber situation comprehension · APT attack · Alert correlation · Log correlation

1 Introduction

With the rapid advancement of the Internet infrastructure and the widely emerged networking applications, the topological structure of information systems has performed complexity and vulnerability. In this situation, network security management has faced significant challenges. To cope with these increasingly complicated and potential security threaten, various detection techniques have been proposed, like vulnerability detection technology, malicious code detection method, intrusion detection system, etc. Almost all the above technologies are aiming to recognize the security issues existing in the information systems. However, the biggest shortcoming of these methods is that they cannot provide real-time recognition of the real threatens in a

© Springer Nature Singapore Pte Ltd. 2019
W. Meng and S. Furnell (Eds.): SocialSec 2019, CCIS 1095, pp. 123–138, 2019.
https://doi.org/10.1007/978-981-15-0758-8_10

comprehensive scope, which limiting the ability of network security administrators to make the most responsive decisions. Recently, to solve the above problem, the concept of Cyber Situation Awareness (CSA) [1] has emerged. The main idea of CSA is to recognize the attack activities scattering among a large amount of the noised data and grasp the whole network security situation macroscopically. In this way, the information system can make the responses appropriately and effectively to reduce the damage caused by the various network attacks as possible. Among these powerful network attacks, Advanced Persistent Threat (APT) is a kind of multiple-steps attack with characteristics of concealment, permeability, and pertinence, which has caused serious threats to all kinds of high-level information systems. To mitigate the negative effects of APT, the key problem needs to be solved is designing the cyber situation core technologies which aiming at APT attack recognition, comprehension and prediction.

To address the problems existing in the previous works, we propose an APT Alerts and Logs Correlation Method, named APTALCM, to achieve the cyber situation comprehension. The main contributions can be summarized as follows: (1) we propose the cyber situation ontology for modeling the concepts and properties that are appropriate for cyber situation awareness; (2) then, we introduce a similarity measures method based on cyber situation ontology providing to situation instances correlation; (3) at last, according to the instance type differences (i.e., alert instance & log instance), we present an APT alert instances correlation method to reconstruct APT attack scenarios and an APT log instances correlation method to detect log instance communities to recognize APT attack intentions.

The rest of the paper organizes as follows. Section 2 summaries the related works of Cyber Situation Awareness. Section 3 presents a cyber situation ontology for modeling the concepts and properties to formalize APT attack activities. Then, we introduce a cyber situation instances similarity measures method based on SimRank method. At last, combining with instance similarity, we further propose the APT alert instances correlation method to reconstruct APT attack scenarios and the APT log instances correlation method to detect the log instance communities. Section 4 gives a view of our experiments and analysis. Section 5 presents some conclusions.

2   Related Work

The situation is a key factor of CSA means the states of various objects in the cyber systems represented by a set of measurement values. In other words, situation is a global concept and all the objects in the cyber systems are synthesized. Any sole states cannot be regarded as a situation that it focuses on the systematic perspective and relationships between the objects in systems. Cyber situation awareness is a cognitive process applied to cyber systems consisted of three phases. First, the original data generated in the system fused and processed gradually to accomplish the semantics extraction of the system states and activities. Then, the recognition procedure will execute to obtain the exiting cyberspace activities and intentions of abnormal activities in the cyberspace. At last, the representational cyber situations acquired based on the effects of recognizing activities and intentions of abnormal activities in the cyber systems. According to the definition and illustration of CSA, we can summarize the whole CSA processes into three specific operations: cyber situation perception, cyber situation comprehension, and cyber situation projection. Among these operations, cyber situation perception completes the measurement data fusion, semantics extraction, and activities recognition. Cyber situation comprehension achieves the recognized activities intentions acquisition. Cyber situation projection estimates the threats incurred by the activities intentions within the cyber systems. There are dialectical unification relations between the three phases of CSA, means that they not only depend on each other but also their outputs used respectively for diverse levels of security management requirement.

Attack intention recognition is one of the primary objectives of cyber situation comprehension and our work is mainly focused on the attack intention recognition of APT. Existing works on attack intention recognition mostly focused on attack scenarios reconstruction while ignoring the related non-aggressive activities' contributions to APT attack and multiple-step attack implementation. In addition to this, the intrusion ontology used in the field of intrusion detection cannot be applied to the CSA paradigm directly. Recently, statistical analysis mechanisms proposed to discover the relationships between attack steps while it can only perform on static databases because of these approaches depend on expert knowledge.

At present, the hot topics of cyber situation comprehension focus on two branches: (1) match the alerts with acquired attack activities based on the priori knowledge; (2) analyze the relationships between the alerts without prior knowledge. Cuppens et al. [2] developed the LAMBDA programming to accomplish the description of templates and matching process. The researchers [3–6] usually divide an attack activity into several stages, like IKC Model [7]. At present, there are mainly two types of methods based on similarity measure: The attribute similarity method and timing sequence method. The key of these methods is definition of suitable similarity measure metric. [8, 9] defined a similarity function and clustered the IDS alerts based on the similarities between attributes. [10] proposed an alert correlation method based on Hidden Markov Model to get the attack sequences with highest possibilities.

3   APT Alerts and Logs Correlation Method

The basic duty of cyber situation comprehension is analyzing the activities (include attack activities) and recognizing the attack intention. We can acquire the activities in two forms: attack alerts and host logs. As the quantity of activities in the information systems is too large, it is impossible to correlate all the activities in the information systems. Thus, we use the following two benchmarks to improve the efficiency of activities correlation: (1) APT attack alerts are essential to be correlated generating the APT attack scenarios; (2) the logs generated in the hosts infected by APT attacks are essential to be correlated detecting the unaggressive malicious activities. According to these two standpoints, the results of cyber situation comprehension contain APT attack scenarios and log instance communities. Moreover, we propose an APT alerts and logs correlation method (APTALCM) to achieve the cyber situation comprehension. The architecture of APTALCM is shown in Fig. 1.

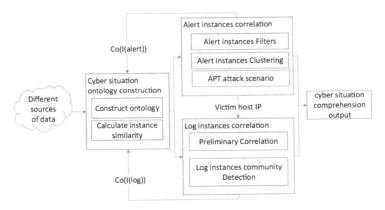

Fig. 1. The architecture of APTALCM

Cyber situation ontology is proposed for modeling the concepts and properties of cyber situation awareness paradigm. At present, there are no ontologies which are enough mature to satisfy the requirement of cyber situation awareness. Therefore, in this paper, we proposed APTALCM that defines a set of representational primitives to model the domain of cyber situation as the cyber situation ontology. The input of this phase is APT alerts and logs affected by APT attacks from various detect sensors and the corresponding output is the cyber situation ontology instances.

After the cyber situation ontology construction, the situation ontology instances will face two operation options according to the different instance types (alert instance & log instance). That is, the alert instances raised from the preceding phase will be fed to the alert instance correlation module (AICM) and the log instances will transmit to the log instance correlation module (LICM). Specifically, the aim of the alert instance correlation module is to recognize APT alert instances could be one part of an APT attack scenario. The log instances correlation module enforces on the log instances generate within the victim host to detect the log instance community and recognize the potential malicious activities.

3.1   Cyber Situation Ontology Construction

According to the APTALCM architecture, the first module of APTALCM will convert the received APT alerts and host logs into cyber situation ontology instances. Thus, our first work is to propose a formal definition of cyber situation ontology. Different from the previously proposed methods directly send the ontology instances to attack scenarios reconstruction module, we introduce a method based on the SimRank method to calculate the similarity between cyber situation instances.

Cyber Situation Ontology Initialization. A widely accepted definition of ontology is shown as follow: the ontology defines a set of representational primitives with which to model a domain of knowledge or discourse. The representational primitives are typically classes (or concepts), attributes (or properties), and relationships (or relations between class members).

According to the ontology definition and the combination of the characteristics of cyber situation, we introduce a formalized definition of the cyber situation ontology as follow: $O = (C, A, D, R, S)$. The elements (C, A, D, R, S) represent the set of classes (alert or log), the set of attributes, the domain of the cyber situation ontology, the set of relationships of the instances, and the set of similarity between the instances (alert instances or log instances), respectively. Then, we define $A(c_i)$ to represent the attributes of a class c_i, $I(c_i)_m$ as an instance of the class c_i. Besides, the attribute value of an instance can be represented as $A(I(c_i)_m)$ and $SIM(I(c_i)_m, I(c_i)_n)$ presents the similarity between instances $I(c_i)_m$ and $I(c_i)_n$.

The APT alert class consists of alert instances converted from APT alert detected by various attack detection sensors and each alert instance represents a suspicious attack step of an APT attack. In this paper, we set seven attributes for APT alert class to analyze the characteristics of APT alerts output from different attack detection sensors: *Timestamp, Alert_Type, Src_Ip, Dest_Ip, Src_Port, Dest_Port*, and *Victim_HostIp*. The attributes values of an alert instance stored in a 7-dimensional vector, A $(I(alert)_m) = (a_1, a_2, a_3, a_4, a_5, a_6, a_7)$.

The host log class consists of the log instances transformed from the log data providing by the application programs, such as *HTTP, Object access, Authentication, Process create* and *WFP connect*. The intrinsic of transforming the log data to log instances is extracting representative attributes. In this work, we select 19 attributes from the log data such as *Tinestamp, Q_Domain, R_Ip, Pid, Ppid, Pname* etc. As the data generate from different application programs, not all the log instances have the same attributes, we also give the log instance type. The attributes value of a log instance can be presented as a 19-dimensional vector: $A(I(log)_m) = (a_1, a_2 \ldots a_{18}, a_{19})$. If a log instance only contains attributes a1, a3, a5, the other elements of its attribute vector are zero.

Calculate Instance Similarity. We proposed a cyber situation instance similarity calculation method to provide a correlation basis for alert correlation module and log correlation module. Each alert or log is an instance of cyber situation ontology and the relationship between them can be presented as a labeled directed graph with similarity. As its graphic character, the proposed method is based on the SimRank mechanism.

The SimRank mechanism provides a similarity measure of structural context where the related objects are connected by directed edges. It defines a recursive function calculating the similarity between object pairs based on the concept of context. The key is objects are similar on the condition that referenced by similar objects.

We measure the similarity between the cyber situation instances, which belong to the same class. In other words, we measure the similarity within the alert class and host log class. To compare the similarity between two cyber situation instances $I(c)_m$ and $I(c)_n$ within the same class, we use the following two sets of parameters:

Attributes: The attributes of each cyber situation instance, $A(I(c)_m)$ and $A(I(c)_n)$

Correlated instances: The instances have already correlated to each cyber situation instance $I(c)_m$ and $I(c)_n$ presented as $Co(I(c)_m)$ and $Co(I(c)_n)$.

The basic similarity measure of cyber situation instances is calculating the similarity between their attributes and the correlated instances. The formalized representation of the similarity between two cyber situation instances is shown in Eq. (1).

$$\mathrm{SIM}\big(\mathrm{I}(c)_m, \mathrm{I}(c)_n\big) = \gamma \mathrm{SIMA}\big(\mathrm{I}(c)_m, \mathrm{I}(c)_n\big) + \beta \mathrm{SIMCo}\big(\mathrm{I}(c)_m, \mathrm{I}(c)_n\big) \tag{1}$$

$$\gamma = \frac{\big|\mathrm{A}(\mathrm{I}(c)_m) \cup \mathrm{A}(\mathrm{I}(c)_n)\big|}{\big|\mathrm{A}(\mathrm{I}(c)_m) \cup \mathrm{A}(\mathrm{I}(c)_n)\big| + \big|\mathrm{Co}(\mathrm{I}(c)_m) \cup \mathrm{Co}(\mathrm{I}(c)_n)\big|}$$

$$\beta = \frac{\big|\mathrm{Co}(\mathrm{I}(c)_m) \cup \mathrm{Co}(\mathrm{I}(c)_n)\big|}{\big|\mathrm{A}(\mathrm{I}(c)_m) \cup \mathrm{A}(\mathrm{I}(c)_n)\big| + \big|\mathrm{Co}(\mathrm{I}(c)_m) \cup \mathrm{Co}(\mathrm{I}(c)_n)\big|}$$

It indicates that $\mathrm{SIMA}\big(\mathrm{I}(c)_m, \mathrm{I}(c)_n\big) \in [0,1]$ and $\mathrm{SIMCo}\big(\mathrm{I}(c)_m, \mathrm{I}(c)_n\big) \in [0,1]$, respectively. The two parameters γ and β are defined to normalize the impact degree where $\gamma + \beta = 1$. Therefore, we can draw the conclusion that $\mathrm{SIM}\big(\mathrm{I}(c)_m, \mathrm{I}(c)_n\big) \in [0,1]$. Then, we will give the formalized representation of $\mathrm{SIMA}\big(\mathrm{I}(c)_m, \mathrm{I}(c)_n\big)$ in a mutually recursive method. $\mathrm{SIMA}\big(\mathrm{I}(c)_m, \mathrm{I}(c)_n\big)$ measures the similarity between cyber situation instances based on attribute similarity, $\mathrm{SIMA}\big(A_i(\mathrm{I}(c)_m), A_i(\mathrm{I}(c)_n)\big)$ measures the similarity between the attributes of each cyber situation instance. Note that the similarity between same instances is 1 and other conditions can be calculated in Eq. (2).

$$\mathrm{SIMA}\big((\mathrm{I}(c)_m, \mathrm{I}(c)_n\big) = \frac{\partial}{|\mathrm{A}(\mathrm{I}(c))|} \sum_{i=1}^{|\mathrm{A}(\mathrm{I}(c))|} \mathrm{SIMA}\big(A_i(\mathrm{I}(c)_m), A_i(\mathrm{I}(c)_n)\big) \tag{2}$$

The similarity between two attributes can be set as 1 on the condition of $A_i\big(\mathrm{I}(c)_m\big) = A_i(\mathrm{I}(c)_n)$. If none of the attributes is the same, $\mathrm{SIMA}\big(\mathrm{I}(c)_m, \mathrm{I}(c)_n\big)$ will be calculated based on Eq. (3) where $\mathrm{Co}_i(\mathrm{I}(c)_m)$ is the correlated instance to $\mathrm{I}(c)_m$. The method of acquiring them will be discussed in Sects. 3.2 and 3.3.

$$\mathrm{SIMA}\big(\mathrm{I}(c)_m, \mathrm{I}(c)_n\big) = \frac{\partial \sum_{i=1}^{|\mathrm{Co}(\mathrm{I}(c)_m)|} \sum_{j=1}^{|\mathrm{Co}(\mathrm{I}(c)_n)|} \mathrm{SIMA}\big(\mathrm{Co}_i(\mathrm{I}(c)_m), \mathrm{Co}_j(\mathrm{I}(c)_n)\big)}{|\mathrm{Co}(\mathrm{I}(c)_m)||\mathrm{Co}(\mathrm{I}(c)_n)|} \tag{3}$$

The $\mathrm{SIMCo}\big(\mathrm{I}(c)_m, \mathrm{I}(c)_n\big)$ measures the similarity between cyber situation instances based on its correlated instances similarity and calculated in Eq. (4). On the condition that either $\mathrm{I}(c)_m$ or $\mathrm{I}(c)_n$ does not have any correlated instance, we will hardly infer any similarity between them.

$$\mathrm{SIMCo}\big(\mathrm{I}(c)_m, \mathrm{I}(c)_n\big) = \begin{cases} 1 & \mathrm{I}(c)_m = \mathrm{I}(c)_n \\ \dfrac{\partial \sum_{i=1}^{|\mathrm{Co}(\mathrm{I}(c)_m)|} \sum_{j=1}^{|\mathrm{Co}(\mathrm{I}(c)_n)|} \mathrm{SIMCo}\big(\mathrm{Co}_i(\mathrm{I}(c)_m), \mathrm{Co}_j(\mathrm{I}(c)_n)\big)}{|\mathrm{Co}(\mathrm{I}(c)_m)||\mathrm{Co}(\mathrm{I}(c)_n)|} & \mathrm{I}(c)_m \neq \mathrm{I}(c)_n \end{cases} \tag{4}$$

3.2   Alert Instances Correlation

As APT attack alerts are essential to be correlated generating the APT attack scenarios, we focus on the APT attack scenarios construction. The APT attack usually performs through a few steps with characteristics of persistent, targeted and aiming at the specific object. The ultimate goal of APT is obtaining confidential data in the information systems. To achieve this goal the attack process usually contains complex multi-step. The alert instances constructed by cyber situation ontology construction module belong to different APT attack step, Table 1 summarizes the matchup between APT attack scenario steps and alert instances.

Table 1. The matchup between APT attack scenario steps and alert instances

Step number	APT Step	Alerts instance
Step 2	(P) Point of entry	$I(p_1)$ Domain_instance
		$I(p_2)$ Disguised_exe_instance
		$I(p_3)$ Hash_instance
Step 3	(C) C&C communication	$I(c_1)$ Domain_flux_instance
		$I(c_2)$ Ip_instance
		$I(c_3)$ Ssl_instance
Step 5	(A) Asset/data discovery	$I(a_1)$ Scan_instance
Step 6	(D) Data exfiltration	$I(d_1)$ Tor_intance

The first step (Intelligence Gathering) contains some passive process and the corresponding alerts are not easily be detected by network traffic sensors. The fourth step (Lateral Movement) is internal traffic within the information system while the APT alerts are generated based on inbound and outbound traffic. Based on the above facts we only correlate the APT alert instances generated in Step 2, Step 3, Step 5 and Step 6 of an APT attack scenario.

The AICM outputs two kinds of correlated alert instance clusters:$Cluster_{full}$ and $Cluster_{sub}$. $Cluster_{full}$ will be generated when AICM has correlated a full APT attack scenario during the correlation duration has every step of an APT attack scenario. $Cluster_{sub}$ will be produced when AICM has correlated two or three rather than all steps of an APT attack scenario during the correlation duration.

Alert Instance Filter (AIF). As the ATP alerts are produced by various detection sensors, the same alert instances have the possibility of generating during a correlation duration. The alert instance filter (AIF) discards the repeated and redundant alert instances. It checks whether the new arriving alert instance has been constructed during the correlation duration through compare the alert instance type and instance attributes value of it with the previous instances. It is obvious that ignoring the invalid alert instances can reduce computation cost of AICM.

Alert Instance Cluster (AIC). Alert instance cluster (AIC) module assigns the alert instances those are most similar to a certain cluster. An APT full steps scenario or sub-steps scenario can present as alert instance clusters. As AIC is based on APT attack scenario it restricts to three rules:

Rule 1. Alert instances, which belong to the same APT attack step, should not be assigned to the same cluster.

Rule 2. The same types of alert instances should not be assigned to the same cluster.

Rule 3. The APT attack alert instances trigger time span should be within the correlation duration and alert instances order should be in accord with the APT attack life cycle.

All the generated alert instance clusters are presented as a directed graph; the scattered alert instances are linked by directed edges based on the similarity. Then the clusters will be consumed by the correlation indexing module. Each cluster is consisted of maximum four ordered alert instances and recorded in an instance_cluster_dataset (ICD). When a new alert instance arrives in the AIC module, we first check to which APT attack step it belongs. Based on the different alert instance type AIC operates different options. We have the conclusion: Point of entry (P) which the second step of APT attack scenario is the first detectable attack step. When AIC get an alert instance $I(p_i)$ it generates a new cluster and sets $I(p_i)$ to instance_1 recorded in ICD. When AIC get an alert instance $I(c_i)$, AIC inquires the similarity $SIM(I(c_i), I(p_i))$ where $I(p_i)$ is the instances already recorded in ICD in the order instance_1 of one existing cluster. AIC adds the $I(c_i)$ to the order instance_2 of the cluster which not only has the largest value of $SIM(I(c_i), I(p_i))$ but also comply with Rule1, Rule 2 and Rule 3. Then we can get the correlated instances of $I(c_i)$:$Co(I(c_i)) = I(p_i)$, and send the $Co(I(c_i))$ back to the cyber situation ontology construction module for later instance similarity calculation. If there are no suitable alert instances $I(p_i)$ to be chosen, AIC generates a new cluster and sets $I(c_i)$ at instance_2 recorded in ICD. The correlation operations of $I(a_i)$ and $I(d_i)$ are similar to above. In general, we correlate the alert instance to the most similar prior step alert instance has recorded. A correlation example is shown in Fig. 2.

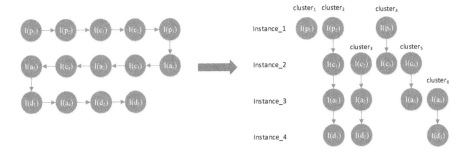

Fig. 2. The alert instance clusters construction

APT Attack Scenario (AAS). APT attack scenario (ASS) module confirms the alert instances belonging to the same alert instance cluster whether can construct a full or sectional APT attack scenario. As we knew each ATP alert instance cluster is constructed incrementally, it has the possibility that later received alert instance reforms the previously correlated alert instances. To address this problem, we add a parameter L_{ij} to the correlated links between every two alert instances, which belong to the same cluster. The parameter L_{ij} has two values: 1 or 0. When the alert instance_i and instance_j has the same *Victim_HostIP* the L_{ij} is set to 1; otherwise, the L_{ij} is set to 0. The ASS will face four state of L_{ij} during the correlation. The four states and corresponding operations are shown in Fig. 3 and described as follow:

$(1,1)$: The APT alert instances can belong to a certain AAS.
$(0,1)$: The latest two alert instances are much more similar than the prior two alert instance. Then the first link should be disconnected and construct a new instance cluster contains the latest two alert instances waiting for coming correlation.
$(1,0)$: No evidences can trigger the disconnection, just waiting for later instances.
$(0,0)$: No evidences can trigger the disconnection, just waiting for later instances.

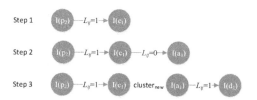

Fig. 3. The constructing AAS states evolution

We also introduce a parameter *LinkNum* to check the clustered APT alert instances and discard the uncorrelated alert instances. *LinkNum* can be formulated as follow.

$$LinkNum_{cluster_k} = \sum^{3}_{\substack{i=1, j=i+1 \\ instance\_i \in cluster_k \\ instance\_j \in cluster_k}} L_{ij} \qquad (5)$$

LinkNum $= 0$. The APT alert instances in the cluster have no effect and cause with each other; they cannot construct an APT attack scenario.
LinkNum $= 1$. The APT alert instances in the cluster can generate a correlation between two alert instances and they can construct a *Cluster_sub* with two steps.
LinkNum $= 2$. The APT alert instances in the cluster can generate correlations between three alert instances and they can construct a *Cluster_sub* with three steps.
LinkNum $= 3$. The APT alert instances in the cluster can generate a correlation between four alert instances constructing a *Cluster_full* and present an APT attack scenario.

Then, we define an ASS vector to record the information of each correlated clusters. The ASS vector is formally defined as follow:

$$assv_k = (cluster_k, LinkNum, Victim\_HostIp, SimDeg) \qquad (6)$$

The $assv_k$ vectors are the sectional output of cyber situation comprehension to be used in future cyber situation projection. Meanwhile the LICM module can get the attribute $Victim\_HostIp$ from ASS vectors to set the correlation hosts range.

Module Implementation. We implement the algorithm of AICM module in C programming language after getting the simulation dataset. The pseudo-code of the AICM module is shown below (Fig. 4).

```
ypedef struct                              else
{                                               arr[i][j] = C * (1.0 + AB) / 2.0;//
    struct TimeStamp                       Compare each attribute and Complete the
    char Alert_Type[20];                   iteration
    char Src_Ip[20];                       }end;
    char Dest_Ip[20];                      }
    int Src_Port;                               Timecmp();//Sort by TimeStamp
    int Dest_Port;                              Check_sort();//Group by type
}Attr;// Structure definition                   //Construct the cluster
main{                                           Linkcourt();//Calculate the linkcount
        readtxt()//Read the information         Print();//Oput the cluster
and convert                                }end
it into a specified format
        sim () {//similarity degree
        do{  If ((edge[i][0] == 1 &&
edge[i][1] == 0 && edge[t][0] == 0 &&
edge[t][1] == 1) || (edge[i][0] == 0 &&
edge[i][1] == 1 && edge[t][0] == 1 &&
edge[t][1] == 0))
        arr[i][j] = C * AB;
```

Fig. 4. The pseudo-code of AICM module

3.3 Log Instances Correlation

Advanced Persistent Threat (APT) attack has multiple stages for the sake of being elusive and stealthy. Besides the APT alerts generated during the multiple stages, this type of attack pattern inevitably leaves some log information spatio-temporally dispersed across victim hosts. LICM exploits the fundamental inter connections between logs and detects the log instances communities. The preliminary correlation module constructs the weighted graphs by correlating log instances generated at the victim hosts (The $Victim\_HostIps$ are got AICM). LICM can also discover the log instance communities hid within the weighted graphs by log instances community detection module.

Preliminary Correlation (PC). The input of preliminary correlation module (PC) is the log instances extracted from log data and the outputs are directed and weighted graphs. In this work, we regard the log instances as nodes and regard the relationships between them as edges. The weights of edges illustrate the similarity between log instances and the directions of edges illustrate the effect and cause relationship between them. Once the LICM gets an ASS vector from the AICM it begins to construct a preliminary correlated graph based on the log instances generated at the victim host. Some preprocessing may leave logs before the significant APT alerts occur, so we correlate the log instances generated before the first alert instance for a short time of τ. As the log instances generated in a timing sequence, preliminary correlation module inquires the similarity from the cyber situation ontology construction module in the same strategy. For example, at a victim host $I(log)_1$ is the first log instance generated within the *CorrelationDuration*. To construct a weighted and directed graph the similarity between the log instances are regarded as weights according to the following strategy:

$\left[I(log)_1, I(log)_2, I(log)_3, \ldots, I(log)_n \right]$ is a log instance sequence generated according to timing sequence. When PC module gets a new log instance $I(log)_i$ by inquiring the $\mathrm{SIM}\left(I(log)_1, I(log)_i \right)$, $\mathrm{SIM}(I(log)_2, I(log)_i)$, $\mathrm{SIM}(I(log)_3, I(log)_i)$,...,$\mathrm{SIM}(I(log)_{i-1}, I(log)_i)$ from the cyber situation ontology construction module. On the condition that $\mathrm{SIM}(I(log)_i, I(log)_j) \neq 0$, create a directed edge from $I(log)_i$ to $I(log)_j$ set $\omega_{ij} = \mathrm{SIM}$ $(I(log)_i, I(log)_j)$, generate a correlated instance of $I(log)_j$ set $\mathrm{Co}_n\left(I(log)_j \right) = I(log)_i$ and pass back $\mathrm{Co}_n\left(I(log)_j \right)$ to cyber situation ontology construction module. Otherwise, $\omega_{ij} = 0$. There are no correlated relationships (edges) between $I(log)_i$ and $I(log)_j$.

The preliminary correlation module acquires the weighted graphs of log instances and sends them to log instance community detection module for acquiring the cyber situation comprehension output.

Log Instance Community Detection (LICD). Taking account for the log instance graphs scale log instance community detection module has the demand of proposing an efficient community detection method to extract the log instance communities from the intricate directed and weighted correlated instance graph. Comparing the existing diverse machine learning method used in communities detection, LICD module owns a log instance community detection method based on the Louvain method, which has the advantage of managing large-scale nodes networks.

At the initial phase of LICD, each log instance in the graph constructed from PC module represents a single log instance community. $\sum_m \omega_{im}$ and $\sum_m \omega_{mj}$ respectively presents the totality weights added on edges associate to log instances $I(log)_i$ and $I(log)_j$,$c_{I(log)_i}$ and $c_{I(log)_j}$ respectively represents the log instance community $I(log)_i$ and $I(log)_j$ belong to. The $\theta - function$ in the LICD module is used to separate the log instances which belong to the different log instance communities, means that

$\theta(i,j) = 1$ if $i = j$, $\theta(i,j) = 0$ otherwise. To compare the density degree of the correlations within the log instance communities with the correlations cross the log instance communities LICD introduces an evaluation index *DenDeg* defined as follow.

$$DenDeg = \frac{\sum_{\mathrm{I}(log)_i, \mathrm{I}(log)_j} \left[\omega_{ij} - \frac{\sum_m \omega_{im} \sum_m \omega_{mj}}{\sum_{\mathrm{I}(log)_i, \mathrm{I}(log)_j} \omega_{ij}} \right] \theta\left(c_{\mathrm{I}(log)_i}, c_{\mathrm{I}(log)_j} \right)}{\sum_{\mathrm{I}(log)_i, \mathrm{I}(log)_j} \omega_{ij}} \quad (7)$$

As soon as the LICD module finishes the log instance initialization, it repeats actions to optimize the index *DenDeg* in the following strategies: for each log instance $\mathrm{I}(log)_k$, shift $\mathrm{I}(log)_k$ from its attached log instance community $c_{\mathrm{I}(log)_k}$ into its correlated log instance $Co_n\left(\mathrm{I}(log)_k\right)$ attached communities. LICD evaluates the value change of index *DenDeg* and places $\mathrm{I}(log)_k$ into the log instance community $c_{\mathrm{I}(log)_{k\_in}}$, which has the most obvious index *DenDeg* increase. If the maximum increase is not positive, the log instance $\mathrm{I}(log)_k$ will not be shifted from its original log instance community. LICD applies this process repeatedly and sequentially to each log instance until no $\Delta DenDeg$ occurs, gets the detected log instance communities as the segmental output of cyber situation comprehension.

Module Implementation. We implement the algorithm of LICM module in Python after getting the log data. The LICM module pseudo-code is provided as follow (Fig. 5):

```
#define MAX_VERTEX_NUM 20                         simrank() //Calculation the similarity degree
typedef struct ArcBox                             { calc_similarity();
{   int tailvex,headvex;                              init_graph(); // Initialization of the graph
    struct ArcBox *hlink,*tlink;                      while(new node occur)//When new nodes arrive,
    InfoType *info;                           renew the graph
}ArcBox; //The struct of edge definition          { ergodic_graph();
typedef struct VexNode                              calc_similarity();
{   VertexType data[20];                            change_graph();
    ArcBox *firstin,*firstout;                      }
}VexNode; //The struct of log nodes definition      print(); //Output the result
typedef struct                                    }
{   VexNode xlist[MAX_VERTEX_NUM];
    int vexnum,arcnum;                            louvain()//Clustering analysis
}OLGraph; //The struct of graph definition        {   calc_modularity(){
//Three main algorithms                                   for(each node) // Evaluation the clustering degree
get_attributes() //Convert the log data into log instance     {
{   key_word log[6]; //Five kinds of log data                get_neighbor();
    init_keyword(); //Initialization of the log data         calc_modularity();
    while()                                               }
    { getline();//Read the log data                       }
    find_keyword()                                    if(new modularity occurs) // Iterative computations
    { if(key_word in log)// Set the attribute vector value     calc_modularity();
        {set 1;                                       else
        }                                                 print();
        else set 0;                               }
    }                                             main()
    }                                             {
    return  A[20];//Output the log instances              get_attirbutes();
}                                                         simrank();
                                                          louvain();
                                                  }
```

Fig. 5. The pseudo-code of LICM module

4   Experimental Evaluation of APTALCM

4.1   Evaluation of the Alert Instance Correlation Module

As there is no available public data set can provide enough APT attack alerts, we adapt to construct a specialized simulation data set. The function of the alert instance correlation module is to recognize various alert instances could belong to a certain APT attack scenario. To significantly evaluate the AICM module, the simulation data set consists of APT alerts belong to APT attack scenarios and other general alerts do not belong to APT attack scenario. The aim of this experiment is to verify whether the AICM module can reconstruct the APT scenarios hidden in the constructed data set.

Data Generation. To construct the simulation data set we use Python to write a script, which constructs two classes of alert: Correlative alerts be part of a $Cluster_{full}$ or $Cluster_{sub}$; scattered alerts do not belong to any of the alert instance cluster.

We set seven attributes to each alert: *Alert_Type*, *Timestamp*, *Src_Ip*, *Dest_Ip*, *Src_Port*, *Dest_Port* and *Victim_HostIp*. To guarantee the randomness of the generated alert we select the *Alert_Type* from the provided eight ATP alert type there in before. We assign a random value start from 01 February 2019 00:00:01 to 30 March 2019 23:59:59 to *Timestamp*. The *Src_Ip* value is assigned based on the selected *Alert_Type*.

The *Dest_Ip* assigned randomly with an IP address on an enterprise network. We select the *Src_Port* randomly from the 49 140 to 65 521 range which is usually allocated dynamically to initiate a connection. We assign a random port number to *Dest_Port* based on the *Alert_Type*. The *Victim_HostIp* is assigned randomly with an IP address on an enterprise network. We have generated 5000 APT alerts for the simulation data set consisted with 150 $Cluster_{full}$, 150 $Cluster_{sub}$ and 4000 random isolated alerts. Then, the simulation data set for evaluate the AICM module has accomplished.

Correlation Performance. We have applied the AICM module algorithm on the constructed simulation data set. The correlation result is shown in Table 2. We choose the False Positive Rate (FPR) and the True Positive Rate (TPR) as the correlation effect measurement parameters. We can find the TPR of the two steps $Cluster_{sub}$ is higher than any other clusters. It is obvious that the TPR is lower with the alert instance cluster steps quantity increaser. This is mainly because more alert instances correlation process will increase the possibility of the random isolated alert instances to be unexpected correlated. When decreasing the TPR, the unexpected random isolated alert instances correlation can also incur the False Positive correlation result. As the larger step

Table 2. Evaluation AICM module correlation result.

APT attack cluster	Correlated quantity	FP	TP	N	P	FPR	TPR
APT two steps cluster	2*83	2*35	2*48	4900	100	1.4%	96%
APT three steps cluster	3*106	3*19	3*87	4700	300	1.2%	87%
APT full scenario	4*121	4*10	4*120	4400	600	0.9%	80%
Total APT cluster	968	167	837	4000	1000	4.2%	83.7%

quantity of the clusters the stronger ability they equipped to amend the previous correlation by the later alert instances, the FPR is lower with the alert instance cluster steps quantity increaser. In general, holistic TPR and FPR are well satisfied.

Performance Comparison Between AICM and Existing APT Detection Systems.
We compared the performance of the developed AICM module with the three typical reconstruction methods of the APT scenarios to show the advantage of our method. The comparative results are shown in Table 3.

Table 3. The comparative results between AICM and other APT scenarios reconstruct method.

APT scenarios reconstruct method	Efficiency	Step quantity	FPR	TPR
AICM	Real-time	Four steps	4.2%	83.7%
Spear phishing based	Real-time	One steps	15.9%	94.3%
TerminAPTor	Real-time	Four steps	25.64%	98.8%
C&C-based	Off-line	One steps	1.2%	79.6%

We can get the obvious results that other three proposed APT scenarios reconstruct method are not able to handle the problem that how to balance the higher TPR and lower FPR properly. As the only method can approximately get to the performance of AICM, the C&C-based method has a disadvantage of failing to accomplish the real-time APT scenarios reconstruct. It is nice to see the AICM has higher TPR with not too high FPR.

4.2   Evaluation of the Log Instance Correlation Module

We implement the algorithm of LICM in Python and take full advantage of the convenience of package python-Louvain to accomplish log instance community detection.

The experiment environment described as follow: (1) a victim Windows 10 64-bit operating system running on a host with an Intel Core i5-7200u 2.0 GHz CPU, 8 GB RAM. (2) an attack Windows 10 64-bit operating system running on a host with an Intel Core i7-8550u 2.53 GHz CPU, 16 GB RAM. We also assign extra roles to the attack host: the FTP server, C&C server and Apache server.

Data Generation. To construct the log data set and evaluate the LICM module algorithm we record the log data from the log providers and the log data quantity of each provider shown as Table 4. We record the log data while using the experimental machine by routinely work without perceiving that some operations have triggered some APT attack activities. We get these log data after a particular attack has launched on the computer system to simulate the APT attack scenario.

Correlation Performance. We have applied the LICM module algorithm on the recorded log dataset to evaluate the performance of log community detection on 7 APT attack scenarios such as Attack on Aerospace (AA), Hacking Team (HT), Tibetan and HK (TH), Russian Campaign (RC), Op-Tropic Trooper (OTT), APT on Taiwan (AT), and Op-Clandestine Fox (OCF). We also choose the FPR and TPR as the correlation

Table 4. APT log instance size.

Log	Quantity	Size (KB)
HTTP	3345	16530
Object access	282	5789
Process create	261	6420
DNS	510	72
WFP	734	18453

effect measurement parameters. The log instances within any detected community are regarded as malicious ones and the others as benign ones. The TRP is the portion of the correctly classified malicious log instance or benign log instance. The FPR is the portion of the actual benign log instances unexpectedly classified to the malicious cluster. From the results shown in Fig. 6, we can see that TPRs of LICM module works well on the 7 typical APT scenarios and the FPRs are also medium.

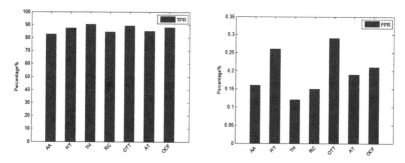

Fig. 6. Evaluation LICM module detection result

5   Conclusion

In this paper, we proposed an APT alerts and logs correlation method to accomplish the cyber situation comprehension. To recognize attack intentions, a similarity measures method based on SimRank is proposed. We also proposed an APT alert instances correlation method to reconstruct APT attack scenarios and an APT log instances correlation method to detect log instance communities. The experimental results show that the APTALCM has higher TPR with acceptable FPR.

References

1. Bass, T.: Intrusion detection systems and multisensor data fusion: Creating cyberspace situational awareness. Commun. ACM **43**(4), 99–105 (2000)
2. Cuppens, F., Ortalo, R.: Lambda: a language to model a database for detection of attacks. In: Proceedings of the 3rd International Workshop on Recent Advances in Intrusion Detection (RAID 2000), Toulouse, vol. 1907, pp. 197–216 (2000)

3. Bhatt, P., Yano, E.T., Gustavsson, P.M.: Towards a framework to detect multi-stage advanced persistent threats attacks. In: Proc. of the IEEE Intel Symposium on Service Oriented System Engineering, Toronto, pp. 390–395 (2014)

4. Roschke, S., Cheng, F., Meinel, C.: A new alert correlation algorithm based on attack graph. CISIS **6694**(11), 58–67 (2017)

5. Albanese, M.: Subrahmanian vs. scalable detection of cyberattacks. CISIM **245**, 9–18 (2016)

6. Mathew, S., Upadhyaya, S., et al.: Situation awareness of multistage cyber attacks by semantic event fusion. In: Proceedings of the Military Communications Conference, London, pp. 1286–1291 (2018)

7. Aleroud, A., Karabatis, G., et al.: Context and semantics for detection of cyber attacks. Int. J. Inf. Comput. Secur. **6**(1), 63–92 (2014)

8. Hutchins, E.M., et al.: Intelligence driven computer network defense informed analysis of adversary campaigns intrusion kill chains. In: Proceedings of the ICIW, Chicago, pp. 113–127 (2011)

9. Julisch, K.: Clustering intrusion detection alarms to support root cause analysis. ACM Trans Inf. Syst. Secur. **48**(4), 443–471 (2016)

10. Ourston, D., et al.: Applications of hidden Markov models to detecting multi-stage network attacks. In: Proceedings of the Hawaii International Conference on System Sciences, Hawaii, pp. 73–76 (2016)

A Secure Fine-Grained Identity-Based Proxy Broadcast Re-encryption Scheme for Micro-video Subscribing System in Clouds

Chunpeng Ge[1], Lu Zhou[2(✉)], Jinyue Xia[3], Pawel Szalachowski[4], and Chunhua Su[2]

[1] Nanjing University of Aeronautics and Astronautics, Nanjing 210000, China
gecp@nuaa.edu.cn
[2] University of Aizu, Aizuwakamatsu 965-8580, Japan
sduzhoulu@gmail.com, chsu@u-aizu.ac.jp
[3] IBM, Research Triangle Park, Durham, NC 27709, USA
jinyue.xia@ibm.com
[4] Singapore University of Technology and Design, Singapore, Singapore
pawel@sutd.edu.sg

Abstract. Micro-video sharing is prevalent nowadays due to the rapid development of personal smart devices, fast growing of network bandwidth and the easy-to-use cloud computing. However, the micro-video sharing system is more vulnerable compared to the conventional video service model because of the vulnerability of the cloud and the hardware computing constraints of personal devices. Ensuring the security and privacy of the micro-videos has become critical for micro-video sharing systems. Recently, a number of encryption schemes have been proposed to protect the security of the micro-videos stored in the cloud. However, these approaches cannot support micro-video sharing functionality. Moreover, the encryption-based method cannot provide the fine-grained access control on encrypted micro-videos. In this paper, we present a notion of fine-grained identity-based broadcast proxy re-encryption to address the issue of fine-grained encrypted micro-video sharing. Further, we present a concrete scheme in the proposed notion and analyze its security. Performance and evaluation show that our proposed scheme is practical and efficient.

Keywords: Micro-video subscribing · Privacy preserve · Identity-based encryption · Attribute-based encryption

1 Introduction

With the advent of smart phones, more and more people are taking micro-videos to record and share things around [25]. With the growth of individual's videos,

© Springer Nature Singapore Pte Ltd. 2019
W. Meng and S. Furnell (Eds.): SocialSec 2019, CCIS 1095, pp. 139–151, 2019.
https://doi.org/10.1007/978-981-15-0758-8_11

people are facing a tough problem of personal video management and maintenance since it is very expensive and impractical for an individual to setup a service infrastructure. Cloud computing, which enables an user to outsource his videos with on-demand storage capability and low cost, is a promising technique to resolve the problem. In current cloud-based video storage and sharing architecture in Fig. 1, the data owner uploads his personal video to a third cloud service provider. Along the video, an access policy defines who is shared with the video is also uploaded. When a data user wants to access the video, he sends a request to the cloud server, then the cloud server returns the corresponding video if and only if the data user satisfies the access policy. However, it is unavoidable that the above mechanism also suffers from the security and privacy problems since video data is stored in a plaintext form in the cloud, which is not fully trusted by the video owner.

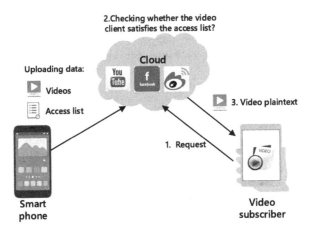

Fig. 1. Current video subscribing system.

Encryption is a basic method for data confidentiality and identity-based encryption (IBE) is a promising representative as it simplifies the public key infrastructure. When the video data is encrypted using the identity-based encryption before it's uploaded to the cloud, video distributing is a basic demand for the video subscribing system. However, traditional identity-based encryption only guarantees the confidentiality of outsourced video. It is incapable for the data sharing functionality.

Here is a potential solution to address the security issue by using traditional IBE. Suppose, in a Micro-Video Subscribing System [21], a video owner encrypts his video $Enc(D, ID)$ using identity-based encryption, where D is the video data and ID is the data owner's identity and then uploads the result ciphertext to the cloud. At some point, the video owner may want to share some specific video with a set of subscribers $U = \{ID_1, \cdots, ID_n\}$, who have paid the video owner. In the traditional identity-based encryption scheme, the video owner should first download the encrypt videos and then decrypt them to obtain the underlying video data. Following that, the video owner encrypts the plaintext video using each subscriber's identity in the set S. Such a phase does not scale well for the above video subscribing scenario as downloading video from the cloud server yields the problem of data maintenance. This problem is even serious for smart phones due to the constrained computation and storage resource. A worse problem is that during the whole sharing phase, the video owner should be online as his private key is involved to decrypt the encrypted video.

Additionally, the traditional identity-based encryption can not support the flexible control of videos. For example, the video owner may only want to share the video satisfying the policy $P = ($ "gender : Male" $\bigwedge$ "age < 30" $\bigwedge$ ("Location : Beijing $\bigvee$ Hongkong")) which means only male subscribers with age under 30 and located in Beijing or Hongkong can visit the video. However the traditional identity-based encryption can not support data match on encrypted ciphertext.

From the above Micro-Video Subscribing System scenario, though the traditional identity-based encryption can support data confidentiality, it is lack of flexible video sharing. The video owner has to download all the encrypted videos and decrypt them locally. However, such a process brings extra burden that is more critical for smart devices.

Naively, one may think that the video owner can store his private key in the cloud. However, in such a solution, the cloud server should be fully trusted. This is impractical since in the cloud computing circumstance the cloud server and the cloud users belong to different trust domains [22].

1.1   Related Work

The concept of identity-based encryption was fist introduced by Boneh et al. [6]. And Cocks [5] in which a user's identity is viewed as his public key. The identity-based encryption simplified the public key infrastructure in traditional public key encryption. Attribute-based encryption (ABE) [18] is a generalized identity-based encryption which enables fine-grained access control on the encrypted data. Attribute-based encryption can be categorized into ciphertext policy ABE (CP-ABE) [1] and key policy ABE (KP-ABE) [10]. In a CP-ABE scheme, the ciphertext is encrypted under an access policy P and the user's private key is described by an attribute set S. A user can decrypt the ciphertext if and only if S satisfies P. While it is reversed in the KP-ABE setting. Following their work, to achieve stronger security and efficiency, many improved ABE scheme were proposed [12,13,23].

To enable encrypted data sharing, Blaze et al. [2] introduced the notion of proxy re-encryption (PRE). In a proxy re-encryption scheme, a proxy with a re-encryption key can transform user Alice's ciphertext to user Bob's ciphertext without knowing the plaintext. Later, Green et al. [11] combined the notion of IBE and PRE and proposed an identity-based proxy re-encryption (IB-PRE) scheme. Shao et al. [19] and Ge et al. [8] extend the notion of IB-PRE to identity-based conditional proxy re-encryption (IB-CPRE) in which only cipher-texts satisfying a certain condition can be transformed. To achieve fine-grained access control, many attribute-based proxy re-encryption (AB-PRE) schemes were proposed [7,9,14–16]. Unfortunately, these approaches can not scale well in the video subscribing scenario in which there are always a set of subscribers. In such a case, the cloud server needs to re-encrypt the original video ciphertext for each subscriber in the list.

In 2009, Chu et al. [3] proposed the notion of broadcast proxy re-encryption (BPRE), in which the proxy can convert a user's ciphertext to a set of users' ciphertext at a time. Following their work, Ge et al. [4] presented a revocable identity-based proxy re-encryption (IB-BPRE) which in which the revoked subscribers can be efficiently revoked. However, although these scheme can achieve the broadcast property of video sharing, they can not support fine-grained control on the encrypted videos.

1.2 Our Contribution

In this work, we adopted the notion of identity-based broadcast proxy re-encryption to the video subscribing system to keep the confidentiality of the video data. Our notion enables the video owner to share the encrypted with a set of subscribers at a time. Moreover, the data owner can achieve fine-grained access control on the encrypted videos. We proposed a concrete fine grained identity-based broadcast proxy re-encryption (ID-BPRE) and analyzed its security for our video subscribing system. Performance and evaluation demonstrate that our proposed scheme is efficient and practical.

2 System Architecture and Definitions

In this section, we first present our fine grained video subscribing system architecture. Following that, we will describe the definition of proposed identity-based BPRE and its threat model in the video subscribing system.

2.1 System Architecture

In the video subscribing system, shown in Fig. 2, there are three entities, the video owner, the cloud server and a set of subscribers. The video is equipped with a smartphone with constrained computation and storage resource. The cloud server is third party cloud service provider with unlimited computing capability and storage (eg, the Ali Cloud and Amazon Cloud). A set of subscribers who wants to view the videos shared by the video owner. The details of each entity are as follows.

- The video owner encrypt the micro-video and then upload the encrypted videos to the cloud. The video owner is also responsible for generating re-encryption keys for different sets of subscribers.

- When received the video request from a subscriber, the cloud re-encrypts the encrypted video with a re-encryption key. And then, responses the subscriber with the re-encrypted ciphertext.
- The subscriber decrypts the re-encrypted video from the cloud with his own private key.

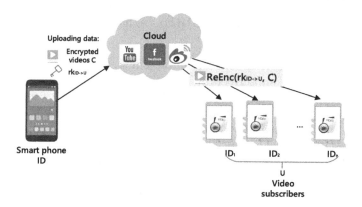

Fig. 2. The proposed system architecture.

2.2   Threat Model

In our video subscribing system, the video is thought to be honest. The cloud server is honest but curious that means he will execute the protocol honestly but curious to collect information to reveal the underlying video. The subscribers are malicious that want to acquire the video without authorized by the video owner. Moreover, the malicious subscribers may collude with the cloud server to reveal the video.

2.3   Fine-Grained IB-BPRE

In this section, we fist present an review of the access policy in our scheme. The access policy in our scheme is defined as an access tree $\mathcal{T}$ which was first introduced by Goyal et al. [10].

Definition 1 (Access tree $\mathcal{T}$). For an access tree $\mathcal{T}$, each non-leaf node of the tree represents a threshold gate, described by its children and a threshold value. For each node x, num_x is the number of its children and k_x is its threshold value, then we have $0 < k_x \leq num_x$. When $k_x = num_x$, it is an AND gate, and when $k_x = 1$, the threshold is an OR gate. For each leaf node x of the its threshold value $k_x = 1$. The root of an access tree is set to be at depth 0. $\overline{LN_{\mathcal{T}}}$ and $LN_{\mathcal{T}}$ denote the set of all non-leaf nodes and leaf nodes respectively. $p(x)$ denotes the parent of the node x. $att(x)$ is defined denotes the attribute associated with a leaf node x. The children of a node x are numbered from 1 to num_x. $inex(z)$ denotes an index associated with the node z.

Satisfying an Access Tree. Let $\mathcal{T}_x$ is a subtree rooted at the node x of $\mathcal{T}$. $\mathcal{T}_x(S) = 1$ denotes the set of attributes S satisfies the access tree $\mathcal{T}_x$. If x is a leaf node, then $\mathcal{T}_x(S) = 1$ if and only if $att(x) \in S$. If x is a non-leaf node, $\mathcal{T}_x(S) = 1$ at least k_x children of node x equal to 1.

Next, we will present the definition of fine-grained IB-BPRE scheme and its security analysis.

Definition 2 (Fine-Grained IB-BPRE). A fine-grained Ib-BPRE scheme comprises the following six algorithms:

- $Setup(1^\lambda, N) \rightarrow (cp, msk)$: The $Setup$ takes a security parameter λ and the maximum number of subscribers N in the system as input. Outputs the master common parameters cp and the PKG's master private key msk.
- $KeyGen(msk, ID) \rightarrow sk_{ID}$: The $KeyGen$ algorithm takes the master private key msk, and an identity ID as input. Outputs user's ID's private key sk_{ID}.
- $Enc(ID, M, S) \rightarrow C$: The Enc algorithms takes a video M, the video owner's identity ID and a set of attributes S as input. Outputs the encrypted video C which can be shared with the subscribers later.
- $ReKey(ID, sk_{ID}, U, \mathcal{T}) \rightarrow rk$: The $ReKey$ algorithm takes an identity ID, private key sk_{ID}, a set of subscribers' identities $U = \{ID_1, \cdots, ID_n\}$ and an access policy $\mathcal{T}$ as input. Outputs a re-encryption key rk. Note that, $ID \notin U$. In our scheme, the access policy is defined as an access tree. Details of the access tree can be found in [10].
- $ReEnc(C, rk) \rightarrow CT$: The $ReEnc$ algorithm takes an original encrypted video C and a re-encryption key rk as input. Outputs the re-encrypted video CT.
- $Dec(sk_{ID}, C/CT) \rightarrow M$: The Dec algorithm takes a private key sk_{ID}, an original encrypted/re-encrypted video C/CT as input. Outputs the video M.

Consistency. The consistency of a fine-grained IB-BPRE scheme implies that the original encrypted video can be decrypted by the video owner and the re-encrypted video can be decrypted by the related subscriber. Formally, for a symmetric key K, $(cp, msk) \leftarrow Setup(1^\lambda, N)$, $sk_{ID} \leftarrow KeyGen(msk, ID)$ and $rk \leftarrow ReKey(ID, sk_{ID}, U, \mathcal{T})$ we have

$$Dec(sk_{ID}, Enc(ID, K, S)) = K;$$
$$Dec(sk_{ID_i}, ReEnc(Enc(ID, K, S), rk)) = K;$$

where $ID_i \in U$, and $\mathcal{T}(S) = 1$. Note that, if an attribute set S satisfies the access policy $\mathcal{T}$, then we define $\mathcal{T}(S) = 1$. Otherwise $\mathcal{T}(S) = 0$.

3   Proposed Scheme

In this section, we present our proposed fine-grained IB-BPRE scheme and analyze its semantic security.

3.1 Proposed IB-BPRE Scheme

Out proposed IB-BPRE Scheme comprise the next six algorithms.

1. $Setup(\lambda, N)$: On input the security parameter λ and the maximum number of subscribers N, the bootstrap first setup a bilinear map [6] (e, p, g, G_1, G_2). Then, chooses $g, h, Z \in G_1$, $\alpha \in Z_p$ randomly, and computes $h_1 = h^\alpha$, $g_i = g^{\alpha^i}$, $i \in \{1, \cdots, N\}$ and $\nu = e(g, h)$. Chooses two target collision resistant hash functions: $H_1 : \{0,1\}^* \to Z_p^*$, $H_2 : \{0,1\}^* \to G_1$, $H_3 : G_2 \to Z_p^*$ and setup the symmetric encryption algorithm AES. The common public key cp is $cp = (G_1, G_2, e, p, g, g_i, i \in \{1, \cdots, N\}, h_1, Z, H_1, H_2, H_3, AES)$, and the master secret key msk is $msk = (\alpha, h)$.

2. $KeyGen(msk, ID)$: On input an identity $ID \in \{0,1\}^*$, the PKG computes

$$sk_{ID} = h^{1/(\alpha + H_1(ID))}.$$

3. $Enc(ID, M, S)$: On input a video M, an identity ID and an attribute set S. Chooses a random AES symmetric key K, and computes the AES ciphertext $C_M = AES.Enc(K, M)$. Then chooses a random element $t \in Z_p^*$ and computes

$$C_K = K \cdot \nu^t, \quad C_1 = g^{t(\alpha + H_1(ID))}, \quad C_2 = Z^t.$$

For each $\omega \in S$, computes $C_\omega = H_2(\omega)^t$. Outputs the ciphertext $C = (S, C_M, C_K, C_1, C_2, (C_\omega)_{\omega \in S})$.

4. $ReKey(ID, sk_{ID}, U, \mathcal{T})$: Randomly chooses $\theta \in G_T$ and a polynomial q_x for each non-leaf node x in $\mathcal{T}$. These polynomials are chosen in an recursion manner from top to down. It calls the procedure $ReKey(\mathcal{T}, H_3(\theta)/H_1(ID))$, which is defined as follows.

For each node x in the tree, set the degree d_x of the polynomial q_x to be $d_x = k_x - 1$. For the root r, set $q_r(0) = H_3(\theta)$ and d_r other random points. For any other node x, set $q_x(0) = q_{p(x)}(index(x))$ and choose d_x other random points randomly. Finally, for each leaf node x, sets $\omega = att(x)$. Then we compute the re-encryption in the following way.

For each leaf node $x \in LN_{\mathcal{T}}$, select a random value $r_x \in Z_p^*$, and computes

$$a_x = sk_{ID} \cdot Z^{q_x(0)} H_2(\omega)^{r_x},$$

$$b_x = g^{r_x(\alpha + H_1(ID))}, \quad c_x = g^{\alpha q_x(0)}.$$

Chooses a random value $r \in Z_p^*$ and computes

$$rk_1 = e(g, h)^r \cdot \theta, \quad rk_2 = h_1^r,$$

$$rk_3 = g^{r \cdot \Pi_{ID \in U}(\alpha + H_1(ID))}.$$

Output the re-encryption key as

$$rk = (\mathcal{T}, \{a_x, b_x, c_x\}_{x \in LN_{\mathcal{T}}}, rk_1, rk_2, rk_3).$$

5. $ReEnc(C, rk)$: To re-encrypt an original ciphertext $C = (S, C_M, C_K, C_1, C_2, (C_\omega)_{\omega \in S})$ with a re-encryption key $rk = (T, \{a_x, b_x, c_x\}_{x \in LN_T}, rk_1, rk_2, rk_3)$. First checks whether $T(S) = 1$, if $T(S) = 0$, the $ReEnc$ algorithms borts and returns an error symbol $\bot$. Otherwise, defines a recursive algorithms $NodeReEnc(C, rk, x)$ that takes input an original ciphertext C, the re-encryption key rk, and a node x in the tree and works as follows.

   (a) If x is a leaf node, let $\omega = att(x)$, if $x \in S$, computes

$$NodeReEnc(C, rk, x)$$

$$= \frac{e(a_x, C_1)}{e(b_x, C_\omega) \cdot e(c_x, C_2)}$$

$$= e(g, h^t) \cdot e(g, Z)^{t \cdot q_x(0) \cdot H_1(ID)}$$

   Else if $x \notin S$, sets $NodeReEnc(C, rk, x) = \bot$.

   (b) If x is a non-leaf node, for all x's children nodes z, it sets $F_z = NodeReEnc(C, rk, z)$. Let T_x be an k_x-sized set of child notes z, such that $F_z \neq \bot$. If no such set exists, sets $NodeReEnc(C, rk_{i,T,S'}, x) = \bot$. Otherwise, let $T'_x = \{index(z) : z \in U\}$, and computes

$$F_x = \prod_{z \in T_x, i=index(z)} (F_z)^{\Delta_{i,T'_x}(0)}$$

$$= \prod_{z \in T_x, i=index(z)} (e(g, h^t) \cdot e(g, Z)^{tq_x(0) \cdot H_1(ID)})^{\Delta_{i,T'_x}(0)}$$

$$= e(g, h^t) \cdot e(g, Z)^{t \cdot H_1(ID) \cdot q_x(0)}.$$

   Finally, computes

$$C'_K = C_K / F_r = K \cdot e(g, Z)^{-t \cdot H_3(\theta)}.$$

   Output the re-encrypted ciphertext

$$CT = (C_M, C'_K, C_2, rk_1, rk_2, rk_3).$$

6. $Dec(sk_{ID}, C/CT)$:
   (a) If C is an original ciphertext. Computes

$$K = C_K \cdot e(sk_{ID}, C_1)^{-1}.$$

   (b) If CT is a re-encrypted ciphertext. Computes

$$\Gamma = \left(e(rk_2'^{-1}, g^{\rho_{i,U}(\alpha)}) \cdot e(sk_{ID}, rk_3) \right)^{\frac{1}{\prod_{j=1, j \neq i}^{U} H_1(ID_j)}}$$

   where $\rho_{i,U}(\alpha) =$

$$\frac{1}{\alpha} \cdot \left(\prod_{j=1, j \neq i}^{U} (\alpha + H_1(ID_j)) - \prod_{j=1, j \neq i}^{U} H_1(ID_j) \right).$$

Then computes

$$\theta = rk_1 \cdot \Gamma^{-1}, \quad K = C'_K \cdot e(g, C_2)^{H_3(\theta)}.$$

Finally, computes $M = AES.Dec(K, C_M)$.

Consistency:

1. If C is an original ciphertext, then we have:

$$K = C_K \cdot e(sk_{ID}, C_1)^{-1}$$
$$= K \cdot e(g, h)^t \cdot e\left(h^{1/(\alpha + H_1(ID))}, g^{r(\alpha + H_1(ID)))}\right)^{-1}$$
$$= K$$

2. If CT is a re-encrypted ciphertext, then we have:

$$\Gamma = \left(e(rk_2'^{-1}, g^{\rho_{i,U}(\alpha)}) \cdot e(sk_{ID}, rk_3)\right)^{\frac{1}{\prod_{j=1, j \neq i}^{U} H_1(ID_j)}}$$
$$= e(g, h)^r,$$

$\theta = rk_1 \cdot \Gamma^{-1}$, and $K = C'_K \cdot e(g, C_2)^{H_3(\theta)}$.

Finally, the user can decrypt the AES ciphertext with the symmetric key K. Thus, the consistency of the proposed scheme is verified.

3.2   Security Analysis

In this subsection, we will analysis the security of our proposed scheme. Our security analysis focus on the following three types of attacker.

1. The semi-honest cloud server. In our scheme, the videos in the cloud are all stored in the ciphertext form. The cloud with the re-encryption key can only convert the encrypted video to the subscribers' encrypted video. Only the with the vide owner's private key or the subscriber's private key, the video plaintext can be achieved. Thus, our proposed scheme can protect the video from a semi-honest cloud server.
2. A malicious subscriber. In the proposed scheme, the cloud can only convert the video owner's encrypted video to the subscriber's encrypted video with the re-encryption key, which is generated by the video owner. Hence, a malicious subscriber cannot reveal the video without authorized by the video owner.
3. A malicious subscriber colludes with the cloud server. In our scheme, though a malicious subscriber can collude with the cloud server to disclose the video plaintext. However, they can only achieve the video original for the subscriber. They cannot collude to disclose other honest subscriber's plaintext video. Thus, the proposed scheme can prevent the video owner and honest subscribers from the collusion attack.

4. Collusion resistant. Our proposed scheme is prevent the collusion resistant attack. In our scheme, when generating a re-encryption key, the delegator's private is randomized by a random element $Z^{q_x(0)}H_2(\omega)^{r_x}$. A malicious cloud server collude with a set of delegatees can only reveal the value of $sk \cdot H_2(\omega)^{r_x}$. The private key of a delegator is encoded by the random value $H_2(\omega)^{r_x}$. Thus, our proposed achieves the collusion resistant property.

5. Non-transferability. In our scheme, though a cloud server collude with a delegatee can transfer the ciphertext to a new delegatee's ciphertext. By the colluding, the can always get the plaintext and then encrypt the plaintext with a new delegatee's public key. However, they cannot collude to generate a new re-encryption key which can transfer the ciphertext without the participant of the cloud server and the colluded delegatee.

Table 1. Computation comparison with [24] and [20].

Schemes	Enc	ReKey	ReEnc	Dec(Or)	Dec(Re)
scheme [24]	$\mathcal{O}(|U|)e$	$\mathcal{O}(|U|)e$	$\mathcal{O}(|T|)(p+e)$	$\mathcal{O}(|U|)e + 2p$	$\mathcal{O}(|U|)e + 3p$
scheme [20]	$\mathcal{O}(|U|)e + p$	$\mathcal{O}(|U|)e + p$	$\mathcal{O}(|U|)e + 8p$	$\mathcal{O}(|U|)e + 8p$	$\mathcal{O}(|U|)e + 7p$
Ours	$\mathcal{O}(|S|)e$	$\mathcal{O}(|S| + |U|)e$	$\mathcal{O}(|T|)(p+e)$	$p + 2e$	$\mathcal{O}(|U|)e + 3p$

4   Performance and Evaluation

4.1   Theoretical Comparison

In this subsection, we compare our scheme with the most recent two identity-based broadcast proxy re-encryption schemes [20,24] in terms of computation cost. The comparison is listed in Table 1. In Table 1 S, T and U represent the size of the attribute set S, an access tree T and the number of subscribers in the broadcast encryption respectively. e denotes the computation cost of an exponential in a group and p denotes the computation cost of a bilinear pairing. We omit the computation cost of hash functions as it is much less than the exponential and bilinear pairing computation.

From Table 1, we can see that our scheme is almost as efficient as [24] and [20] in Enc, $ReEnc$ and $Dec(Re)$ algorithms. In the $ReKey$ algorithm, our scheme is a bit less efficient than [24] and [20]. However, this makes sense as our scheme provides the fine-grained access control on encrypted data which is note achieved in both [24] and [20].

Table 2. Execute time.

Algorithms	Enc (ms)	RKeyGen (ms)	ReEnc (ms)	Dec(Or) (ms)	Dec(Re) (ms)
$|S| = 30$	32.438	51.031	61.828	2.962	39.863
$|S| = 40$	43.105	64.003	84.612	2.876	41.068
$|S| = 50$	55.112	74.757	113.391	3.003	41.986
$|S| = 60$	68.375	86.953	136.153	3.026	38.772
$|S| = 70$	80.025	99.687	161.664	2.915	39.016

4.2 Implementation

To implement our scheme, we use the PBC package [17] which is written in Golang. The PBC package offers structures for building pairing-based cryptosystems. The implement hardware is Intel(R) Core(TM) i5-8250U CPU @ 1.60 GHZ 8 GB RAM with Linux Mint 18.1 Serena operation system. We use the GO 1.9 programming language.

In the PBC library, we set the elliptic curve to be $Y^2 = X^3 + X$ with 160 bit group order. For each time, we run each experiment for 20 times to obtain the average execution time.

In our experiment we set the broadcast subscribers' size to be $U = 20$. We varied the attribute set size $|S|$ from 30 to 70 with step 10. The execute time is summarized in Table 2.

Table 2 plot the execution time of the algorithms run by the data user and the proxy. We observe that the execution time of $Dec(Or)$ and $Dec(Re)$ algorithms are almost constant. While the execution time of Enc, $RKeyGen$ and $ReEnc$ algorithms are almost linear with the size of S. The experiment results demonstrate the theoretical analysis in Table 1.

5 Conclusions

In this paper, we studied the security and privacy problems of the exist micro-video system and presented the notion of fine-grained identity-based broadcast proxy re-encryption. Moreover, we proposed a concrete scheme under the proposed notion. Furthermore, we analyzed its security in the threat model. While this work has solved the issues of secure micro-video subscribing, there are still some interesting problems to be solved in the micro video subscribing system such as designing fine-grained identity-based proxy re-encryption schemes with hidden identities. This is critical in the micro-video subscribing scenario as the video owner may not want to disclose his subscribers.

Acknowledgments. Chunpeng Ge is supported by the National Natural Science Foundation of China (Grant No. 61702236) and Changzhou Sci & Tech Program (Grant No. CJ20179027). Chunhua Su is supported by JSPS Kiban(B) 18H03240 and JSPS Kiban(C) 18K11298.

References

1. Bethencourt, J., Sahai, A., Waters, B.: Ciphertext-policy attribute-based encryption. In: IEEE Symposium on Security and Privacy, SP 2007, pp. 321–334. IEEE (2007)
2. Blaze, M., Bleumer, G., Strauss, M.: Divertible protocols and atomic proxy cryptography. In: Nyberg, K. (ed.) EUROCRYPT 1998. LNCS, vol. 1403, pp. 127–144. Springer, Heidelberg (1998). https://doi.org/10.1007/BFb0054122
3. Chu, C.-K., Weng, J., Chow, S.S.M., Zhou, J., Deng, R.H.: Conditional proxy broadcast re-encryption. In: Boyd, C., González Nieto, J. (eds.) ACISP 2009. LNCS, vol. 5594, pp. 327–342. Springer, Heidelberg (2009). https://doi.org/10.1007/978-3-642-02620-1_23
4. Chunpeng, G., Liu, Z., Xia, J., Liming, F.: Revocable identity-based broadcast proxy re-encryption for data sharing in clouds. IEEE Trans. Dependable Secure Comput. (2019)
5. Cocks, C.: An identity based encryption scheme based on quadratic residues. In: Honary, B. (ed.) Cryptography and Coding 2001. LNCS, vol. 2260, pp. 360–363. Springer, Heidelberg (2001). https://doi.org/10.1007/3-540-45325-3_32
6. Boneh, D., Franklin, M.: Identity-based encryption from the Weil pairing. In: Kilian, J. (ed.) CRYPTO 2001. LNCS, vol. 2139, pp. 213–229. Springer, Heidelberg (2001). https://doi.org/10.1007/3-540-44647-8_13
7. Ge, C., Susilo, W., Fang, L., Wang, J., Shi, Y.: A CCA-secure key-policy attribute-based proxy re-encryption in the adaptive corruption model for dropbox data sharing system. Des. Codes Cryptogr. **86**, 2587–2603 (2018)
8. Ge, C., Susilo, W., Wang, J., Fang, L.: Identity-based conditional proxy re-encryption with fine grain policy. Comput. Stand. Interfaces **52**, 1–9 (2017)
9. Ge, C., Susilo, W., Wang, J., Huang, Z., Fang, L., Ren, Y.: A key-policy attribute-based proxy re-encryption without random oracles. Comput. J. **59**(7), 970–982 (2016)
10. Goyal, V., Pandey, O., Sahai, A., Waters, B.: Attribute-based encryption for fine-grained access control of encrypted data. In: ACM Conference on Computer and Communications Security, pp. 89–98 (2006)
11. Green, M., Ateniese, G.: Identity-based proxy re-encryption. In: Katz, J., Yung, M. (eds.) ACNS 2007. LNCS, vol. 4521, pp. 288–306. Springer, Heidelberg (2007). https://doi.org/10.1007/978-3-540-72738-5_19
12. Hohenberger, S., Waters, B.: Attribute-based encryption with fast decryption. In: Kurosawa, K., Hanaoka, G. (eds.) PKC 2013. LNCS, vol. 7778, pp. 162–179. Springer, Heidelberg (2013). https://doi.org/10.1007/978-3-642-36362-7_11
13. Lewko, A., Waters, B.: New proof methods for attribute-based encryption: achieving full security through selective techniques. In: Safavi-Naini, R., Canetti, R. (eds.) CRYPTO 2012. LNCS, vol. 7417, pp. 180–198. Springer, Heidelberg (2012). https://doi.org/10.1007/978-3-642-32009-5_12
14. Liang, K., Fang, L., Susilo, W., Wong, D.S.: A ciphertext-policy attribute-based proxy re-encryption with chosen-ciphertext security. In: 2013 5th International Conference on Intelligent Networking and Collaborative Systems (INCoS), pp. 552–559. IEEE (2013)
15. Liang, X., Cao, Z., Lin, H., Shao, J.: Attribute based proxy re-encryption with delegating capabilities. In: International Symposium on Information, Computer, and Communications Security, pp. 276–286 (2009)

16. Luo, S., Hu, J., Chen, Z.: Ciphertext policy attribute-based proxy re-encryption. In: Soriano, M., Qing, S., López, J. (eds.) ICICS 2010. LNCS, vol. 6476, pp. 401–415. Springer, Heidelberg (2010). https://doi.org/10.1007/978-3-642-17650-0_28
17. Nik-U: PBC package (2015). https://github.com/Nik-U/pbc
18. Sahai, A., Waters, B.: Fuzzy identity-based encryption. In: Cramer, R. (ed.) EURO-CRYPT 2005. LNCS, vol. 3494, pp. 457–473. Springer, Heidelberg (2005). https://doi.org/10.1007/11426639_27
19. Shao, J., Wei, G., Ling, Y., Xie, M.: Identity-based conditional proxy re-encryption. In: 2011 IEEE International Conference on Communications (ICC), pp. 1–5. IEEE (2011)
20. Sun, M., Ge, C., Fang, L., Wang, J.: A proxy broadcast re-encryption for cloud data sharing. Multimed. Tools Appl. **77**(9), 10455–10469 (2018)
21. Vimeo: https://vimeo.com/upgrade?vcid=35201&utm_medium=cpc&utm_source=google&gclid=EAIaIQobChMI-bTsz_m34QIVgw4rCh0LNQSNEAMYASAAEgIG5fD_BwE&gclsrc=aw.ds
22. Wang, C., Wang, Q., Ren, K., Lou, W.: Privacy-preserving public auditing for data storage security in cloud computing. In: 2010 Proceedings IEEE INFOCOM, pp. 1–9. IEEE (2010)
23. Waters, B.: Ciphertext-policy attribute-based encryption: an expressive, efficient, and provably secure realization. In: Catalano, D., Fazio, N., Gennaro, R., Nicolosi, A. (eds.) PKC 2011. LNCS, vol. 6571, pp. 53–70. Springer, Heidelberg (2011). https://doi.org/10.1007/978-3-642-19379-8_4
24. Xu, P., Jiao, T., Wu, Q., Wang, W., Jin, H.: Conditional identity-based broadcast proxy re-encryption and its application to cloud email. IEEE Trans. Comput. **65**(1), 66–79 (2015)
25. YouTube: https://www.youtube.com/

Exploit in Smart Devices: A Case Study

Zian Liu[1], Chao Chen[1], Shigang Liu[1], Dongxi Liu[2], and Yu Wang[3(✉)]

[1] School of Software and Electric Engineering, Swinburne University of Technology,
Melbourne, VIC, Australia
929319519qq@gmail.com, {chaochen,shigangliu}@swin.edu.au
[2] Data61, CSIRO, Sydney, Australia
Dongxi.Liu@data61.csiro.au
[3] School of Computer Science, Guangzhou University, Guangzhou, China
yuwang@gzhu.edu.cn

Abstract. With the rapid development of Internet of Things (IoT) and smart devices, an increasing number of home security devices are produced and deployed in our daily life. To improve the awareness of the security flaws of these household smart devices, we perform a demo attack in this paper, which utilizes the vulnerability of a security camera to do the exploit. We set up the malicious Wi-Fi environment and our assuming victim in the experiment uses Samsung GALAXY Note 10.1. We demonstrate how to steal the victim's credential log in information after tricking him into connecting to the malicious Wi-Fi. Our experiment shows that those smart devices lack high-standard security. In our experiment, we show it is trivial and cheap to steal the users credential using a malicious Wi-Fi.

Keywords: Smart things · Cyber attack · Information leak

1   Introduction

Internet of Things (IoT) devices, known as nonstandard computing devices that connect wirelessly to a network and have the ability to send sensor data or surveillance information, are popularly used in various industrial manufacturers because it can bring many advantages to their production process such as work-flows optimization, costs-saving etc. [13]. Researchers in the community have shown that people's daily life will continue to be effectively changed with the deployment of SmartThings (e.g., home monitoring sensors, surveillance cameras, and displays, vehicles) [19]. However, previous study has shown that IoT devices are vulnerable to cyber attack, and sometimes can be utilized by hackers to amplify the attack [12]. For example, [5] reported 20 vulnerabilities found in Samsung SmartThings Hub, which works as a center for managing multiple smart devices by means of Zigbee, Z-Wave, Ethernet, or Bluetooth. Exploiting of such smart device hub can enable attackers to do many malicious actions such as unlock smart locks, spy on people through smart cameras, disable motion

© Springer Nature Singapore Pte Ltd. 2019
W. Meng and S. Furnell (Eds.): SocialSec 2019, CCIS 1095, pp. 152–164, 2019.
https://doi.org/10.1007/978-981-15-0758-8_12

detectors, and even control thermostats. Therefore, it is of great importance to study the security problem of real-world home-based IoT devices.

In this paper, we study one of the in-market household security monitoring devices, which is D-Link Mini HD Wi-Fi Camera. We find that the security camera's working process is vulnerable, which could be exploited to leak users' credential information. The working process is as following. Firstly, users need to connect the security camera. The camera constantly uploads monitoring videos to D-Link's Server, after being connected to Wi-Fi. All the live and history videos are stored on the manufacturer's server. Secondly, users log into the mydlink app to view the monitoring videos. The connections in the whole process are based on TLS Protocol to ensure the data sent through the Internet is encrypted. The data should only be decrypted by the user and the server in the communication.

In order to illustrate the security problem of using D-Link Mini HD Wi-Fi Camera, we demonstrate how to attack the camera. The attacker's goal is to intercept the legitimate user's login information. Then, he can log into this user's account, and view the stored video. The assumption in our demonstration is that the legitimate user has already been tricked into connecting to a malicious Wi-Fi controlled by the attacker, through social-engineering techniques. Once the users log into the mydlink apps, their confidential information such as username and password can be retrieved by the attacker. However, our study discovered that even the attacker retrieved this information, he still cannot log into the legitimate user's account due to extra authentication process implemented by the manufacturer. This extra process contains validating more fields in the login request such as timestamp, signature, and etc. Hence, the extra step for the attacker is to figure out how each of these fields can be forged by reverse-engineering mydlink app. Once the attacker has the ability to change these fields to the correct values, he can forge such log in requests to log into the legitimate users' account. The contributions of this paper are:

- We demonstrate how to forge a TLS certificate that D-Link Mini HD Wi-Fi Camera (model DCS-8000LH) can accept.
- We demonstrate how to forge the login request from mydlink app to bypass the server side authentication process. This is done by reverse-engineering the client side mydlink app.

2   Background

2.1   DNS (Domain Name System)

According to [3], the DNS can resolve a given domain into its corresponding IP address. For example, when a user tries to visit a website www.google.com, before the connection is established, the DNS first translates the domain name into the IP address (e.g., 216.58.196.142).

The DNS working process is described as follows. Once the user in the network has a DNS request, firstly the request is sent to the gateway. If the gateway has the cached DNS record, it will respond to the DNS query directly. If the gateway does not has the cached DNS record, the gateway will do the multiple layered DNS queries as shown in Fig. 1. This process starts from querying the root name server, then layer by layer, to obtain the IP address from the target name server (UWCS in Fig. 1).

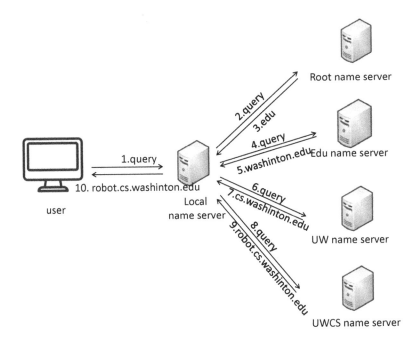

Fig. 1. Multiple layered DNS query

2.2   Transport Layer Security (TLS) Protocol

According to [11], the TLS protocol is a cryptography protocol aimed at improving the computer network's communication security. The server and the client in the TLS protocol use the symmetric key for transmitting data to each other. The symmetric key is negotiated by the client and the server based on the TLS handshake protocol.

The flowchart of the TLS handshake protocol is shown in Fig. 2 [11]. In brief, as in Fig. 2, the steps before the Application Data are referred to as the TLS handshake process. The aim is to make the client and the server agree upon a master secret key, which is used later for generating the symmetric encryption key for the Application Data.

In this paragraph, we briefly introduce the TLS handshake process. As per [11], *ClientHello* and *ServerHello* each contains a random number, which is later used for generating the master secret key and the symmetric encryption key. A

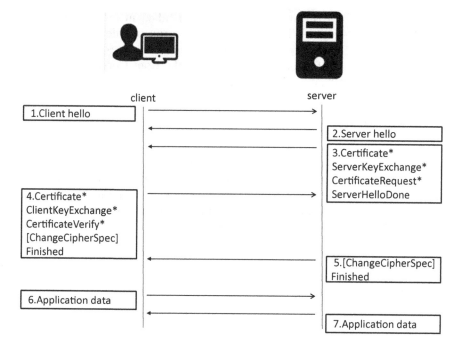

Fig. 2. The TLS handshake protocol

certificate is used for authentication and contains the public key, which can be in either RSA or Diffie-Hellman format. When the public key information is not enough in *Certificate*, *ServerKeyExchange* can provide extra information. After the *ClientKeyExchange*, the client and the server should be able to agree upon a pre-master secret key. Then both sides use this pre-master secret key with the client and server random numbers to generate the master secret key.

2.3   Certificate

As per [15], a certificate is used in the TLS connection for authentication. It binds the identity of a party to a pair of keys. That is, each party can own a certificate, with its public key known to the public, while keeping its private key secret. A party's private key can be used for signing other parties' certificates. Hence, it can be easy to verify that other parties' certificates are signed by that party using the signing party's public key.

2.4   Certificate Authority (CA)

A CA is a party that issues certificates. Each CA owns a certificate that signed by its own private key. This certificate is known as the Root Certificate. This Root Certificate also contains the public key corresponding to its own private key. The CA's Root Certificate is trusted and installed in most browsers and mobile devices by default. When the browsers or the mobile devices connect to a server through TLS protocol, the server usually provides a certificate. To validate the server's certificate, the public key in the Root Certificate is used to check the server's certificate is indeed signed by that Root Certificate.

2.5   Certificate Chain

A certificate chain represents a chain of trust. There are two categories of CAs: root CAs and intermediate CAs. To validate a TLS certificate chain, each node in the chain must be signed by its preceding certificate, and the first node should be signed by Root Certificate. For example, as depicted in Fig. 3 [4], suppose that we have installed the Root Certificates in the browser or the mobile device. We can use the Root Certificate's public key to validate that the Intermediate Certificate is signed by the Root Certificate. Then we can use the Intermediate Certificate's public key to validate that the End-entity Certificate is signed by the Intermediate Certificate. In a similar way, we can validate the remaining part of the certificate chain block by block.

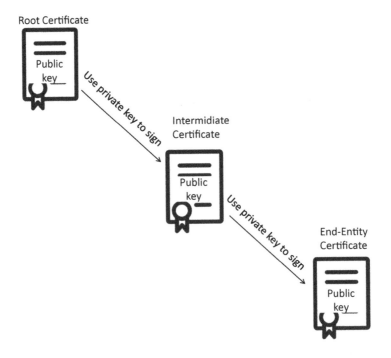

Fig. 3. The trust chain

2.6   Hypertext Transfer Protocol Secure (HTTPS) Protocol

From [16], HTTPS protocol is encrypting the HTTP data by TLS or Secure Sockets Layer (SSL). So HTTPS is also referred to HTTP over TLS or HTTP over SSL. Due to the encryption of the TLS or SSL, HTTPS is considered secure against the man-in-the-middle attack. Analog to HTTP protocol, HTTPS also provides the same set of requests for the client (e.g., GET, POST, PUT, and etc.).

3   Related Work

Many works have been done concerning the cyber attacks on IoT devices. Some of these works focus on the vulnerabilities within the devices, others need the participation of a controlled Wi-Fi. [18] introduced the risk of connecting to a public Wi-Fi, including the attack of Sniffers, Evil Twin, Man-in-the-Middle Attacks, and Sidejacking.

Jyoti et al. [10] summarised the general attack approaches on the IoT devices. This includes physical attacks (e.g., node tampering, RF interference on RFIDs, node jamming in WSNs, malicious node injection, physical damage, social engineering, sleep deprivation attack, and malicious code injection), network attacks (e.g., traffic analysis attacks, RFID spoofing, RFID cloning, RFID unauthorized access, sinkhole attack, man in the middle attacks, denial of service, routing information attacks, sybil attack), software attacks (e.g., phishing attack, virus, worms, trojan horse, spyware and adware, malicious scripts, denial of service), encryption attacks (e.g., Side-Channel attacks, Cryptanalysis Attacks).

Gunes et al. [6] presented two web-based attacks against IoT devices on the local area network (LAN). In the scenario, since the victim IoT devices have open HTTP servers, once they visit a website containing malicious codes, they can be infected.

Zoran et al. [8] introduced the essence of Main In the Middle (MITM) attack used in IoT devices. In this paper, they also included common methods used in a MITM attack. Mauro et al. [9] did a survey on the MITM attack based on different spoofing techniques and different network protocols.

[7] described the Domain name Server (DNS) service and its relevant vulnerabilities, which include cache poisoning. Simar et al. [17] demonstrated various DNS spoofing approaches in more detail in their paper.

Even though the TLS protocol is proved to have high security, it still contains several vulnerabilities. Chris et al. [14] mentioned some of these vulnerabilities, for example, lack of Certificate Pinning.

4   Attacking Demo

4.1   Environment Setting

Gateway. Our gateway is a RaspberryPi, which is connected to the desktop through the SSH protocol, in order to access the Internet. This RaspberryPi also acts as a hotspot, which creates a Wi-Fi, by running the open-sourced program create_ap [1]. In the experiment, our gateway IP address is 192.168.12.1.

DNS Caching. To perform the DNS spoofing, the attacker needs to install the malicious DNS cache into the gateway in advance. To achieve this, when running the create_ap program, we set this program to take into account additional hosts file using the command "-e". Hence we created this additional host file named dnsmasq.hosts, which contains 4 lines:

192.168.12.1	mp-sg-dcdda.auto.mydlink.com
192.168.12.1	api.auto.mydlink.com
192.168.12.1	mp-sg-openapi.auto.mydlink.com
192.168.12.1	mp-sg-dcdda.auto.mydlink

As shown in these lines, when answering the DNS requests, the gateway will resolve the domain names in the right column into the IP address in the left column. Therefore, all these domain names will be resolved into the IP address, 192.168.12.1, which is our gateway.

To open up a hotspot named liuzian with DNS spoofing capability, the attacker types the following line into the command window in the RaspberryPi:
sudo create_ap wlan0 eth0 -e /etc/dnsmasq.hosts liuzian.

4.2 Mydlink App

Mydlink is a mobile app designed for managing home security devices, by the smart camera's manufacturer. A user can combine his account with multiple home devices. As long as their home security devices are connected to the Internet, these devices keep sending monitoring data to the server. When users want to view the device's content, they can log into their accounts to manage their devices. The process behind logging into this app is introduced below.

Once a user opens up his mydlink app on the mobile device and tries to log into the account, the app firstly sends the DNS query about api.auto.mydlink.com to the gateway. The gateway will respond to this query by firstly looking up its cached record. Once such a record exists, the gateway will respond using this record. Otherwise, the gateway starts the multilayered DNS query as shown in Fig. 1.

Once retrieved the IP address in the response, the app tries to establish an HTTPS connection to the server with that IP address. To establish the HTTPS connection, the first step is to establish a TLS connection. After the TLS connection is established, the app will send an HTTP request encrypted by this TLS protocol to the server. The request includes the user-typed username and the MD5-encrypted password, along with other tokens such as the timestamp, the signature and etc., for server-side authentication.

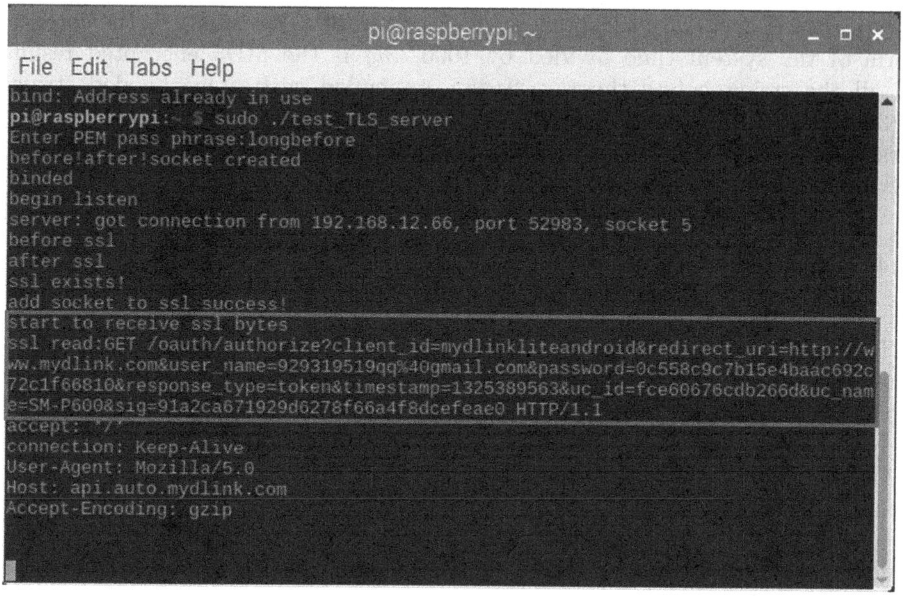

Fig. 4. The account information interception (Color figure online)

4.3   Mydlink App Log in HTTPS Request

As we introduced in the last paragraph, the HTTP request contains many fields. In this paragraph, we will introduce these fields in detail. Figure 4 shows an example of such HTTP request. The HTTP request contains both encrypted fields (e.g., field password is encrypted by MD5 hash) and plain-text fields (e.g., field username). Even though the attacker can obtain the password in cipher form, he is still unable to log into the legitimate user's account, as the server side requires other fields in the request for validation. The HTTP GET request is highlighted in Fig. 4 is as follows:

GET   /oauth/authorize?client_id=mydlinkliteandroid&redirect_uri=http://
www.mydlink.com&user_name=929319519qq%40gmail.com&password=dd71a46
0c42b71c6e9f3fdc578bd6c28&response_type=token&timestamp=1547686112&uc_
id=fce60676cdb266d&uc_name=SM-P600&sig=ec383858369c41f7b901f41d9765f
703   HTTP/1.1

This request contains multiple fields. Among these fields, *client_id*, *response_type*, *uc_id*, and *uc_name* are fixed values depending on the mobile device. They represent the Mydlink app version, response type, device identification, and device name respectively. *User_name* is the plain-text username that the user entered.

Password is the MD5 encrypted account password. *Timestamp* is the integer form of the system time divided by 1000. *Sig* is the MD5 encrypted result of all the string before the tag "&sig", appended with a hard-coded string "83EB5870943E44A1B483C8E9BE5A36BC". The above introductions are all based on the reverse-engineer analysis of the Android mydlink app, which is performed using Android Studio.

4.4   Charles Proxy

According to [2], Charles is an HTTP proxy. It helps the user to debug the HTTP/HTTPS connections by deploying between the user and the server. Installing the Charles Root Certificate on the user side ensures the connection between the user and Charles can be set up. To establish the connection to the server, Charles forges the Certificate Chain according to the original Certificate Chain provided by the user, which maximizes the possibility that the server can accept this certificate.

Once Charles is deployed between the user and the server, it provides multiple functionalities to the user such as blocking requests, modifying requests in both directions and etc.

4.5   Scenario

Our experiment scenario is that the legitimate user is tricked into connecting to a malicious Wi-Fi. Initially, the legitimate user is tricked into connecting to the server in step 1. We deliberately set the fake DNS records as in subsection *DNS caching*. As a result, in step 2, a forged DNS record is used as the response to the DNS query. So the app will regard the gateway as the server and tries to set up the TLS connection with the gateway as in step 3. In order to accept this TLS connection, the attacker runs a TLS server program on the gateway. Due to the app side authentication request, the attacker needs to prepare a forged certificate chain on the server side as 4. After the app side's validation, the TLS connection is established. Now the server side can decrypt the HTTPS data sent in 5 using the symmetric TLS key. The program on the server side is also programmed to be able to record the plain-text HTTPS data through this TLS connection (Fig. 5).

4.6   Attacking Steps

Forging the Certificate. As denoted in Fig. 2, in some cases, within the TLS handshake protocol, the certificate authentication only occurs at one side. Since in our assumed attacking scenario, the attacker uses the fake server (gateway) to send a fake certificate chain to the user, the attacker needs to imitate the original Certificate Chain to forge the fake one. Figure 6 depicts the original certificate chain sent from the real server that is to be validated by the mydlink app in the normal scenario.

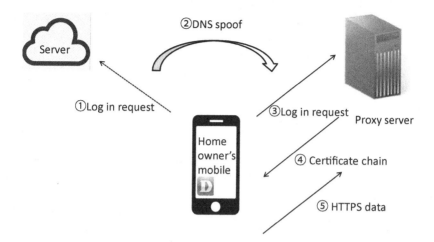

Fig. 5. The flowchart of our experiment scenario

▷ Certificate:(id-at-commonName=*.auto.mydlink.com,id-at-organizationName
  Certificate
▷ Certificate:(id-at-commonName=GlobalSign Organization Validation CA - SI
  Certificate
▷ Certificate:(id-at-commonName=GlobalSign Root CA,id-at-organizationalUn

Fig. 6. Server's certificate chain in normal scenario

```
(id-at-countryName=BE)
(id-at-organizationName=GlobalSign nv-sa)
(id-at-organizationalUnitName=Root CA)
(id-at-commonName=GlobalSign Root CA)
```

Fig. 7. The Root Certificate

```
(id-at-countryName=BE)
(id-at-organizationName=GlobalSign nv-sa)
(id-at-commonName=GlobalSign Organization Validation CA - SHA256)
```

Fig. 8. The Intermediate Certificate

The server's certificate chain shown in Fig. 6 contains 3 certificates. The Root Certificate is GlobalSign Root, its information is shown in Fig. 7.

The second certificate is signed by the Root Certificate, also known as the Intermediate Certificate. Its information is shown in Fig. 8.

The last certificate in the chain is signed by the Intermediate Certificate. This certificate is owned by the mydlink corporation and also known as the End-entity Certificate. Its information is depicted in Fig. 9.

```
(id-at-countryName=TW)
(id-at-stateOrProvinceName=Taipei)
(id-at-localityName=Taipei)
(id-at-organizationalUnitName=IT Dept)
(id-at-organizationName=D-Link Corporation)
(id-at-commonName=*.auto.mydlink.com)
```

Fig. 9. The End-entity Certificate

Based on the observations described above, we can forge the certificate chain. The forged End-entity Certificate should be forged to at least contain the same value of commonName, organizationName, organizationUnitName, localityName, stateOrProvinceName, and contryName in the legitimate End-entity Certificate. At this stage, we do not know the server side certificate authentication process, which means there might be additional validation on the Intermediate Certificate or Root Certificate. Hence we try to guess how to forge it from the minimum requirements. This minimum requirement assumes that the server side only validates the End-entity certificate's fields, such as commonName, organizationName, organizationUnitName, localityName, stateOrProvinceName, and contryName.

To test and improve our guessing benchmark, we have performed the experiment on an Android device, Samsung Galaxy Note 10.1. Since the Android mydlink app only trusts the system certificate, in the real attack, we can purchase a legitimate Intermediate Certificate from one of the Android trusted root CAs. Then we can use our purchased Intermediate Certificate to sign the End-entity Certificate. However, in the experiment, for simplicity, we replaced this step with an equivalent step, by creating our own Root Certificate and embedding it into the system trusted store. Then we used our created Root Certificate to forge the certificate chain. Our forged certificate chain is depicted in Fig. 10.

```
▷ Certificate: 3082045b30820243a003020102020209009060fd325e29b0e2... (id-at-commonName=*.auto.mydlink.com,id-at-organizati
  Certificate Length: 1295
▷ Certificate: 3082050b308202f3a003020102021100abc49193d9427913... (id-at-organizationName=Example,id-at-countryName=GB)
```

Fig. 10. The forged Certificate Chain

The forged certificate chain contains 2 certificates. We discarded the Intermediate Certificate in the forged chain because we started our guessing from the minimum requirement, that the server side only validates the End-entity certificate. The Root Certificate's information is shown in Fig. 11.

The End-entity Certificate is directly signed by our Root Certificate. Its information is depicted in Fig. 12.

Intercepting HTTPS Information on the Gateway. As introduced before, since we have forged the DNS cached record, when the Android app tries to set

```
(id-at-countryName=GB)
(id-at-organizationName=Example)
```

Fig. 11. The forged Root Certificate

```
(id-at-countryName=TW)
(id-at-stateOrProvinceName=Taipei)
(id-at-localityName=Taipei)
(id-at-organizationName=D-Link Corporation)
(id-at-organizationalUnitName=IT Dept)
(id-at-commonName=*.auto.mydlink.com)
```

Fig. 12. The forged End-entity Certificate

up the TLS connection and send the user account information to the server, it actually connects to the gateway. On the fake server (gateway), we opened up a C program that will listen to and accept the TLS connecting request. The functionality of this C program is introduced here. After the mydlink app connects to this program, this C program will record all the information sent through this connection in plain-text form. In order to set up the connection with the app, this program will send the forged certificate chain. In our experiment the TLS handshake was successful. The intercepted HTTPS request is introduced in *Mydlink app log in HTTPS request.*

Logging into Legitimate User's Account. At this step, the attacker has obtained the legitimate user's account information, but it is not enough for intruding into the user's account. After reverse engineering, we found that except username and password, the server side also validates the signature and timestamp. Hence to forge the HTTPS request, two more fields (timestamp and sig) need to be modified. Therefore we have implemented a simple Javascript program to refresh the real-time timestamp value for our reference. The timestamp value is updated on the web page every second.

To forge the request, the attacker only needs to calculate the *timestamp* and *sig* in advance. The rules for modifying these two fields are also manually written into Charles by us ahead. For example, since at this stage, we know how the app produces each of these fields if a user sends the login request 5 min later. We can instantly calculate the value of each these fields if it is being sent 5 min later. Then we tell Charles what value each field is to be modified to. Then we manually send the login request in 5 min. Charles will stop the request and modify each field to the desired value before sending it to the server.

5   Conclusion

In this paper, we have demonstrated a possible attack on the Wi-Fi camera. Our assuming scenario is that the attacker can trick the user into connecting to a malicious Wi-Fi. Then the attacker uses reverse engineering results and the intercepted account data to intrude into the user's account. We have shown that even though the communication protocol the smart device based on is secure enough, a cyber attack is still possible using other measures together with social engineering techniques. The smart device manufacturers should implement a more complex authentication process for the TLS certificate on the app side. The users should always be aware of the Wi-Fi security they are connected to.

References

1. https://github.com/oblique/create_ap . Accessed 05 Dec 2018
2. https://www.charlesproxy.com/. Accessed 24 Nov 2018
3. What is DNS?—How DNS works. https://www.cloudflare.com/learning/dns/what-is-dns/. Accessed 20 Nov 2018
4. How certificate chains work (2018). https://knowledge.digicert.com/solution/SO16297.html. Accessed 28 Nov 2018
5. Researchers reveal 20 vulnerabilities in Samsung Smartthings Hub (2018). https://www.csoonline.com/article/3292942/researchers-reveal-20-vulnerabilities-in-samsung-smartthings-hub.html. Accessed 28 Jan 2019
6. Acar, G., Huang, D.Y., Li, F., Narayanan, A., Feamster, N.: Web-based attacks to discover and control local IoT devices. In: IoT S&P@SIGCOMM (2018)
7. Al-Hajeri, A.: DNS spoofing attack support of the cyber defense initiative (2014)
8. Cekerevac, Z., Dvorak, Z., Prigoda, L., Cekerevac, P.: Internet of things and the man-in-the-middle attacks-security and economic risks. MEST J. 5(2), 15–25 (2017)
9. Conti, M., Dragoni, N., Lesyk, V.: A survey of man in the middle attacks. IEEE Commun. Surv. Tutor. 18(3), 2027–2051 (2016)
10. Deogirikar, J., Vidhate, A.: Security attacks in IoT: a survey. In: 2017 International Conference on I-SMAC (IoT in Social, Mobile, Analytics and Cloud) (I-SMAC), pp. 32–37, February 2017
11. Dierks, T., Allen, C.: The TLS protocol version 1.0. Technical report (1998)
12. Kolias, C., Kambourakis, G., Stavrou, A., Voas, J.: DDoS in the IoT: Mirai and other botnets. Computer 50, 80–84 (2017)
13. Lee, I., Lee, K.: The Internet of Things (IoT): applications, investments, and challenges for enterprises. Bus. Horiz. 58, 431–440 (2015)
14. Stone, C.M., Chothia, T., Garcia, F.: Spinner: semi-automatic detection of pinning without hostname verification, pp. 176–188 (2017)
15. Prodromou, A.: TLS/SSL Explained – TLS/SSL Certificates, Part 4 (2017). https://www.acunetix.com/blog/articles/tls-ssl-certificates-part-4/. Accessed 23 Nov 2018
16. Rescorla, E.: HTTP over TLS. Technical report (2000)
17. Preet Singh, S., Maini, A.: Spoofing attacks of domain name system internet (2011)
18. Private WiFi: The hidden dangers of public WiFi (2014)
19. Zanella, A., Bui, N., Castellani, A., Vangelista, L., Zorzi, M.: Internet of things for smart cities. IEEE Internet Things J. 1(1), 22–32 (2014)

Retrieve the Hidden Leaves in the Forest: Prevent Voting Spamming in Zhihu

Jun Zhang$^{(\boxtimes)}$ and Houda Labiod$^{(\boxtimes)}$

INFRES, Telecom Paris, Institut Polytechnique de Paris, Paris, France
{jun.zhang,houda.labiod}@telecom-paris.fr

Abstract. Nowadays, more and more people start posting their opinions on online social networks, such as commercial product evaluation websites, forums, and crowdsourcing $Q\&A$ websites. In practice, most majority vote schemes cannot reveal the true distribution of opinions, due to the spam problem. Many public relationship companies can recruit people or use automatic commenting machines to promote target products and ruin the reputation of their opponents. In such a sense, the opinions on these websites may not be reliable. In the literature, there are a lot of studies contributed to detect such spams, based on the characteristics of posted content, social relationship, user activity, posting time, etc. We find that most spam detection schemes rely heavily on the experience and preference of experts. This is dangerously as it can lead to bias and dictatorship. In this work, we take Zhihu - one popular Chinese $Q\&A$ website as a case study, and propose a *time diversity* based voting scheme to reduce the impact of voting spamming. We illustrate that, our proposed opinion tolerant system can maintain a good balance in the appearance of different opinions.

Keywords: Social networks · Question and answer community · Ranking algorithm · Spam

1 Introduction

In the era of Web 1.0, the communication is often single directional. People can only read static documents posted by the creators of websites. Their relationship is similar to consumer/producer. The situation has been improved significantly in the era of Web 2.0. Users are allowed to interact with each other by posting text or multimedia content. Lots of websites based on user generated content grow up in this era, such as youtube [12], wikis [11], forums, and blogs. In order to organize massive information over the Internet, these websites may employ different evaluation mechanisms to control the visibility of information, based on users' comment (voting up or voting down). The posts that get higher ranks have higher chances to be propagated. Websites for online shopping and production evaluation, such as Amazon [1], Ebay [2], IMDb [5] also rely on users' comments to quantify the quality of products. Recently, the crowdsourcing

© Springer Nature Singapore Pte Ltd. 2019
W. Meng and S. Furnell (Eds.): SocialSec 2019, CCIS 1095, pp. 165–180, 2019.
https://doi.org/10.1007/978-981-15-0758-8_13

Q&A websites become popular, such as Quora [8], Stack Overflow [9], and Zhihu [13]. In a crowdsourcing manner, people submit questions to such websites, and corresponding answers are evaluated by other users.

Traditional comment/opinion evaluation mechanism is based on the wisdom of majority, i.e., opinions that get more agreement are thought to be more reliable/close to the truth/representative. However, due to the impact of OSNs (online social networks), product evaluation websites, and crowdsourcing $Q\&A$ websites, many professional public relationship companies start to post untruthful information and evaluation on these sites to affect the preference of users who trust the credibility of these websites. The majority rule does not work under this mechanism, as it is easy to create an account online and is cheap to buy an account (or recruit people) to post biased information [23, 27].

In this paper, we investigate the vulnerability of voting system for the current crowdsourcing $Q\&A$ websites, and take the voting campaign in Zhihu [13] as a case study. We analyze the statistics related to the distribution of answers and votes, and show that Zhihu's current ranking policy may cause bias in the visibility of answers with different opinions. In general, it is hard to judge that whether a user is a spammer or not if he plays the game smartly. Instead of proposing a spam detection system, we propose a spam tolerant voting system, which can maintain answers' diversity, to encourage good answers with better chance to be displayed.

The organization of the paper is as follows. In Sect. 2 we present our motivation to analyze the spam attacks on crowdsourcing $Q\&A$ websites. In Sect. 3, we take the voting campaign from Zhihu [13] as a case study. In Sect. 4, we propose a spam-tolerant voting system and evaluate its performance. Finally, we conclude the paper in Sect. 5.

2   Our Motivation

2.1   Introduction on Crowdsourcing $Q\&A$ Websites

A typical crowdsourcing $Q\&A$ website, such as Quora [8], Stack Overflow [9], and Zhihu [13] operates in the following manner. Users are allowed to raise questions, post comment on questions or answers, and vote up or vote down answers. Each question is attached with several topics, so that users can access similar questions that belong to the same topic. Users can follow other users, so that the activity of the followed users can appear in their timeline. The ranking of answers relies on how many voteups and votedowns are received by them, in addition to some other criteria, such as the aging of the answer, the weight of voters, etc.

Below are some unique features making crowdsourcing $Q\&A$ websites different from other types of online social networks.

– Compared with user-centric online social network, such as twitter [10] and facebook [3], $Q\&A$ websites are more content-centric. Registered users can access the answers even when they do not have a connection with other users. For certain $Q\&A$ websites, even unregistered users have access to answers.

- Compared with websites on product evaluation, such as Amazon [1] and IMDb [5], answers in *Q&A* websites do not have explicit scores on the question.
- For tradition forums, threads are often ranked in either ascending or descending orders according to when the threads are generated. In comparison, answers in *Q&A* websites are ranked according to how many voteups and votedowns are received, while ranking policies may be different from site to site.

2.2 Spam Detection Difficulty in Crowdsourcing Q&A Websites

Similar to Twitter [10] and Facebook [3], crowdsourcing *Q&A* websites are not immune to spamming attacks by nature. Public relationship companies can recruit people or use programs like "Internet Water Army" [15], to generate biased answers, and maliciously vote answers up or down, to maximize the influence of promotion or defame their opponents.

The traditional spam detection schemes may not perform well for such crowdsourcing *Q&A* websites, due to the following reasons:

Disadvantage of connectivity-based schemes: The schemes based on the connectivity between users, such as SybilGuard [32], SybilLimit [31], Sybil-Infer [18], SybilDefender [28], and Sybil shield [22], detect spam users based on the assumption that the community of spam users are sparsely connected with normal communities. However, in practise, it is difficult to identify normal users since the network ID is not bound to the real personal ID. In addition, users can post answers directly in *Q&A* websites, without propagating information to the whole online social network. Spammers can communicate with each other via various applications, hiding the real connections between them.

Disadvantage of feature-based schemes: In the literature, there are many studies using machine learning algorithms to help detect spams based on the features in online social network, such as [16, 19–21, 25, 26, 30, 33]. In particular, content-based features can be used to detect spam messages, and user-based features can be used to detect spammers. Some typical features include the number of URLs and pictures contained in the message, the number of similar message pairs, the number of followees/followers, the generation time of messages, and the behavior of users reflected by the state transition graph in the clickstream model in [25, 30]. However, it is hard to apply these approaches for detecting spams in Q&A websites, due to the following reasons. (1) The training examples require explicitly labeling both spams and non-spams. This heavily relies on the experience and preference of experts. Such dependence is dangerous as it can lead to bias and dictatorship, according to the Arrow's impossible theorem [14]. (2) More publication relationship companies tend to recruit normal users to send bias answers, or give bias votes occasionally. These users are very difficult to be detected based on just their average performance. (3) Some malicious users can manipulate the rank of answers by sending a large amount of voteups or votedowns. Since they do not send answers, these spams may not be detected by those schemes based on the content-based features.

3   A Case Study of the Voting Campaign in Zhihu

In this section, we present a case study based on a typical Chinese $Q\&A$ website named Zhihu [13]. We briefly introduce its voting system in Sect. 3.1, and we then show that such a system is easily to be cheated by spammers in Sect. 3.2. As an example, we illustrate the statistics of one voting campaign in Sect. 3.3.

3.1   Voting System in Zhihu

The system of Zhihu [13] composes of three parts: questions, answers and users. Questions and their associated answers are categorized by themes. The answers corresponding to a certain question are ordered by either the ranking policy defined by Zhihu, or by time. Users can choose to follow other users, so that they can observe their recent actions (raising question/answering/commenting/voting). They can also be informed of new questions and answers by following certain themes (topics). Based on the behavior, a user can act as a questioner, respondent (writer), voter, or a commenter. The voter can send voteups or votedowns to answers, which can influence the ranking of answers. A respondent (writer) is regarded as a voter who votes up for himself automatically. An example of one $Q\&A$ session in Zhihu is shown in Fig. 1.

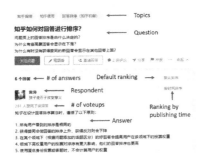

Fig. 1. An example of one $Q\&A$ session in Zhihu

Considering one $Q\&A$ voting campaign for a certain question, we denote the set of answers as $A = \{a_1, a_2, \ldots, a_m\}$, the set of corresponding respondents (writers) as $W = \{w_1, w_2, \ldots, w_m\}$, and the set of all voters as $V = \{v_1, v_2, \ldots, v_n\}$. The publishing time of each answer a_i is denoted as $T(a_i)$. We define *supporting voters* for a certain answer a_i, as the set of voters that send voteups to the answer a_i, denoted as $V^{up}(a_i)$; and *opposing voters* for the answer a_i, as the set of voters that send votedowns to the answer a_i, denoted as $V^{dn}(a_i)$.

$A^{up}(v_i)$ and $A^{dn}(v_i)$ denote the set of answers that are voted up or voted down by the voter v_i, respectively.

The normalized supporting ratio of each answer a_i is

$$\hat{p}(a_i) = \frac{\sum_{j \in V^{up}(a_i)} (e_j) + e_i}{\sum_{j \in V^{up}(a_i)} (e_j) + \sum_{j \in V^{dn}(a_i)} (e_j) + e_i}, \tag{1}$$

such that the efficient e_i is relevant to its past behavior of user v_i, like the number of its voteups and votedowns received in the past.

According to the official response in [4], the ranking policy in Zhihu is inspired by the Wilson interval [29], which is a generation of the supporting ratio even when the size of samples is small. The score of one answer a_i is the minimal bound of the Wilson interval for its normalized supporting ratio, that is

$$score(a_i) = \frac{1}{1 + \frac{1}{k(a_i)} z^2} \tag{2}$$

$$\times \left[\hat{p}(a_i) + \frac{1}{2k(a_i)} z^2 - z \sqrt{\frac{1}{k(a_i)} \hat{p}(a_i)(1 - \hat{p}(a_i)) + \frac{1}{4k(a_i)^2} z^2} \right].$$

Here $k(a_i) = |V^{up}(a_i)| + |V^{dn}(a_i)| + 1$ is the number of voters who have a judgement of the answer a_i, and z is the parameter to decide the confidence interval, which is set as 1.96 in general for 95% confidence. All answers are ranked according to their scores in the descending order.

3.2 Spammers in Zhihu

The Wilson interval based ranking policy in Zhihu tries to give a higher possibility for answers that receive less voteups to be visible, preventing users who have many followers to be the dominate respondents. For example, suppose an answer a_1 receives 1000 voteups and 200 votedowns, and an answer a_2 receives 10 voteups and 1 votedown. The latter has a higher rank under Zhihu's policy, since it has a larger support from its readers. However, such system may fail to reveal the true distribution of opinions when there exist spammers.

Taking the popular chatting software QQ [7] as an example, there are many groups in QQ that recruit spammers for Zhihu. These groups recruit people to send voteups or votedowns to certain answers, as shown in Fig. 2.

These groups can strictly control the number of followers for a dedicate user, and the number of voteups for a dedicate answer. Therefore, under this condition, it is very hard to distinguish whether a user with more followers is a trusted user, and whether an answer with more voteups is of high quality. Moreover, these groups also offer the business to recruit people to maliciously send votedowns, and write biased answers, with a higher payment.

To ensure the effect, the organizer of spammers tend to recruit users that have good record in Zhihu, and require these users to behave normally when they execute the action (following/voting/writing), i.e., leaving the corresponding pages open for at least one minute. In this case, such spammers cannot be

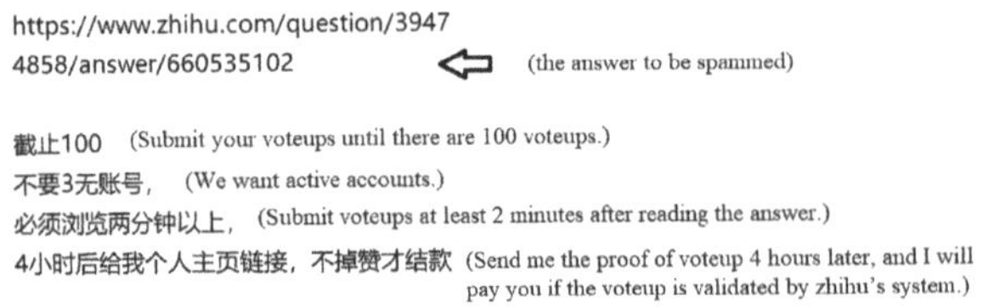

https://www.zhihu.com/question/3947
4858/answer/660535102   ⇐   (the answer to be spammed)

截止100   (Submit your voteups until there are 100 voteups.)
不要3无账号,   (We want active accounts.)
必须浏览两分钟以上,   (Submit voteups at least 2 minutes after reading the answer.)
4小时后给我个人主页链接, 不掉赞才结款 (Send me the proof of voteup 4 hours later, and I will
                                          pay you if the voteup is validated by zhihu's system.)

Fig. 2. An example of recruiting spammers to send voteups for one answer in Zhihu

easily detected by either the feature-based spammer detection schemes, or the clickstream-based models [25,30].

3.3   Study of a Voting Campaign in Zhihu

To observe how spammers work in Zhihu, we study one $Q\&A$ voting campaign in Zhihu from [6]. The question is about "whether genetic modified organism (GMO) is harmful to the health or the environment?". Up to 2017/10/17, we collect 120 answers (not including those are folded), which received 3048 voteups from 2656 different voters. Due to the system settings, the number of votedowns is not visible to public. Thus, in the following, the voters is considered as supporting voters by default.

Since this question is a Yes-No one, we manually divide answers into three groups: *Pro, Con*, and *Mid*, which respectively represents that *"supporting the idea that GMO is risky"*, *"against the idea that GMO is risky"*, and *"not sure"*. For each answer a_i, we define its idea (preference/attitude) as

$$I(a_i) = 1, a_i \text{ is in the } Pro \text{ group} \tag{3}$$
$$= 0, a_i \text{ is in the } Mid \text{ group}$$
$$= -1, a_i \text{ is in the } Con \text{ group.}$$

We also divide voters into three groups: *Pro, Con*, and *Mid*, based on their average opinions. For each voter v_i, we define its idea according its average preference in answers (i.e., the set of answers that it sends voteups), because votedowns is invisible. We define the idea of a voter v_i as

$$I(v_i) = \sum_{a \in A^{up}(v_i)} I(a)/|A^{up}(v_i)|. \tag{4}$$

v_i is assigned to the *Pro* group when $I(v_i) \geq 0.5$, to the *Con* group when $I(v_i) \leq -0.5$, and to the *Mid* group otherwise.

Distribution and Visibility of Answers. Table 1 shows the statistics of the number of answers and voteups belonging to different groups. We can see the posting rate is far from a constant, but rather busty. More than half of the answers were posted at the date 2017/10/7, and more than 80% of answers were posted in the nearby three days. In other days, the number of answers per day is usually not bigger than four. The answers in the *Pro* and *Con* groups are more busty than the *Mid* group, possibly due to the communities in these two groups. However, it is still hard to tell an answer posted in the peak dates was from a spammer or not, as the number of answers posted from different groups are balanced.

Nevertheless, answers were not balanced regarding voteups. More than half of the answers received zeros voteup, and more than 85% answers received less than 10 voteups. The number of voteups received by answers in different groups were quite imbalanced. We observe that respondents show a smaller interest in judging other answers, especially the respondents in the *Mid* group. As a result, the votes from respondents contribute marginally on the total number of voteups.

Table 1. Statistics of answers and voteups by groups

Distribution of answers by dates					Distribution of received voteups by answers			
Date	# of answers	Groups of answers						
		Pro	Mid	Con				
9/3	1		1		Range of received voteups		Groups of answers	
10/4	8	3	2	3			Pro	Mid	Con
10/5	1		1		≥ 81	0	0	4
10/6	12	8		4	41-80	0	2	2
10/7	62	14	26	22	11-40	6	1	2
10/8	24	10	8	6	1-10	8	7	10
10/9	3		3		0	21	38	19
10/10	1		1		Total received voteups	158	190	2725
10/11	1		1					
10/12	4		3	1	Voteups from respondents (excluding self voteups)	19	7	18
10/16	1			1				
10/17	2		2					
In total	120	35	48	37				

The imbalanced assignment of voteups may result in a appearance loss of the diversity of answers. As quoted in [17][1], burying an answer can be achieved by sending many votedowns and creating certain amount of answers to hide it from readers. This is because an answer with a lower ranking has a lower possibility to be visible.

We show the imbalance of the appearance of answers in Table 2. The left part shows the top 25 answers ranked by the policy in Zhihu, and the right part shows the top 25 answers ranked by the amount of voteups received. In the top

---

[1] Where does a wise man hide a leaf? In the forest. But what does he do if there is no forest? He grows a forest to hide it in.
By G.K. Chesterton, The Innocence of Father Brown, [17].

Table 2. Top 25 answers by different ranking policies

By Zhihu's ranking policy			By voteups		
Order	Group	Voteups	Order	Group	Voteups
1	**Con**	2114	1	**Con**	2114
2	**Con**	104	2	**Con**	175
3	Mid	76	3	**Con**	146
4	**Con**	146	4	**Con**	104
5	Mid	75	5	**Con**	79
6	**Con**	53	6	Mid	76
7	**Con**	175	7	Mid	75
8	**Con**	16	8	**Con**	53
9	Mid	31	9	Pro	35
10	**Con**	79	10	Mid	31
11	Mid	0	11	Pro	30
12	**Con**	10	12	Pro	26
13	**Con**	1	13	Pro	17
14	**Con**	6	14	**Con**	16
15	**Con**	0	15	**Con**	13
16	Pro	26	16	Pro	11
17	Pro	17	17	Pro	11
18	Pro	11	18	Pro	10
19	Pro	35	19	**Con**	10
20	Pro	5	20	Pro	6
21	Pro	30	21	Pro	5
22	**Con**	3	22	**Con**	3
23	**Con**	3	23	**Con**	3
24	Mid	2	24	Pro	3
25	Pro	10	25	**Con**	2

25 answers ranked by Zhihu's policy, the answers in the *Con* group dominate the top 10 list, while the answers in the *Pro* group have a quite low ranking. All the answers in the *Pro* group are ranked lower even than two answers that receive zero voteup (the 11th answer and the 15th answer). We also can see that, two answers in the *Mid* group with 76 and 31 voteups cannot appear in the top 25. This indicates that, quite a few answers in the *Mid* group and the *Con* group received many votedowns.

We use the metric *diversity of visibility* to formally illustrate the extent of the balance of ideas (opinions) among groups, as shown in Appendix A. The value of *diversity of visibility* for k groups is between 1 and k, while a larger *diversity of visibility* indicates the visibility of ideas from different groups are more balanced.

We compare the *diversity of visibility* for four ranking policies: Zhihu's policy, ranking by number of voteups in the descending order, ranking by time in the ascending order (past first), and ranking by time in the descending order (current first). The set of answers are selected from top t ones, where $t \in [5, 10, 15, 20, 25]$. As shown in Table 3, Zhihu's policy in general has a lower diversity of visibility. This is because answers in the *Con* group dominate the appearance. The diversity by the voteup policy is marginal better than the Zhihu's policy, showing that it provides better resistance to the voting spamming attack. When answers are ordered by time, the diversity can achieve a similar level close to three, indicating that readers are possible to retrieve answers from different groups. We notice that, the visibility by time- for the top5 or top10 answers is low, while it is acceptable as most answers in such a case are in the *Mid* group.

Table 3. Diversity of visibility by different ranking policies (Decay factor $\lambda = 0.8$). time+: ranked by time in ascending order, time−: ranked by time in descending order.

Policy	Diversity of visibility				
	Top 5	Top 10	Top 15	Top 20	Top 25
Zhihu	1.9	1.8	1.9	2.1	2.1
voteup	1	1.8	2.0	2.1	2.1
time+	3.0	3.0	3.0	3.0	3.0
time−	1.9	1.3	2.8	2.6	2.8

Distribution of Voters. In Table 4, we summarize the distribution of voters by their preference in answers and the numbers of voteups sent by them. We can find that most voters only send one or two voteups. Therefore, it is hard to distinguish normal voters and spam voters. The latter can launch a voting campaign by cooperatively sending a large amount of voteups or votedowns, to intentionally raise or reduce particular answers. Voters who are more active are not necessarily spammers, as they do not contribute too much in the total voting.

Table 4. Distribution of voters that send h voteups, $h \in [1, 15]$

h	Voters by group		
	Pro	Mid	Con
1	77	89	2250
2	7	46	103
3	7	8	39
$4 \leq h \leq 15$	5	9	16

4   Spam-Tolerant Voting System

As it is hard to detect spamming answers and spamming voters directly from their behavior, it is more desirable to design a voting system that is tolerant to the voting spamming attacks. In this section, we propose the concept of *time diversity* and *idea diversity*, which can investigate the interaction between voters and answers. Then we propose the voting system based on such diversities, which can achieve a high diversity of visibility between different groups.

4.1   Idea Diversity

We introduce the concept of *idea diversity* to measure whether an answer is maliciously biased. Each answer is derived by the diversity of the ideas of the supporting voters for the corresponding answer. The intuition is that, an answer that receives voteups from groups with different ideas is less likely to be promoted by spammers.

We define the friend set of an answer a_i, $F(a_i)$, as the set of answers that receive voteups from a_i's supporting voters, i.e., $F(a_i) = \{a \in A^{up}(v)|v \in V^{up}(a_i)\}$.

Then the friend set by ideas can be defined as

$$F_{Pro}(a_i) = \{a \in \sum_{v \in V^{up}(a_i)} A(v)|I(a) = 1\},$$

$$F_{Mid}(a_i) = \{a \in \sum_{v \in V^{up}(a_i)} A(v)|I(a) = 0\},$$

$$F_{Con}(a_i) = \{a \in \sum_{v \in V^{up}(a_i)} A(v)|I(a) = -1\}. \tag{5}$$

Let $\phi(v, a)$ denote the binary indices to represent the interaction between the voter v and the answer a. $\phi(v, a) = 1$ means that the voter v sends a voteup to the answer a, and $\phi(v, a) = 0$ otherwise. Then the total amount of voteups received by a group of answers g from a_j's supporting voters $V^{up}(a_j)$ is

$$w_g(a_i) = \sum_{v \in V^{up}(a_i), a \in g} \phi(v, a). \tag{6}$$

Let $G_{idea}(a_i) = \{F_{Pro}(a_i), F_{Mid}(a_i), F_{Con}(a_i)\}$ denote the idea-based set of groups of friend answers of a_i, we define *idea-based voteup ratio* of each group $g \in G_{idea}(a_i)$ as

$$q_{idea}(g, a_i) = \frac{w_g(a_i)}{\sum_{g' \in G_{idea}(a_i)} w_{g'}(a_i)}, \tag{7}$$

The *idea diversity* $D_{idea}(a_i)$ for each answer a_i can be computed as

$$D_{idea}(a_i) = \exp\left(-\sum_{g \in G_{idea}} q_{idea}(g, a_i) \ln(q_{idea}(g, a_i))\right). \tag{8}$$

4.2   Time Diversity

It is subjective to measure the idea diversity for answers depends on personal preference. Therefore, we introduce another concept of *time diversity* to measure the diversity of supporting voters for a certain answer in a more objective manner.

The definition of *time diversity* is similar to *idea diversity*, except for the groups of friend set. For each answer a_i, its friend set is divided by time into three groups as

$$F_-(a_i) = \{a \in \sum_{v \in V^{up}(a_i)} A(v) | T(a) < T(a_i) - \varepsilon\},$$

$$F_0(a_i) = \{a \in \sum_{v \in V^{up}(a_i)} A(v) | |T(a) - T(a_i)| \leq \varepsilon\},$$

$$F_+(a_i) = \{a \in \sum_{v \in V^{up}(a_i)} A(v) | T(a) > T(a_i) + \varepsilon\}. \tag{9}$$

The publishing time of answer a, $T(a)$ is calculated in the virtual unit, i.e., the ascending order of the posting time. The variable ε is used to specify the range of answers that can be considered as posted during the same period.

The corresponding *time-based voteup ratio* of each group $g \in G_{time}(a_i)$ is

$$q_{time}(g, a_i) = \frac{\omega_g(a_i)}{\sum_{g' \in G_{time}(a_i)} \omega_{g'}(a_i)}, \tag{10}$$

where $G_{time}(a_i) = \{F_-(a_i), F_0(a_i), F_+(a_i)\}$ denotes the idea-based set of groups of friend answers of a_i,

The *time diversity* $D_{time}(a_i)$ for each answer a_i can be computed as

$$D_{time}(a_i) = \exp\left(-\sum_{g \in G_{time}} q_{time}(g, a_i) \ln(q_{time}(g, a_i))\right). \tag{11}$$

Considering the voting campaign in [6], we study the relationship between *idea diversity* and *idea diversity* when ε is set as 0 and 10, respectively. We observe a high correlation between these two kinds of diversity, i.e., 0.9383 for $\varepsilon = 0$, and 0.9451 for $\varepsilon = 10$. This is because spamming voters usually vote once, and their voted answers usually both have a lower *time diversity* and *idea diversity*. This phenomenon indicates that *time diversity* should be a good approximator for *idea diversity*.

4.3   Evaluation Based on Time Diversity

Considering that *time diversity* can well approximate *idea diversity*, we propose to use it as the ranking metric to rank answers in order to avoid loss of diversity of ideas, under the voting spamming attack. Intuitively, a voter that votes for answers posted in different periods is less likely to be burst and its voted answer is less likely to be a spammer.

The time diversity based voting system only uses voteups rather than both voteups and votedowns, as voteups are already sufficient to express the idea of voters, while votedowns can be maliciously used to lower targeted answers. In this system, all answers are sorted in the descending order of their *time diversities*.

Table 5. Diversity of visibility by different ranking policy (Decay factor $\lambda = 0.8$) (TD (time diversity), ID(idea diversity))

Policy		Diversity of visibility				
		Top 5	Top 10	Top 15	Top 20	Top 25
TD	ε					
	0	1.98	2.00	2.00	2.11	2.12
	1	2.85	2.73	2.69	2.69	2.70
	2	2.85	2.79	2.73	2.74	2.74
	3	2.85	2.75	2.69	2.69	2.69
	4	2.85	2.75	2.70	2.69	2.70
	5	2.42	2.63	2.57	2.58	2.59
ID		2.66	2.92	2.94	2.95	2.95
Zhihu		1.86	1.80	1.91	2.06	2.08
voteup	1		1.82	2.03	2.09	2.10

Scenarios Regarding the Campaign in [6]. We evaluate the performance in terms of both the diversity of visibility and the time diversity, as shown in Table 5, for the same campaign of [6].

We found that, by increasing ε from zero to one, there is a significant increase in the diversity of visibility. This is because it punishes busty voting for sequential answers that express similar ideas. Compared with the ranking policy by Zhihu, our *time diversity* based voting scheme has a better performance in general. For $\varepsilon = 2$, the proposed scheme achieves a similar performance as the *idea diversity* based scheme.

Synthetic Scenarios. We further investigate the performance of our voting system in a synthetic scenario. We consider that there are 120 answers, and the number of voters are 3000. We equally divide the answers and voters into the group of *Pro*, *Mid* and *Con*. We assume that, the voteups and votedowns received by each answer follow the exponential distribution with mean value as 26 and 20, respectively.

Table 6 shows the diversity of visibility of different ranking polices, when there is no voting spamming attack, voting down spamming attack and voting up spamming attack. The spamming attack sends v_a votedowns for each answer

Table 6. Diversity of visibility by different ranking policies in the synthetic scenarios without voting spamming attack (Decay factor $\lambda = 0.8$) time+: ranked by time in ascending order), time−: ranked by time in descending order

Policy	Diversity of visibility				
	Top 5	Top 10	Top 15	Top 20	Top 25
Without attack					
time-diversity	2.1	2.4	2.4	2.4	2.4
Zhihu	2.7	2.7	2.7	2.7	2.7
voteup	1.5	2.2	2.2	2.3	2.3
time+	2.9	3.0	3.0	3.0	3.0
time−	2.7	2.7	2.8	2.8	2.8
Under voting down spamming attack					
time-diversity	1.4	2.3	2.4	2.4	2.4
Zhihu	1.6	1.9	1.9	2.0	2.0
voteup	1.5	2.2	2.2	2.3	2.3
time+	2.9	3.0	3.0	3.0	3.0
time−	2.7	2.7	2.8	2.8	2.8
Under voting up spamming attack					
time-diversity	2.2	2.4	2.4	2.4	2.4
Zhihu	1.0	1.0	1.0	1.0	1.0
voteup	1.0	1.0	1.0	1.0	1.0
time+	2.9	3.0	3.0	3.0	3.0
time−	2.7	2.7	2.8	2.8	2.8

a that has v_a voteups, in order to lower their order in display. The voting up attack sends voteups to the answers in the *Con* groups, ensuring that the received voteups of the top 20 answers (by voteups) in the *Con* group are at least larger than the voteups received by the most favorite answers in the *Pro* group. We can see that, the visibility by Zhihu's policy is sensitive to such attacks, while our *time-diversity* base policy shows a good performance in the cases with/without attacks.

5   Conclusion

In this paper, we perform a case study to investigate the answer ranking in the Q&A website - Zhihu [13]. We show that the imbalance appearance of answers with different preferences is caused not necessarily by the imbalance of posted answers, but the imbalance in the voting. We use the diversity of visibility to indicate the robustness of the voting system in defeating voting spamming attacks, and show that the current ranking policy of Zhihu is more vulnerable than the

simple ranking policy defined by the number of votes in certain cases. By analyzing the interaction between voters and answers, we propose a *time diversity*
based voting system to mitigate the impact of voting spamming attacks. In this
system, the credibility of an answer depends on the behavior of its supporting
voters on other answers. In the future work, we will study how to make this
voting system scalable and immune to targeted spamming attacks, and apply it
on other *Q&A* websites.

A   Definition of Diversity of Visibility

In order to formally evaluate the appearance of the diversity of answers, we
borrow the concept of the *true diversity* from [24]. Considering a set of groups
G and supposing the proportion of each group $g_i \in G$ is q_i, the true diversity
with 1-mean is

$$D = \exp\left(-\sum_{g_i \in G} q_i \ln(q_i)\right). \tag{12}$$

A large number of true diversity indicates that there is a good balance between
the proportion of species.

In our case, the diversity is not only related with number of answers in
different groups, but also their positions. Let us denote the position of an answer
a under the ranking policy p as $L(a,p)$. We consider the fact that the visibility
of an answer decreases with the decreasing of its position. Therefore we define
the *visibility index* of an answer at position L as λ^L, where λ is the decay
factor, under the assumption that there is an exponential decrease of visibility
by rankings. For a set of answers N, we denote the set of its groups as $G(N)$,
such that

$$\forall g \in G(N), g \in 2^N$$
$$\forall g_i, g_j \in G(N), g_i \cap g_j = \varnothing$$
$$\cup_{g \in G(N)} = N. \tag{13}$$

The total visibility index of each group $g \in G(N)$ is

$$V(g,p) = \sum_{a \in g} \lambda^{L(a,p)}. \tag{14}$$

The corresponding *visibility ratio* of each group $g \in G(N)$ is

$$q(g,p) = \frac{V(g,p)}{\sum_{g' \in G(N)} V(g',p)}. \tag{15}$$

Then the *diversity of visibility* of a set of answers N under the ranking policy
p is defined as the true diversity of the visibility of groups. Formally, it is defined
as

$$D_{vis}(N,p) = \exp\left(-\sum_{g \in G(N)} q(g,p) \ln(q(g,p))\right). \tag{16}$$

References

1. Amazon. http://www.amazon.com/
2. Ebay. https://www.ebay.com/
3. Facebook. https://www.facebook.com/
4. How answers are ranked in Zhihu? https://zhuanlan.zhihu.com/p/19902495/
5. Imdb. https://www.imdb.com/
6. Is GMO harmful to health or envrionment? https://www.zhihu.com/question/64850604/
7. QQ International. http://www.imqq.com/English1033.html/
8. Quora. https://www.quora.com/
9. Stack overflow. http://stackoverflow.com/
10. Twitter. https://www.twitter.com/
11. Wikipedia. https://www.wikipedia.org/
12. Youtube. https://www.youtube.com/
13. Zhihu. http://www.zhihu.com/
14. Arrow, K.: A difficulty in the concept of social welfare. J. Polit. Econ. **58**(4), 328–346 (1950)
15. Chen, C., Wu, K., Srinivasan, V., Zhang, X.: Battling the internet water army: detection of hidden paid posters. In: IEEE/ACM ASONAM, pp. 116–120 (2013)
16. Chen, Y., Chen, H.: Opinion spam detection in web forum: a real case study. In: WWW, pp. 173–183 (2015)
17. Chesterton, G.K.: The Innocence of Father Brown. John Lane Company (1911)
18. Danezis, G., Mittal, P.: SybilInfer: detecting sybil nodes using social networks. In: NDSS, pp. 1–15 (2009)
19. Ghosh, A., Kale, S., McAfee, P.: Who moderates the moderators? Crowdsourcing abuse detection in user-generated content. In: ACM EC, pp. 167–176 (2011)
20. Harris, C.G.: Detecting deceptive opinion spam using human computation. In: Workshops at AAAI on AI (2012)
21. Morris, M.R., Counts, S., Roseway, A., Hoff, A., Schwarz, J.: Tweeting is believing? Understanding microblog credibility perceptions. In: CSCW, pp. 441–450 (2012)
22. Shi, L., Yu, S., Lou, W., Hou, Y.T.: SybilShield: an agent-aided social network-based sybil defense among multiple communities. In: IEEE INFOCOM, pp.1034–1042 (2013)
23. Thomas, K., McCoy, D., Grier, C., Kolcz, A., Paxson, V.: Trafficking fraudulent accounts: the role of the underground market in twitter spam and abuse. In: USENIX Security, pp. 195–210 (2013)
24. Tuomisto, H.: A consistent terminology for quantifying species diversity? Yes, it does exist. Oecologia **164**(4), 853–860 (2010)
25. Wang, G., Konolige, T., Wilson, C., Wang, X., Zheng, H., Zhao, B.Y.: You are how you click: clickstream analysis for sybil detection. In: USENIX Security, pp. 241–256 (2013)
26. Wang, G., et al.: Social turing tests: crowdsourcing sybil detection. http://arxiv.org/pdf/1205.3856.pdf (2012)
27. Wang, G., et al.: Serf and turf: crowdturfing for fun and profit. In: ACM WWW, pp. 679–688 (2012)
28. Wei, W., Xu, F., Tan, C., Li, Q.: SybilDefender: defend against sybil attacks in large social networks. In: IEEE INFOCOM, pp. 1951–1959 (2012)
29. Wilson, E.B.: Probable inference, the law of succession, and statistical inference. J. Am. Stat. Assoc. **22**(158), 209–212 (1927)

30. Yang, Z., Wilson, C., Wang, X., Gao, T., Zhao, B.Y., Dai, Y.: Uncovering social network sybils in the wild. ACM Trans. Knowl. Discov. Data **8**(1), 1–29 (2014)
31. Yu, H., Gibbons, P.B., Kaminsky, M., Xiao, F.: SybilLimit: a near-optimal social network defense against sybil attacks. In: IEEE S&P, pp. 3–17 (2008)
32. Yu, H., Kaminsky, M., Gibbons, P.B., Flaxman, A.: Sybilguard: defending against sybil attacks via social networks. SIGCOMM **36**(4), 267–278 (2006)
33. Zhenga, X., Zenga, Z., Chen, Z., Yua, Y., Rong, C.: Detecting spammers on social networks. Neurocomputing **159**, 27–34 (2015)

Online Event Detection in Social Media with Bursty Event Recognition

Wanlun Ma$^{(\boxtimes)}$, Zhuo Liu$^{(\boxtimes)}$, and Xiangyu Hu$^{(\boxtimes)}$

School of Information and Communication Engineering,
University of Electronic Science and Technology of China,
Chengdu 611731, People's Republic of China
mawanlun0@gmail.com, 201721010807@std.uestc.edu.cn, alxe24@163.com

Abstract. The emergence of social media opens tremendous research opportunities. Many individuals, mostly teens and young adults around the world, share their daily lives and opinions about a wide variety of topics (e.g., crime, sports, and politics) on social media sites. Thus, social media becomes a valuable repository for data of different types, which could provide insights of social events happening around the world. However, it is still a challenge to identify the bursty and disruptive events from the massive and noisy user-generated content on social media sites. In this paper, we present a novel event detection framework for identifying surrounding real-world events that can support decision making and emergency management. Our proposed framework consists of four main components, including data pre-processing, event-related tweets classifying, online clustering, and bursty event recognition. We conducted a series of experiments on the real-world social media dataset collected from Twitter. The experimental results demonstrated the effectiveness of our proposed method.

Keywords: Event detection · Social media · Text mining · Information extraction

1 Introduction

Online Social Networks (OSNs), such as Twitter and Facebook, have become an integral part of individuals' daily life. Due to the fast dissemination nature of information on OSNs, they are now served as the major news consumption tool for users. In a survey recently conducted by Pew Research Centre (PRC), two-thirds of Americans get at least some of their news on social media with one-in-five doing so frequently and about three-in-four Twitter users get news on the site [17]. Social network users share their views and broadcast news and information about ongoing events. Online social media platforms serve as real-time "sensors" for social trends and incidents [21], which is very useful for supporting decision making and public management. Some research has shown the importance of social media in disaster warning system design and emergency management. For

© Springer Nature Singapore Pte Ltd. 2019
W. Meng and S. Furnell (Eds.): SocialSec 2019, CCIS 1095, pp. 181–190, 2019.
https://doi.org/10.1007/978-981-15-0758-8_14

instance, Palen [15] stated that social media was a significant and accurate tool for the crisis event management during the Virginia Tech shootings and the Southern California wildfire.

Although many researchers have proposed models and techniques for the purpose of detecting events from social media contents, the existing approaches suffer from several key challenges. Firstly, it is hard for real-time event detection due to the large number of social media records (e.g., tweets) and the continuous appearance of new events. In addition, user-generated content in social media consists of incomplete and even wrongly structured sentences due to abbreviations, irregular expressions, abnormal words, and slang terms. Secondly, the event-related tweets classification can filter most noisy and irrelevant content, but the effectiveness of classifying the event-related posts is limited due to the performance of the classifier. Moreover, it is difficult to conduct further analysis of the ongoing events from the massive event clusters generated by online clustering.

To overcome these issues, we propose a novel event detection framework which can recognize the bursty and disruptive events from social media. Our contributions can be summarised as follows:

- We proposed a novel event detection framework which can identify surrounding bursty events, such as terrorist attacks. Our proposed framework consists of four main components, including data pre-processing, event-related tweets classifying, online clustering and bursty event recognition.
- In the bursty event recognition module, we employed the temporal bursty feature and the news value of events to distinguish the significant and bursty events from the event clusters.
- In the evaluation, we conducted extensive experiments on the real-world social media dataset, and the experimental results demonstrated the effectiveness of our proposed method.

2   Related Work

There are many research works that focus on event detection and tracking [1, 6,7], topic discovery and evolution [8,11,20], and information summarization [16]. These works extract various types of events from social media, such as Arab Spring uprisings [1], terrorist attacks [6], sports games [16,20], and disease outbreak [9].

Becker et al. [3] proposed an online clustering and filtering framework to identify events with different types. This approach extracted temporal, social, topical, and twitter centric features of tweets clusters and then classified these clusters into real-world event clusters and non-event clusters. Moreover, Alsaedi et al. [1] implemented a similar clustering method using three sets of features (temporal, spatial and textual features) to identify whether a message cluster belonging to the group of real-world events or not. In the literature, Latent Dirichlet Allocation (LDA) [4] and non-negative matrix factorization (NMF) [13] are two widely used topic models for event detection. Xing et al. [20] extended the

LDA method to model the relationship between hashtags and topics of tweets, and then discovered events based on event-related hashtags. Both Kalyanam [11] and Chen [8] employed the NMF method to model the evolution of topics in social media. Similarly, Shin et al. [18] proposed an NMF-based approach using both spatial and temporal information from tweets to detect anomalous events. Besides, Chen et al. [7] proposed a clustering-based approach using a similarity metric and low dimensional representations of events which were learned from a neural network with an attention mechanism. While Liu et al. [14] had a similar idea that they exploited a recurrent neural network with a cross-lingual attention gate to identify events from multiple languages. In addition to the text source, Schinas et al. [16] proposed a multimodal clustering method using not only the textual information but also the image content from social media.

In general, most existing research firstly models bursty frequency patterns along with time or space, and then extract events using classification or clustering methods. However, most existing approaches showed an unsatisfactory performance of recognizing bursty and important events from the massive extracted events.

3   Online Event Detection

In this section, we describe the framework of our event detection and tracking method, which consists of four components - data pre-processing, event-related tweets classifying, online clustering and bursty event recognition. Figure 1 provides an overview of our proposed event detection framework. First of all, the data pre-processing component applied several text pre-processing techniques to clean the tweets. Then, the event-related tweets classification component identifies event-related tweets from noisy and irrelevant posts. After filtering non-event tweets, the online clustering component groups similar event-related tweets into the same event cluster. Then, the bursty event recognition component distinguishes the significant and bursty events from the massive event clusters.

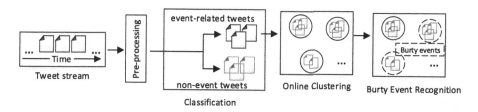

Fig. 1. Event detection framework for twitter stream

3.1 Data Pre-processing

Tweets usually consist of incomplete and even wrongly structured sentences due to abbreviations, irregular expressions, abnormal words, and slang terms. Therefore, we applied some pre-processing techniques to clean the tweets and consequently improve their quality for the subsequent event detection analysis.

In addition to the traditional text pre-processing techniques (e.g., stop words removal), we performed word segmentation and parts-of-speech (POS) tagging for each tweet and then employed name entity recognition (NER) to extract various kinds of name entities, including mentioned users, organizations, locations. An example of the data pre-processing is shown in Fig. 2.

raw tweet		#Trump says second summit with #KimJongUn will happen after the midterms https://t.co/OtXi13wYXA						
after preprocessing	words	Trump	says	second	summit	KimJongUn	happen	midterms
	NER	PER	-	-	-	PER	-	-
	POS	NOUN	VERB	ADJ	NOUN	NOUN	VERB	NOUN

Fig. 2. An example of the data pre-processing. The results of NER denotes names for a certain specific person (PER), location(LOC), or organization (ORG). And each word has one of the ten following POS tags: verbs (VERB), nouns (NOUN), pronouns (PRON), adjectives (ADJ), adverbs (ADV), adpositions (ADP), conjunctions (CONJ), cardinal numbers (NUM), particles or other function words (PRT), and others (X).

3.2 Event-Related Tweets Classifying

As OSNs contain various types of content posted by users, such as personal updates, random thoughts and opinions, and information sharing, it is necessary to separate "event" and "non-event" content on OSNs. Generally, the classification aims to identify event-related tweets from noisy and irrelevant posts and eliminate non-event tweets. Since the following online clustering component only considers the event-related tweets, filtering non-event tweets consequently reduces the number of tweets to be processed in subsequent steps. In the classification, we applied a well-known supervised machine learning algorithms - random forest [5] - for filtering non-event tweets. Features are critical in a machine learning based classification task. Therefore, based on the Sriram's work [19], we chose nine features to represent the tweets, including the number of words, the ratio of capitalized words, the ratio of hashtag words. Table 1 lists all the features used in the task.

We used a manually sampled dataset which was composed of 1737 event-related tweets and 1900 non-event tweets to train the Random Forest classifier. Then, this pre-trained classifier can be used to identify the "event" and "non-event" posts in the streaming tweets.

Table 1. 9 features used in the classification

Features	Examples
The number of words	The count of words in a tweet
The ratio of capitalized words	BBC, CNN, NEWS
The number of name entities	London, Troy, FBI
The ratio of hashtag words	#Brexit, #Tradewar
The ration of mentioned users	@ReutersPolitics, @TheEconomist
The ratio of non-English words*	Trade, summit
The ratio of opinion words	Think, tell, believe, deem
The ratio of personal sentiment words	God, thanks, hell, stupid
The number of question expression word	Where, why, what

*The example words are translated from the originals.

3.3 Online Clustering

The event-related tweets classification separates the event-related tweets from the noisy and messy tweet stream. In order to identify the topic of an event, we applied an unsupervised online clustering approach [2] to group similar event-related tweets into the same event cluster.

Each tweet is represented as a vector T whose values are weighted based on the POS of each word and the results of NER. Based on the empirical study, name entities (e.g., locations, organizations and celebrities) are weighted as 1.2, noun and verb are weighted as 1, and other words are weighted as 0.5. The similarity function used to measure the similarity between the tweet and the existing clusters $(C_1, C_2, ..., C_n)$ is defined as:

$$similarity = \frac{T \cdot C_i}{|T| \cdot |C_i|} \qquad (1)$$

Whether a tweet T belongs to an existing cluster C_i or not is determined by the threshold parameters τ. Different from the work [2], we dynamically tune the threshold τ based on the number of words in a tweet. In the empirical study, τ is set as 0.4, 0.45, 0.55 respectively, when the length of the tweet is greater than 13, 6 or 0.

3.4 Bursty Event Recognition

The event-related tweets classification can filter the most noisy and irrelevant content, but the effectiveness of classifying the event-related posts is limited depending on the performance of the classifier. Moreover, it is difficult to conduct a further fine-grained analysis of the ongoing events from the massive event clusters generated by online clustering. In order to address these issues, we applied bursty event recognition to the generated event clusters to distinguish the significant and bursty events for further analysis.

In the bursty event recognition module, we employed the temporal bursty feature and the news value of events to recognize the bursty events from the event clusters. In each event cluster C_i, there are n tweets $(T_1, T_2, ..., T_n)$ which are sorted by the post time. In other words, let PT_k represents the post time of T_k, then PT_j is earlier than PT_k when j is smaller than k. Thus, the temporal bursty feature (TBF) for an event cluster C_i is defined as:

$$TBF = min |PT_k - PT_{k+w}| \tag{2}$$

where w is the time window. Intuitively, social media users are likely to update many posts in a short time to share information with others when a bursty event (e.g., terrorist attacks) is happening around them. Thus, the temporal bursty features (TBFs) of bursty events are supposed to be smaller than that of general events. Therefore, the temporal bursty feature (TBF) of an event under the threshold τ is identified as a bursty event.

Furthermore, we applied the news value of events to recognize the bursty events from the event clusters. In order to assess the news value of events, we use three indicators, including the max number of retweets, the number of keywords (e.g., breaking news, breaking, and news post) and the number of name entities about locations (LOC). Table 2 shows the three indicators used to assess the news value of events. The news value of an event cluster is set to 1 when two of the indicators are over the thresholds respectively; otherwise, it is set to 0. In general, an event cluster is identified as a bursty event when TBF is under the threshold τ and the news value is equal to 1.

Table 2. News value indicators

Indicators	Examples
The max number of retweets	The max number of retweets for a tweet in the same cluster
The number of keywords words	Breaking, #news, #breaking, #breakingnews
The number of name entities about locations (LOC)	Manchester, London bridge

4   Experimental Evaluation

4.1   Dataset and Experiment Setting

The performance of the proposed model was evaluated on real-world data collected using Twitter public API. The raw data was collected during 2017 U.K. General Election from May 19th to June 6th, considering two severe terrorist attacks (i.e., the Manchester Arena bombing and 2017 London Bridge attack)

Table 3. The statistics of the real-world datasets

Country	Time period	#Tweets (million)	#Events
UK	05/19/2017–06/06/2017	11.36	120

happened during this time period. We also collected 120 events from May 19th to June 6th through several news websites and evaluated the proposed model based on these background events. The detailed statistics of the datasets are listed in Table 3.

All the experiments were implemented by Python and conducted on a computer running Windows 10 with a memory of 16 G and a processor of 3.0 GHz Intel Core i5.

4.2 Baseline Methods

To validate the effectiveness of the proposed framework, we compare our approach with the following methods:

1. *BHS* [12]: BHS models the tweet stream by an infinite-state automaton, in which the burst appearance of a topic or event is viewed as a state transition process. We set the threshold as 3 for detecting the high-intensity state of the bursty events.
2. *AED* [1]: AED is a detection framework for identifying disruptive events. AED applies a Naive Bayes model for event-related tweets classification and a similar online clustering method to detect disruptive events.

4.3 Evaluation Metrics

In order to evaluate the performance of our proposed method and the baselines, we employed the same evaluation method as in [7, 10]. Detected events are judged by two humans whether the events are meaningful and important. Since it is a time-consuming task, only 40 events are judged in the work [7]. Thus we only analyzed 100 events in our experiments. The performance of our approach and baseline methods are evaluated in terms of precision, recall, and F-measure.

4.4 Model Comparisons and Results

We evaluated the proposed approach by comparing with the baseline methods in Sect. 4.2. The experimental results on the real-world dataset are shown in Table 4. We can observe that the performance of our approach is better than the baseline methods in terms of precision, recall, and F-measure. Specifically, the F-measure of our method is improved by 16% and 11% respectively, compared to BHS and AED. BHS considers the bursty and hierarchical structure of the stream tweet data and models the arrival times (i.e., post times) of tweets in an event cluster to identify bursts that have high intensity. Therefore, a non-bursty

Table 4. The results of different methods

Method	Precision	Recall	F-measure
BHS	0.5670	0.7333	0.6395
AED	0.6176	0.7590	0.6810
Our method	**0.7735**	**0.8283**	**0.7999**

Table 5. Sample events detected by our method

Events	Sample tweets
Tory candidate Craig Mackinlay charged over election expenses	Tory election expenses explained: Craig Mackinlay charged https://t.co/sDAO810uBb via @cmackinlay @Channel4News #GE2017
	Craig Mackinlay (Con, South Thanet) has been charged with election offences for the 2015 election campaign in the South Thanet constituency
Election campaigning suspended after London Bridge attack	Safety over freedom: Social media users call for General Election to be suspended following the London Bridge attack https://t.co/ATL0VSJykG
	UK Govt considering indefinitely cancelling election following terror attacks in London Sat. which killed at least 7

event cluster will be wrongly identified as a bursty one if the post timings of several tweets are very close. As a result, BHS has the lowest performance. The main difference between our method and AED is that we incorporated the bursty event recognition for the generated event clusters. This result demonstrates the importance of employing the bursty event recognition component in the proposed framework. To further show the effectiveness of our method, some examples from our detected events are shown in Table 5.

As discussed in Sect. 3.4, the time threshold of the temporal bursty feature (TBF) highly affects the performance of our proposed framework. In other words, an event cluster will be identified as a bursty event under the condition that its TBF is less than the threshold τ. Therefore, we evaluated the performance of our framework under different TBF thresholds. As shown in Fig. 3, the precision decreases with the increase of the threshold τ, in contrast, recall, and F-measure increase. Besides, the result demonstrates that the F-measure almost remains stable when the threshold τ is over 3 min. Thus, we set the threshold τ as 3 in practice.

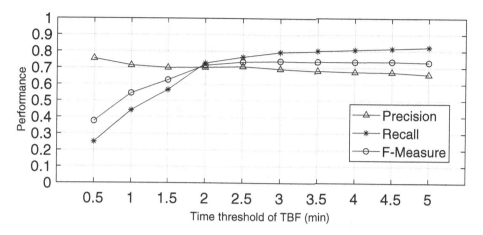

Fig. 3. The performance of our framework under different time thresholds of TBF.

5   Conclusion

In this work, we study the problem of event detection from the massive and noisy content in social media. The major challenge of event detection stems from bursty event recognition on which existing methods showed unsatisfactory performance. In order to tackle this problem, we proposed a novel event detection framework which can identify surrounding bursty events, such as terrorist attacks. Particularly, in the bursty event recognition module, we employed the temporal bursty feature and the news value of events to distinguish the significant and bursty events from the event clusters. Experimental results show that our proposed event detection method achieves significant improvement over existing approaches.

For future work and improvements, there are two main directions including (i) more appropriate semantic representation methods for tweets, such as Word2vec model, (ii) utilizing external information of tweets in the clustering process, like tweets' locations and URLs, (iii) further investigating the temporal and spatial characteristics of bursty events and designing more effective and accurate features to identify bursty events.

References

1. Alsaedi, N., Burnap, P.: Arabic event detection in social media. In: Gelbukh, A. (ed.) CICLing 2015. LNCS, vol. 9041, pp. 384–401. Springer, Cham (2015). https://doi.org/10.1007/978-3-319-18111-0_29
2. Alsaedi, N., Burnap, P., Rana, O.: Can we predict a riot? Disruptive event detection using twitter. ACM Trans. Internet Technol. (TOIT) **17**(2), 18 (2017)
3. Becker, H., Naaman, M., Gravano, L.: Beyond trending topics: real-world event identification on twitter. In: ICWSM, vol. 11, pp. 438–441 (2011)

4. Blei, D.M., Ng, A.Y., Jordan, M.I.: Latent Dirichlet allocation. J. Mach. Learn. Res. **3**(Jan), 993–1022 (2003)
5. Breiman, L.: Random forests. Mach. Learn. **45**(1), 5–32 (2001)
6. Burnap, P., Williams, M.L., Sloan, L., Rana, O., Housley, W., Edwards, A., Knight, V., Procter, R., Voss, A.: Tweeting the terror: modelling the social media reaction to the Woolwich terrorist attack. Soc. Netw. Anal. Min. **4**(1), 206 (2014)
7. Chen, G., Kong, Q., Mao, W.: Online event detection and tracking in social media based on neural similarity metric learning. In: IEEE International Conference on Intelligence and Security Informatics, pp. 182–184 (2017)
8. Chen, Y., Zhang, H., Wu, J., Wang, X., Liu, R., Lin, M.: Modeling emerging, evolving and fading topics using dynamic soft orthogonal NMF with sparse representation. In: 2015 IEEE International Conference on Data Mining (ICDM), pp. 61–70. IEEE (2015)
9. Ghenai, A., Mejova, Y.: Catching Zika fever: application of crowdsourcing and machine learning for tracking health misinformation on twitter. arXiv preprint arXiv:1707.03778 (2017)
10. Guille, A., Favre, C.: Mention-anomaly-based event detection and tracking in twitter. In: 2014 IEEE/ACM International Conference on Advances in Social Networks Analysis and Mining (ASONAM 2014), pp. 375–382. IEEE (2014)
11. Kalyanam, J.: Leveraging social context for modeling topic evolution. In: ACM SIGKDD International Conference on Knowledge Discovery and Data Mining, pp. 517–526 (2015)
12. Kleinberg, J.: Bursty and hierarchical structure in streams. Data Min. Knowl. Disc. **7**(4), 373–397 (2003)
13. Lee, D.D., Seung, H.S.: Learning the parts of objects by non-negative matrix factorization. Nature **401**(6755), 788–791 (1999)
14. Liu, J., Chen, Y., Liu, K., Zhao, J.: Event detection via gated multilingual attention mechanism. Statistics **1000**, 1250 (2018)
15. Palen, L.: Online social media in crisis events. Educ. Q. **31**(3), 76–78 (2008)
16. Schinas, M., Papadopoulos, S., Petkos, G., Kompatsiaris, Y., Mitkas, P.A.: Multimodal graph-based event detection and summarization in social media streams. In: ACM International Conference on Multimedia, pp. 189–192 (2015)
17. Shearer, E., Gottfriend, J.: News use across social media platforms 2017. Pew Research Center (2017)
18. Shin, D.S., et al.: STExNMF: spatio-temporally exclusive topic discovery for anomalous event detection. In: 2017 IEEE International Conference on Data Mining (ICDM), pp. 435–444. IEEE (2017)
19. Sriram, B., Fuhry, D., Demir, E., Ferhatosmanoglu, H., Demirbas, M.: Short text classification in twitter to improve information filtering. In: Proceedings of the 33rd International ACM SIGIR Conference on Research and Development in Information Retrieval, pp. 841–842. ACM (2010)
20. Xing, C., Wang, Y., Liu, J., Huang, Y., Ma, W.Y.: Hashtag-based sub-event discovery using mutually generative LDA in twitter. In: AAAI, pp. 2666–2672 (2016)
21. Zhao, L., Sun, Q., Ye, J., Chen, F., Lu, C.T., Ramakrishnan, N.: Multi-task learning for spatio-temporal event forecasting. In: Proceedings of the 21th ACM SIGKDD International Conference on Knowledge Discovery and Data Mining, pp. 1503–1512. ACM (2015)

Predicting Users' Emotional Intelligence with Social Networking Data

Xiangyu Wei[1], Jin Li[2], Zhen Han[1], and Wei Wang[1,3]([⊠])

[1] Beijing Key Laboratory of Security and Privacy in Intelligent Transportation, Beijing Jiaotong University, Beijing 100044, China
{weixiangyu,zhan,wangwei1}@bjtu.edu.cn
[2] School of Computer Science, Guangzhou University, Guangzhou 510006, China
lijin@gzhu.edu.cn
[3] Division of Computer, Electrical and Mathematical Sciences and Engineering (CEMSE), King Abdullah University of Science and Technology (KAUST), Thuwal 23955-6900, Kingdom of Saudi Arabia

Abstract. Social networks have integrated into daily lives of most people in the way of interactions and of lifestyles. The users' identity, relationships, or other characteristics can be explored from the social networking data, in order to provide more personalized services to the users. In this work, we focus on predicting the user's emotional intelligence (EI) based on the social networking data. As an essential facet of users' psychological characteristics, EI plays an important role on well-being, interpersonal relationships, and overall success in people's life. Most existing work on predicting users' emotional intelligence is based on questionnaires that may collect dishonest answers or unconscientious responses, thus leading in potentially inaccurate prediction results. In this work, we are motivated to propose an emotional intelligence prediction model based on the sentiment analysis of social networking data. The model is represented by four dimensions including self-awareness, self-regulation, self-motivation and social relationships. The EI of a user is then measured by the four numerical values or the sum of them. In the experiments, we predict the EIs of over a hundred thousand users based on one of the largest social networks of China, Weibo. The predicting results demonstrate the effectiveness of our model. The results show that the distribution of the four EI's dimensions of users is roughly normal. The results also indicate that EI scores of females are generally higher than males'. This is consistent with previous findings.

Keywords: Emotional intelligence · Sentiment analysis · User profile · Social networks

1 Introduction

In recent years, cyberspace has become parallel to physical world along with the rise of social networks. Although social networks bring a lot of convenience

© Springer Nature Singapore Pte Ltd. 2019
W. Meng and S. Furnell (Eds.): SocialSec 2019, CCIS 1095, pp. 191–202, 2019.
https://doi.org/10.1007/978-981-15-0758-8_15

to people's daily life, people have paid more and more attention on the risk of security and privacy on the social networks. The nature of social networks, such as the large amount of data and the rich information contained in the message, makes it possible to analyze users' characteristics and private information. Previous work [11, 19, 26] on users' attributions revolves around users' demographics, such as age, gender and location. In addition, many researchers [3, 4, 12, 13, 20, 29] mined users' psychological traits through social networks. However, there is no related work on predicting users' emotional intelligence with social networking data.

Emotional intelligence [23] is a type of user's characteristics that involve the ability to monitor one's own emotions as well as others' so as to discriminate them and to use the information to guide one's thinking and actions. Emotional intelligence [18] includes four dimensions: emotional perception and expression, emotional thinking, emotional understanding, and emotional management.

Thorndike et al. [25] proposed the concept of Social Intelligence in 1920 and Alexander et al. [1] proposed the concept of Non-intellectual Factors in 1938. In 1987, Gardner et al. [8] proposed Multiple Intelligence. In fact, the concept of emotional intelligence develops from these early ideas and theories. In 1990, American psychologists Salovey and Mayer [23] reinterpreted emotional intelligence and formally proposed systematic theory. Bar-On also proposed his own definition. Bar-On [2] first proposed the concept of the emotional quotient in 1985 and published his Emotional Quotient Inventory. There also exist work on predicting validity of emotional intelligence in various scenarios [5–7], and many studies revealed that emotional intelligence has an important impact on motivation, emotional regulation, stress, decision-making, work performance and job satisfaction [2, 9, 10].

The traditional emotional intelligence model is based on questionnaires with a number of samples. However, there are some factors affecting the measurement in the self-reported questionnaire. For example, the respondent has a response set, such as extreme, avoidance and carelessness. Or rather, respondents fail to know their own situations and understand the grading standards. Meanwhile, respondents' answers to some questions were affected by unstable factors, such as emotions and motives at that time, which means that the test results may not truly reflect the psychological level of the person. Moreover, emotional intelligence is constantly changing as the living environment changes [22]. In contrast, social networks provide a good platform for measurement of users' EI, as it contains rich information for profiling a very big number of users and most users in social networks are honest to convey themselves.

In this work, we propose an emotional intelligence model based on the sentiment analysis of social networking data. The model is represented by four dimensions including self-awareness, self-regulation, self-motivation and social relationships. The EI of a user is then measured by four numerical values or the sum of them. In the experiments, we predict the EIs of over a hundred thousand users based on one of the largest social networks of China, Weibo. The predicting results demonstrate the effectiveness of our model.

We make the following contributions:

- We propose an emotional intelligence model based on social networking data to measure users' ability to control emotions. The model includes self-awareness, self-regulation, self-motivation and social relationship according to the psycho-emotional intelligence theory. To the best of our knowledge, this is the first work towards predicting users' emotional intelligence based on social networking data.
- We test our model on one of the largest social networks in China, Weibo, and predict emotional intelligence of over a hundred thousand users of Weibo. The prediction results verify the effectiveness of our model.

The reminder of this paper is organized as follows. The model for predicting emotional intelligence is proposed in Sect. 2. The experiments and results are presented in Sect. 3. Concluding remarks follow in Sect. 4.

2   Prediction Model of Emotional Intelligence

The model is based on four dimensions including self-awareness, self-regulation, self-motivation as well as social relationships according to the psycho-emotional intelligence theory.

The self-awareness (A) reflects the ability to accurately identify own emotions and appraisal and expression of emotions encompassing the ability to be sensitive to the slight variations between emotions. The self-regulation (R) includes the ability to manage disruptive emotions and impulses. Therefore, emotionally intelligent individuals often pay attention to harness emotions. The self-motivation (M) measures whether the user's emotions are always in a positive state and the recovery from disappointment is rapid. The social relationships (S) measures the ability of infecting others' emotions, and the harmonization in the process of interpersonal interaction. Emotional intelligence helps individuals to behave appropriately, which allows them to maintain good relationships with others.

First, we need to set a time window for analyzing the text. The experimental time window is day. Assuming a time window contains W sentences, the expect sentiment value in the time window j is

$$E_j = \frac{1}{W} \sum_{i=1}^{W} e_i \tag{1}$$

where e_i is the sentiment value of the sentence i in the time window j.

Variance of sentiment values is defined as follows:

$$\sigma_j = \frac{1}{W} \sum_{i=1}^{W} (e_i - E_j)^2 \tag{2}$$

Emotional change value is defined as follows:

$$\delta_j = E_j - E_{j-1} \tag{3}$$

Then we calculate the values of the four dimensions of emotional intelligence.

2.1   Self-awareness

Self-awareness is the ability to recognize own and others' emotions. There are 21 categories of sentiment words, and the each category has five intensities. The proportion of sentiment words in the whole text reflects the frequency of expressing emotions. The proportion of sentiment words with different categories reflects the richness of the user's emotions. The proportion of sentiment words with different intensities in the same category reflects the ability of identifying slight variations between emotions. In addition, whether the emotion can be expressed accurately or not is influenced by the user's emotion. Therefore, the sentiment value of the text E_i is also an important indicator of cognitive ability. The self-awareness is defined as follows:

$$A = \frac{1}{k} \sum_{i=0}^{k} (\frac{w_s}{w_n} + \frac{w_i}{w_p} + \frac{w_p}{w_s}) E_i \tag{4}$$

Where w_s is the number of sentiment words, w_i is the number of different intensities of sentiment words, w_p is the number of the categories of the sentiment words. w_n is the number of words. E_i is the expect sentiment value in the time windows i. k is the number of time windows.

2.2   Self-regulation

Self-regulation reflects the ability to manage own emotions. When the variance of the user's sentiment value in a time window exceeds 0.1, it indicates that the user's emotion has fluctuated. The high value of self-regulation manifests a high mean of sentiment value and low variance. At the same time, the entropy value is introduced to indicate the fluctuations of the user's emotions. The smaller the entropy is, the more stable the mood is and the less emotional fluctuations. Assuming m represents the number of positive emotions of the user, and n represents the number of negative emotions. The equation for entropy is

$$entropy = \frac{-m}{m+n} \times \log \frac{m}{m+n} - \frac{n}{m+n} \times \log \frac{n}{m+n} \tag{5}$$

The self-regulation is defined as follows:

$$R = \frac{1}{k} \sum_{i=0}^{k} \frac{E_i + 1}{(\sigma_i \times entropy \times \log t) + 1} \tag{6}$$

Where t is average time window intervals between the window where variance value does not exceed 0.1 and the average sentiment value is larger than 0.5 and the window where the mood swing appears.

2.3   Self-motivation

Self-motivation can be measured by the time of the recovery from the depressed stage to emotional stable stage, and the proportion of positive emotions in the whole time. When the average sentiment value of a user in a window is less than 0.5, the window can be viewed as a depressed stage. The t_l is calculated by the average number of time window from less than 0.5 to more than 0.5 for the first time, and self-motivation is also affected by the user's current emotional level. Therefore, self-motivation is defined as follows:

$$M = (\arctan \frac{1}{k} \sum_{i=0}^{k} \frac{w_p \times E_i \times 25}{w_s \times \log t_l}) \times 2 \div \pi \qquad (7)$$

Where w_p is the number of positive words, w_s is the number of the sentiment words. 25 is an amplification factor.

2.4 Social Relationships

The social relationships reflects the harmony of relationships and the ability of emotional contagion. In other words, we measure the extent of the impact on users' emotion by the number of mood-swing, comments and retweet. Emotional change value which is greater than 0.2 is viewed as a mood swing. The number of comments and retweet are quantitative indicator to determine the influence of the text. Additionally, whether the text conveys a positive attitude to others can be considered. As the transmission of positive information, people can form a positive relationship. Therefore we add the average sentiment value to the formula. The social relationships is defined as follows:

$$S = \left(\arctan \frac{1}{k} \sum_{i=1}^{k} \log \left(\frac{N_{ci} \times N_{ti}}{N_{di}} \right) \times E_i \right) \times 2 \div \pi \qquad (8)$$

Where N_{ci} is the ratio of the number of comments to the number of followers. N_{ti} is a ratio that takes into the number of retweet and followers in the time window i. N_{di} represents the number of the mood swings. In order to achieve the overall convergence of the value, the value after the calculation is processed by the inverse tangent function.

2.5 Measurement

We calculate the values of the four dimensions of emotional intelligence through the Eq. 4, the Eq. 6, the Eq. 7 and the Eq. 8. The result is shown in Table 1 and the values of EI of a user after data standardization is shown in Fig. 1.

There are two methods to measure users' EI. As shown in Table 1, we use the sum of the four dimensions of EI as the first method. This method can reflect the user's comprehensive score, however the size of value of each dimension cannot be distinguished. The second method, shown in Fig. 1, use values of the four dimensions of EI to measure users' EI. This method can figure out the difference of each dimension.

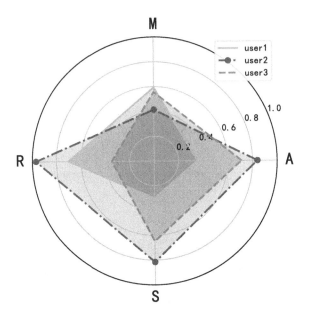

Fig. 1. The distribution of the values of EI. A represents self-awareness, M represents self-motivation, R represents self-regulation, S represents social relationship.

Table 1. The values of the four dimensions of emotional intelligence

User	A	M	R	S	Sum
1004762303	0.65760	0.65899	1.26609	0.31275	2.8954
1004434392	1.27210	0.52058	1.145383	0.809535	2.9437
1000755992	1.10951	0.63020	1.01585	0.64672	3.404

3   Experiments and Results

3.1   Data Set

We measure users' EI based on the weibo data that was collected by Fudan NLP Group. The data set consists of 1.5 billion tweets and more than 2 million users. As shown in Table 2, the user information includes user identifier, number of comments, number of retweet, source, publishing time, post. In addition, we have the number of followers and the number of following. Weibo data is used as the training data set for the naive Bayesian method.

We choose one hundred thousand users with the number of tweets more than 500, the number of friends and followers more than 10 in the experiment. The number of micro blog is 105176341.

The micro-blog is very short (140 words), and there are @, tags, URLs and other noise information that are relatively unimportant for sentiment analysis in a single micro-blog. The text needs to denoising and word segmentation.

Table 2. Weibo data

userid	retweets	comments	source	time	text
1427652963	0	0	iPhone	2012-06-10 21:49:00	什么时候狠，什么时候软也真是一门艺术. 善良过了头，就成了软弱 (Harshness or kindness is an art. Extreme kindheartedness is considered a kind of weakness)

3.2　Chinese Sentiment Analysis

In order to recognize the expression of emotions and calculate the value of self-awareness, we analyze the lexicon in the text published by the user through the Chinese emotional vocabulary [14]. The vocabulary containing 27466 sentiment words is divided into 7 major categories and 21 subcategories.

Moreover, we expand the vocabulary by calculating the word semantic similarity through the words of HowNet and the word forest [31]. According to the distribution of the word, a dynamic weighting strategy of considering both HowNet and CiLin is used to calculate the word similarity.

For the sake of calculating the values of the four dimensions of EI, we should know each sentence's sentiment. Emoticons in the user's post are closely related to the content. Accordingly, we extract emoticons to obtain the sentiment value of a sentence.

Firstly, the Sina weibo data is deduplicated and a total of 341,067 emoticons are extracted. We removed the error-extracted emoticons. Then, we choose emoticons with the number of occurrences more than 400 times. Finally, we obtain 1818 emoticons including some the traditional Chinese characters' emoticons. And after counting all the 1818 emoticons, we find that the top 10% of emoticons account for 96.3% of all emoticons. Therefore, we manually annotated the top 10% of emoticons.

1 is the positive emoticon and -1 is viewed as the negative emoticon. Assuming that the number of the positive emoticon is N_p and the number of the negative emoticon is N_n. The sentiment value of a sentence is as follows:

$$s = \begin{cases} -1 \text{ for } N_p < N_n \\ 1 \;\; \text{ for } N_p \geq N_n \end{cases} \tag{9}$$

After classification according to above the formula, the number of positive micro-blogs is 14125, and the number of negative micro-blogs is 5793. Additionally, we have 7134 positive micro-blogs and 8257 negative micro-blogs that are manually annotated, including micro-blog emotional evaluation data set of China Computer Federation International Conference on Natural Language Processing and Chinese Computing (NLPCC) in 2014. Those data set are trained for sentiment analysis using the naive Bayesian method.

The naive Bayesian method is used to construct a text sentiment classifier. Based on the prior probability, we obtain the probability of observing different features under a given hypothesis. We define the category as

$$C = \arg\max P(C_j) \prod_{i=1}^{n} P(w_i, C_j)^{wt(w_i)} \qquad (10)$$

Where $P(C_j)$ represents the prior probability of category C_j, $P(w_i, C_j)$ is the posterior probability of the characteristic word in the category C_j, $wt(w_i)$ is the weights of the word w_i in the testing corpus.

The naive Bayesian method is used to classify the text sentiment in a positive probability. The positive probability which is greater than or equal 0.6 means a positive emotion. The positive probability which is less than 0.6 means a negative emotion.

3.3   Experimental Result Analysis

As described in Sect. 2, we obtain the values of four dimensions of EI. In order to evaluate the validity of our model, we analyze the distribution of these values, the relationships between users' gender and EI.

The Distribution of Values of EI. We analyze the histogram of four dimensions of emotional intelligence in Fig. 2, and discover that they obey normal distribution.

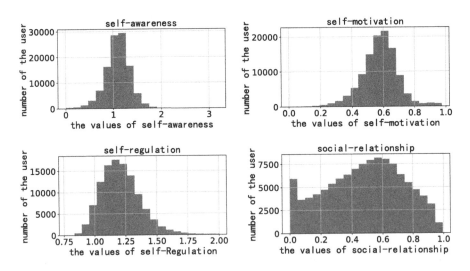

Fig. 2. The distribution of the four dimensions of emotional intelligence

The distribution area of the value of self-awareness is smaller to narrow than the value of self-motivation and mostly concentrate on the low-value region. The value of self-regulation is also distributed in the low-value region.

On the one hand, the deviation of identifying sentiment words results in lower values. On the other hand, user inclines to publish more positive text, therefore the category of sentiment words is less. The number of low values of social relationships is larger than high values, owing to the number of comments and retweet is small in most cases.

Gender Difference. From Table 3, we note a relationship between emotional intelligence and gender. EIs of females are higher than those of males that supports the hypothesis that women have more emotional intelligence. Intuitively, females are mostly expected to be more expressive of feelings in the culture. This result is in accordance with the previous work [15,16,24].

Table 3. The relationship between EI and gender

Gender	A	M	R	S	Sum
Female	1.147648	0.605886	1.244395	0.479632	3.477561
Male	1.040861	0.557913	1.215466	0.476139	3.290380

Topic Analysis. We rank sum of the four values to obtain the top 1000 high-score users and the last 1000 low-score users, then we use Latent Dirichlet Allocation (LDA) to retrieve key information in the two groups. Through contrasting the key top 30 words in 6 topics, we discover that the topics mostly concentrate on health, politics, economics and posts are much longer in low-score groups. However, the high-score users prefer to publish posts which reflect inner feeling compared with the low-score users. A part of words are shown in Tables 4 and 5. The results suggest that the stronger the motivation of users to express their emotions, the higher the users score. In other words, aiming at the user with different motivations, we can design different features based on the present models in the future.

Table 4. Six topics in low-score of EI group

Topic	Words
topic1	we, nothing, ourselves, can, that is, life, people, health...
topic2	market, company, international, price, project, bank, US Dollar, gold...
topic3	china, development, hospital, work, Japan, security, construction, reform...
topic4	society, children, treatment, organization, investigation, impact, media, life...
topic5	economy, China, investment, experts, food, real estate, sector, policy...
topic6	USA, journalists, services, news, activities, support, reporting, about...

Table 5. Six topics in high-score of EI group

Topic	Words
topic1	photography, love, transfer, cake, Beijing, sun, good morning, tomorrow...
topic2	Hip-hop, watch, like, greedy, warm, fans, enjoy, opportunity...
topic3	breeze, support, thank you, friends, flowers, efforts, expectations, sunshine...
topic4	awesome, laugh, happiness, roses, wedding, wedding dress, music, cheers...
topic5	thank you, gifts, movies, studios, fun, evening, coffee, wishes...
topic6	Aha, applause, constellation, Child Star, appreciation, simple, delicious, restaurant...

4 Concluding Remarks

In this work, we propose a prediction model to measure users' Emotional Intelligence (EI) through analyzing texts and interactive information in social networks. To the best of our knowledge, this is the first work that emotional intelligence models are proposed based on social networking data.

The model is expressed with four dimensions including self-awareness, self-regulation, self-motivation and social relationships. We test our model on one of largest social network of China, Weibo. In the experiments, we predict EIs of over a hundred thousand users in Weibo with four numerical values and the sum of these values. The experimental results show that the distribution of users' EIs is normal. The results also indicate that EIs of females are higher than those of males.

We mine potentially psychological information in the users' posts and interactive information. The model is based on sentiment analysis, thus the stronger the motivation of users to express their emotions, the better the predictive effect of the model. However, most users in social networks are motivated by social interaction and self-presentation [30]. For instance, users post self-relevant information to interact with others, companies run advertisement campaigns, and journalists gather information and express ideas. Meanwhile, the extracted features depend on expert knowledge. All these may lead to inaccurate prediction models.

There exists the measurement of emotional intelligence based on the questionnaire [17,21,27,28]. The measurement of EI remains controversial. To evaluate the validity of the model, we can use the cross-validation. We preliminary use the relationship between EI and gender and the distribution of the values of EI. In the future, we will compare the relationship between EI and personality. In addition, we plan to employ questionnaires to optimize the models and apply the models onto twitter.

In the future, we are also planing to design more fine-grained features to better predict users' emotional intelligence with social networking data.

Acknowledgements. The work reported in this paper was supported in part by the Natural Science Foundation of China, under Grant U1736114 and by the National Key R&D Program of China, under Grant 2017YFB0802805.

References

1. Alexander, W.P.: Intelligence, concrete and abstract: note. Br. J. Psychol. **29**(1), 74 (1938)
2. Bar-On, R.: The development of an operational concept of psychological well-being. Ph.D. thesis, Rhodes University (1985)
3. Burrus, J., Betancourt, A., Holtzman, S., Minsky, J., Maccann, C., Roberts, R.D.: Emotional intelligence relates to well-being: evidence from the situational judgment test of emotional management. Appl. Psychol. Health Well-Being **4**(2), 151–166 (2012)
4. Chen, J., Liu, Y., Zou, M.: User emotion for modeling retweeting behaviors. Neural Netw. **96**, 11–21 (2017)
5. Davis, S.K., Humphrey, N.: Emotional intelligence predicts adolescent mental health beyond personality and cognitive ability. Pers. Individ. Differ. **52**(2), 144–149 (2012)
6. Ferrando, M., et al.: Trait emotional intelligence and academic performance: controlling for the effects of IQ, personality, and self-concept. J. Psychoeduc. Assess. **29**(2), 150–159 (2011)
7. Gardner, D.K.J., Qualter, P.: Concurrent and incremental validity of three trait emotional intelligence measures. Aust. J. Psychol. **62**(1), 5–13 (2011)
8. Gardner, H.: The theory of multiple intelligences. Ann Dyslexia **37**(1), 19–35 (1987)
9. Joseph, D.L., Newman, D.A.: Emotional intelligence: an integrative meta-analysis and cascading model. J. Appl. Psychol. **95**(1), 54–78 (2010)
10. O'Boyle Jr., E.H., Humphrey, R.H., Pollack, J.M.: The relation between emotional intelligence and job performance: a meta-analysis. J. Organ. Behav. **32**(5), 788–818 (2011)
11. Jurgens, D., Finethy, T., Mccorriston, J., Yi, T.X., Ruths, D.: Geolocation prediction in twitter using social networks: a critical analysis and review of current practice. In: International Conference on Weblogs and Social Media (2015)
12. Kosinski, M., Bachrach, Y., Kohli, P., Stillwell, D., Graepel, T.: Manifestations of user personality in website choice and behaviour on online social networks. Mach. Learn. **95**(3), 357–380 (2014)
13. Kosinski, M., Stillwell, D., Graepel, T.: Private traits and attributes are predictable from digital records of human behavior. Proc. Natl. Acad. Sci. U.S.A. **110**(15), 5802–5805 (2013)
14. Xu, L., Lin, H., Pan, Y., Ren, H., Chen, J.: Constructing the affective lexicon ontology. J. China Soc. Sci. Tech. Inf. **27**(2), 180–185 (2008)
15. Lopez-Zafra, E., Gartzia, L.: Perceptions of gender differences in self-report measures of emotional intelligence. Sex Roles **70**(11–12), 479–495 (2014)
16. Valadez Sierra, M.D., Borges del Rosal, M.A., Ruvalcaba Romero, N., Villegas, K., Lorenzo, M.: Emotional intelligence and its relationship with gender, academic performance and intellectual abilities of undergraduates. Electron. J. Res. Educ. Psychol. **11**, 395–412 (2013)
17. Mayer, J.D., Salovey, P., Caruso, D.R., Sitarenios, G.: Measuring emotional intelligence with the MSCEIT V2.0. Emotion **3**(1), 97–105 (2003)

18. Mayer, J.D., Salovey, P., Caruso, D.: Models of emotional intelligence. Ed. by R.J. Sternberg (2000)

19. Minkus, T., Ding, Y., Dey, R., Ross, K.W.: The city privacy attack: combining social media and public records for detailed profiles of adults and children. In: ACM on Conference on Online Social Networks (2015)

20. Modarresi, K.: Recommendation system based on complete personalization. Procedia Comput. Sci. **80**, 2190–2204 (2016)

21. Petrides, K.V.: Psychometric properties of the trait emotional intelligence questionnaire (TEIQue). In: Parker, J., Saklofske, D., Stough, C. (eds.) Assessing Emotional Intelligence. The Springer Series on Human Exceptionality, pp. 85–101. Springer, Boston (2009). https://doi.org/10.1007/978-0-387-88370-0_5

22. Bar-On, R.: BarOn Emotional Quotient Inventory: Technical Manual. Multi-Health Systems Inc., Toronto (1997)

23. Salovey, P., Mayer, J.D.: Emotional intelligence. Imagin. Cogn. Pers. **9**(6), 217–236 (1990)

24. Schutte, N.S., et al.: Development and validation of a measure of emotional intelligence. Pers. Individ. Differ. **25**(2), 167–177 (1998)

25. Thorndike, E.L.: Intelligence and its uses. Concours Med. **72**(18), 227–235 (1920)

26. Weinsberg, U., Bhagat, S., Ioannidis, S., Taft, N.: BlurMe: inferring and obfuscating user gender based on ratings. In: ACM Conference on Recommender Systems (2012)

27. Wong, C.S., Law, K.S., Wong, P.M.: Development and validation of a forced choice emotional intelligence measure for Chinese respondents in Hong Kong. Asia Pac. J. Manag. **21**(4), 535–559 (2004)

28. Wood, L.M., Parker, J.D.A., Keefer, K.V.: Assessing emotional intelligence using the emotional quotient inventory (EQ-i) and related instruments. In: Parker, J., Saklofske, D., Stough, C. (eds.) Assessing Emotional Intelligence. The Springer Series on Human Exceptionality, pp. 67–84. Springer, Boston (2009). https://doi.org/10.1007/978-0-387-88370-0_4

29. Yarkoni, T., Westfall, J.: Choosing prediction over explanation in psychology: lessons from machine learning. Perspect. Psychol. Sci. **12**(6), 1745691617693393 (2017)

30. Zhang, D., Feng, X., Chen, P.: Examining microbloggers' individual differences in motivation for social media use. Soc. Behav. Pers. **46**(4), 667–682 (2018)

31. Zhu, X., Ma, R., Sun, L., Chen, H.: Word semantic similarity computation based on HowNet and CiLin. J. Chin. Inf. Process. **30**(4), 29–36 (2016)

Design and Implementation of Medical Dispute Governance Based on Blockchain

Xiaofeng Wang[1(⊠)], Qilin Zhang[2], Zhenni Shi[2], and Ziyuan Ye[1]

[1] School of Communication, Shenzhen University, Shenzhen 518060, China
freewxf@szu.edu.cn
[2] School of Political Science and Public Management, Wuhan University,
Wuhan 430072, China

Abstract. Electronic medical record is the core component of hospital information system, and it is also an important evidence in solving social security and governance such as medical disputes, medical insurance cash and fraud. The most advanced digital certificates and other technologies have effectively solved a series of important security issues such as "identity camouflage" and "man-in-the-middle attacks" and have been granted certain legal effects. However, due to their dependence on trusted third-party organizations, there are facts. Technical loopholes and serious trust crises. Blockchain technology is considered to be the best solution for current data security due to its decentralized distributed storage, non-tamperable, consensus computing and other characteristics, and has received widespread attention. Based on the alliance blockchain architecture, the research project supported by this paper selects the health service and management organization of Nanshan District of Shenzhen as the social programming practice scenario; builds the alliance blockchain network based on Fabric super account, writes and deploys intelligent contracts, and collects the core of electronic medical records. The data item (desensitization) generates a HASH digest, and stores the HASH digest on the alliance blockchain network; the user can select the network node to download the corresponding HASH digest, and perform the two-way comparison to complete the electronic medical record security credit, thereby realizing Key governance of medical disputes. The experimental results show that the system can effectively complete the protection and acceptance of electronic medical records, and has a good social security and governance application prospects.

Keywords: Blockchain · Electronic medical record · Fabric · Medical dispute · Governance

Foundation projects: China Post-doctoral Foundation Project (2016M602370), Ministry of Education Key Research Base of Humanities and Social Sciences (Foundation No. 15JJD630009), Shenzhen Philosophy and Social Sciences "Thirteenth Five-Year Plan Project" (SZ2018B031) Author's brief introduction: Wang Xiaofeng (1981-), male, from Jingzhou, Hubei Province, doctor of computer science and post-doctoral of public administration, assistant professor of Communication College of Shenzhen University, deputy director of Health Management Research Institute of Shenzhen Academy of Accurate Academy of Mass Evidence-based Medicine, whose main research directions are machine learning and network information security. Zhang Qilin (1969-), male, Doctor of Management. He is currently a professor and doctoral supervisor of the Social Security Research Center of Wuhan University, and a visiting scholar of the Institute of Social and Policy of Yale University from 2000 to 2001. His main research fields are international comparison of medical security system, social policy, charity and non-profit organizations.

© Springer Nature Singapore Pte Ltd. 2019
W. Meng and S. Furnell (Eds.): SocialSec 2019, CCIS 1095, pp. 203–222, 2019.
https://doi.org/10.1007/978-981-15-0758-8_16

1 Introduction

On August 26, 2016, the Political Bureau of the Central Committee of the Communist Party of China deliberated and adopted the "Healthy China 2030" plan outline, pointing out: "National health is the foundation of a well-off society for all. Integrating health into all policies and guaranteeing people's health in an all-round and full-cycle way is the action guide for promoting the construction of a healthy China in the next 15 years." However, in recent years, malignant medical attacks and medical disturbances have emerged in endlessly, which makes the management of medical disputes by health management institutions become the focus of public attention. The problems existing in the mechanism of medical damage appraisal are also manifested in the large difficulty, the long period and the low rate of withdrawal in the hearing of medical disputes.

Table 1. Classification, causes and proportion of medical disputes (Data were collected from three hospitals in Nanshan District, Futian District and Luohu District respectively in Shenzhen City)

Type	The proportion of frequency	The proportion of litigation
A [Medical Satisfaction] For example, inappropriate speech, etc.	60%	0%
B [Medical quality (subjective feeling)] For example, the medical process is normal, but the result does not meet the expectations of the patient	15%	5%
C [Medical quality (objective error)] For example, medical malpractice caused by doctor's misconduct in the process of medical treatment, resulting in disputes	15%	95%
D [unreasonable trouble] For example, the patient recovers after transfer to another hospital and then disputes with the previous hospital about medical expenses	20%	0%

We investigated the core insititutions in dealing with medical disputes of each People's Hospitals in three different districts of Shenzhen City (Nanshan District, Futian District and Luohu District respectively), including: Doctor-patient relationship department, legal system department, medical risk prevention department, medical record department, etc. As shown in Table 1, the survey results reflect that the current medical disputes caused by medical malpractice mainly refer to the type C in the table, that is, disputes and disputes caused by medical malpractice (medication, surgery, etc.) in the medical process. Although its proportion of frequency is only 15%, it accounts for 95% in the proportion of litigation, and almost 100% of the cases will be based on electronic medical records (or medical records) as important evidence in the process of litigation. The targeted object of this system is exactly the type C medical disputes in Table 1, that is, medical disputes caused by medical accidents. According to the data disclosed by the 3rd China Internet Medical Congress in December 2017, there were 107,000 medical disputes and 42 typical violent injuries in China in 2016. Among them, the electronic medical records involved 85% of the cases, and the closure and withdrawal rates of disputes were 10% lower than the civil cases in the same period.

The above data highlight that the electronic medical record, which records medical services such as clinical diagnosis and treatment, guidance and intervention by medical institutions, is not only the core component of the hospital information system, but also an important evidence and ontology for solving social problems such as medical disputes, insurance disputes and disclosure of privacy data of diagnosis and treatment. At present, the platform of regional health information has been built all over the country, and its core system includes electronic medical record database. However, these electronic medical record systems are constructed and managed by hospitals and health institutions, which makes the objectivity and authenticity of electronic medical record information questioned and affected. Among them, the phenomenon of interest-driven medical record tampering and fabrication is indeed unavoidable, which results in untrue and inaccurate statistics, and seriously infringes on the legitimate rights and interests of patients.

To sum up, in the context of the development of big health and big data, health industry and management are facing more and more public supervision. It is urgent to establish an effective trust mechanism between patients and health departments. Ensuring the objectivity and authenticity of core data in electronic medical records is the most difficult problem in medical dispute management and litigation (disputes occur in hospitals and core data are kept in hospitals),which contains "information asymmetry" and "trust crisis". Essentially, the problem is caused by the difficulty in solving the "de-centralization" of data preservation and protection. The governance system designed in this paper will take electronic medical record data as the core data source and utilize alliance block chain technology to achieve the goal of "decentralization and trust" of core data, realizing the reliable acceptance of electronic medical records (desensitization collection and reliability guarantee) and being effectively applied in medical dispute management services.

2 Design of Governance System

2.1 Research Status and Framework Design

At present, the mainstream technologies of electronic file storage and protection can be divided into three categories: one-way hash function-based message digest and message authentication code-based electronic file verification and protection methods, digital signature and trusted digital timestamp-based electronic file protection methods, and the current cutting-edge "Distributed Storage and Consensus Protection Based on Block Chain Technology" [1]. In view of these three types of research, the following will carry out a review of research.

(1) A Method of Electronic Document Verification and Protection Based on One-way Hash Function Message Summary and Message Authentication Code Technology

The core of message digest technology is Hash algorithm, which maps binary strings of arbitrary length to binary strings of fixed length (e.g. 256 or 512 bits). This smaller binary string is called message digest or Hash hash value (hereinafter referred to as Hash digest). Since it is almost impossible to find two different inputs of the same Hash digest, the Hash digest is also called the "fingerprint" of electronic information. On the basis of message digest technology, message authentication code first combines the symmetric key shared by both sender and receiver, and then generates the Hash digest as a whole. Although Hash abstract can well protect the integrity of electronic information, it can not resist "camouflage" because it does not solve the problem of key distribution.Message authentication code adds authentication function on the basis of Hash digest, but this authentication is only between sender and receiver. It can not provide "proof to third party" or "denial afterwards" and can not become the basis of legal effect.

(2) Digital Signature and Electronic Document Protection Method Based on Trusted Digital Time Stamp Issued by Institutions

The core technology of digital signature technology is based on asymmetric encryption (RSA public key encryption algorithm) and Hash digest. The sender generates a Hash digest based on the electronic file, and encrypts it with the sender's private key (signature digital signature), then passes the original text (either plaintext or public key encryption based on the recipient, for example) and the encrypted Hash digest to the recipient at the same time. The receiver decrypts the encrypted Hash digest with the sender's public key (verifying digital signature) to get the original Hash digest, and then applies the Hash algorithm to the received electronic files to generate a new Hash digest. If the two Hash abstracts are aligned, it means that the information has not been destroyed or tampered with (content confirmation) in the transmission process cycle, or vice versa. Although digital signatures can provide "authentication to third parties" or "denial after the event", they cannot resist man-in-the-middle attacks because they cannot guarantee the reliability of public key transmission.

Digital time-stamp (DTS) is an encrypted certificate document. Based on digital signature technology, it is signed by a third-party trusted institution to the public key of the recipient. Its working process is as follows: The recipient registers the public key in the third party organization, and the institution signs the trusted practice and digital signature certificate to the recipient's public key; the sender confirms the validity of the recipient's public key after obtaining the certificate from the third party organization, and encrypts the message with the recipient's public key and sends it to the recipient. Finally, the recipient decrypts the message with its own private key. It can be seen that the trusted digital timestamp can not only guarantee the correctness of the public key in the digital signature process, but also uniquely identify the time, ownership and integrity of the content of the data object [5]. On November 14, 2010, the Symposium on Credible Time Stamp and Legal Effectiveness of Electronic Medical Records, organized by the Ministry of Health in the 5th Conference Room of the 2nd National Recruitment, confirmed that credible time stamp is an effective way to solve the legal effectiveness of electronic medical records. Trusted digital timestamp guarantees the transmission of public key and adds time label on the basis of digital signature. It is considered to be the most perfect and effective method of electronic document protection at present. However, the actual signer of trusted timestamp (including digital signature) is DTS certification authority, which includes Time Stamp Authority and Certificate Authority, which essentially require third-party authoritative agencies to endorse credit, are still a centralized technology lacking trust, and there are de facto loopholes and shortcomings in credibility and security [5].

(3) Data Distributed Storage and Consensus Protection Based on Block Chain

Block chain is a new programming framework which integrates encryption technology, point-to-point transmission, distributed storage and consensus computing technology. It can ensure that the distributed and inter-agency trusted data storage and verification system can be implemented by computer algorithm to solve the problems in multi-party cooperation and trusted processing without participation, which is widely considered to be the technological cornerstone of "the programmable credit society" [9]. As shown in Fig. 1, the development of block chains has gone through three important stages: digital currency (Bitcoin), de-centralized application platform (ETF), and social programming framework (Super Account). Using this technology in the protection of patient privacy and sensitive data (especially electronic medical records) can realize the protection, arbitration and notarization of electronic medical records, even the safe sharing of large data [15]. It can not only protect the rights and interests of patients, but also significantly enhance the credibility of health management departments. Block chain technology is currently mainly used in the financial field (digital money, real-time bank reconciliation system, etc.). There are few cases that can be used for reference in health management and social governance. Since its birth, the technology has produced three macro-structures: private chain (centralization), public chain (non-centralization), alliance chain (multi-centralization) and a variety of complex open source platforms [14]. In order to control and put it into practice, it is necessary not only to sort out the business process of health informatization in hospital and out-of-hospital areas, but also to dig and accumulate the technical details and philosophical principles of block chain (Chen Chun, 2017) and social application scenarios.

Fig. 1. The development of blockchain technology

To sum up, this paper aims to research and implement a multi-point consensus and autonomous electronic medical record acceptance system based on the block chain network of alliance chain architecture (multi-centralization, centralization and de-centralization compromise means), as shown in Fig. 2, which combines hospital electronic medical record database and health management platform. We collect disputes related data of electronic medical record by desensitization, generate HASH summary and store it to the link node of alliance block. By using multi-point broadcasting and consensus mechanism of alliance node, we can realize distributed and reliable storage that can not be tampered with afterwards. By downloading and comparing Hash abstracts with trusted nodes, patients can achieve reverse credit information, improve the governance efficiency of medical disputes, improve doctor-patient relationship, and greatly enhance the credibility of government management departments. This project has acquired a large number of data sets of scientific research cooperation, including the historical data (desensitization) of the hospital medical record system of the urban people's hospital in recent three years, and the online data set built with the regional health platform (the Health Planning Commission and the Administrative Bureau). Experiments on these data sets will fully verify and test the effectiveness and robustness of the system.

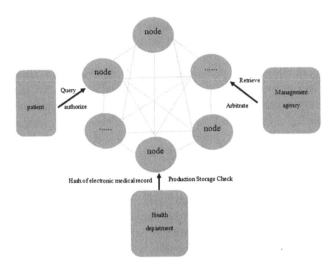

Fig. 2. Framework of medical dispute management system based on Consortium Blockchain

As shown in Fig. 2, circular nodes come from health service organizations and health management organizations, which together form a block chain network. Patients, judicial and arbitration departments are all users of the block chain network.

2.2   System Design Scheme from the Perspective of Social Programming

As shown in Fig. 3, the overall implementation plan of this project is from the perspective of social programming (the working principles of peer node, anchor peer node and order node are quoted from the underlying architecture of open source fabrics). The plan requires to build Alliance Block Chain Network System, which consists of two organizations: the health service department (Nanshan Hospital, Shekou Hospital) and the administrative department (Nanshan Health Planning Bureau, Nanshan Social Security Bureau, etc.).

(1) Channel is an important concept in fabrics. There are many channels in a block chain network system. Data between different channels is not shared (channel, can be regarded as independent data logical flow), and data privacy protection or business logic isolation can be achieved. Obviously, this project only needs one channel (i.e. HASH storage channel for electronic medical records).

(2) All the organizations in the two organizations are a node in the block chain network, which can be divided into three types: peer node, anchor peer node and order node. The whole network/channel can only have one anchor peer node, and

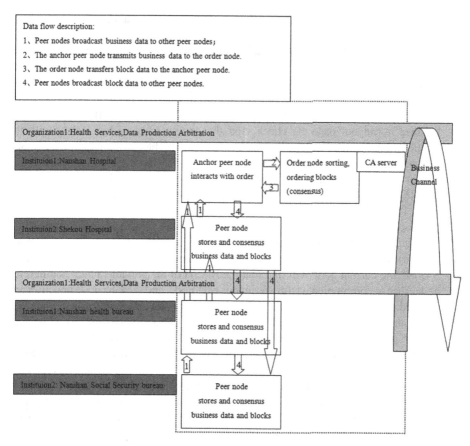

Fig. 3. Overall implementation plan from the perspective of social programming

each organization can have one order node. In order to simplify the system or save experimental resources, the whole network can have only one anchor peer node and one order node, and even the same node can act as both anchor peer node and order node. In fact, this system adopts the simplest design pattern (as described in Table 2). From the angle of communication network, all peer nodes (including the anchor peer node) are in the same communication network, and there is broadcast communication between peer nodes and other peer nodes, while the order node is outside the communication network. However, there is a dedicated communication link between the order node and the anchorpeer node. Applications deployed in different nodes (also known as smart contracts) achieve important functions such as data storage and consensus (tamper-proof), which gradually form a block chain.

(3) The main functions of peer node are: (a) Storing local business data (more general than transaction data), broadcasting business data (such as data stream 1) to other peer nodes, and storing business data from other peer nodes after verification. For this system, the business data is only the hash value of the medical record data items,

and there is no amount verification similar to the financial transfer, so the so-called business data verification is only to prevent duplicate submission of the same data; (b) Receiving block data from the anchor peer node, broadcasting block data to other peer nodes (e.g. data stream 4), and storing block data from the anchor peer node and other peer nodes after verification; (c) When the data in the historical block is tampered, and no auxiliary header HASH modification is made to all subsequent blocks, all block data after the historical block in the node will be invalidated because it can not pass the check, and the correct copy of block data will be duplicated from other nodes. (d) The data in historical blocks are tampered, and all subsequent blocks are modified by auxiliary head HASH. If the current node is an anchor peer node, when the latest block is formed, other peer nodes will find that the HASH of the previous block is different and thus, refuse to communicate with that node. Then the anchor peer node will become an isolated node and be excluded from the block chain network system, which will lead to the whole system paralysis (this is a manifestation of the immaturity of the block chain system based on fabirc at present). If the current node is not an anchor peer node, when the latest block is formed, the current node will find that the HASH of the previous block is different and refuse to communicate with the anchor peer node, and then the node becomes an isolated node and is excluded from the block chain network system.

(4) To configure a node (with high computing and storage performance) to be the anchor peer node. The anchor peer node performs three important functions: (a) Summarizing the business data of all peer nodes with data production behavior, such as data stream 1; (b) Communicating with the order node (trans-fering all data to the order node, such as data stream 2; receiving block data generated by the order node, such as data stream 3); (c) The newly generated block data and the HASH of the previous block in the node are broadcasted to all peer nodes for network-wide distributed storage, such as data stream 4.

(5) To configure a node (with high computing and storage performance) to be the order node. The order node performs two important functions: (a) Receiving business data from the anchor peer node, such as data stream 2, sorting the data according to the time and organization information in business data, and gener-ating block data structure. (b) The block data structure (HASH excluding the previous block) is returned to the anchor peer node, such as data stream 3.

2.3 System Design Scheme from Technical Perspective

As shown in Fig. 4, it is the specific technical architecture design of "Medical Dispute Governance Database System". It should be emphasized that the system in the dotted line frame corresponds to the health service (hospital) institutions one by one. (The number of hospitals is equal to the number of systems in the dotted frame; note that "upload program" uploads the data of a hospital only to the network node of the block chain corresponding to the hospital. The operation and data flow within the block chain network are shown in Sect. 4). That is to say, taking the block chain network formed by four hospitals as an example, the system in the dotted frame should implement four sets independently; taking the block chain network formed by two hospitals and two

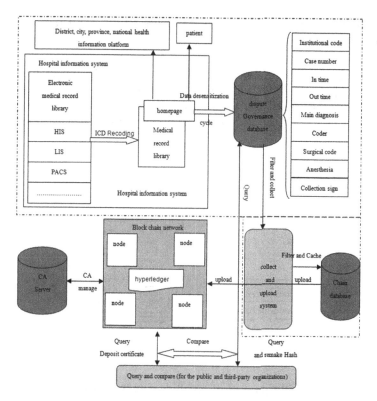

Fig. 4. Overall implementation plan from a technical perspective

administrative agencies as an example, the system in the dotted frame should implement two sets independently. For the case that the number of network nodes in block chain is N, it can be synthetically analogized (except for the case where the regional unified health information database has been built).

Considering the limitation of the actual situation (the business of this project is in the stage of scientific research and experiment, but has not landed in the actual business/administration), the Nanshan District of Shenzhen City is selected as the simulated experimental environment for this project, including: Block chain network simulation hospital 2 institutions (Shenzhen Nanshan People's Hospital, Shenzhen Nanshan Shekou Hospital), administrative agencies (Nanshan Health Planning Bureau, Nanshan Social Security Bureau). For the deployment in the actual production environment, the actual situation will be more complex: block chain network simulates x hospital institutions (hospital 1, hospital 2,... Hospital x, administrative organs y (administrative organ 1, administrative organ 2...administrative organ y). The number of X and Y and the selection of institutions depend on the actual situation of social services and administration.

3 Technical Implementation of Alliance Block Chain Network System

As shown in Fig. 5, the environment deployment diagram of the alliance block chain in this project is presented. We will build the top-level sub-project fabrics based on hyperledger in open source operating system ubuntu, which mainly includes three parts: block chain network node, block chain network system and chain program.

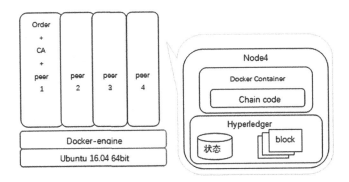

Fig. 5. Environmental deployment diagram

As shown in Fig. 6, the purpose of installing docker in this project is not to install fabric in docker, but to run intelligent contracts in the virtual machine environment of docker (the intelligent contracts in Ethernet workshop take EVM as virtual machines in Ethernet workshop) (Shown in Fig. 6b); of course, we can also do all this in a docker container (Shown in Fig. 6a). When the work is completed, it can be published as a docker image for others to use (or reuse) and greatly improve the efficiency of environmental deployment.

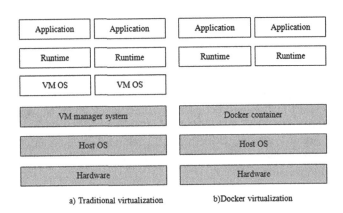

Fig. 6. Docker virtualization deployment

3.1   Building Alliance Block Chain Network

Based on the framework of social programming, this project selected four organizations in Nanshan District of Shenzhen City (two business organizations: Nanshan Hospital and Shekou Hospital; two administrative agencies: Nanshan District Health Bureau and Nanshan District Social Security Bureau) to form an alliance block chain network. By means of distributed certificate storage and arbitration of electronic medical record evidence, medical disputes management based on decentralized structure was realized. Correspondingly, in this section, we will build an alliance chain block chain network in four servers deployed to support the environment. The network consists of four nodes: four peer nodes and one order node (one peer node server also acts as an orderer node to provide order services for the other four nodes). Specific parameters are shown in Table 2.

Table 2. Basic support software list and installation configuration

ID	IP address	Node identification	Hostname	Organization
Server1	10.0.0.92	orderer_sp1(The node acts as both an anchor peer node and an order node)	peer1.org1.example.cn	Nanshan Hospital
Server2	10.0.0.93	sp2	peer2.org1.example.cn	Shekou Hospital
Server3	10.0.0.94	Sp3	peer1.org2.example.cn	Nanshan District Health Bureau
Server4	10.0.0.95	Sp4	peer2.org2.example.cn	Nanshan District Social Security Bureau

As shown in Table 3, in the process of building the HyperLedger Fabric environment, defining three configuration files correctly would be important, otherwise the alliance chain network will not work as planned. The three key core configuration files are:

Table 3. Core configuration file

File name	Function
crypto-config.yaml	Generating digital certificates for each node
configtx.yaml	Define institutions and configure relevant information to build Genesis blocks. (Before building the Genesis Block, you need to create a collection of validation files for all the nodes that correspond to it.) Among them, there is an OrdererType parameter in the configuration of Orderer information, which can be configured as "solo" and "kafka". The environmental configuration of this project is the consensus of Kafka nodes
order.yaml	Configure the digital certificate of the order node, the IP address of the extranet, etc.
core.yaml	Configure the digital certificate of peer node, IP address of external network, storage path of blocks, etc.

Deployment contract demonstration code:
CORE_PEER_MSPCONFIGPATH =/opt/fabric-cfg/crypto-config/peerOrganizations/
org1.bl.com/users/Admin@org1.bl.com/msp/./peer chaincode install-n VoteChain-v 10
4-p github.com/VoteChain

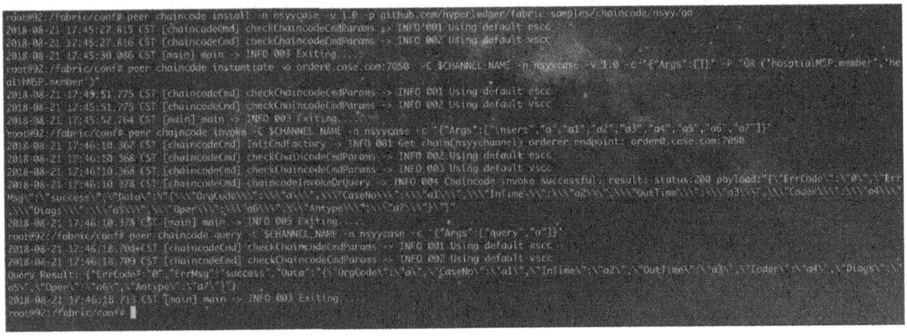

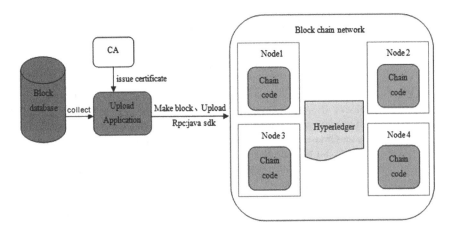

Fig. 7. Deploy and invoke smart contracts to implement data chaining and querying

As shown in Fig. 7, the core system of the federated block chain network is successfully deployed based on Fabric environment. The federated block chain network will be used for all-network storage (distributed storage + tamper-proof arbitration) electronic medical record feature data (HASH abstract), which can be effectively applied to medical dispute management. Next, we will mainly implement the application-level functions, such as feature data extraction, chaining, query, comparison and so on.

3.2   Upload key data to the Alliance Block Chain Network to form a consensus book

As shown in Fig. 8, we can write Java programs based on fabric JDK to remotely call the runtime of remote call (RPC,Remote Procedure Call) in block chain network system (such as fabric, bitcoin, Ethernet workshop), in order to achieve the purpose of

Fig. 8. Data packing and winding function module

operation and control of block chain network. The RPC interface of block chain system has two main forms: http_post (which can be implemented in any programming language or even web/js) and SDK of java/python/go. Because fabrics have many complex data such as identity and ca, it is generally not recommended to use RPC interface in the form of http, but RPC interface in the form of SDK which is easy to use after encapsulation (this project is based on Java sdk). The core implementation code ('Go' language intelligence contract) is shown in the Appendix A.1.

4   Technical Implementation of Governance Application System

Figures 9 and 10 shows the function module of Query and Comparison Governance System. Once medical disputes arise, we need to collect electronic medical record data as proof of lawsuit. We only need to query and generate HASH abstract of hospital department data from "Dispute Governance Database", and then query HASH abstract of original data based on decentralized certificate from alliance block chain. By comparing the two, we can arbitrate and judge whether there is data tampering. On this basis, we can greatly improve the effectiveness and credibility of medical dispute management.

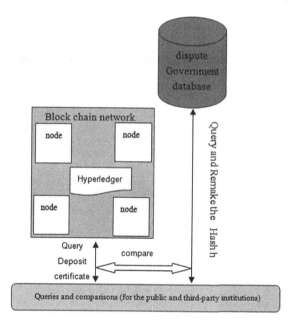

Fig. 9. Query raw data and deposit data to achieve dispute management (Macro structure)

4.1   Function Implementation of Searching Storage Card from Block Chain

As shown in Fig. 11, the user still needs to enter a query URL (page address and query search ID) in the web application. In order to improve the query efficiency, when the

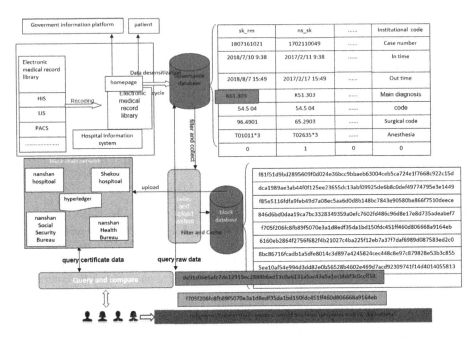

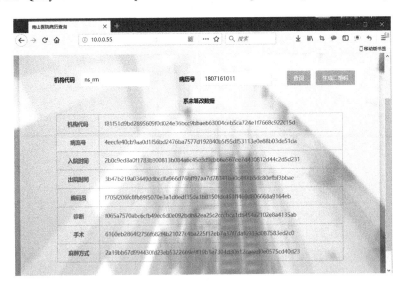

Fig. 10. Query raw data and deposit data to achieve dispute management (Detailed process)

Fig. 11. Patient index query the original certificate HASH in the blockchain

patient user discharges from hospital, the URL can be generated and stored offline (e.g. directly printed on the electronic medical record). When the user needs to initiate the query, the HASH value of the stored data can be obtained by scanning the two-dimensional code directly, which is very simple and efficient. Firstly, the users of the system are mainly oriented to arbitration institutions that have been set up beforehand, and ordinary users could complete registration and login only through identity card number, mobile phone number and authentication number. Secondly, although it is necessary to provide the institution number and medical record numbers as parameters when inquiring, queries with inconsistent ID card numbers and medical record numbers would be rejected. Finally, all the data queried are not plaintexts, but in the form of hashed abstracts, which do not have any readability and therefore do not cause privacy disclosure. The core implementation code (java calls fabric SDK) is shown in the Appendix A.2.

4.2 "Governance" by Querying the Stored Certificate Data and the Original Data

As shown in Figs. 12 and 13, the system has been put into use as a scientific research test in the Nanshan Hospital Group of Shenzhen City. The test results show that whether it is a judicial institution, an arbitration institution or a user, they can effectively arbitrate the data tampering behavior by querying and comparing the original certificate HASH and the corresponding data HASH in the database. Meanwhile, it can also improve the governance efficiency and credibility in the process of medical disputes.

4.3 "Governance" by Querying the Stored Certificate Data and the Original Data

There are still some defects in the system, such as:

(1) The system adopts RFTB (Byzantine Fault Tolerance) consensus algorithm. If tampering exists on two-thirds of the nodes, the tampered data is considered correct.
(2) The tampering behavior of the anchor peer node will directly lead to the isolation of this anchor peer node by the block chain network. As shown in Fig. 3, since the anchor peer node is unique and necessary in the whole coalition block chain, this will inevitably lead to the collapse and discontinuation of the whole governance system.

Fig. 12. Contrasting query arbitration for tampering data

Fig. 13. User scans the QR code to complete the self-service query

(3) As shown in Fig. 4, the bi-directional data of arbitration governance (original data and certificate data in the block chain) of the system actually come from the "Business Governance Database" of the business organization. However, extracting data from hospital's business system to "Business Governance Database" allows time difference (based on internal norms of the organization, reasonable adjustment of data, such as errors made by the attending physician or intern, standardization adjustment of medical data, standardization adjustment of medical data by data archiving staff, etc.). If there is pre-falsification at the source within the time difference, the system can not be arbitrated.

In view of (1) and (2) of the above shortcomings, considering that all network nodes are credible government agency nodes, tampering will not occur easily; Even if tampering occurs, it requires a lot of tedious operations on multiple nodes at the same time (from historical data to current real-time data, all blocks of the chain and HASH are needed to be tampered); In terms of defect (3), it is a defect existing in all other systems, Unless the process(from the production of business data to archiving and utilizing) happens instantaneously and in real time. However, it obviously does not conform to the actual management system of any hospital.

5   Conclusion

To sum up, this paper aims to research and implement a multi-point consensus and autonomous electronic medical record acceptance system based on the block chain network of alliance chain architecture (multi-centralization, centralization and de-centralization compromise means), as shown in Fig. 2, which combines hospital electronic medical record database and health management platform. We collect disputes related data of electronic medical record by desensitization, generate HASH summary and store it to the link node of alliance block. By using multi-point broadcasting and consensus mechanism of alliance node, we can realize distributed and reliable storage that can not be tampered with afterwards. By downloading and comparing Hash abstracts with trusted nodes, patients can achieve reverse credit information. This project can not only improve the governance efficiency of doctor-patient disputes, improve the doctor-patient relationship, and greatly enhance the credibility of government management departments, but also provide scientific practice cases for the block chain social programming framework, and promote the legislative process of a new type of electronic document protection technology.

Appendix

A.1 Go language intelligence contract

```
func (t *NsyyChaincode) insert(stub shim.ChaincodeStubInterface, args []string) pb.Response {
    if len(args) != 8 {
        return shim.Success(processError("Incorrect number of arguments. Expecting 8"))
    }
    nsyycase:=new (NsyyCase)
    nsyycase.OrgCode=args[0]
    nsyycase.CaseNo=args[1]
    nsyycase.InTime=args[2]
    nsyycase.OutTime=args[3]
    nsyycase.Coder=args[4]
    nsyycase.Diags=args[5]
    nsyycase.Oper=args[6]
    nsyycase.Antype=args[7]
    nsyyJsonByte, err := json.Marshal(nsyycase)
    if err != nil {
        return shim.Success(processError("insert Failure to serialize case objects"))
    }
    err= stub.PutState(args[0]+args[1],nsyyJsonByte)
    if(err!=nil){
        return shim.Success(processError("Failure to store case data"))
    }
```

A.2 Java calls fabric SDK

```java
public ModelAndView redicalRecorePage(String orgCode, String caseNo) {
        ModelAndView mv = new ModelAndView("mobileIndex");
        try {
            hfClient = getClient();

            nsyyChannel = geChannel(hfClient);
            String[] chaincodeArgs = new String[1];
            chaincodeArgs[0] = Sha256Util.getSHA256Str(orgCode) + Sha256Util.getSHA256Str(caseNo);
            String result = InvokeChainCode.invokeChainCode(hfClient, nsyyChannel, chaincodeArgs, "query");
            JSONObject obj = JSONObject.fromObject(result);
            String errCode = (String) obj.get("ErrCode");

            if ("0".equals(errCode)) {
                String queryOne = "select orgCode,caseNo,inTime,outTime,coder,diags,oper,antype from
BL_HP_MEDICALRECORD where caseNo =? and orgCode=?";
                List<MedicalRecordBean> medicalRecordBean = jdbcTemplate.query(queryOne, new
BeanMapper(), caseNo, orgCode);
                if (medicalRecordBean.size() == 0) {
                    mv.addObject("message", "The data has been deleted");
                    return mv;
                }
                String OrgCode = Sha256Util.getSHA256Str(medicalRecordBean.get(0).getOrgCode());
                String CaseNo = Sha256Util.getSHA256Str(medicalRecordBean.get(0).getCaseNo());
                String InTime = Sha256Util.getSHA256Str(medicalRecordBean.get(0).getInTime());
                String OutTime = Sha256Util.getSHA256Str(medicalRecordBean.get(0).getOutTime());
                String Coder = Sha256Util.getSHA256Str(medicalRecordBean.get(0).getCoder());
                String Diags = Sha256Util.getSHA256Str(medicalRecordBean.get(0).getDiags());
                String Oper = Sha256Util.getSHA256Str(medicalRecordBean.get(0).getOper());
                String Antype = Sha256Util.getSHA256Str(medicalRecordBean.get(0).getAntype());

                JSONObject dataJson = JSONObject.fromObject(obj.get("Data"));

                if (!OrgCode.equals(dataJson.getString("OrgCode"))) {
                    OrgCode = OrgCode + "(The data has been tampered)";
                }
                if (!CaseNo.equals(dat aJson.getString("CaseNo"))) {
                    CaseNo = CaseNo + "(The data has been tampered)";
                }
                if (!InTime.equals(dataJson.getString("InTime"))) {
                    InTime = InTime + "(The data has been tampered)";
                }
                if (!OutTime.equals(dataJson.getString("OutTime"))) {
                    OutTime = OutTime + "(Th e data has been tampered)";
```

```
        }
        if (!Coder.equals(dataJson.getString("Coder"))) {
            Coder = Coder + "(The data has been tampered)";
        }
        if (!Diags.equals(dataJson.getString("Diags"))) {
            Diags = Diags + "The data has been tampered";
        }
        if (!Oper.equals(dataJson.getString("Oper"))) {
            Oper = Oper + "(The data has been tampered)";
        }
        if (!Antype.equals(dataJson.getString("Antype"))) {
            Antype = Antype + "(The data has been tampered)";
        }
        mv.addObject("OrgCode", OrgCode);
        mv.addObject("CaseNo", CaseNo);
        mv.addObject("InTime", InTime);
        mv.addObject(" OutTime", OutTime);
        mv.addObject("Coder", Coder);
        mv.addObject("Diags", Diags);
        mv.addObject("Oper", Oper);
        mv.addObject("Antype", Antype);
        return mv;
    }
} catch (Exception e) {
    e.printStackTrace();
}
```

References

1. Zhang, N., Zhong, S.: Block privacy-based personal privacy protection mechanism. Comput. Appl. **37**(10), 2787–2793 (2017)
2. Yuan, Y.: Research on the protection of electronic documents. Chin. Inf. (3) 2017
3. Tao, Y., Zhou, X.: Mobile two-way authentication protocol based on Hash function. Comput. Appl. **36**(3), 657–660 (2016)
4. Wang, W., Li, Z.: Trusted electronic medical record system based on digital signature. Chin. Digit. Med. **11**(3), 19–21 (2016)
5. Zhang, X., Huang, M.: Application of trusted time stamp in electronic file security protection. Beijing Arch. **1**, 38–40 (2015)
6. Huang, X.: Blockchain creates trust——interview with chen chun, academician of the Chinese academy of engineering. High Technol. Ind. **7**, 30–33 (2017)
7. Yukihiro.: Graphical cryptography, vol.6, 229–251 (2016)
8. Xing, S., Feng, W.: Research on confidential electronic document protection scheme based on blockchain technology. Inf. Secur. Res. **3**(10) (2017)
9. Zyskind, G., Alex, N.O.: Decentralizing privacy: using blockchain to protect personal data. In: IEEE Security and Privacy Workshops, pp. 180–184. IEEE Computer Society (2015)

10. Yan, Z., Gan, G.: BC-PDS: protecting privacy and self-sovereignty through BlockChains for OpenPDS. In: Service-Oriented System Engineering. IEEE (2017)
11. Reijers, W.: Governance in blockchain technologies & social contract theories. Ledger **1**, 134–151 (2016)
12. Fu, D., Fang, L.: Blockchain-based trusted computing in social network. In: IEEE International Conference on Computer and Communications, pp. 19–22. IEEE (2017)
13. Ichikawa, D., Kashiyama, M., Ueno, T.: Tamper-resistant mobile health using blockchain technology. Jmir Mhealth Uhealth **5**(7), e111 (2017)
14. Kshetri, N.: Blockchain's roles in strengthening cybersecurity and protecting privacy. Telecommun. Policy **41**(10), 1027–1038 (2017)
15. Ubacht, J., Janssen, M.: Blockchain in government: Benefits and implications of distributed ledger technology for information sharing. Government Information Quarterly (2017)
16. Zhang, Q., Li, P.: Government trust, interpersonal trust and institutional dependence: an interpretation framework for urban and rural distress. Qinghai Soc. Sci. (5), 123–129 (2016)

Greedily Remove k Links to Hide Important Individuals in Social Network

Jie Ji, Guohua Wu, Chenjian Duan, Yizhi Ren, and Zhen Wang$^{(\boxtimes)}$ (ID)

School of Cyberspace, Hangzhou Dianzi University, Hangzhou, Zhejiang, China
{171270004,wugh,171270001,renyz,wangzhen}@hdu.edu.cn

Abstract. Closeness centrality is a type of measure that usually used in social network analysis (SNA). For personal privacy, we study how to help important individuals avoid being detected by closeness centrality analysis. In this paper, we present an optimization problem of finding k edges removed to minimize leader node closeness value to hide leader. We consider this problem in the undirected graph and prove its NP-completeness by reduction from the Hamiltonian cycle problem. Hence, we propose a greedy algorithm with a $(1 - \frac{1}{e})$ - approximation lower bound and design *UpdateCloseness* algorithm to reduce time cost by Breadth-First Search algorithm. Experimental results confirm the effectivity of our greedy scheme.

Keywords: Social network analysis · Closeness centrality · Hiding individuals · Greedy algorithm

1 Introduction

1.1 Background

Nowadays, there are still many issues in social network analysis (SNA) need to solve and one of the problems is "How to help individuals avoid being detected by social network analysis ?" (first proposed by Waniek [32]). Since social network analysis, such as centrality analysis and community-detection algorithms, plays vital roles in sociology, geography [27], economic [28], and counter terrorism [20], there is an urgent need to address the personal privacy disclosure problem caused by the misuse of social network analysis tool, which has been proved in [35].

In this paper, we try to handle the above problem by *closeness centrality*, which is a widely used centrality measure. It measures node importance by the inverse of the average of shortest path to all other nodes. A node with higher closeness value is closer to the other node in the network and may be more "influential" or knows better of the whole network [4]. The attacker may make use of closeness centrality analysis to find the important member in the network and obtain individuals' private information by analysing the public information [35].

Therefore, to guarantee the privacy of important individuals, we ask the question:"How to help important individuals avoid being detected by closeness

© Springer Nature Singapore Pte Ltd. 2019
W. Meng and S. Furnell (Eds.): SocialSec 2019, CCIS 1095, pp. 223–237, 2019.
https://doi.org/10.1007/978-981-15-0758-8_17

Table 1. Comparison with related work

Scheme	Edges updated	Measurement	Selection range	Hidden effect
Waniek [32]	Addition & Removal	Degree centrality [26]	Neighbours	Yes
Crescenzi [9]	Addition	Harmonic centrality [16]	Neighbours	No
This paper	Removal	Closeness centrality [2]	Entire network	Yes

centrality analysis?" In our work, we consider this problem as an optimization problem that how to minimum the leader node's closeness by removing limited edges in network. We take the limited edges into consideration for minimum disconnected cost and network topology change. The edge deletion can be seen as the relationship between two members are disconnected, for example, the user "unfriend" another user in Twitter [32]. This optimization problem makes sense because traditionally attacker uses the top-k closeness algorithm to find the leader nodes, the defender (who has the highest closeness value) does not know the exact value of k and has to minimize his closeness by limited network reduction to avoid being detected by attacker.

1.2 Related Work

The goal of our work is to hide the important node by solving the optimization problem of minimize closeness value by removing limited edges. There are two schemes which are similiar to our work. Table 1 compares our work with the published schemes. Our work is distinct from others in some aspects as follows.

– Note that Crescenzi [9] chooses the harmonic centrality to compute the closeness centrality instead of the original one [2]. Research [21] shows that harmonic centrality can be only a more prominent in the unconnected graph and in our work we assume that the graph is connected. Therefore, we choose the original *closeness centrality* to measure node importance.
– Differ from the other two schemes [9,32], we choose the deletion edges set in the whole network to make the result obtained by our scheme more accurate despite that it would increase time cost.

To date, there exists numerous research about closeness computing or ranking in mainly three aspects: closeness approximation algorithm, effective top-k closeness algorithm and update closeness in dynamic network. The existing work as follows:

Approximate Computing Closeness. In the traditional scheme, we have to run a breadth first search (BFS) to compute closeness, so it is infeasible to obtain every node's closeness for large-scale networks. Therefore, closeness approximation algorithm has been subject to considerable discussion. Cohen [8] proposed a closeness approximation algorithm by sampling some nodes and it can be applied in directed and undirected graph in near linear time complexity. Eppstein and Wang [31] proposed a closeness approximation algorithm to reduce the time of estimating all nodes' closeness in $O(\frac{\log n}{\epsilon^2}(n \log n + m))$ within a $(1+\epsilon)$ additive error. There are some other schemes to approximately compute closeness [7,30].

Fast Closeness Ranking. Although there have been studies on closeness approximation algorithms, in real-life scenarios, people tend to pay more attention to the closeness rank of node and top-k algorithm attracts most researchers' attention. The first study of top-k closeness algorithm was reported by Okamoto [18], and many researchers later proposed improved algorithms in this respect [3,6,15,19]. Bisenius [5] first proposed dynamic top-k closeness algorithm to compute top-k closeness after edge-addition or edge-deletion.

Dynamic Updating Closeness. Most of the above algorithms can only be used in the static graph. However, as edge connections and deletions occur frequently in real-life complex network, dynamic update closeness algorithm is particularly necessary. Saxena [25] proposed a heuristic dynamic closeness ranking algorithm to obtain one node's rank in $O(\alpha \cdot m)$ time. Tong [29] analysed the effects of edge deletions and additions on centrality and proposed scalable algorithm to find the edges that improve network information dissemination. Santos [23] proposed an approximate closeness algorithm that can be used after edge deletion in dynamic graphs. Sarıyüce [24], Kas [13] and Yen [34] proposed their unique update closeness algorithm in the dynamic graph.

1.3   Our Contributions

In this paper, we study the problem that how to minimize the leader node's closeness value by removing limited edges. We prove that this optimization problem is hard to solve in polynomial time unless $P = NP$ and try to propose a greedy algorithm with a pruning algorithm *UpdateCloseness* to reduce the number of traverse edges and nodes when calculate closeness. We estimate the approximate of our *UpdateCloseness* algorithm and compare our approximate scheme with the optimal solution and the other edge deletion schemes in various datasets to prove its efficiency and accuracy.

2   Preliminaries

2.1   Network Notation

Let $G = (V, E)$ be a connected, undirected and unweighted graph with $n := |V|$ nodes and $m := |E|$ edges. The edge between a pair of nodes, $u, v \in V$, is denoted as (u, v). We refer to the neighbors of the node u as $N(u) = \{v | (u, v) \in E\}$. We denote the shortest-path distance between node u and node v as dis_{uv} (we does not consider the case that there is no path from u to v).

Given a set of edges $R \subset E$, we denote by $G(R)$ the subgraph after removing the set of edges R in G, i.e. $G(R) = (V, E/R)$. Also, after removing a set of edges R, the distance between the chosen node u and node v can be denoted as $dis_{uv}(R)$.

2.2 Closeness Centrality

The concept of *closeness centrality* in network analysis was introduced by Beauchamp [2]. This measure qualifies the importance of a given node according to the shortest-path distance from this node to all other nodes. For a given node u, the normalized *closeness centrality* is defined as follows:

$$clo_u = \frac{n-1}{\sum_{v \in V \setminus \{u\}} dis_{uv}} \qquad (1)$$

3 Problem Definition and Analysis

3.1 Theoretical Definition

In this section, we define the main theoretical problem of our work. As is mentioned in Sect. 1, we try to minimize the leader node's *closeness* by removing some edges in the network. We formally define this problem as Leader Node Closeness Minimization (LNCM) problem as follows.

Definition 1 (Leader Node Closeness Minimization Problem). *We defined the problem by a tuple (G, u, R, k). Let $G = (V, E)$ be a network which is unweighted, undirected and connected, $u \in V$ is the leader node with maximum closeness value, $R \subset E$ is the set of edges that can be removed, $k \in \mathbf{Z}$ denotes the maximum of the edges can be removed. The problem is to find a set of edges, $R \subset E$ and $|R| \leq k$, and $G(R) = (V, E \setminus R)$ is connected, and R is in:*

$$\underset{R \subset E, |R| \leq k}{\arg \min} \quad clo_u(G(R)). \qquad (2)$$

In this problem, we assume that the modified network $G(R)$ is still connected after removing edges to remain the integrity of the network. We consider a budget k to limit the passive impact of removing edges to the network. For ease in explanation, we only consider the case in the *undirected* graph.

3.2 Hardness Analysis

In this section, we study the optimization problem from the computational point of view. We prove the NP-completeness of the LNCM problem by Theorem 1 as follows.

Theorem 1. *Leader Node Closeness Minimization Problem is NP-complete.*

Proof. Due to space constraints, we prove the LNCM problem is NP-complete in Fig. 1 by the Hamiltonian cycle problem to our problem.   □

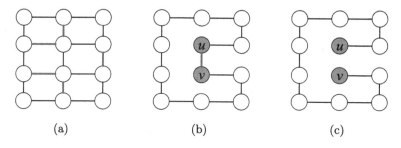

(a)   (b)   (c)

Fig. 1. The reduction from the Hamiltonian cycle problem to the LNCM problem

4 Approach

In Sect. 3, we define the optimization problem and prove the NP-completeness of the LNCM problem. In order to solve this problem in real-life scenarios, in this section, we design an approximation algorithm to find a deletion edges set to minimize leader node's closeness. Intuitively, we consider a greedy algorithm to obtain the approximate solution of the optimization problem in polynomial time, and the detail of the greedy algorithm is shown in Algorithm 1.

Algorithm 1. GreedyReduction

Input: A network, $G = (V, E)$, the leader node u, and a selected integer
　　$k \in \mathbf{N}$;
Output: A set of removed edge $R \subset E$ and $|R| \leq k$;
1 $R := \varnothing$;
2 **while** $|S| < k$ **do**
3 　**foreach** $e \in E$ **do**
4 　　**if** $G(V, E \backslash e)$ *is connected* **then**
5 　　　Compute $clo_u(e)$
6 　$e_{min} = \arg\min clo_u(e)$
7 　$R := R \cup e_{min}$
8 **return** R;

We first prove that the greedy algorithm of the optimization problem can have a $(1 - \frac{1}{e})$ - approximation lower bound solution [17] .

Theorem 2. *The LNCM problem subject to a cardinality constraint admits a $1 - \frac{1}{e}$ approximation algorithm*

Proof. We prove the monotone and submodular of the shortest-path sum function $\sum_{v \in V \backslash \{u\}} dis_{uv}(R)$ for every possible solution of LNCM to find an approximate solution in a lower bound $1 - \frac{1}{e}$.   □

Now, we show that our greedy algorithm has a solution of the LNCM optimization problem in a lower bound $1 - \frac{1}{e} \approx 0.63$. In Sect. 5, we find that the solution of the greedy algorithm is usually more accurate than this lower bound.

4.1   Greedy Improving Algorithm

In this section, we try to improve the computing time of the greedy approximation algorithm by decreasing the nums of traversing edges and nodes. Traditional way to compute the closeness of a node has to run a BFS algorithm in the whole network and its time complexity is $O(m + n)$. Therefore, we can find that the time complexity of the greedy algorithm in worst case is $O(k \cdot m \cdot (m + n))$ and it is infeasible in real-life complex networks. In order to reduce the running time of closeness computing at line 5 in Algorithm 1, we provide a *UpdateCloseness* algorithm inspired by Yen's work [34].

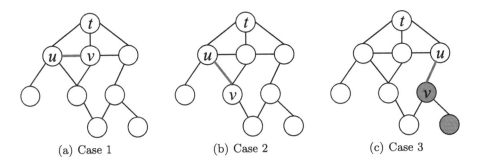

(a) Case 1   (b) Case 2   (c) Case 3

Fig. 2. The three cases of the edge deletion

Example. To illustrate our *UpdateCloseness* algorithm, we obtain a BFS tree by running a BFS algorithm in an arbitrary graph $G = (V, E)$ with the leader node t in Fig. 2. Now, we delete an arbitrary edge $e = (u, v) \in E$ (guarantee connectivity) and the distance from the leader node t to the other nodes in the graph will be divided into three cases as follows.

- Case 1. In Fig. 2(a), the two nodes of the removed edge (u, v), u and v, are in the same level of the BFS tree. In this case, it is evident that $\sum_{v \in V \setminus \{t\}} dis_{tv}(e) = \sum_{v \in V \setminus \{t\}} dis_{tv}$.
- Case 2. In Fig. 2(b), we find that u and v are not in the same level of the BFS tree, i.e. $dis_{tv} > dis_{tu}$. However, the node v still has a neighbor node in the upper level and there is a shortest path with same distance from t to v. Hence, $dis_{tv}(e) = dis_{uv}$ and $\sum_{v \in V \setminus \{t\}} dis_{tv}(e) = \sum_{v \in V \setminus \{t\}} dis_{tv}$
- Case 3. In Fig. 2(c), we find that u and v are not in the same level of the BFS tree, i.e. $dis_{tv} > dis_{tu}$. Differ from Case 2, the node u has no neighbors in the topper level of the BFS tree after edge deletion, so we have to update

the distances between t and a set of affected nodes, which are blacked out in Fig. 2(c), include v and its child nodes which has no neighbors in the upper level of the BFS tree.

Algorithm 2. FindAffectSet

Input: A network, $G = (V, E)$, the leader node t, edge $(start, end)$,
            shortest-path array dis'
Output: The Affect set of node S
1 $S := \emptyset$, $Q := \emptyset$;
2 $Q := Q \cup end$;
3 **while** $Q \neq \emptyset$ **do**
4 $\quad$ $x := Q.dequeue()$;
5 $\quad$ $S := S \cup x$;
6 $\quad$ **foreach** $y \in N_x$ and $dis_{uy} > dis_{ux}$ **do**
7 $\quad\quad$ **if** $!\exists z \in N_y$ not in the upper level of BFS tree **then**
8 $\quad\quad\quad$ $Q := Q \cup y$;

9 **return** S;

Our UpdateCloseness Algorithm. In our *UpdateCloseness* algorithm, our goal is to reduce the time cost by running a BFS to compute the shortest-path distance between the leader node and other nodes. As mentioned above, our dynamic *UpdateCloseness* algorithm tries to reduce time cost of the BFS algorithm by updating only the distance of the affected set of nodes exploited by Algorithm 2. In detail, Algorithm 2 returns the affected set of node S which is similar to Case 3 above. We denote end as the node of the removed edge $e \in E$ which is in the lower level of the BFS tree. We design a queue Q to run a pruned search in the child nodes of the lower node end (lines 3–11). For each neighbor nodes of the node extracted from the queue, if there are no neighbors in the upper level of the BFS tree (line 7), we push it into the queue Q. Algorithm 2 repeats this procedure until the queue Q is empty.

In Algorithm 3, we aims at computing the updated shortest-path array dis' by a pruned search. First, in lines 1–9, if the removed edge $e \in V$ is the same situation of the Case 1 or Case 2 mentioned in the example above, the algorithm return the original closeness value and original distance array dis. In line 10, we use Algorithm 2 to find the affected set of the nodes, which corresponds to Case 3. For each node extracted from S, if it has neighbor nodes in the same level of the BFS tree, we update its distance from its neighbor node which is nearest to the leader node t and update the total of all distances to t (lines 13–16). This procedure will be repeated untill all nodes in S have been updated.

Algorithm 3. UpdateCloseness

Input: A network, $G = (V, E)$, the number of nodes $N = |V|$, the leader node
t, edge $e = (start, end) \in E$, shortest-path array dis, the original total
distance ToD

Output: The updated closeness $clo_{up} := (N - 1)/ToD'$ and the updated
shortest-path array dis

1   $S := \varnothing$;

2   **if** $dis_{t,start} == dis_{t,end}$ **then**

3     $\lfloor$ **return** $(N - 1)/ToD$;

4   **foreach** $x \in N_{end}$ **do**

5   **if** x *in the upper level of BFS tree* **then**

6       $\lfloor$ **return** $(N - 1)/ToD$;

7   $S := FindAffectSet$

8   **while** $S \neq \varnothing$ **do**

9     $x := S.dequeue()$

10   **if** $\exists y \in N_x$ *in the same level of BFS tree* **then**

11      $dis_{ux}(e) = Min(dis_{uy}) + 1$;

12      $ToD' := ToD - dis_{ux} + dis_{ux}(e)$;

13 **return** $(N - 1)/ToD'$;

Analyse Time Complexity. We analyse the time complexity of our greedy algorithm to prove its efficiency. In our greedy algorithm, we employ the *Update-Closeness* algorithm to prune the number of nodes that has to traverse. The number of the traverse nodes and edges is defined as τ_{mn}, whose worst case is $O(m+n)$. We can find that the time complexity of our updatecloseness is $O(\tau_{mn})$ and greedy algorithm's time complexity is $O(k \cdot m \cdot \tau_{mn})$.

5 Experiments

In this section, we evaluate the efficiency and accuracy of our algorithm by some experiments. First, we evaluate the efficiency of our *UpdateCloseness* algorithm in different kinds of and sizes of networks. Second, we compare the solutions of our greedy algorithm with the optimal results. What's more, we compare our greedy algorithm with other algorithms which using different edge deletion strategies. We run all program codes of experiments on the computer which has a Intel i5-8500 CPU(3.0 GHz) with 6 cores and 16 GB memory.

5.1 Datasets

To measure our algorithm, we have selected several real-life networks and generated different types of random networks. There are mainly three types of random

Table 2. Real-life datasets that used in the experiments

Network	$|V|$	$|E|$	Network type
WTC	36	64	Terrorist network
Jazz	198	2742	Collaboration network
FB-tvshow	3892	17262	Social network
FB-politician	5908	41729	Social network
FB-government	7057	89455	Social network

generation networks as follows: Random graph [10], Small-world network [33] and Scale-free network [1]. These random networks are respectively denoted as ER, BA and WS.

Also, we select some real-life datasets which are commonly used in complex network analysis. Table 2 shows the details of every real-life network. WTC network [14] is the terrorist network of the WTC 911 attack. Jazz [12] is the collaboration network in a band which selected from the Alex Arenas Website. FB-tvshow, FB-politician and FB-government [22] are the social networks in Facebook obtained from SNAP.

Table 3. Complex network datasets used in evaluating the efficiency of our *Update-Closeness* algorithm

Graph	$|V|$	$|E|$	Speed up ratio
ER - 5	3000	15057	35.01
ER - 12.5	3000	37572	31.26
BA - 2	3000	5996	31.56
BA - 5	3000	14975	30.08
WS - 2	3000	6000	30.04
WS - 5	3000	15000	31.85
FB-tvshow	3892	17262	28.95
FB-politician	5908	41729	32.59
FB-government	7057	89455	36.15

5.2 Evaluate UpdateCloseness Algorithm

To assess our *UpdateCloseness* algorithm, we design comparative experiments between our algorithm with the BFS algorithm. Since the efficiency of our update algorithm is depend on the specific structure of the network, we evaluate *Update-Closeness* algorithm in the following two ways:

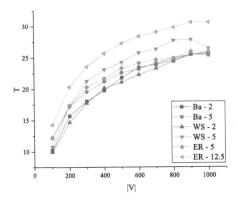

Fig. 3. The average speed up ratio T in different sizes and kinds of random networks

- Randomly generate graph of different sizes and randomly select a node $v \in V$ in each graph. Repeatedly calculate closeness value by BFS and *UpdateCloseness* in 5000 times after randomly edge deletion and calculate average value.
- Randomly select a node $v \in V$ in a large-scale network G and randomly remove an edge $e \in E$, compute the closeness value by BFS and *UpdateCloseness*, repeat 5000 times and calculate average value.

Note that, in the first experiment, the node size of the random generated network is range from 100 to 1000 and the edge size of the every graph is 2 or 5 times of the node size (ER is 5 or 12.5 times). The ratio of the average time cost by BFS and *UpdateCloseness* algorithm is used to measure the efficiency of *UpdateCloseness*, i.e. speed up ratio $T = \frac{t_{BFS}}{t_{update}}$.

Table 3 and Fig. 3 show the results of the two experiments. We observe that our update algorithm can reduce at least 9 times the computing time compared to BFS regardless of the random generated model. In the large scale networks, our algorithm is nearly 30 times of the BFS algorithm because of using pruning strategy to reduce the number of edges and nodes that have to traverse. Hence, we find that the time cost by *UpdateCloseness* algorithm change a little in different networks and we ascertain that our algorithm can significantly reduce the traverse edges and nodes when calculating node closeness regardless of network structure.

5.3   Compare Approximate Solution with the Optimal Solution

In this section, we select several networks to evaluate our greedy algorithm and compare with the optimal solutions. The edge deletion budget k is range from 1 to 7 and we compare the greedy result with the optimal one in every k value in three random generated networks and a real-life network. Considering that the time to calculate the optimal solution increases exponentially with the increasing number of deleted edges, we only select small-scale networks (about 30 nodes and 60 edges). Table 4 shows the detail of four networks. We choose the worst

Table 4. Datasets used in comparing greedy solutions with the optimal solutions

Graph	$|V|$	$|E|$	Min Appro Ratio
WTC [14]	36	64	0.9632
Random graph	30	55	0.8511
Scale-free	30	56	0.9437
Small-world	30	60	0.9174

Table 5. Datasets used in comparing greedy solution with the other algorithms

Graph	$|V|$	$|E|$
WTC	36	64
Jazz	198	2742
FB-tvshow	3892	17262
FB-politician	5908	41729
BA - 2	1000	1996
BA - 5	1100	5475
WS - 2	1000	2000
WS - 5	1000	5000

case in every k budget as the *minimum approximation ratio* (denoted by Min Appro Ratio) and Table 4 shows the ratio of evert networks. We observe that the worst case of our algorithm is far better than the theoretical approximation ration $(1 - \frac{1}{e} \approx 0.63)$ proved in Sect. 4.

Figure 4 shows that the differences of the closeness value of the target node between the optimal solution and greedy one in every budget k. Obviously, our greedy algorithm can significantly reduce the target node closeness and the result is still very close to the optimal solution. What's more, our algorithm can reduce the time cost from several days to just one second when the budget k is 7 and we assure that it can reduce much time in the complex network in practice. The above results prove that our greedy algorithm can obtain significant approximate results in limited time in practice.

5.4   Compare Approximate Algorithm with Other Algorithms

In this section, we compare our greedy algorithm with other algorithms with different edge selection strategies as follows:

(1) uniformly and randomly choose k edges in the whole network.(**Random**)
(2) choose k edges whose nodes have the highest degree sum.(**Top-k degree**)

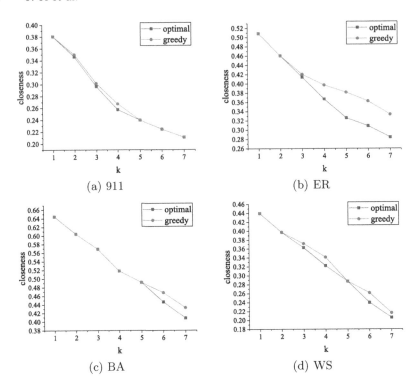

Fig. 4. The comparison of the optimal and greedy closeness results in experiment 2

(3) choose k neighbor edges whose nodes have the highest degree. (**Top-k neighbor degree**)

(4) choose k edges whose nodes have the highest closeness sum. (**Top-k closeness**)

The first comparison algorithm above is easy to understand and the other three comparison algorithms choose edges by different top-k strategies. The third algorithm is a variant of ROAM algorithm (proposed by Waniek [32]) . To compare our greedy algorithm with the algorithm above, we select several random and real-life networks and details are shown in Table 5. We set the edge deletion budget k in range from 1 to 10.

Figure 5 shows the different results in random networks or real-life networks. We observe that our greedy algorithm works better than other four comparison algorithms in general and the three top-k algorithms can only c obtain lower approximation results. **Random** algorithm performs poor in all networks because there are limited edges whose deletion can contribute to closeness decrement in complex network.

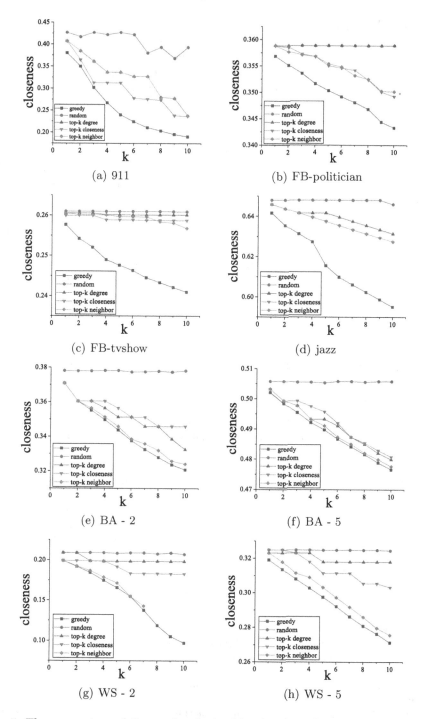

Fig. 5. The comparison of the results obtained by the algorithms in experiment 3 in real-life networks and random networks

6   Conclusions

In this paper we have presented a feasible method for minimizing node closeness by limited k edges deletion in the whole network. We first prove the NP-complete of the optimization scheme and propose an greedy algorithm. We find the lower bound of the greedy algorithm by theoretical analysis and design *UpdateCloseness* algorithm to reduce the time cost by BFS. In experiment, we evaluate the efficiency of *UpdateCloseness* and test our greedy algorithm with the optimal results or approximate results obtained by other algorithms. Thanks to our greedy algorithm, we are able to obtain the approximate results in seconds (where optimal results would take days to compute) and the results has *minimum approximation ratio* in more than 0.85.

Since the study is limited to minimize closeness value, it is not possible to consider the closeness rank of the target node and edge deletions may block the normal communication in network. Hence, in future, our work may include the extension of our algorithm to other centrality measures, such as betweenness [11], and proposing faster or more accurate schemes. We also plan to apply our algorithm in closeness rank.

References

1. Barabási, A.L., Albert, R.: Emergence of scaling in random networks. Science **286**(5439), 509–512 (1999)
2. Beauchamp, M.A.: An improved index of centrality. Behav. Sci. **10**(2), 161–163 (1965)
3. Bergamini, E., Borassi, M., Crescenzi, P., Marino, A., Meyerhenke, H.: Computing top-k closeness centrality faster in unweighted graphs. In: ALENEX, pp. 68–80. SIAM (2016)
4. Berno, B.: Network formation with closeness incentives. In: Naimzada, A.K., Stefani, S., Torriero, A. (eds.) Networks, Topology and Dynamics, vol. 613, pp. 95–109. Springer, Heidelberg (2009). https://doi.org/10.1007/978-3-540-68409-1_4
5. Bisenius, P., Bergamin, E., Angriman, E., Meyerhenke, H.: Computing top-k closeness centrality in fully-dynamic graphs. In: ALENEX, pp. 21–35. SIAM (2018)
6. Borassi, M., Crescenzi, P., Marino, A.: Fast and simple computation of top-k closeness centralities. arXiv preprint arXiv:1507.01490 (2015)
7. Chan, S.Y., Leung, I.X., Liò, P.: Fast centrality approximation in modular networks. In: CNIKM, pp. 31–38. ACM (2009)
8. Cohen, E., Delling, D., Pajor, T., Werneck, R.F.: Computing classic closeness centrality, at scale. In: COSN, pp. 37–50. ACM (2014)
9. Crescenzi, P., Dangelo, G., Severini, L., Velaj, Y.: Greedily improving our own closeness centrality in a network. TKDD **11**(1), 9 (2016)
10. ERDdS, P., R&wi, A.: On random graphs i. Publ. Math. Debrecen **6**, 290–297 (1959)
11. Freeman, L.C.: A set of measures of centrality based on betweenness. Sociometry, pp. 35–41 (1977)
12. Gleiser, P.M., Danon, L.: Community structure in jazz. Adv. Complex Syst. **6**(04), 565–573 (2003)
13. Kas, M., Carley, K.M., Carley, L.R.: Incremental closeness centrality for dynamically changing social networks. In: ASONAM, pp. 1250–1258. ACM (2013)

14. Krebs, V.E.: Mapping networks of terrorist cells. Connections **24**(3), 43–52 (2002)
15. Le Merrer, E., Le Scouarnec, N., Trédan, G.: Heuristical top-k: fast estimation of centralities in complex networks. Inf. Process. Lett. **114**(8), 432–436 (2014)
16. Marchiori, M., Latora, V.: Harmony in the small-world. Phys. A Stat. Mech. Appl. **285**(3–4), 539–546 (2000)
17. Nemhauser, G.L., Wolsey, L.A., Fisher, M.L.: An analysis of approximations for maximizing submodular set functions-i. Math. Program. **14**(1), 265–294 (1978)
18. Okamoto, K., Chen, W., Li, X.-Y.: Ranking of closeness centrality for large-scale social networks. In: Preparata, F.P., Wu, X., Yin, J. (eds.) FAW 2008. LNCS, vol. 5059, pp. 186–195. Springer, Heidelberg (2008). https://doi.org/10.1007/978-3-540-69311-6_21
19. Olsen, P.W., Labouseur, A.G., Hwang, J.H.: Efficient top-k closeness centrality search. In: ICDE, pp. 196–207. IEEE (2014)
20. Ressler, S.: Social network analysis as an approach to combat terrorism: past,present, and future research. Homel. Secur. Aff. **2**(2) (2006)
21. Rochat, Y.: Closeness centrality extended to unconnected graphs: the harmonic centrality index. Technical report (2009)
22. Rozemberczki, B., Davies, R., Sarkar, R., Sutton, C.: Gemsec: graph embedding with self clustering (2018)
23. Santos, E.E., Korah, J., Murugappan, V., Subramanian, S.: Efficient anytime anywhere algorithms for closeness centrality in large and dynamic graphs. In: IPDPSW, pp. 1821–1830. IEEE (2016)
24. Sariyuce, A.E., Kaya, K., Saule, E., Catalyurek, U.V.: Incremental algorithms for network management and analysis based on closeness centrality. arXiv preprint arXiv:1303.0422 (2013)
25. Saxena, A., Gera, R., Iyengar, S.: A faster method to estimate closeness centrality ranking. arXiv preprint arXiv:1706.02083 (2017)
26. Shaw, M.E.: Group structure and the behavior of individuals in small groups. J. Psychol. **38**(1), 139–149 (1954)
27. Takhteyev, Y., Gruzd, A., Wellman, B.: Geography of twitter networks. Soc. Netw. **34**, 73–81 (2012)
28. Ter Wal, A.L., Boschma, R.A.: Applying social network analysis in economic geography: framing some key analytic issues. Ann. Reg. Sci. **43**(3), 739–756 (2009)
29. Tong, H., Prakash, B.A., Eliassi-Rad, T., Faloutsos, M., Faloutsos, C.: Gelling, and melting, large graphs by edge manipulation. In: CIKM, pp. 245–254. ACM (2012)
30. Ufimtsev, V., Bhowmick, S.: An extremely fast algorithm for identifying high closeness centrality vertices in large-scale networks. In: IAAA, pp. 53–56. IEEE Press (2014)
31. Wang, D.E.J.: Fast approximation of centrality. Gr. Algorithms Appl. **5**(5), 39 (2006)
32. Waniek, M., Michalak, T.P., Wooldridge, M.J., Rahwan, T.: Hiding individuals and communities in a social network. Nat. Hum. Behav. **2**(2), 139 (2018)
33. Watts, D.J., Strogatz, S.H.: Collective dynamics of "small-world" networks. Nature **393**(6684), 440 (1998)
34. Yen, C.C., Yeh, M.Y., Chen, M.S.: An efficient approach to updating closeness centrality and average path length in dynamic networks. In: ICDM, pp. 867–876. IEEE (2013)
35. Zhou, B., Pei, J., Luk, W.: A brief survey on anonymization techniques for privacy preserving publishing of social network data. ACM Sigkdd Explor. Newsl. **10**(2), 12–22 (2008)

Blockchain-Based Threshold Electronic Voting System

Borui Gong, Xingye Lu, Lau Wang Fat, and Man Ho Au[✉]

The Hong Kong Polytechnic University, Hong Kong, China
{borui.gong,xingye.lu}@connect.polyu.hk,
{franky.wf.lau,mhaau}@polyu.edu.hk

Abstract. In this paper, we propose a secure blockchain-based electronic voting (e-voting) system with distributed authorities. Specifically, we employ threshold blind signature to distribute trust for registration; and threshold ElGamal decryption to distribute trust in ballots tallying. Combining these techniques with decentralized blockchain technology, our system can achieve verifiability, eligibility, fairness and anonymity with reduced trust. We also analyze the efficiency of our system by implementing the proposed e-voting system on a typical laptop for performance evaluation. Our system is efficient enough to be employed in practice based on the experiment results.

Keywords: Electronic voting · Blockchain · Threshold cryptosystem · Blind signature

1 Introduction

As an important social function, voting has been studied extensively. With the rapid development of the Internet, electronic voting (e-voting) has gained considerable amount of interest over the years. The notion of e-voting was first put forth by Chaum [8] in 1981. It empowers voters to cast their ballots remotely through the network. Security and accuracy are two important issues that must be considered [15]. They are usually provided through the use of cryptographic techniques. Typically, the following cryptographic approaches are adopted, namely, Mix-net [8], homomorphic encryption [28], linkable ring signature [23] and blind signature [9].

Mix-net removes the link between ballots and voters by shuffling the ballots in system. Homomorphic encryption can allow the entity to operate the ballots in ciphertext domain without decryption. It enables fast tallying by adding all votes in encrypted form together, followed by a single decryption to obtain the final result. A subtle issue involved in the use of these two approaches is the need for a responsible party to produce proof of correctness of these operations. Due to this requirement, their computation cost is usually very high. Besides, homomorphic encryption is more suitable for voting systems with a small number of choices. Linkable ring signature is also usually used to construct a secure voting

© Springer Nature Singapore Pte Ltd. 2019
W. Meng and S. Furnell (Eds.): SocialSec 2019, CCIS 1095, pp. 238–250, 2019.
https://doi.org/10.1007/978-981-15-0758-8_18

system. It can prevent unauthorized voter to cast ballots while maintain privacy of legitimate voters. However, at least one operation has computation complexity linear to the size of anonymity set (i.e. the number of legitimate voters in the case of e-voting) in all existing linkable ring signatures. Consequently, it is inefficient if the number of legitimate voters is high. Blind signature is also another common approach to construct voting system. Voters can obtain certified ballots from the authorities in a privacy-preserving manner based on blind signatures. However, the authority could create as many ballots as it wish without being detected.

By adopting these cryptographic techniques, an e-voting system can achieve the commonly defined security requirements. However, usually a public bulletin board is needed to publish the final voting results. The bulletin board also has to be trusted by all the participants. To address this issue, recent e-voting schemes adopt blockchain as the underlying technique to instantiate the public bulletin board. McCorry et al. [25] presented the first implementation of a decentralized and self-tallying e-voting protocol. Some companies like The Blockchain Voting Machine [18], FollowMyVote [5] also proposed solutions of adopting blockchain as a ballot box. However, all these solutions are platform dependent. More recently, Yu et al. [35] proposed a new approach to construct platform-independent secure voting system based on blockchain.

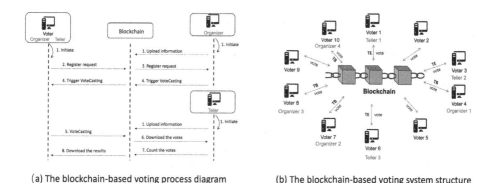

(a) The blockchain-based voting process diagram   (b) The blockchain-based voting system structure

Fig. 1. Overview of our blockchain-based electronic voting system

Taking computation cost and efficiency into consideration, we employ blind signature, encryption and blockchain with threshold techniques to construct our e-voting system. We made trade-offs between efficiency, anonymity and whether or not trusted party has to be completely eliminated. In our construction, we use threshold blind signature for voter registration. For a large group size, the approach is more efficient than linkable ring signature. The trade-off here is that a threshold number of registration authority is trusted not to abuse its powerful and allow registration of unauthorized voters. Ballot in our system is encrypted using ElGamal encryption in which the corresponding decryption key is distributed to a set of authorities using threshold techniques. Our system does achieve the property of fast tallying for systems based on homomorphic encryption. Besides, we emphasize that the efficiency of our system is practical enough to be developed in the real world based on our experiment results. The overview of our construction is showed in Fig. 1.

1.1 Related Work

Mix-net [8], homomorphic encryption [28], linkable ring signature [23] and blind signature [9] are the common cryptographic approaches adopted to achieve anonymity and verifiability in the e-voting systems.

Mix-net was proposed by Chaum [8] in 1981. It consists of a number of mixes, which can shuffle and remask the ballots in order to break the link between voters and their ballots. To reduce the trust assumption, the concept of universal verifiability has been developed [30]. It means that each mix should proof the completely correctness of its operation. In 2002, Jakobsson et al. [19] proposed a new technique called RPC mix net to make the voting systems robust, without proving the completely correctness. However, such proofs are usually hard to generate and verify due to its computation efforts while its first implementation has not been made until 2002 [16]. The efficiency of this approach was further improved in [17] but its time consumed in proving is still a bottleneck.

Homomorphic encryption proposed in [28] is another commonly used approach to preserve anonymity in voting system. Generally, existing e-voting systems mainly adopts Paillier encryption [29,34] and ElGamal decryption [21,22]. Based on the models set by Benaloh et al. [6,7,10], Cramer proposed a new cryptographic protocol for multi-authorities [11], which can distribute authorities. It was further strengthened in [12], which is the first optimal solution for large-scale systems through threshold techniques. This system is not a general construction since the choices of voters are binary (yes or no). In addition, as no single ballot is decrypted, the casted ballots must be proven correct by using zero-knowledge proof. Thus, it cannot be employed on multi-choices voting systems easily due to its huge computation cost. Compared with mix-net, it is more suitable for voting systems with small number of candidates (e.g. yes/no voting) [4]. Nonetheless, it can be used to provide additional properties: In [31], it was combined with mix-net to improve the efficiency in voting system.

Linkable ring signature was proposed in [23], which can be used to ensure authenticity of the ballots. Its signature size is linear to the group size. Some works aims to reduce signature size [14,32]. However, the time consumed in signing or verification process is still linear to the group size. Blind signature [9] is commonly used to register voters. Specifically, in the registration phase, a legitimate voter will receive a blind signature on a random value. This signature-value pair can be used to prove authenticity of the voter. This method was first used in a secret e-voting mechanism by Fujioka et al. in 1992 [15]. Okamoto proposed the first practical receipt-free voting schemes for large-scale election in [26]. However, compared with the linkable ring signature, adopting blind signature requires the signer to be trusted. If the signer is compromised, the attacker will be able to cast as many ballots as he wishes. To address this issue, threshold techniques [13] can be applied. Juang et al. [20] proposed a scheme to support distributed authorities by applying threshold techniques. Recently, Mateu et al. [24] proposed a threshold voting system by achieving the property of public verifiability.

1.2   Overview of Our Approach

We construct our e-voting system by combining a (t, n)-threshold blind signature $\mathcal{TB}$, a (t^*, n^*)-threshold ElGamal decryption scheme $\mathcal{TE}$ with blockchain technology. The conceptual construction is outlined as follows.

To register, t organizers co-operate to issue a threshold blind signature, using $\mathcal{TB}$, for the eligible voter. When an eligible voter casts his/her ballot, he/she encrypts his/her ballot with threshold ElGamal scheme $\mathcal{TE}$, whose encryption key is publicly available. The encrypted ballot, together with the signature obtained from the registration phase, is submitted to the blockchain. In the vote counting phase, co-operations of at least t^* tellers is needed to decrypt the encrypted ballots. The results are also published on the blockchain. As long as there are less than t (resp. t^*) malicious organizers (resp. tellers), the votes must be casted by legitimate users. Also, thanks to the blindness of $\mathcal{TB}$, no one will be able to link the ballot to a voter. In addition, since each user only receives one signature-random value pair, double ballots can therefore be detected and discarded. This ensure fairness. Looking ahead, the threshold techniques employed in $\mathcal{TB}$, $\mathcal{TE}$ are both one-round, meaning that the communication process can be simply conducted through the public blockchain efficiently.

1.3   Our Contributions

In our paper, we propose an e-voting system using distributed blind signature, encryption and blockchain. Specifically, we system offers the following features.

1. *Our system does not rely on a single trusted third party.* Using a threshold blind signature scheme, the role of registration authority is played by n organizers in our system. Likewise, n^* tellers play the role of tallying authority. Through combining these two techniques, our system does not rely on a single trusted third party.
2. *Our system is distributed.* We distribute the capability of registration and tallying in a round efficient manner. This matches the inherent decentralized nature of blockchain perfectly. Thus, our system can is truly distributed.
3. *Our system is anonymous.* We use blind signature to protect the voters' identity. Specifically, even if the set of registration authority colludes, they will not be able to link a ballot to a registered voter.
4. *Our system is efficient.* We implement our system to evaluate its efficiency. From the experimental results, the performance of our system is efficient enough to be adopted in practice. Notably, the time and complexity at the user side is constant.

1.4   Outline

In the next section, we review hardness assumptions, threshold blind signature scheme, threshold ElGamal decryption scheme, followed by the syntax of e-voting systems with its security requirements. We propose our e-voting system and its security analysis in Sects. 3.1 and 3.2 respectively. We give our implementation results with efficiency analysis in Sect. 4. We conclude the paper in Sect. 5.

2   Preliminaries

2.1   Hardness Assumptions

Let group $\mathbb{G}_1$ be a group with prime order q, whose generator is P. We review the well-known hard cryptographic problems.

- **CDH (Computational Diffie-Hellman) Problem.** Given a triple $(P, P^a, P^b) \in \mathbb{G}_1$, where $a, b \in \mathbb{Z}_q^*$, find the element P^{ab}.
- **DDH (Decision Diffie-Hellman) Problem.** Given a quadruple $(P, P^a, P^b, P^c) \in \mathbb{G}_1$, where $a, b, c \in \mathbb{Z}_q^*$, decide whether $c = ab$.
- **GDH (Gap Diffie-Hellman) Problem.** A class of problems where CDH problem is hard but DDH problem is easy.

GDH Group. Groups where the CDH problem is hard but DDH problem is easy are called GAP Diffie-Hellman (GDH) groups.

2.2   Threshold Blind Signature

The (t, n)-threshold blind signature [33], based on GDH hard problem, containing the following four algorithms, namely, Setup algorithm TBU, Key Generation algorithm TBK, Signature Generation algorithm TBS and Signature Verification algorithm TBV, where TBK and TBS are two interactive algorithms. Let n players in this protocol denoted as $\{L_1, L_2, ..., L_n\}$.

1. *Setup Algorithm* TBU
   On input security parameter 1^λ, this algorithm outputs public parameters param $= (\mathbb{G}_1, \mathbb{G}_t, q, P, H, \hat{e})$. $\mathbb{G}_1$ is a GDH group with order q, P is its generator and $H : \{0,1\}^* \to \mathbb{G}_1$ denotes a one-way function. $\mathbb{G}_t$ denotes a pairing group and $\hat{e}$ denotes the pairing operation, i.e., $\hat{e}(\mathbb{G}_1, \mathbb{G}_1) \to \mathbb{G}_t$. Looking ahead, these parameters will be uploaded to the blockchain in our e-voting system. It is an implicit input to the following algorithms.
2. *Key Generation Protocol* TBK
   The interactions between the players, $\{L_i\}_{i=1}^n$, are described as follows.
   - L_i conducts the following computations.
     (a) Picks up the parameters a_{ij} $(j = 0, 1, 2, .., t - 1)$ randomly in the following polynomial $f_i(x)$:

$$f_i(x) = a_{i0} + a_{i1}x + ... + a_{i,t-1}x^{t-1}.$$

(b) Computes and broadcasts $P^{a_{ij}}$ for $j = 0, 1, ..., t-1$; sends $f_i(j)$ to each player L_j for $j = 1, 2, ..., n$; $j \neq i$.

– L_i receives the information from other players.

(a) After receiving $f_j(i)$ from L_j for $j = 1, 2, ..., n$; $j \neq i$, player L_i verifies if

$$P^{f_j(i)} = \prod_{k=0}^{t-1} P^{a_{jk} \cdot i^k}.$$

If the check fails, L_i broadcasts a complaint against L_j.

(b) L_i computes the secret share $s_i = \sum_{k=1}^{n} f_k(i)$ and the public share $Q_i = P^{s_i}$, which will be broadcasted to other players. The public key in this algorithm will be set as $Q = \prod_{i=1}^{n} P^{a_{i0}}$, which can be computed using Q_i.

After executing TBK protocol, the public key is set as $Q = P^s$ where the secret key is $s = \sum_{i=0}^{n} a_{i0}$, which is distributed to the n players but does not appear explicitly in the protocol.

3. *Signature Generation Protocol* TBS

This protocol allows user A to obtain a blind signature on message m from t signers. Let $S = \{L_i | 1 \leq i \leq t\}$ denote the set of t signers. For the ease of presentation, we use w_i to denote $\prod_{j \in S, \, j \neq i} \frac{j}{j-i}$.

(a) User A randomly chooses $r \in \mathbb{Z}_q^*$ and blinds message m by computing $m' = H(m)^r$. A sends m' to every signer $L_i \in S$.

(b) Signer L_i computes and sends σ_i to user A's address on the blockchain after receiving m', where

$$\sigma_i = m'^{w_i s_i}.$$

(c) User A validates σ_i by checking if the following equation holds.

$$\hat{e}(\sigma_i, P) \stackrel{?}{=} \hat{e}(m'^{w_i}, Q_i).$$

If this does not hold, A sends m' to the signer L_i again. Otherwise, A computes the signature σ on m as,

$$\sigma = \left(\prod_{i \in S} \sigma_i \right)^{-r}.$$

4. *Key Verification Algorithm* TBV

The signature σ on the message m is accepted if

$$\hat{e}(\sigma, P) = \hat{e}(H(m), Q).$$

2.3 Threshold ElGamal Decryption Scheme

The (t^*, n^*)-threshold ElGamal decryption scheme [27] consists of the following four algorithms, namely, TEU, TEK, TEC, TED, where TEK and TED are interactive algorithms. It is based on the DDH problem. Let $\{T_1, T_2, ..., T_{n^*}\}$ denote the set of n^* players.

1. *Setup Algorithm* TEU:
   On input security parameter 1^λ, this algorithm outputs public parameters param $= (\mathbb{G}_1, \mathbb{G}_t, q, P, \hat{e})$, where $\mathbb{G}_1$ is an elliptic curve group of order q with P as its generator. $\mathbb{G}_t$ is a pairing group and $\hat{e}$ denotes the pairing operation, i.e., $\hat{e}(\mathbb{G}_1, \mathbb{G}_1) \to \mathbb{G}_t$. Looking ahead, param will be uploaded to blockchain and it is an implicit input of the following algorithms.

2. *Key Generation Protocol* TEK:
   Same as the TBK protocol of the threshold blind signature scheme, each user T_i randomly selects a_{ij} in the $(t^* - 1)$ degree polynomial $f_i(x)$, where

   $$f_i(x) = a_{i0} + a_{i1}x + \ldots + a_{i,t^*-1}x^{t^*-1},$$

   and sends $f_i(j)$ to T_j. The public share of T_i is $Q_i^* = P^{s_i^*}$, which will be broadcasted. Its corresponding secret is $s_i^* = \sum_{k=1}^{n^*} f_k(i)$. The resulting public key is set as $Q^* = \prod_{i=1}^{n^*} P^{a_{i0}}$ and secret key is $s^* = \sum_{i=0}^{n^*} a_{i0}$. The whole algorithm can be written as: TEK $\to (Q^*, s^*, Q_i^*, s_i^*)$, for $i \in \{1, 2, .., n^*\}$.

3. *Encryption Algorithm* TEC:
   On input with message m and public key Q^*, the ciphertext is computed as,

   $$C = (C_1, C_2) = (P^k, mQ^{*k}),$$

   where k is a random number: $k \overset{\$}{\leftarrow} \mathbb{Z}_q$.

4. *Decryption Protocol* TED:
   The decryption protocol takes ciphertext C as input. t^* players in list $S^* = \{T_i | 1 \le i \le t^*\}$ decrypt the ciphertext as follows together.
   (a) Each player computes and broadcasts $m_i = C_1^{-w_i s_i}$, where

   $$w_i = \prod_{j \in S^*,\ j \neq i} \frac{j}{j - i}.$$

   (b) After receiving m_i, verifies if

   $$\hat{e}(m_i, P) = \hat{e}(C_1^{-w_i}, Q_i).$$

   If the above equation does not hold, broadcasts a complaint on T_i.
   (c) Finally, the resulting decrypted message is computed as

   $$m = C_2 \cdot \prod_{i=1}^{t^*} m_i.$$

Correctness. The decrypted message, m, has the form,

$$m = C_2 \cdot \prod_{i=1}^{t^*} m_i = C_2 \cdot \prod_{i=1}^{n^*} C_1^{-w_i s_i}$$

$$= C_2 \cdot \prod_{i=1}^{n^*} C_1^{-\frac{j}{j-i} \cdot s_i}$$

$$= C_2 \cdot C_1^{-s^*}$$

When we derive the above result, we use the Lagrange interpolation and we can see that the decrypted message is correct.

2.4   E-Voting

Syntax. The e-voting system contains the following three kinds of entities, namely, **Voters, Organizers** and **Tellers**.

- **Voters.** The eligible voter can only votes one ballot during voting.
- **Organizers.** Organizers can give voters voting rights through registering.
- **Tellers.** The tellers will count the ballots after voting.

An e-voting system consists of the following four phases, namely, **KeyGen, Register, VoteCasting** and **VoteCounting**.

1. **KeyGen.** The voters, organizers and tellers generate their own public and secret keys respectively.
2. **Register.** Voters get voting rights from organizers through registering.
3. **VoteCasting.** Each voter casts their ballot in the system.
4. **VoteCounting.** Tellers count the ballots and publish the results.

Security Requirements. The security properties of the e-voting system are summarized as following four points.

- **Verifiability.** It means that individual voter can verify whether his/her ballot has been counted correctly or not.
- **Eligibility.** This property requires that only eligible voters are allowed to cast votes only once. Besides, only valid ballots will be counted.
- **Fairness.** This property requires that no early results can be obtained before the end of voting. It guarantees that the choice of voters cannot be influenced by current voting results.
- **Anonymity.** The anonymity property requires that no one can reveal the owner of a ballot. In other words, voters can cast their ballots anonymously.

3   Construction and Security Analysis

3.1   Our Construction

We adopt blockchain technology, a (t, n) threshold blind signature $\mathcal{TB}$ - (TBU, TBK, TBS, TBV), a (t^*, n^*) threshold ElGamal encryption scheme $\mathcal{TE}$- (TEU, TEK, TEC, TED) and a signature scheme $\Pi^{sig} - \{\mathsf{KeyG}, \mathsf{Sign}, \mathsf{Verify}\}$ to construct our blockchain-aided e-voting system.

Entities. Three entities involved in our e-voting system is described as follows.

- **Voters.** Assume that there are l eligible voters, i.e., $V_i \in \{V_1, V_2, .., V_\ell\}$.
- **Organizers.** Organizers are played by n eligible voters, i.e., $L_i \in \{L_1, L_2, .., L_n\}$.
- **Tellers.** Tellers are played by n^* eligible voters, i.e., $T_i \in \{T_1, T_2, .., T_{n^*}\}$.

Detailed Construction. There are five phases in our voting system, namely, **Setup, KeyGen, Register, VoteCasting** and **VoteCounting**.

1. **Setup**: On input security parameter 1^λ, it outputs param $= (\mathbb{G}_1, q, P, H)$ and broadcasts it. $\mathbb{G}_1$ is a GDH group with order q, P is its generator. $H : \{0,1\}^* \to \mathbb{G}_1$ is a one-way function. param is an implicit input to the following algorithms.
2. **KeyGen**: Each voter V_i first generates public key and secret key pair in Π^{sig}, i.e., $(pk_i, sk_i) \leftarrow$ KeyG. l players in $\mathcal{TB}$ will be randomly selected from n eligible voters, i.e., $\mathcal{L} = \{L_1, L_2, .., L_n\}$. l^* players in $\mathcal{TE}$ are randomly picked from n^* eligible voters and we denote them as $\mathcal{T} = \{T_1, T_2, .., T_{n^*}\}$. Finally, run TBK with players in $\mathcal{L}$ and TEK with players in $\mathcal{T}$ to get,
   - Public and secret shares of L_i are set as, $Q_i = P^{s_i}$ and s_i. Q_i will be broadcasted on blockchain.
   - The public key in $\mathcal{TB}$ is set as $Q = P^s$, with secret key s.
   - Public and secret shares of T_i are set as, $Q_i^* = P^{s_i^*}$ and s_i^*. Q_i^* will be broadcasted on blockchain.
   - The public key in $\mathcal{TE}$ is set as $Q^* = P^{s^*}$, with secret key s^*.
3. **Register**: Every voter V_i can get a blind signature on its public key pk_i, by interacting with t players L_i on TBS protocol, i.e., (σ_i, pk_i).
4. **VoteCasting**: Each voter V_i encrypts its ballot b by running TEC algorithm under the public key Q^*,

$$\mathsf{TEC}_{Q^*}(b) \to C_i.$$

   V_i then uses its registered secret key sk_i to sign on the ciphertext, e.g., $\mathsf{Sign}_{sk_i}(C_i) \to \sigma_i'$ and puts the quadruple $(pk_i, \sigma_i, C_i, \sigma_i')$ on the blockchain.
5. **VoteCounting**: When counting the ballots, tellers T_i first run TBV protocol to verify the signature σ_i on the voter's public key pk_i, followed by validating signature σ_i' on ciphertext C_i. That is,

$$In\ \mathcal{TB}.\mathsf{TBV} : \hat{e}(\sigma_i, P) \overset{?}{=} \hat{e}(H(pk_i), Q);$$

$$In\ \Pi^{sig}.\mathsf{Verify} : \mathsf{Verify}(C_i, \sigma_i') \overset{?}{=} 1.$$

If all the verifications are passed, t^* tellers decrypt C_i together to get the ballot b. Ballot b will be added to the quadruple, i.e., $(pk_i, \sigma_i, C_i, \sigma_i', b)$. The quadruple will then be broadcasted on blockchain.

3.2   Security Analysis

Our e-voting system can achieve four properties, namely, verifiability, eligibility, fairness and anonymity.

- **Verifiability.** The result will be put behind the quadruple as $(pk_i, \sigma_i, C_i, \sigma_i', b)$. Each user can verify whether his or her ballot has been counted correctly.

- **Eligibility.** This property is guaranteed by the unforgeability in blind signature. The malicious adversary cannot forge a new valid signature pair in blind signature, hence he cannot forge a valid ballot in the form of $(pk_i, \sigma_i, C_i, \sigma'_i)$; The other way of destroying the voting system's eligibility is to vote multiple times by using the same identity. This cannot be achieved because the quadruple $(pk_i, \sigma_i, C_i, \sigma'_i)$ reveals pk_i of the voter. Tellers can recognize it immediately if same voter casts ballots for multiple times.
- **Fairness.** This property can be guaranteed by the security in threshold ElGamal decryption scheme. The ballots casted by voters are encrypted by using ElGamal Decryption scheme, anyone cannot obtain the final result before vote counting phase.
- **Anonymity.** This property is guaranteed by the blindness in threshold blind signature. As every voter gets the signature on their public key blindly. Besides, we use blockchain to broadcast all the information, identity of the voters cannot be leaked. Our system achieves highly anonymous in this way.

4   Implementation and Performance

4.1   Implementation Setup

We implement our voting system on a MacBook Pro with 3.1 GHz Intel Core i5 processor and 16 GB memory. We use PBC library [2] and Crypto++ library [1] to implement our system. We choose the parameters suggested in Type A internals [3]. Our implementation results are given by parallel computing to simulate the real situation.

4.2   Results and Performance Evaluation

As **Setup** and **KeyGen** can be seen as the preparation process of voting, we evaluate **Register**, **VoteCasting** and **VoteCounting** phases in our system with holding $(7, 10)$-threshold. The results of our experiments are as follows.

From Table 1, we can see that time consumed in each phase for each voter is a roughly constant value, with maintaining parameters in threshold. The total time consumed in each stage is linear to the number of voters in the system.

Besides, we also test our system by changing parameters (t, n) in threshold blind signature scheme and threshold ElGamal decryption scheme. The average time consumed in each stage has slight linear relation with parameter t, while the additional operation only costs little time while increasing t. The number in n set does not have impact on the average consumed time.

In particular, when using a $(7, 10)$ threshold, it takes roughly 11-ms to count one vote. For 1 million votes, it takes about 3.06 h to complete vote counting on a laptop. We stress that our final results are based on experiments over a laptop. When the system is deployed on a real server, the efficiency can be improved. Furthermore, the efficiency can be further optimized with moving the process of validation on signature ahead, in vote casting phase. Thus, our whole system is efficient and practical enough to be adopted in the real world.

Table 1. Time Consumed in Each Phase with $(7, 10)$ Threshold

Time consumed t'	Number of voters n'				
	1000	2000	3000	4000	5000
Total time in **Register** (min)	0.3	0.6	0.9	1.22	1.49
Average time in **Register** = Total time/n (ms)	18.007	17.987	18.001	18.255	17.919
Total time in **VoteCasting** (min)	0.1	0.19	0.29	0.39	0.48
Average time in **VoteCasting** = Total time/n (ms)	5.829	5.835	5.838	5.874	5.792
Total time in **VoteCounting** (min)	0.18	0.37	0.55	0.74	0.91
Average time in **VoteCounting** = Total time/n (ms)	11.058	11.011	11.060	11.084	10.973

5   Conclusion

In this paper, we combine threshold signature scheme, threshold ElGamal decryption and blockchain to build a distributed e-voting system. We show that our system achieves the commonly defined security requirements for any e-voting systems. We also implement our system and evaluate its performance. The results show that it is practical for typical scenarios.

Acknowledgment. We appreciate the anonymous reviewers for their valuable suggestions. Part of this work was supported by the National Natural Science Foundation of China (Grant No. 61602396), Early Career Scheme research grant (ECS Grant No. 25206317) from the Research Grant Council of Hong Kong, the Innovation and Technology Support Programme of Innovation and Technology Fund of Hong Kong (Grant No. ITS/356/17), and the MonashU-PolyU-Collinstar Capital Joint Lab on Blockchain.

References

1. Crypto++ library. https://www.cryptopp.com/
2. Pbc library. https://crypto.stanford.edu/pbc/manual/
3. Pbc library - type a internals. https://crypto.stanford.edu/pbc/manual/ch08s03.html
4. Aditya, R., Boyd, C., Dawson, E., Viswanathan, K.: Secure e-voting for preferential elections. In: Traunmüller, R. (ed.) EGOV 2003. LNCS, vol. 2739, pp. 246–249. Springer, Heidelberg (2003). https://doi.org/10.1007/10929179_44
5. Aradhya, P.: Distributed ledger visible to all? ready for blockchain? (2016). https://www.huffpost.com/entry/are-we-ready-for-a-global_b_9591580
6. Benaloh, J., Yung, m.: Distributing the power of a government to enhance the privacy of voters. Association for Computing Machinery Inc., August 1986
7. Benaloh, J.D.C.: Verifiable secret-ballot elections. PhD thesis, New Haven, CT, USA (1987). AAI8809191

8. Chaum, D.: Untraceable electronic mail, return addresses, and digital pseudonyms. Commun. ACM **24**(2), 84–90 (1981)

9. Chaum, D.: Blind signatures for untraceable payments. In: Chaum, D., Rivest, R.L., Sherman, A.T. (eds.) Advances in Cryptology, pp. 199–203. Springer, Boston, MA (1983). https://doi.org/10.1007/978-1-4757-0602-4_18

10. Cohen, J.D., Fischer, M.J.: A robust and verifiable cryptographically secure election scheme. In: Proceedings of the 26th Annual Symposium on Foundations of Computer Science, SFCS 1985, Washington, DC, USA, pp. 372–382. IEEE Computer Society (1985)

11. Cramer, R., Franklin, M., Schoenmakers, B., Yung, M.: Multi-Authority secret-ballot elections with linear work. In: Maurer, U. (ed.) EUROCRYPT 1996. LNCS, vol. 1070, pp. 72–83. Springer, Heidelberg (1996). https://doi.org/10.1007/3-540-68339-9_7

12. Cramer, R., Gennaro, R., Schoenmakers, B.: A secure and optimally efficient multi-authority election scheme. In: Fumy, W. (ed.) EUROCRYPT 1997. LNCS, vol. 1233, pp. 103–118. Springer, Heidelberg (1997). https://doi.org/10.1007/3-540-69053-0_9

13. Desmedt, Y., Frankel, Y.: Threshold cryptosystems. In: Brassard, G. (ed.) CRYPTO 1989. LNCS, vol. 435, pp. 307–315. Springer, New York (1990). https://doi.org/10.1007/0-387-34805-0_28

14. Dodis, Y., Kiayias, A., Nicolosi, A., Shoup, V.: Anonymous identification in *Ad Hoc* groups. In: Cachin, C., Camenisch, J.L. (eds.) EUROCRYPT 2004. LNCS, vol. 3027, pp. 609–626. Springer, Heidelberg (2004). https://doi.org/10.1007/978-3-540-24676-3_36

15. Fujioka, A., Okamoto, T., Ohta, K.: A practical secret voting scheme for large scale elections. In: Seberry, J., Zheng, Y. (eds.) AUSCRYPT 1992. LNCS, vol. 718, pp. 244–251. Springer, Heidelberg (1993). https://doi.org/10.1007/3-540-57220-1_66

16. Furukawa, J., Miyauchi, H., Mori, K., Obana, S., Sako, K.: An implementation of a universally verifiable electronic voting scheme based on shuffling. In: Blaze, M. (ed.) FC 2002. LNCS, vol. 2357, pp. 16–30. Springer, Heidelberg (2003). https://doi.org/10.1007/3-540-36504-4_2

17. Furukawa, J., Mori, K., Sako, K.: An implementation of a mix-net based network voting scheme and its use in a private organization. In: Chaum, D., et al. (eds.) Towards Trustworthy Elections. LNCS, vol. 6000, pp. 141–154. Springer, Heidelberg (2010). https://doi.org/10.1007/978-3-642-12980-3_8

18. Hertig, A.: The first bitcoin voting machine is on its way (2015). http://motherboard.vice.com/read/the-first-bitcoin-voting-machine-ison-its-way

19. Jakobsson, M., Juels, A., Rivest, R.L.: Making mix nets robust for electronic voting by randomized partial checking. In: Proceedings of the 11th USENIX Security Symposium, pp. 339–353. USENIX Association, Berkeley (2002)

20. Juang, W.S., Lei, C.L., Liaw, H.T.: A verifiable multi-authority secret election allowing abstention from voting. In: The Computer Journal 2002, vol. 45, pp. 672–682. IEEE (2002)

21. Kiayias, A., Yung, M.: Self-tallying elections and perfect ballot secrecy. In: Naccache, D., Paillier, P. (eds.) PKC 2002. LNCS, vol. 2274, pp. 141–158. Springer, Heidelberg (2002). https://doi.org/10.1007/3-540-45664-3_10

22. Lee, B., Kim, K.: Receipt-free electronic voting scheme with a tamper-resistant randomizer. In: Lee, P.J., Lim, C.H. (eds.) ICISC 2002. LNCS, vol. 2587, pp. 389–406. Springer, Heidelberg (2003). https://doi.org/10.1007/3-540-36552-4_27

23. Liu, J.K., Wei, V.K., Wong, D.S.: Linkable Spontaneous anonymous group signature for ad hoc groups. In: Wang, H., Pieprzyk, J., Varadharajan, V. (eds.) ACISP 2004. LNCS, vol. 3108, pp. 325–335. Springer, Heidelberg (2004). https://doi.org/10.1007/978-3-540-27800-9_28

24. Mateu, V., Sebé, F., Valls, M.: Blind certificates for secure electronic voting. In: 2013 10th International Conference on Information Technology: New Generations, pp. 20–26, April 2013

25. McCorry, P., Shahandashti, S.F., Hao, F.: A smart contract for boardroom voting with maximum voter privacy. In: Kiayias, A. (ed.) FC 2017. LNCS, vol. 10322, pp. 357–375. Springer, Cham (2017). https://doi.org/10.1007/978-3-319-70972-7_20

26. Okamoto, T.: Receipt-free electronic voting schemes for large scale elections. In: Christianson, B., Crispo, B., Lomas, M., Roe, M. (eds.) Security Protocols 1997. LNCS, vol. 1361, pp. 25–35. Springer, Heidelberg (1998). https://doi.org/10.1007/BFb0028157

27. Pedersen, T.P.: A threshold cryptosystem without a trusted party. In: Davies, D.W. (ed.) EUROCRYPT 1991. LNCS, vol. 547, pp. 522–526. Springer, Heidelberg (1991). https://doi.org/10.1007/3-540-46416-6_47

28. Rivest, R.L., Adleman, L., Dertouzos, M.L.: On Data Banks and Privacy Homomorphisms. Foundations of Secure Computation, pp. 169–179. Academia Press, Ghent (1978)

29. Ryan, P.Y.A.: Prêt à voter with paillier encryption. Math. Comput. Model. **48**(9–10), 1646–1662 (2008)

30. Sako, K., Kilian, J.: Receipt-free mix-type voting scheme. In: Guillou, L.C., Quisquater, J.-J. (eds.) EUROCRYPT 1995. LNCS, vol. 921, pp. 393–403. Springer, Heidelberg (1995). https://doi.org/10.1007/3-540-49264-X_32

31. Sebé, F., Miret, J.M., Pujolàs, J., Puiggalí, J.: Simple and efficient hash-based verifiable mixing for remote electronic voting. Comput. Commun. **33**, 667–675 (2010)

32. Tsang, P.P., Wei, V.K.: Short linkable ring signatures for e-voting, e-cash and attestation. In: Deng, R.H., Bao, F., Pang, H.H., Zhou, J. (eds.) ISPEC 2005. LNCS, vol. 3439, pp. 48–60. Springer, Heidelberg (2005). https://doi.org/10.1007/978-3-540-31979-5_5

33. Vo, D., Zhang, F., Kim,K.: A new threshold blind signature scheme from pairings (2002)

34. Xia, Z., Schneider, S.A., Heather, J., Traoré, J.: Analysis, improvement and simplification of prêt à voter with paillier encryption. In: Proceedings of the Conference on Electronic Voting Technology, EVT 2008, pp. 13:1–13:15. USENIX Association, Berkeley (2008)

35. Yu, B., et al.: Platform-independent secure blockchain-based voting system. In: Chen, L., Manulis, M., Schneider, S. (eds.) ISC 2018. LNCS, vol. 11060, pp. 369–386. Springer, Cham (2018). https://doi.org/10.1007/978-3-319-99136-8_20

PassGrid: Towards Graph-Supplemented Textual Shoulder Surfing Resistant Authentication

Teng Zhou[1], Liang Liu[1(✉)], Haifeng Wang[2], Wenjuan Li[3], and Chong Jiang[4]

[1] College of Computer Science and Technology, Nanjing University of Aeronautics
and Astronautics, Nanjing, China
liangliu@nuaa.edu.cn

[2] NARI Technology Co., Ltd. State Key Laboratory of Smart Grid Protection
and Control in China, Nanjing, China

[3] Department of Computer Science, City University of Hong Kong,
Hong Kong S.A.R., China
wenjuan.li@my.cityu.edu.hk

[4] School of Computer Science, Guangzhou University, Guangzhou, China

Abstract. With the rapid development of intelligent mobile devices and network applications, user authentication plays an important role to help protect people's privacy and sensitive information. A large number of authentication textual and graphical schemes have been proposed in the literature, but the majority of them are vulnerable to shoulder surfing attacks, or have to sacrifice usability. Motivated by this challenge, we propose a graph-supplemented textual shoulder surfing resistant authentication system, called PassGrid. With a series of one-time login indicators and cyclic movable blocks with textual elements, PassGrid prevents attackers from guessing the passwords even with the help of a camera. To reduce users' workload, they only have to memorize one set of the password. Our user study shows that PassGrid can achieve good performance regarding security and usability, i.e., average login time consumption of 22s with a small password length.

Keywords: Graphical authentication · Textual password · Shoulder surfing resistant · User authentication · Security and usability

1 Introduction

With the rapid development of mobile devices, more applications are associated with users' private information like online transaction, which may allow attackers to gain unauthorized access to the device. Shoulder surfing is a kind of intrusion that attackers watch over a user's shoulder to gain the information. There are two ways to launch shoulder surfing attack [16–18,25]: (1) attacker users naked eyes, or (2) attacker uses camera-based device. In general, shoulder surfing attack tends to take place in the crowd, users will not easily figure out the attackers

© Springer Nature Singapore Pte Ltd. 2019
W. Meng and S. Furnell (Eds.): SocialSec 2019, CCIS 1095, pp. 251–263, 2019.
https://doi.org/10.1007/978-981-15-0758-8_19

due to chaotic environment. Some attackers will capture videos that record the authentication scenes one or more times, and they are able to analyze users' behavior and then crack the password.

Texture password is the most widely used method during authentication [24]. People prefer to setting their passwords with ordinary words, phrases and symbols, making them easy to memorize. However texture password is too fragile to resist shoulder surfing attack. Users often input their password by pressing the buttons on the screen directly, which makes attackers to recover their passwords easily by shoulder surfing. In order to resist shoulder surfing attack, researchers proposed various graphic password schemes [3–7]. Graphic password consists of a series graphs and pictures, users need to select some graphs or pixels and upload them as passwords. A random indicator is always used with the graphic password to make passwords hard to be cracked. Though graphic password shows great advantages of resisting shoulder surfing attack, most applications authenticate users by texture passwords and most of the users still like to use texture passwords due to their habits. And only users in the crowd or insecure environments will be more likely to suffer from shoulder surfing attack, they can still log into the system by utilizing texture password in private occasions. Thus it is a trouble to memorize two completely different set of passwords for users. The ideal scheme is utilizing a new system based on texture password, learning from graphic password scheme to resist shoulder surfing attack.

In this paper, we focus on shoulder surfing attacks and propose a hybrid authentication system called *PassGrid*, which combines the features from both textual and graphical password authentication. PassGrid can provide one-time indicators and cyclic movable blocks with textual elements. Based on the random indicators, users have to move the blocks to the proper location with the correct inputting sequence. Our contributions can be summarized as below:

- We design a graph-supplemented textual shoulder surfing resistant authentication system named *PassGrid*, which can provide good usability and security with a small password length.
- We implemented a prototype of *PassGrid* and conducted a user study to evaluate the performance of *PassGrid* in the aspects of security and usability.

This paper is organized as follows: Sect. 2 provides the related studies regarding graphical password-based authentication system. Section 3 introduces our proposed system, and Sect. 4 conducts a user study to evaluate our scheme. Section 5 discuss some challenges and Sect. 6 concludes our work.

2   Background and Related Works

Textural password based authentication scheme was firstly introduced in the 1960s. It has become the most common authentication scheme nowadays. Textural passwords that comprised of numbers, upper- and lower-case letters and tokens are considered strong enough to resist brute attacks. However, complicate textural password is hard to memorize and still unable to restrict shoulder surfing attack.

From long ago, due to the limited graphic support of handheld devices, it is very difficult to design a good graphic authentication system. Jermyn et al. proposed an authentication system called Draw-A-Secret (DAS) [1]. This system makes users be able to draw a secret shape on the grids as a password. It will record the coordinates that the shape occupied. Users should draw the shape almost the same as stored one to pass authentication. Blonder [2] designed a graphic password scheme, the scheme generates password by clicking on the several locations on an image. During authentication, the user clicks the tolerant location where the user set up. It claims that the image can assist users to recall the password. Thus this schema may be more convenient than texture passwords. PassPoint system is proposed by Wiedenbecket et al. [3] Such password consists of a sequence of PassPoints on one image. The users should select some pixels and touch the screen to create their password. To log into the system, they have to select the pixels they picked before and click them in a tolerant area and in a correct sequence.

Most existing textural and graphic password schemes above are still vulnerable to shoulder surfing attacks. To address this issue, Sobrado and Birget developed a graphic password technique [4]. The system displays a number of 3 pass-objects that pre-selected by users among several other objects. The user has to click inside the triangle formed by the 3 pass-objects when they are authenticated. The Spy-Resistant Keyboard, a novel interface that allows users to enter private text without revealing it to an observer. The keyboard looks like an on-screen keyboard. A user study has been conducted, based on the study, users require more time to enter the password but they are prevented from observation attack [20].

PassBYOP is a new graphic authentication system, in which user presents the image to a system camera and then enter their password as a sequence of selections on live video of the token. Highly distinctive optical features are extracted from these selections and used as the password. They present three feasibility studies of PassBYOP examining its reliability, usability, and security about shoulder surfing attack [19]. Hung-Min Sun et al. proposed a shoulder surfing resistant authentication system named PassMatrix by using special graphic password [13]. In their system, there are random indicators and two circulative bars. It divides a picture into 7×11 parts and users choose one part as a digit of the password. During authentication, users will get an indicator, and then they need to align the corresponding letters on the horizontal bar and the vertical bar with the selected part of the picture. Some other relevant graphical passwords can refer to [5–12, 22].

3 Our Proposed Scheme

Textual password is the most widely used authentication method, but is too fragile to resist shoulder surfing attack. Many graphical password schemes were also proposed in the literature [1–4, 13]. However, the existing authentication systems often have the following problems: (1) most textual and graphical password

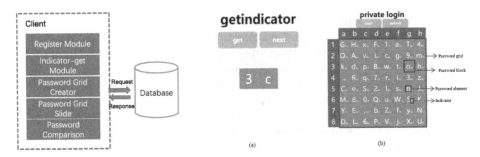

Fig. 1. The high-level architecture of PassGrid.

Fig. 2. (a) Indicator-get Module (b) Password
grid creator Module.

schemes are vulnerable to shoulder surfing attacks; (2) some password schemes
are too complicated to reduce the usability; and (3) some schemes require users
to memorize too much information or steps. In this work, our goal is to design
a graph-supplemented textual shoulder surfing resistant authentication system
without reducing the usability.

3.1 Architecture

The architecture of our system is shown in Fig. 1, which consists of the following
components:

- *Register module.* Users should have an account with user name and password
  in text strings.
- *Indicator-get module.* The system creates the coordinate of the first character
  of the password (As shown in Fig. 2(a)). In particular, it uses the number of
  1–8 as a horizontal coordinate, and the letter of *a–h* as a vertical coordinate.
  The horizontal and vertical coordinates will be generated randomly. To get
  an indicator, we adopt the methods proposed in [13]. There are two ways: the
  indicator could be shown on the display directly, or can be delivered by an
  audio signal through the ear buds or Bluetooth.
- *Password grid creator module.* As shown in Fig. 2(b), we create a $M \times N$
  matrix and select all printable characters as password elements. In addition,
  we assume the password grid is divided into a *8 × 8* matrix including numbers
  from 0 to 9, lowercase letters from *a* to *z*, uppercase letters from *A* to *Z*, and
  two token , and . as valid password elements. There is a random textual
  indicator in the lower right of every block, representing the next password
  character location.
- *Password grid slide module.* As shown in Fig. 3, users can drag each block by
  their finger in four directions and the whole password grid can move cyclic in
  rows and columns.
- *Password comparison module.* In this module, our system collects all textual
  elements that users input and constructs a password sequence. Then the
  system (or a server) can make a comparison to verify the password.

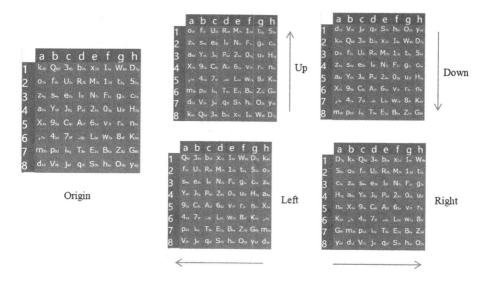

Fig. 3. Password grid slide module.

– *Database.* It mainly contains a *user table* that records usernames and passwords, and a *LoginData table* that records the login data for all users.

In this work, we mainly consider two conditions: private and public environment. For the former, users can log into the system by inputting texture password directly. For the latter, as shown in Fig. 2(a), users have to receive an indicator that represents the location of the first character of the password before entering texture password. The indicator is a 2D coordinate like $(3, c)$. When a user performs password verification, as shown in Fig. 2(b), a password grid sequence will be generated according to the password length. Each password character corresponds to a password grid, which is composed of several password blocks. A password element is displayed in the middle and the indicator is displayed in the lower right corner.

3.2 PassGrid Design

As mentioned earlier, based on different environments, our scheme considers two conditions: a Normal Login phase and a Private Login phase.

– Normal Login phase. If the user is authenticated in a private environment, he or she just needs to input username and password directly.
– Private Login phase. If the user is authenticated in a public place, then the detailed procedures are shown below:
  • Step 1: as shown in Fig. 4(a), the user has to first input the username to verify whether there is valid user.
  • Step 2: the index of a password character in a password is denoted by i, which is initialized as 1.

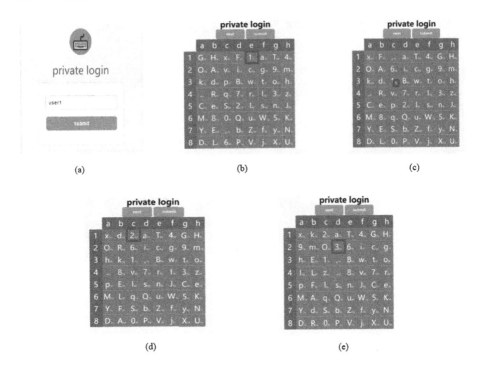

Fig. 4. Private login phase

- Step 3: as shown in Fig. 2(a), the user then presses the *'get' button* to obtain a random indicator *ind*. The user should memorize the indicator and then move to the next step.
- Step 4: the system creates a password grid and the user moves the block containing the *ith* password character to the location, where the indicator *ind* points to. The user needs to memorize the indicator *nextInd* in the lower right corner of the block containing the *ith* password character, and then presses the *'next' button*. After that, *i:=i+1, ind := nextInd*.
- Step 5: the user repeats step 4 until he/she acknowledges he/she has finished inputting the password. Then the user presses the *'submit' button*.
- Step 6: password sequence *pwd* will be generated by password comparison module, and then the system or server will compare *pwd* with the correct password *pwd'*. If successful, the user passes the authentication; otherwise, the authentication process fails.

The password grid-based authentication is summarized in Algorithm 1. As an example, we assume that a user sets 'user1' as the account name and '123' as the password. In a public environment, the user has to firstly input the username and obtain the indicator (see Fig. 2(a)) in the Indicator-get module, which is '3c'. The next step is to move the textual password block with the number of '1' to the location of $(3, c)$ (see Fig. 4(b)). Then the user should press the 'next' button

---

Algorithm 1. Password grid-based authentication

Initialization:

    1. Password sequence users input is *pwdlist* and password sequence users pre-defined is *pwd*. Initial pwdlist as NULL.

    2. Generate L password grid matrixs $\{MA_1, MA_2, \ldots, MA_L\}$, where L is the length of *pwd*. In each matrix, there are MN password elements $MA_i[j][k]$ and indicators $ind_i [j][k]$. $i \in \{1,2,\ldots,L\}$, $j \in \{1,2,\ldots,M\}$, $k \in \{1,2,\ldots,N\}$

    3. The current indicator is denoted by *ind*, which is initialized as NULL. get the first indicator *ind1*, and *ind = ind1*

while *Ture* **do**

    generate a new password grid

    look for the location *ind* points to and move the block with element *pwd[i]* to the location. Get the password element $MA_i[j][k]$ from the block in MA_i and append $MA_i[j][k]$ into *pwdlist*, and *ind = ind_i[j][k]*, *i = i+1*

    if *the user acknowledges he/she has finished inputting password and chooses to submit* **then**

        break;

generate *pwdlist* as a string

if *pwdlist is equal to pwd* **then**

    the user passes the authentication

else

    the user fails to pass the authentication

---

to continue. As shown in Fig. 4(c), the indicator of the next password character is displayed in the lower right of the previous texture block. It is worth noting that as indicators will be recreated in every round. Then the user should drag the right password block to the proper location and repeat previous step for the next password (as shown in Fig. 4(d) and Fig. 4(e)). When the user completes the whole password, he or she can press the submit button and wait for verification.

4   User Study

We designed a user study that requires participants to register three different accounts with three different passwords, and they need to login about five times in each account. We set the length of the passwords: a short one (1–3 digits), a medium one (4–6 digits) and a long one (above 6 digits). We adopted two common metrics to help evaluate the performance of PassGrid in the aspects of both accuracy and usability.

– Accuracy. In the study, we investigate whether participates can log into the system successfully with different length of passwords. To analyze the accuracy, each participant was required to register three different accounts.
– Usability. In this study, we measured the system usability by recording time consumption by all participants on different length of passwords.

Participants. We recruited 15 participants (M = 23 years; SD = 3; 6 females), who are volunteers and have an interest in our study. All participants are graduate students from different disciplines such as Mathematics, Computer Science and so on. After an informal interview, we found all participants are common smartphone users, but were unfamiliar with graphical authentication system. This work received an approval from the Department and all participants have to make an agreement before they started.

Study phases. In the study, we have three main phases:

- *Introduction phase.* We explained the basic idea and our goals to all participants. We also provided a presentation on how to use the prototype system and answered any questions from participants.
- *Practice phase.* Participants were required to register three different accounts with different password lengths. Before the study, they could have several trials until they believe that they have been familiar with the system.
- *Login phase.* After practice, participants were requested to log into the system five times for each account. The login phase would be repeated once, that is, there are two rounds of login trials.

Accuracy. We recorded the login information after each of the Private Login phase. We defined the *Total Accuracy* as below:

$$Total\ Accuracy = \frac{Successful\ Times}{Total\ Times} \tag{1}$$

Figure 5 shows the total accuracy in the login session with three different password lengths. It is found that when users utilized a short password, they could achieve a higher successful rate like 96% and 98% in two rounds. Intuitively, it is easily understand that all participants were more proficient in the second round. In addition, the successful rate was found to decrease with the increase of password length. While participants could improve the rate in the second round, i.e., from 76% to 86%, and from 72% to 80%. We particularly surveyed participants to investigate why the successful rate would drop with a longer password length. In addition to memory limitation, we also found that participants might conduct many errors, i.e., accidentally moving the block to the wrong place, or pressing the next button carelessly. These errors could be avoided when they are more careful during the authentication process.

Usability. As mentioned above, we evaluate the usability of PassGrid by computing the time consumption for all participants in each round, those who could successfully pass the private authentication phase.

- It is found that participants spent less time handling the passwords with a smaller length. With the increase of length, participants have to spend more time in authentication. For example, the average time consumption is around 24.4 s for the password length with 3 letters or less. The time consumption could increase to over 82 s for the middle-length and long-length passwords.

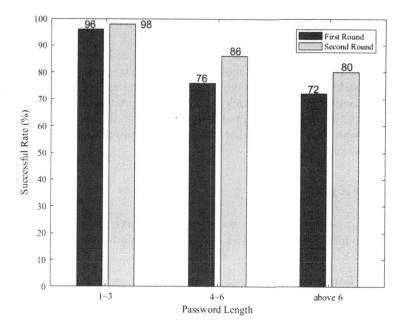

Fig. 5. Successful rate of different passwords' length in two rounds

– In addition, participants can perform better in the second round, where the average time consumption is around 22 s for the short password length, and over 74.2 s for the middle-length and long-length passwords. This observation validates that PassGrid can provide good usability when participants get familiar with the system, i.e., after several practice trials.

Limitation Discussion. In our informal interview with all participants, we found that most of them positively rated our system to be acceptable and usable in practice, by considering the enhanced security provided by PassGrid, i.e., against shoulder surfing attacks. However, as our work is at an early stage, we acknowledge there existing many issues and challenges.

– Based on the data, it is observed that PassGrid could reach good performance in the aspects of accuracy and usability, when the password length is small, i.e., 22 s for the short password length. As a reference, PassMatrix [13] provided an average time consumption of 30 s. However, with a larger password length, the time consumption of PassGrid could keep increasing. This is actually an open issue for most shoulder surfing resistant schemes including PassMatrix. We acknowledge this is the major limitation of PassGrid, and it is one of our future work to investigate how to reduce the time consumption.
– As an ongoing research study, we only involved 15 participants in the evaluation part, and all of them are graduate students. We acknowledge that more participants with diverse background are desirable in practice. We plan to

involve more than 50 participants in our future work and validate the results obtained in this work.

- In this work, we only analyze the security of PassGrid against several typical attacks. We acknowledge that more efforts should be provided to explore the practical performance. One of our future directions is to perform a shoulder surfing attack or guessing attack with the attempt to compromise our system. Each participant is expected to have many trials, like 10 times [13], to crack our system. We believe that this study can provide statistical data and validate the performance.

5   Security Discussion

In this section, we mainly discuss the security of PassGrid against three typical attacks: brute force attack, shoulder surfing attack, and smudge attack.

5.1   Brute Force Attack

To perform the brute force attack, intruders have to enumerate all possible passwords. We assume that users set the password in n characters. Considering one character from a password, we divided one password grid into a $M \times N$ matrix, which represents the password space is $(M \times N)$. On the other hand, the possibility that attackers can crack one character is $1/(M \times N)$. We used location indicators to increase the randomness of PassGrid. This means only when attackers can input the right former password sequence, they can get the next right character of the password. Thus, the probability of cracking the whole authentication scheme is $1/(M \times N)^{2n}$. In our prototype, we assume $M = 8$ and $N = 8$, then our system can reach the above possibility of $(0.024\%)^n$. We believe it is should be sufficient to defend against brute force attacks.

5.2   Shoulder Surfing Attack

Most of the textural or graphical password authentication systems cannot succeed in resisting shoulder surfing attacks, which have been a real threat and challenge. In our scheme, there is no need for users to click the button or input the password on the screen directly. They only need to drag the textural blocks and ensure the password character being moved to the correct location.

The password spaces of other schemes such as those in CAPTCHA-based method [21], Pass-icons [23] and Color-rings [15] can be narrowed down by camera-based shoulder surfing attacks. While in our system, the order of password elements on each password grid is totally distinct, i.e., the first location indicator is given randomly to ensure that users can obtain it in a private way. The indicator in the lower right of each block is also randomly recreated in every round. That is, even if an attacker can capture users' authentication phase by using camera or other recording devices, it is still hard to determine the correct blocks which the user moves in each round.

5.3   Smudge Attack

When users interact with phone screens, they will leave oily residues, or smudges. This attack allows intruders to examine *smudge* on the phone screen after users inputting their sensitive information [14]. In our scheme, the smudge can be any shape, e.g., irregular, and not easy to identify, since the password grid is cyclic in rows and columns, and users can drag any block many times. In this case, it is very difficult for attackers to extract useful information based on the complicated and vague smudges.

6   Conclusion

For most current authentication schemes, shoulder surfing attack is one of the major threats, where attackers can compromise the authentication process by watching over people's shoulder or recording videos through some camera-based devices. The use of graphical passwords can alleviate shoulder surfing attack to some degree, whereas people are accustomed to textual password and cannot memorize completely distinct password sequences.

To overcome this challenge, we propose a graph-supplemented textual shoulder surfing resistant authentication system, called PassGrid, which only requires users to set textual password, based on randomly generated indicators and cyclic movable texture blocks. Users have to move password blocks to the right location according to the location indicator instead of touching the screen or inputting directly, which can effectively prevent shoulder surfing attack. In the evaluation, we conducted a users study to investigate the performance of PassGrid. Our results indicate that PassGrid can provide good security and usability when the password length is small, while the usability would be degraded with the increase of password length. In future work, we plan to investigate how to simplify the authentication process and decrease the login time. In addition, we plan to compare our system with other related schemes.

References

1. Jermyn, I., Mayer, A., Monrose, F., Reiter, M., Rubin, A.: The design and analysis of graphical passwords. In: Proceedings of the 8th Conference USENIX Security Symposium, vol. 8 (1999)
2. Blonder, G.E.: Graphical passwords. United States Patent 5559961 (1996)
3. Wiedenbeck, S., Waters, J., Birget, J., Brodskiy, A., Memon, N.: Passpoints: design and longitudinal evaluation of a graphical password system. Int. J. Hum.-Comput. Stud. **63**(1–2), 102–127 (2005)
4. Sobrado, L., Birget, J.C.: Graphical passwords. The Rutgers Scholar, An Electronic Bulletin for Undergraduate Research, vol. 4 (2002)
5. Meng, Y., Li, W., Kwok, L.-F.: Enhancing click-draw based graphical passwords using multi-touch on mobile phones. In: Janczewski, L.J., Wolfe, H.B., Shenoi, S. (eds.) SEC 2013. IAICT, vol. 405, pp. 55–68. Springer, Heidelberg (2013). https://doi.org/10.1007/978-3-642-39218-4_5

6. Meng, W.: RouteMap: a route and map based graphical password scheme for better multiple password memory. Network and System Security. LNCS, vol. 9408, pp. 147–161. Springer, Cham (2015). https://doi.org/10.1007/978-3-319-25645-0_10

7. Meng, W.: Evaluating the effect of multi-touch behaviours on android unlock patterns. Inf. Comput. Secur. **24**(3), 277–287 (2016)

8. Meng, W., Li, W., Wong, D.S., Zhou, J.: TMGuard: a touch movement-based security mechanism for screen unlock patterns on smartphones. In: Manulis, M., Sadeghi, A.-R., Schneider, S. (eds.) ACNS 2016. LNCS, vol. 9696, pp. 629–647. Springer, Cham (2016). https://doi.org/10.1007/978-3-319-39555-5_34

9. Meng, W., Lee, W.H., Au, M.H., Liu, Z.: Exploring effect of location number on map-based graphical password authentication. In: Pieprzyk, J., Suriadi, S. (eds.) ACISP 2017. LNCS, vol. 10343, pp. 301–313. Springer, Cham (2017). https://doi.org/10.1007/978-3-319-59870-3_17

10. Meng, W., Li, W., Kwok, L.F., Choo, K.K.R.: Towards enhancing click-draw based graphical passwords using multi-touch behaviours on smartphones. Comput. Secur. **65**, 213–229 (2017)

11. Meng, W., Fei, F., Jiang, L., Liu, Z., Su, C., Han, J.: CPMap: design of click-points map-based graphical password authentication. SEC **2018**, 18–32 (2018)

12. Meng, W., Liu, Z.: TMGMap: designing touch movement-based geographical password authentication on smartphones. In: Su, C., Kikuchi, H. (eds.) ISPEC 2018. LNCS, vol. 11125, pp. 373–390. Springer, Cham (2018). https://doi.org/10.1007/978-3-319-99807-7_23

13. Sun, H.-M., Chen, S.-T., Yeh, J.-H., Cheng, C.-Y.: Shoulder surfing resistant graphical authentication system. IEEE Trans. Dependable Secure Comput. **15**(2), 180–193 (2018)

14. Aviv, A., Gibson, K., Mossop, E., Blaze, M., Smith, J.: Smudge attacks on smartphone touch screens. In: Proceedings of USENIX 4th Workshop on Offensive Technologies (2010)

15. Zhao, H., Li, X.: S3pas: a scalable shoulder-surfing resistant textual-graphical password authentication scheme. In: Proceeding of the 21st International Conference Advances Information Network Applications Workshops, vol. 2, pp. 467–472 (2007)

16. Long, J., Mitnick, K.: No tech hacking: a guide to social engineering, dumpster diving, and shoulder surfing (2011). https://www.hackersforcharity.org/files/NTH_SAMPLE.pdf

17. Kwon, T., Shin, S., Na, S.: Covert attentional shoulder surfing: human adversaries are more powerful than expected. IEEE Trans. Syst. Man Cybern. Syst. **44**(6), 716–727 (2014)

18. Google glass snoopers can steal your passcode with a glance. http://www.wired.com/2014/06/google-glass-snoopers-can-steal-your-passcode-with-a-glance/

19. Bianchi, A., Oakley, I., Kim, H.S.: PassBYOP: bring your own picture for securing graphical passwords. IEEE Trans. Hum.-Mach. Syst. **46**(3), 2168–2291 (2015)

20. Tan, D., Keyani, P., Czerwinski, M.: Spy-resistant keyboard: towards more secure password entry on publicly observable touch screens. In: Proceedings of OZCHIComputer- Human Interaction Special Interest Group (CHISIG) of Australia, Canberra, Australia. ACM Press. Citeseer (2005)

21. Wang, L., Chang, X., Ren, Z., Gao, H., Liu, X., Aickelin, U.: Against spyware using captcha in graphical password scheme. In: Proceeding of the 24th IEEE International Conference on Advanced Information Networking and Applications, pp. 760–767. IEEE (2010)

22. Yu, X., Wang, Z., Li, Y., Li, L., Zhu, W.T., Song, L.: EvoPass: evolvable graphical password against shoulder-surfing attacks. Comput. Secur. **70**, 179–198 (2017)

23. Wiedenbeck, S., Waters, J., Sobrado, L., Birget, J.-C.: Design and evaluation of a shoulder-surfing resistant graphical password scheme. In: Proceedings of the working conference on Advanced Visual Interfaces, ser. AVI 2006, pp. 177–184. ACM, New York (2006)

24. Suo, X., Zhu, Y., Owen, G.S.: Graphical passwords: a survey. In: Proceedings of the 21st Annual Computer Security Applications Conference, ACSAC, pp. 463–472. IEEE Computer Society, USA (2005)

25. Takada, T.: Fakepointer: an authentication scheme for improving security against peeping attacks using video cameras. In: Proceedings of the 2nd International Conference Mobile Ubiquitous Computer, System, Service Technology, pp. 395–400 (2008)

Learning from Imbalanced Data: A Comparative Study

Yu Sui(✉), Mengze Yu, Haifeng Hong, and Xianxian Pan

Program and Research Center, Guangdong Power Grid Corporation,
Guangzhou, China
suiyugxzx@163.com

Abstract. Learning from imbalanced data is a great challenge when we use machine learning techniques to solve real-world problems. Imbalanced data can result in a classifier's sub-optimal performance. Moreover, the distribution of the testing data may differ from that of the training data, thus the true mis-classification costs is hard to predict at the time of learning. In this paper, we present a comparative study on various sampling techniques in terms of their effectiveness in improving machine learning performance against class imbalanced data sets. In particular, we evaluate ten sampling techniques such as random sampling, cluster-based sampling, and SMOTE. Two widely used machine learning algorithms are applied to train the base classifiers. For the purpose of evaluation, a number of data sets from different domains are used and the results are analysed based on different metrics.

Keywords: Data mining · Machine learning · Class imbalance · Data sampling

1 Introduction

The class imbalance problem is a challenge to data mining and machine learning, and it is of crucial importance since last decade in many domains, such as network intrusion detection, financial engineering, medical diagnostics, surveillance, and even in-flight helicopter gearbox fault monitoring [13]. In certain cases, this has caused a significant bottleneck in the performance attainable by traditional data mining algorithms, which tend to bias to the majority class. That is, the accuracy for majority class is high while the performance is poor for minority class. For example, if a data sample contains of 95% of majority class and 5% of minority class, thus an accuracy rate of 95% (which is in general a good accuracy) can be achieved by classifying all examples to majority class. However, such a model has no practical value in real-world problems. It is typically the minority class in which the practitioners are more interested. Therefore, a natural question is how to empower the classification performance when the data set is imbalanced?

Supported by Guangdong Power Grid Research Project 030000QQ00180019.

© Springer Nature Singapore Pte Ltd. 2019
W. Meng and S. Furnell (Eds.): SocialSec 2019, CCIS 1095, pp. 264–274, 2019.
https://doi.org/10.1007/978-981-15-0758-8_20

Class imbalance problem has been studied by many researchers [9,11,16]. So far, a common solution is using data sampling techniques to re-distribute the data across classes. Generally speaking, a pre-sampling method balances the training set, either by oversampling the minority class or undersampling the majority class. A large amount of data sampling techniques have been proposed in the past and some of them have been applied to address the class imbalance problem. The simplest over-sampling method is to randomly duplicate some of the minority instances (ROS), while a more complex version is the synthetic minority class over sampling (SMOTE) [5] technique which artificially creates new minority examples from known examples. Han et al. [8] proposed a Borderline-SMOTE over sampling approach, which improves upon SMOTE by only oversampling minority class samples which are believed to be on the border of the decision regions. Cluster-based oversampling (CBOS) [14] attempts to even out the between-class imbalance as well as the within-class imbalance. Meanwhile, the simplest under-sampling method is random under-sampling (RUS), which randomly reduces data of the majority class. One-sided selection (OSS) [15], which removes the majority class samples that are considered either redundant or noisy, is one of the earliest attempts to improve upon the performance of random resampling. In addition, Wilson's editing (WE) [1] uses the kNN (Nearest Neighbor) technique with $k = 3$ to classify each sample in the training set by using the remaining class, and remove those majority class which are misclassified. Various data sampling techniques have been explored. However, there is no universal solution and it is worth to explore which kind of data sampling technique is more effective and efficient in balancing class distribution in terms of the type of data and classifiers.

This paper presents an extensive experimental study on a variety of data sampling techniques, with a focus on their effectiveness in terms of boosting the classification performance of machine learning algorithms on class imbalanced data sets. In particular, we use two popular algorithms, i.e., C4.5 Decision Tree and Support Vector Machines, to train the base classifiers. The study is based on a number of different imbalanced data sets from the PROMISE repository software engineering databases [20]. To our knowledge, this is the first comprehensive empirical investigation in comparing the performance of these data sampling techniques among imbalanced data sets from different application domains.

The rest of the paper is organised as follows. Section 2 introduces the related work, while the details of data sets and methodology are presented in Sect. 3. Section 4 discusses the experimental results on different performance measures. Conclusions and future work are provided in Sect. 5.

2   Related Work

Data-Perspective Approaches. Generally speaking, approaches to classification with imbalanced data issues involve two main categories, i.e., data perspective and algorithm perspective. In this work, we mainly focus on sampling techniques that is related to our study.

Random Over-Sampling (ROS): The minority oversampling randomly selecting a training example from the minority class, and then duplicating it. This may usually cause over-fitting and longer training time during imbalance learning process.

Random Under-Sampling (RUS): Majority under-sampling draws a random subset from the majority class while discarding the rest instances. In doing so, the class distribution can be balanced, however, some important information may be lost when examples are removed from the training data set at random, and especially when the data set is small.

Synthetic Minority Over-Sampling Techniques (SMOTE or SM) [5]: This technique adds new artificial minority attribute examples by extrapolating instances from the k nearest neighbours (kNN) to the minority class instances. In our experiments, the parameter k is set to five.

Border-SMOTE (BSM) [8]: BSM is an attempt to improve upon SMOTE by only oversampling minority class instances which are considered to be on the border of the minority-decision region. It can be described as follows: First, determine kNN for each original sample $x_i \in S_{min}$ and identify the number of nearest neighbours that belong to the majority class, then if $\frac{k}{2} < t < k$ is true, $x_i \in S_{min}$ is considered as borderline instance, finally, SM is applied to create new examples by using borderline samples.

Wilson's Editing (WE) [1]: WE applies the kNN classifier with $k = 3$ to classify each example in the training set by using all the remaining examples, and removes those majority class instances whose class label does not agree with the class associated with the largest number of the k neighbours.

Cluster-Based Oversampling (CBOS) [14]: Before performing random oversampling, CBOS first uses k-means algorithm to cluster the minority and majority classes separately. All clusters in the majority class, except for the largest one, are randomly oversampling as the same number of the training examples as the largest cluster. Then the total number of the majority clusters are even out to each cluster of minority clusters.

Cluster-Based Undersampling (CBUS) [18]: CBUS is not to balance the data ratio of majority class of minority class into 1:1, instead to reduce the gap between the numbers of minority class and minority class. Different from CBOS, this method only clusters the majority class into K clusters and regard each cluster as one subset of the majority class samples. After that CBUS combines each cluster with the whole minority class, and then thecombined data sets will considered as the updated training data sets. Finally, CBUS classifies all the K data sets with a learning algorithm and chose the data set with the highest accuracy for building the training model.

One-Sided Selection (OSS) [15]: Similar to the idea of BSM, OSS aims to create a training set consisting of safe cases by removing the considered either redundant or noisy examples of the majority class examples. When using OSS, Borderline and noisy cases are detected by Tomek links.

Ensemble Oversampling Algorithm (ENOS) [22]: ENOS integrates the information decomposition algorithm, cluster-based oversampling and random oversampling approaches. In specific, first the algorithm assumes that there are missing instances which caused the data set to be imbalanced and the missing instances are recovered by using information decomposition algorithm. After that, the classification models from random oversampling and cluster-based oversampling techniques are combined together, where majority voting is used to obtain the final result.

Algorithm-Perspective Approaches. The goal of algorithm level learning is to optimize the performance of the learning model on unseen data. Various algorithms have been proposed in last decades. For example, cost-sensitive learning is regard as an important approach for the class imbalance problem. Many cost-sensitive methods have been proposed, for instance, cost-sensitive boosting [21], meta cost [7], adjusting misclassification costs algorithm [3], Genetic Programming (GP) [10], and kernel-based one-class classifier via optimizing its parameters [24]. Yang et al. [23] explore the use of cost-based soft-margin maximization method, which is used to penalize certain misclassified examples and treats the positive and negative example differently. Besides, one-class learning methods such as one-class SVMs [19] and neural networks [12] were proposed to combat the over-fitting problem.

3   Methodology

3.1   Data Sets

In this work, we use data sets from the PROMISE repository software engineering databases [20], which are listed in Table 1. Detailed information includes data set name, data set size, the amount of minority class data, and the percentage of minority class data, and the class attribute. As can be seen in the table, the data sets we use in this study cover a variety of sizes and imbalance levels. More specifically, the percentage of minority class data varies from 2.2% (highly imbalanced which can be regarded as imbalance due to rare minority instances) to 12.4%. Besides, the size of data varies from the smallest data set with 253 data points to the largest data set with 17186 data points. Moreover, these data sets represent different application domains.

3.2   Machine Learning Algorithms

In this paper, we employ two classic machine learning algorithms to build classifier models using unbalanced training data and evaluate their performance by

Table 1. Data sets

Dataset	Size	#min	%min	#attr
MW1	253	27	10.7	38
MC1	1988	46	2.3	39
pc1	705	61	8.7	38
pc2	745	16	2.2	37
pc3	1077	134	12.4	38
pc4	1458	178	12.2	38
pc5	17186	516	3.0	39

unseen test data. These two algorithms are popular and widely used in the real world. For the purpose of evaluation, we use the implementation of these algorithms provided in Matlab 8.0.

C4.5 Decision Tree [17]. C4.5 improves upon ID3 by adding support for handling missing values and tree pruning. It builds decision trees using an entropy-based splitting criterion, which is sensitive to class imbalance in the training data. This is because C4.5 works globally while not paying much attention to specific data points.

Support Vector Machine (SVM) [6]. SVM is a classifier that for binary classification, which attempt to find out a linear combination of the variables that best divide the samples into two groups. The ideal separation is that the optimal linear combination of variables can maximize the distance between the classes. However, when the perfect separation is not possible, the optimal linear combination will be determined by a criterion in order to minimize the number of mis-classifications.

3.3   Performance Measure

In this work, we consider the minority class as the positive class and the majority class as the negative class. Overall classification accuracy is not a good metric for measuring the performance of classifiers in the face of imbalanced data. Thus the evaluation of the classification models should be done by other criteria rather than overall accuracy. In this work, we carry out the comparative study using four performance metrics, which are based on the confusion matrix metrics including true positive (TP), false positive (FP), true negative (TN), and false negative (FN). The definition of performance metrics are described as follows.

Precision is the positive predictive value that measures the proportion of positive results in classification that are true positive. The metric is widely used in the evaluation of machine learning results. In particular, we focus on the precision of the minority class in this work, which can be obtained through the following equation.

$$Precision = \frac{TP}{TP + FP}$$

G-Measure (GM) is the geometric mean of the classification accuracy between classes, and each class of poor accuracy will cause low GM value, which in turn indicates that at least one class cannot be identified effectively. G-Measure can be calculated using the following formula.

$$GM = \sqrt{Recall \cdot Precision}$$

Cohen's Kappa rate, which evaluates the merit of the classifier, is an alternative measure to accuracy because it compensates for random hits. Previous studies [4] show that Kappa rate penalizes all-positive or all-negative predictions. The value of Cohen's Kappa ranges from -1 (total disagreement) to 0 (random classification) to 1 (total agreement). It can be derived as follows.

$$Kappa = \frac{N \sum\limits_{i=1}^{k} x_{ii} - \sum\limits_{i=1}^{k} x_i x_i}{N^2 - \sum\limits_{i=1}^{k} x_i x_i}$$

Matthew's Correlation Coefficient is a single performance measure that considers both error rates and mutual accuracy on both the minority class and majority class in terms of confusion matrix. It will be less influenced by imbalanced data sets. The value of MCC ranges from 1 (perfect prediction) to -1 (the worst prediction), while 0 indicates that the model produces random results. According to an earlier study [2], MCC is regarded as a good singular measure for imbalance learning problem.

$$MCC = \frac{TP \times TN - FP \times FN}{\sqrt{(TP + FP)(TP + FN)(TN + FP)(TN + FN)}}$$

3.4   Experimental Design

In this comparative study, we randomly choose 60% of the original data points as training data and the other 40% are used as unseen testing data. We note that all the data sampling techniques are only used to process the training data, while the testing data are left alone. In this way, the testing data can better reflect the real class distribution in real world problems. Therefore, the approach is more practical and applicable.

Regarding the data sampling parameters, undersampling techniques are performed at 20%, 50%, 70%, and 90% of the majority class, while oversampling are performed at 200%, 500%, 700%, 900% of the minority class. For example, running RUS_20 means 20% of majority class will be removed after applying RUS method to the training data set. Similarly, ROS 200 means the data size of minority class will be raised to 200% of the original. Moreover, BSM_even, CBOS_even, CBUS_even, OSS_even, ROS_even, RUS_even, SM_even, WE_even, and Ensemble_even are also considered in the evaluation. It means that the data size of the minority class and majority class is even. For example, ROS_even means that the minority class and the majority class of each data set has the same number of instances after applying ROS method with minority samples. In addition, original data set are also divided into 60% for training the model and the other 40% for testing in order to provide baseline for our experiments. Hence, the classification results obtained from the original data without data sampling are denoted as "None" in the results.

Table 2. Precision results across data sets

Classifier	Data set	Approach									
		None	BSM	CBOS	CBUS	OSS	ROS	RUS	SM	WE	ENOS
C4.5	MW1	0.44	0.35	0.40	0.38	0.50	0.67	0.71	**0.83**	0.43	**0.83**
	MC1	0.38	0.30	0.43	0.43	0.28	0.71	0.56	0.63	0.38	**0.94**
	pc1	0.44	0.24	0.43	0.44	0.43	0.74	0.61	0.72	0.33	**0.90**
	pc2	0.13	0.14	0.25	0.33	0.17	0.86	0.57	0.57	0.13	**1.00**
	pc3	0.30	0.26	0.26	0.31	0.33	0.70	0.61	0.64	0.30	**0.77**
	pc4	0.58	0.38	0.58	0.54	0.54	0.77	0.74	0.77	0.47	**0.83**
	pc5	0.49	0.53	0.55	0.51	0.51	0.76	0.70	0.72	0.52	**0.78**
SVM	MW1	0.40	0.32	0.43	0.40	0.43	0.54	0.62	0.43	0.38	**0.58**
	MC1	0.08	0.09	0.13	0.50	0.08	**0.17**	0.12	0.09	0.08	**0.17**
	pc1	0.21	0.22	0.43	0.56	0.20	0.38	0.27	0.23	0.21	**0.65**
	pc2	0.07	0.06	0.13	0.25	0.11	**0.40**	0.17	0.17	0.07	**0.40**
	pc3	0.24	0.24	0.35	0.29	0.25	0.37	0.25	0.24	0.24	**0.40**
	pc4	0.33	0.34	0.29	0.30	0.32	**0.74**	0.33	0.39	0.33	**0.66**
	pc5	0.29	0.31	0.57	0.56	0.30	0.30	0.29	0.34	0.31	**0.58**

4   Results

The best Precision, GM, Kappa, and MCC results obtained by each sampling technique are presented in Tables 2, 3, 4 and 5 respectively. We can see that in most situations, the data sampling techniques can improve the performance of the machine learning classifiers. In particular, the ENOS algorithm benefits both the C4.5 and SVM classifiers most by increasing all the metrics in most data sets.

It is worth to notice that not all of the sampling techniques result in better results than the model built directly from the original data set (i.e., the None column in the tables) on Precision measure. Take Precision for C4.5 classifier from Table 2 as an example, we can see that the methods such as BSM, CBOS, CBUS, OSS, and WE perform worse than None. However, we are more interested in the models that can correctly identify more minority class samples that may

Table 3. GM results across data sets

Classifier	Data set	Approach									
		None	BSM	CBOS	CBUS	OSS	ROS	RUS	SM	WE	ENOS
C4.5	MW1	0.4	0.44	0.32	0.42	0.46	**0.78**	0.57	0.64	0.34	**0.78**
	MC1	0.24	0.22	0.26	0.47	0.34	0.75	0.52	0.62	0.24	**0.86**
	pc1	0.39	0.3	0.44	0.54	0.43	0.8	0.61	0.68	0.36	**0.84**
	pc2	0.14	0.15	0.2	0.33	0.33	0.76	0.5	0.5	0.14	**0.8**
	pc3	0.36	0.32	0.3	0.41	0.39	0.78	0.69	0.71	0.37	**0.8**
	pc4	0.53	0.5	0.57	0.54	0.58	0.79	0.71	0.76	0.5	**0.81**
	pc5	0.49	0.51	0.53	0.53	0.57	0.75	0.68	0.7	0.54	**0.76**
SVM	MW1	0.47	0.42	0.48	0.47	0.48	0.62	0.67	0.48	0.45	**0.68**
	MC1	0.20	0.20	0.22	0.22	0.21	0.35	0.30	0.21	0.20	**0.36**
	pc1	0.40	0.39	0.46	0.47	0.40	**0.57**	0.48	0.44	0.40	**0.57**
	pc2	0.18	0.12	0.24	0.20	0.24	0.39	0.34	0.31	0.18	**0.40**
	pc3	0.42	0.43	0.41	0.41	0.44	0.46	**0.46**	0.42	0.42	**0.46**
	pc4	0.54	0.56	0.60	0.66	0.53	0.63	0.55	0.58	0.54	**0.67**
	pc5	0.52	0.54	0.54	0.54	0.53	0.52	0.52	0.56	0.54	**0.57**

Table 4. Kappa results across data sets

Classifier	Data set	Approach									
		None	BSM	CBOS	CBUS	OSS	ROS	RUS	SM	WE	ENOS
C4.5	MW1	0.34	0.34	0.25	0.34	0.36	0.74	0.51	0.59	0.27	**0.75**
	MC1	0.21	0.19	0.22	0.45	0.31	0.74	0.50	0.61	0.21	**0.85**
	pc1	0.32	0.22	0.38	0.48	0.38	0.78	0.57	0.65	0.30	**0.82**
	pc2	0.12	0.14	0.19	0.31	0.18	0.74	0.49	0.49	0.12	**0.77**
	pc3	0.28	0.23	0.21	0.31	0.32	0.74	0.65	0.67	0.28	**0.78**
	pc4	0.46	0.40	0.52	0.47	0.47	0.77	0.68	0.72	0.43	**0.79**
	pc5	0.47	0.50	0.51	0.51	0.55	0.74	0.67	0.69	0.52	**0.75**
SVM	MW1	0.39	0.31	0.41	0.39	0.41	**0.56**	0.62	0.41	0.36	**0.56**
	MC1	0.10	0.11	0.16	0.14	0.10	**0.25**	0.17	0.12	0.10	**0.25**
	pc1	0.23	0.24	0.37	0.42	0.22	0.47	0.32	0.27	0.23	**0.52**
	pc2	0.08	0.06	0.16	0.14	0.14	0.31	0.24	0.23	0.08	**0.32**
	pc3	0.26	0.27	0.29	0.29	0.28	**0.32**	0.27	0.26	0.25	**0.32**
	pc4	0.37	0.39	0.48	0.59	0.35	0.57	0.38	0.44	0.38	**0.60**
	pc5	0.42	0.44	0.45	0.51	0.42	0.42	0.42	0.47	0.44	**0.53**

have a lower overall accuracy. To be more specific, Table 3 shows that CBOS, CBUS, OSS, ROS, RUS, SM, and ENOS perform better than None for most times. This is because GM measures the classification accuracy from both posi-

Table 5. MCC results across data sets

Classifier	Data set	Approach									
		None	BSM	CBOS	CBUS	OSS	ROS	RUS	SM	WE	ENOS
C4.5	MW1	0.34	0.35	0.25	0.34	0.37	0.75	0.53	0.60	0.28	**0.76**
	MC1	0.23	0.20	0.25	0.45	0.32	0.74	0.51	0.61	0.23	**0.86**
	pc1	0.33	0.22	0.38	0.49	0.38	0.78	0.57	0.65	0.30	**0.83**
	pc2	0.12	0.14	0.19	0.31	0.29	0.75	0.49	0.49	0.12	**0.74**
	pc3	0.29	0.23	0.21	0.32	0.32	0.75	0.65	0.68	0.28	**0.78**
	pc4	0.46	0.42	0.52	0.47	0.50	0.77	0.68	0.72	0.43	**0.79**
	pc5	0.47	0.50	0.51	0.52	0.56	0.74	0.67	0.69	0.52	**0.75**
SVM	MW1	0.39	0.32	0.41	0.39	0.41	0.57	0.62	0.41	0.37	**0.63**
	MC1	0.15	0.16	0.18	0.18	0.16	**0.33**	0.27	0.17	0.15	**0.33**
	pc1	0.31	0.30	0.39	0.43	0.30	**0.52**	0.41	0.35	0.30	**0.52**
	pc2	0.12	0.07	0.20	0.15	0.18	0.36	0.30	0.27	0.12	**0.37**
	pc3	0.32	0.33	0.30	0.31	0.35	**0.37**	0.36	0.32	0.31	**0.37**
	pc4	0.45	0.46	0.52	0.61	0.43	0.57	0.46	0.50	0.45	**0.61**
	pc5	0.50	0.52	0.52	0.51	0.50	0.50	0.50	0.54	0.52	**0.55**

tive and negative perspectives, and low accuracy on either class will lead to low GM value. While Table 4 demonstrates that almost all the sampling techniques (except BSM and WE) can achieve higher Kappa value than None. Because the Kappa rate penalises all-positive or all-negative predictions, and its value 1 means total agreement. Obviously, we can see that sampling methods such as CBOS, ROS, RUS and ENOS can improve the imbalanced learning performance in terms of Kappa performance measure while the rest are close with each other, which are not much better than None. Finally, as we discussed before, MCC is less influenced by imbalanced unseen test sets. Table 5 shows that ROS, RUS and ENOS can result in higher MCC values in terms of average results.

Tables 2, 3 and 4 also show that when the data set is slightly imbalanced, most of the sampling techniques do not perform much improvement in imbalanced learning. However, when the datasets becomes more imbalanced (e.g., pc2, pc5, and MC1), almost all the sampling techniques perform better, which means such sampling techniques can improve the performance of imbalanced learning. Practically speaking, ROS, RUS and ENOS are the top three sampling techniques when facing different kinds of imbalance ratio on different performance measures.

In summary, we find that the ENOS algorithm boosts the performance of C4.5 classifier in all metrics including Precision, GM, Kappa, and MCC in most data sets, while ROS achieves the second best results. The case for the SVM classifier is similar, ENOS performs the best for most of the times. Next comes the ROS algorithm.

5   Conclusions

In this paper, we present a comparative study for machine learning with imbalanced data. A variety of imbalanced data sets are used in the evaluation. The main goal is to examine the performance of various data sampling approaches, in terms of the boosting of the classification performance of C4.5 Decision Tree and Support Vector Machines on class imbalance data, so as to provide practical guidance to machine learning practitioners when facing imbalanced learning problem. Based on our extensive experiments, we find that data sampling techniques can improve the performance of machine learning when data sets are severely imbalanced. Besides, we find that the ensemble oversampling algorithm and random oversampling achieve the top performance in most data sets and both classifiers.

References

1. Barandela, R., Valdovinos, R.M., Sánchez, J.S., Ferri, F.J.: The imbalanced training sample problem: under or over sampling? In: Fred, A., Caelli, T.M., Duin, R.P.W., Campilho, A.C., de Ridder, D. (eds.) SSPR /SPR 2004. LNCS, vol. 3138, pp. 806–814. Springer, Heidelberg (2004). https://doi.org/10.1007/978-3-540-27868-9_88
2. Bekkar, M., Djemaa, H.K., Alitouche, T.A.: Evaluation measures for models assessment over imbalanced data sets. J. Inf. Eng. Appl. **3**(10) (2013)
3. Bhowan, U., Johnston, M., Zhang, M.: Developing new fitness functions in genetic programming for classification with unbalanced data. IEEE Trans. Syst. Man Cybern. Part B **42**(2), 406–421 (2012). https://doi.org/10.1109/TSMCB.2011.2167144
4. Cano, A., Zafra, A., Ventura, S.: Weighted data gravitation classification for standard and imbalanced data. IEEE Trans. Cybern. **43**(6), 1672–1687 (2013). https://doi.org/10.1109/TSMCB.2012.2227470
5. Chawla, N.V., Bowyer, K.W., Hall, L.O., Kegelmeyer, W.P.: SMOTE: synthetic minority over-sampling technique. J. Artif. Intell. Res. **16**, 321–357 (2002). https://doi.org/10.1613/jair.953
6. Cortes, C., Vapnik, V.: Support-vector networks. Mach. Learn. **20**(3), 273–297 (1995). https://doi.org/10.1007/BF00994018
7. Domingos, P.: Metacost: a general method for making classifiers cost-sensitive. KDD **99**, 155–164 (1999)
8. Han, H., Wang, W.-Y., Mao, B.-H.: Borderline-SMOTE: a new over-sampling method in imbalanced data sets learning. In: Huang, D.-S., Zhang, X.-P., Huang, G.-B. (eds.) ICIC 2005. LNCS, vol. 3644, pp. 878–887. Springer, Heidelberg (2005). https://doi.org/10.1007/11538059_91
9. He, H., Garcia, E.A.: Learning from imbalanced data. IEEE Trans. Knowl. Data Eng. **21**(9), 1263–1284 (2009). https://doi.org/10.1109/TKDE.2008.239
10. He, H., Shen, X.: A ranked subspace learning method for gene expression data classification. In: Arabnia, H.R., Yang, M.Q., Yang, J.Y. (eds.) Proceedings of the 2007 International Conference on Artificial Intelligence, ICAI 2007, Las Vegas, Nevada, USA, 25–28 June 2007, vol. I, pp. 358–364. CSREA Press (2007)

11. Hulse, J.V., Khoshgoftaar, T.M., Napolitano, A.: Experimental perspectives on learning from imbalanced data. In: Ghahramani, Z. (ed.) Machine Learning, Proceedings of the Twenty-Fourth International Conference (ICML 2007), Corvallis, Oregon, USA, 20–24 June 2007, vol. 227, pp. 935–942. ACM International Conference Proceeding Series, ACM (2007). https://doi.org/10.1145/1273496.1273614
12. Japkowicz, N.: Supervised versus unsupervised binary-learning by feedforward neural networks. Mach. Learn. **42**(1/2), 97–122 (2001). https://doi.org/10.1023/A:1007660820062
13. Japkowicz, N., Myers, C., Gluck, M.A.: A novelty detection approach to classification. In: Proceedings of the Fourteenth International Joint Conference on Artificial Intelligence, IJCAI 1995, Montréal Québec, Canada, 20–25 August 1995, vol. 2, pp. 518–523. Morgan Kaufmann (1995). http://ijcai.org/Proceedings/95-1/Papers/068.pdf
14. Jo, T., Japkowicz, N.: Class imbalances versus small disjuncts. SIGKDD Explorations **6**(1), 40–49 (2004). https://doi.org/10.1145/1007730.1007737
15. Kubat, M., Matwin, S.: Addressing the curse of imbalanced training sets: one-sided selection. In: Fisher, D.H. (ed.) Proceedings of the Fourteenth International Conference on Machine Learning (ICML 1997), Nashville, Tennessee, USA, 8–12 July 1997, pp. 179–186. Morgan Kaufmann (1997)
16. Lin, M., Tang, K., Yao, X.: Dynamic sampling approach to training neural networks for multiclass imbalance classification. IEEE Trans. Neural Netw. Learn. Syst. **24**(4), 647–660 (2013). https://doi.org/10.1109/TNNLS.2012.2228231
17. Quinlan, J.R.: C4.5: programs for machine learning. Elsevier (2014)
18. Rahman, M.M., Davis, D.: Cluster based under-sampling for unbalanced cardiovascular data. Proc. World Congr. Eng. **3**, 3–5 (2013)
19. Raskutti, B., Kowalczyk, A.: Extreme re-balancing for svms: a case study. SIGKDD Explorations **6**(1), 60–69 (2004). https://doi.org/10.1145/1007730.1007739
20. Shirabad, J.S., Menzies, T.J.: The promise repository of software engineering databases. School of Information Technology and Engineering, University of Ottawa, Canada 24 (2005)
21. Sun, Y., Kamel, M.S., Wong, A.K.C., Wang, Y.: Cost-sensitive boosting for classification of imbalanced data. Pattern Recogn. **40**(12), 3358–3378 (2007). https://doi.org/10.1016/j.patcog.2007.04.009
22. Wang, C., Hu, L., Guo, M., Liu, X., Zou, Q.: imdc: an ensemble learning method for imbalanced classification with mirna data. Genet. Mol. Res. **14**(1), 123–133 (2015)
23. Yang, S., Khot, T., Kersting, K., Kunapuli, G., Hauser, K., Natarajan, S.: Learning from imbalanced data in relational domains: a soft margin approach. In: Kumar, R., Toivonen, H., Pei, J., Huang, J.Z., Wu, X. (eds.) 2014 IEEE International Conference on Data Mining, ICDM 2014, Shenzhen, China, 14–17 December 2014, pp. 1085–1090. IEEE Computer Society (2014). DOI: https://doi.org/10.1109/ICDM.2014.152
24. Zhuang, L., Dai, H.: Parameter optimization of kernel-based one-class classifier on imbalance learning. JCP **1**(7), 32–40 (2006). https://doi.org/10.4304/jcp.1.7.32-40

Author Index